W9-ACN-438

UNDEFEATED

UNDEFEATED

The Life of Hubert H. Humphrey

Dan Cohen

Foreword by Muriel Humphrey

Introduction by G. Theodore Mitau

LERNER PUBLICATIONS COMPANY / MINNEAPOLIS

Library of Congress Cataloging in Publication Data

Cohen, Dan.
Undefeated.

Includes bibliographical references and index.
1. Humphrey, Hubert Horatio, 1911-1978. 2. Legislators—United States—Biography. 3. United States. Congress. Senate—Biography. 4. Vice-President—United States—Biography. 5. United States—Politics and government—1945- I. Title.
E748.H945C63 973.923′092′4 [B] 78-53933
ISBN 0-8225-9953-8

Manufactured in the United States of America

CONTENTS

FOREWORD

Undefeated is a most appropriate title for this account of Hubert Humphrey's life and work, for although Hubert experienced losses as well as victories at the polls, the word "defeat" was never part of his vocabulary. Throughout his long and challenging political career—from the mayor's office in Minneapolis to the Senate in Washington, and on to the Vice-Presidency—Hubert always found something stimulating in every situation he encountered.

On his first visit to Washington, before we were married, he wrote me these words: "Washington, D.C., thrills me to my very finger tips; I simply revel . . . in this realm of politics and government." Throughout his career, that initial enthusiasm for political life never faded.

During my forty-one years with Hubert, he and I were fortunate to have a genuine partnership in both our public and our private lives. In that same letter from Washington he wrote, "You'll help me, I know. Together we can do things, I am sure. Never let me get lazy or discouraged. You be my inspirational force, Muriel, and always encourage me in what you feel will be right for me to do." I did encourage him, and he always encouraged me. In the following years our respect for each other and our deep, abiding love saw us through many difficulties.

We matured during the devastating period of the depression, the dust bowl, and World War II. Our experiences during those years taught us that we could survive under the worst circumstances, no matter what the setbacks were. In addition, our observations of Franklin Roosevelt's efforts to solve the nation's immense problems had a lasting influence on our thinking. We came out of those hard times with tremendous confidence in ourselves and a feeling of being well-prepared for the uncertainties of holding elective office.

We faced difficulties, too, in balancing our public and private lives. One of the greatest challenges for us came during Hubert's first Senate term, when our children were small. I was constantly torn between what

I felt were my responsibilities to Hubert in his public life and my responsibilities to our children. Despite the many demands on Hubert, he, too, wanted to make certain that he spent time with the children. Later on, our home at Waverly, Minnesota, became a real family haven. The weekends and summers that we were able to spend there during the children's school years were our salvation from the pressures of Washington life. There we had time to talk and to be together as a family.

"My Dad used to say," Hubert once observed, "that there are some unnecessary expenses that I would find very necessary in life. That's our home in Waverly. No matter where we go, Waverly is home; Waverly is peace."

Of course, Hubert always had to make decisions that took him away from that peaceful place. But neither of us ever regretted those decisions. In 1972, for example, Hubert and I spent several weeks discussing whether he should seek the nomination for President. The decision, a difficult one, had to be made soon. So it was on my mind as I worked at our Waverly home while Hubert was at work in the Senate.

Finally, I phoned his Washington office. "You'd better get your track shoes out," I said, "I'm running you as my candidate."

Since this was to be our eleventh campaign for public office, I knew how much of our time and energy it would take. But I had confidence in the strong and innovative leadership that Hubert could give our country, and I was happy to travel and speak again on his behalf. He had such drive. There was so much that he wanted to do—that he could do—if given the opportunity. As always, I wanted to help him to do it.

Sometimes I felt discouraged, but Hubert never did. Perhaps the real impact of Hubert's public career is best summed up in a statement made to me by the mayor of Rochester, Minnesota, back in 1948. It was toward the end of the Senate campaign, on a rainy Sunday afternoon in a park in Rochester where Hubert was speaking. I was tired and discouraged. Suddenly, the mayor turned to me and said, "Muriel, no matter what happens in this election, you can know that Hubert has given the state the best political education it has ever had."

I have never forgotten that statement. In all of our campaigns and efforts in public life, it has given me encouragement. For Hubert's speeches *did* teach and inspire. Whether we won or lost, what was important, I believe, was the contribution that he made toward promoting a better understanding of critical public issues and democratic processes among the people of our nation.

MURIEL HUMPHREY

PREFACE

The idea for this book originated during a brainstorming meeting of the Lerner Publication editorial staff in the summer of 1977. The Lerner people felt there was a need that had not yet been met for a special kind of book about Hubert H. Humphrey, who was at that time beginning his fifth term as a United States senator. There were a few Humphrey biographies in existence, but they had become dated; the most recent book about Humphrey was an autobiography, which, though well written, suffered from a format that seemed too formal for its ebullient subject. What was needed was a joyous book, one that would stress Humphrey's warmth, his energy, and his indomitable spirit.

The Lerner staff was excited about the project from the outset and started work on it the afternoon of the meeting. Mark Lerner began collecting material for the book and then, as he had long planned, left for London to continue his education. By that time, I had become interested in the project and ready to assume the responsibilities of authorship. Although I am not a scholar, my long acquaintance with Minnesota politics provided a useful background for a book such as this, as well as access to many sources of valuable information. As would be expected, most of my sources were Democrats. In Minnesota, members of opposing political parties contend fiercely on a public level while usually remaining friendly on a private basis—one of Hubert Humphrey's legacies to the state. Despite notorious Republican tendencies on my part, most of the Minnesota Democrats that I sought to interview were cooperative. A few weren't.

Many people outside the confines of Minnesota political life also contributed to the project by submitting to interviews and exchanging correspondence with us. Some are quoted in the book; others were interviewed but not quoted directly. Among those who provided excellent background material were David Cohen of Common Cause, Earl Larson, Mason Mallory, Deschler Welch, Lee Loevinger, Dick Scammon, Forrest Harris, George Doerr, Gordon Twiss, Gerald Brekke, and Laurene Tibbetts. Dr. G. Theodore Mitau was kind enough to read the book in manuscript stage and to give me the benefit of his advice. I am also grateful for the assistance given the project by Betty South of Senator Humphrey's office, by the staff of the Minnesota Historical Society, and by Dorothy Burke, Ruth Angell, and the staff of the Minneapolis History Collection in the Minneapolis Public Library, who clipped and carefully saved so many Humphrey newspaper articles.

In writing this book, I made use of many excellent secondary sources, particularly *The Education of a Public Man* by Hubert H. Humphrey; *Almost to the Presidency* by Albert Eisele; *Hubert Humphrey: A Candid Biography* by Winthrop Griffith; the section on Humphrey by Charles Bailey in *Candidates 1960,* edited by Eric Sevareid; *Not So Wild a Dream* by Eric Sevareid; *The Making of the President, 1960, The Making of the President, 1964, The Making of the President, 1968,* and *The Making of the President, 1972,* all by Theodore White; *Marathon* by Jules Witcover; an unpublished monograph by Arthur Naftalin on the history of the Farmer-Labor Party in Minnesota; the *Minneapolis Star,* the *Minneapolis Tribune,* the *St. Paul Dispatch-Pioneer Press,* and, of course, the *New York Times.*

I am also deeply indebted to an understanding publisher, Harry Lerner, and to the overworked staff of Lerner Publications for their aid. Sylvia Johnson contributed coherence and a sense of pace in her editing of the book; without her help, the project could not have been completed. Emily Kelley provided invaluable assistance as a researcher and record keeper, as well as a manuscript typist. She and Adeline Toftness not only typed hundreds of manuscript pages but also, on more than one occasion, saved me from some glaring misstatement or grammatical atrocity. Richard Hannah devoted many hours of painstaking work to the book's complicated design; Cynthia Bix handled the enormous job of indexing; and Emily Kelley and Stephanie Satz compiled the appendix of election results. Finally, George Overlie, Elizabeth Petersen, Peg Pursell, Susan Stan, Diane Larson, L'Enc Matte, Fran Hanson, Sandy Heinen, Gary Hansen, and Richard Trombley each contributed their skills with professional competence and dedication.

DAN COHEN

INTRODUCTION

G. Theodore Mitau

To Hubert H. Humphrey, politics represented a way of life—the testing of religious convictions in a world that cried out for men and women who would "walk humbly with their Lord, love mercy, and do justice." With his intellectual roots in Midwest populism, Wilsonian idealism, and Rooseveltian pragmatism, Humphrey had unlimited faith in the essential goodness of the human race and of democracy. This faith proved profoundly inspiring and infectious to the thousands of Americans who cherished him and to whom he, in turn, looked for support and comradeship in the course of a long career that spanned enormous achievement and great personal disappointments.

The first major achievement of Humphrey's political career took place in 1944, when he served as a catalyst in the merger of the Democratic and Farmer-Labor parties in Minnesota. Before that time, Farmer-Laborites had deeply distrusted city Democrats, many of whom in turn suspected both the urban and rural radicalism of the hyphenated party. Much talk and effort expended over the years to build a powerful alternative had come to naught; the Republicans, meanwhile, were winning most of the elections.

Finally, under the impetus of improving the victory prospects of the Roosevelt-Truman ticket in Minnesota, Humphrey enticed key national figures in the Democratic Party to lend their support to the fusion of the two parties, while he prodded and cajoled and successfully out-maneuvered recalcitrant leaders and factions. With the 1944 presidential ticket winning the state solidly, thirty-three-year-old Humphrey clearly emerged as a major leader in the newly formed Democratic-Farmer-Labor Party. His remarkable qualities as a prodigious worker and a pragmatic yet uplifting politician were soon readily apparent, and he was urged to become a candidate for mayor of Minneapolis. When Humphrey was elected to that office in 1945, his political career had its start. Before it was over, it would take him to the United States Senate, to the office of the vice-president, and almost to the White House.

Throughout his career, Hubert Humphrey's political interests, causes, and programs were wide in scope and variety, but they reveal, nevertheless, considerable consistency as well as vision. The central thrust of his political thought, so frequently reflected in his speeches, was that government in democracy must do for the people what the people cannot do for themselves. Within the general framework of this political philosophy, Humphrey offered vigorous leadership in at least four basic areas: the development of international cooperation; the advancement of human rights; the implementation of the New Deal; and the elevation of practical politics to a high level of responsibility and dedication.

Developing International Cooperation. Even before the impact of Pearl Harbor and World War II shook the nation, Humphrey strongly advocated international cooperation and collective security as policies best assuring peace and a more orderly world. Addressing workers in union halls, farmers at county fairs and plowing contests, students and faculties at university assemblies—traveling the speaker circuits to chambers of commerce, church meetings, and neighborhood rallies—campaigning at innumerable district and state conventions—Humphrey hammered home the imperative need to aid embattled Britain and to strengthen the national effort against the rising tide of Fascist and Japanese aggression.

After his first election to the U.S. Senate, Humphrey worked aggressively for a great number of crucial programs aimed at international cooperation and peace. The most prominent that enlisted his enthusiasm included: the Peace Corps, foreign aid, support of NATO, Food for Peace, the Nuclear Test Ban Treaty, the establishment of the Arms Control and Disarmament Agency, and international negotiations that sought to encourage cooperation in science and medical research. Traveling abroad, Humphrey established bonds of friendship and communication with leaders throughout the world. He counted his eight-and-a-half hour Kremlin dialogue with Nikita Khrushchev in 1958 as among his most fascinating meetings with a foreign head of state. As a member of the prestigious Senate Foreign Relations Committee, as assistant Senate majority leader, as vice president (within Johnson-fixed perimeters and priorities), and finally as "elder statesman," Humphrey also spoke and worked energetically to advance the role of the United States as a UN partner and leader of the Western world.

Advancing Human Rights. To Humphrey, loving one's fellow human beings—transcending differences in race, religion, sex, and national origin—always constituted a deeply held personal as well as spiritual imperative that was to be applied in everyday life and in every action and policy of government

Born into a remarkably warm and caring family, with a socially sensitive father whom he admired greatly, Humphrey developed quite early a genuine concern for the victims of social and economic injustice. Later, during a year of graduate study in political science at Huey Long's Louisiana State University, he was offended by the human degradation and despair caused by Southern segregationist practices.

As mayor of Minneapolis—a city well known in the 1940s for its occasional but ugly manifestations of anti-Semitic, anti-black, and anti-Indian sentiments—Humphrey created the nation's first mandatory municipal Fair Employment Practices Commission as well as one of the best examples of a human relations program for police officers. Humphrey's deep friendships and personal ties forged with key members of the city's various minority groups during the early struggle for human rights survived unimpaired throughout his career.

National prominence as a courageous spokesman for civil liberties came to Humphrey as early as 1948. Heading the Minnesota delegation to the Democratic Convention in Philadelphia in that year, the brash young mayor acted as one of the floor leaders for a greatly strengthened civil rights plank in the party platform. Humphrey's dramatic speech in support of the plank threw the assembly into an uproar, but when the roll call was taken, his bitterly fought "minority plan" had prevailed. Hubert Humphrey had begun the process that would eventually lead his party out of "the shadow of states' rights" and into "the bright sunshine of human rights."

Implementing the New Deal. In a world where powerful technological and economic forces contributed so greatly to personal insecurity and social interdependence, Franklin Roosevelt's "New Deal" sought to assign to government a distinctly more positive role as an active partner in the battle against the ravages of unemployment, sickness, and poverty. Hubert Humphrey was proud to consider himself a New Deal Democrat. On the campaign trails in Minnesota and throughout the nation, as senator, vice-president, and candidate for president, as majority whip and national chairman of the Americans for Democratic Action, he emphasized the principles of the New Deal with unvarying consistency and tenacity.

Humphrey passionately believed that if modern democracy were to remain strong and dynamic, then government would have to perform many functions and services traditionally considered too restrictive, too costly, or too socialistic to be undertaken. If local or state governments did not or would not respond to these newer demands because of insufficient resources, expertise, or political will, then Washington represented quite clearly the people's most practical means to corrective action. To make this federal-state "partnership" more effective, Humphrey advocated improvements in the processes of inter-governmental relations, reforms in the federal income tax, and more vigorous enforcements of anti-trust laws and regulations. As a legislator, he worked for numerous bills and programs that would improve the lives of American farmers, laborers, small businessmen, home buyers, and others who found their well-being threatened by the increasing complexity of modern industrial society.

Advocating "the Politics of Joy." In his book *The Education of a Public Man,* Humphrey readily acknowledged that his use of the expression "the politics of joy" during his 1968 presidential campaign was a serious blunder. As a campaign theme, "the politics of joy" proved disastrous; as a description of Humphrey's style of politics and of life, however, nothing could have been more appropriate. Hubert Humphrey loved life, politics, and people. Whereas so many politicians affect concern for others, Humphrey's concern was genuine. Whereas so many politicians either ignore the misery of poverty or seek to exploit it, Humphrey responded to human suffering as a challenge calling for the development of programs of action or reform.

Despite instances of rhetorical extremes and not infrequent hyperbole, Humphrey was in some ways the most political of men, comfortable with compromise and moderation. Unlike so many earlier voices of Midwest populism, notably those of A. C. Townely and Ignatius Donnelly, Humphrey's brand of politics stressed coalition-building and consensus. He never ceased reminding some of his more radical and righteous followers that incremental gains in programs or policy can in fact add up to something important; that victory goes to those who can gain a majority where it counts most—on election day.

To make such a system of pragmatic politics work, however, politicians must be able to skillfully blend strongly held principles with the "art of the possible." For a politician to succeed as impressively as Humphrey, and for as long a time, requires in addition enormous personal fortitude and a nearly inexhaustible capacity to "forgive and forget."

Hubert Humphrey possessed all these abilities, and he put them into practice every day of his life. When defeated or ignored, he redoubled his efforts; when called a "visionary" he regaled his colleagues with homey illustrations to point up the essential practicality of his proposals; when assailed for bankrupting the nation by urging huge deficit spending, he responded by adding up the costs of human misery, disillusionment, and unemployment; when criticized for encouraging socialism, he referred to the Sermon on the Mount, to Thomas Jefferson, Andrew Jackson, and Franklin Roosevelt, and to the principles of social justice they extolled; when personally abused and slandered during the Vietnam disaster, he held to a vice-presidential oath of loyalty to his president despite deep personal misgivings and disagreements with policies that rent the nation; when accused of surrendering his convictions and integrity for reasons of personal ambition or expediency, he attempted to rise above the battle, to ignore the very real hurt, and then to go on to persuade his critics of underlying factors that may have been to them initially less apparent or relevant.

Missing by the narrowest of margins an American politician's most dearly sought prize—the presidency—did not long dent or dim Humphrey's good humor, personal warmth, and extraordinary resilience. His faith in himself, in his God, and in his political roots was profound, and his charisma real. If it is the essence of political genius to be able to rally men and women of decency and good will behind a vision of the public weal that can transcend considerations of greed or gain, then Hubert Humphrey must be ranked as one of the preeminent American politicians of recent times.

G. Theodore Mitau is Distinguished Service Professor of Political Science in the Minnesota State University System.

chapter 1

DOLAND

"Just think of it, boys, . . . here we are in the middle of this great continent—here in South Dakota —with the land stretching out for hundreds of miles, with people who can vote and govern their own lives—with riches enough for all, if we will take care to do justice."

Hubert Humphrey, Sr.

We looked over the countryside as we came by. Of course we saw the drought, but I must tell you in all honesty that I remember the days in the '30s—It doesn't look anywhere near as bad now as it did then. And I think that despite the adversity that we face now of bad weather that we are going to come through it alright. We've learned how to take care of our soil a little better. I think the farmers are much better and everybody has better equipment and we are going to do alright. I saw a lot of irrigation too and if I can put in a plug to do more of it, as long as there is water in the river, we ought to be able to get it on the ground.

HUBERT H. HUMPHREY
SPEECH GIVEN IN DOLAND,
SOUTH DAKOTA, JUNE 14, 1976

The town of Doland, South Dakota, lies on the eastern edge of a vast semi-arid region of grazing and marginal farm land that stretches into Montana. Heavy rain clouds roll in from the west, but they carry their payloads beyond the Dakota plains, eastward into Minnesota. The land around Doland is flat from horizon to horizon—not parched or stark, but not exactly green either. Though better plowing methods and tree planting programs have done much to restore the soil since dust bowl days, even today thoughts of rain and the need for it are never very far from mind. "It's a wonderful country if you get rain. This soil here will produce some wonderful crops if you get a little rain at the right time. And it don't take a lot to do it,"[1] says Homer Krentz, a Doland farmer and a long-time resident.

Hubert and Christine Humphrey

Hubert Horatio Humphrey was born about fifty miles away from Doland in Wallace, South Dakota, on May 27, 1911. His family had roots in the dry soil of the region, although they did not run very deep. The Humphreys were pre-revolutionary Yankees who had lived in New England, then in Ohio, and later in Minnesota, moving from one farm to another. Hubert's father broke the family farming tradition when he became a pharmacist after graduating from the Drew School of Pharmacy in Minneapolis. He opened his first drugstore in Lily, South Dakota, in 1903. On the maternal side, Hubert's ancestors had come to South Dakota by way of Norway. His mother's father, Guttorn Sannes, was a Norwegian merchant sailor who had somehow become landlocked on the midwestern prairies. After conceiving a plan to pilot riverboats on the Missouri, he learned that neither the scheme, nor the riverboats, nor his skills in and about the fjords of his native land were transferable to South Dakota. He, too, became a farmer.

In 1906, Sannes' daughter Christine met and married Hubert Humphrey, Sr., in Lily. Soon after their marriage, an old friend offered Humphrey a partnership in another drugstore, and Hubert and Christine moved to Granite Falls, Minnesota, where their first son, Ralph, was born in 1907. After a fire destroyed the store in Granite Falls, the family moved to Wallace, where Hubert was born in a room above his father's new drugstore. Humphrey, Sr., sold the store in Wallace in 1915, and they moved again, this time to Doland. Hubert's sister Frances was born that same year; the last child, another sister, Fern, was born in 1919.

Hubert Humphrey, Jr., at age two

Hubert (left) and his brother Ralph

Christine Sannes Humphrey

Christine Humphrey, Hubert's mother, was a sweet-natured, hard-working, God-fearing Republican woman whose life was given over to the concerns of her family. "She would make up little poems for us and tell us stories of the Troll. She also read us Dickens and the classics,"[2] recalled Frances of those early days. The endless political discussions and discourses that animated the elder Humphrey and his son Hubert left Mrs. Humphrey overwhelmed and overtired. As the rest of the family talked into the night, she would head for bed. "You sleep for all of us, Mother," the elder Humphrey would call to her affectionately. Hubert and his Dad would talk for hours. "I can never remember going to bed before midnight since I was twelve years old, except when I was sick,"[3] Hubert said later.

Hubert Humphrey, Sr., was the single most profound influence on his son throughout his life. One of five Democrats in a town of six hundred

Hubert Humphrey, Sr., in the late 1930s

souls, a nonchurchgoer on the fringes of the Bible Belt, and a vigorous advocate of his personal views, he dispensed politics with every pill, yet he managed to retain the friendship and goodwill of creditor, debtor, political opponent, of nearly all who knew him. It was a gift, perhaps the greatest gift that he passed on to his son.

Humphrey, Sr., was a man of enormous enthusiasms. As the town agnostic, he was fond of quoting the words of the notorious Robert Ingersoll to his devout Lutheran wife—until the day that young Hubert and Ralph decided to join the Methodist church. Humphrey, Sr., was baptized in the Methodist faith the same day as his two sons, but he was too embarrassed to have the ceremony performed in church in front of his new co-parishioners. Instead, he got Reverend Hartt to conduct the rite in the local doctor's office. Soon Humphrey was an ardent church member, drawing hundreds to the Sunday School classes that he taught and sometimes bringing groups of his students back home to an astonished wife for Sunday dinner and an evening of radio sermonizing with Reverend Cannon or Harry Emerson Fosdick.

Music was another of Humphrey's passions. He stocked his drugstore with unsellable records, and on one occasion, when the craving for a live performance overwhelmed him, he drove to Minneapolis to see a touring company of the Metropolitan Opera. This excursion was made all the more memorable because he began it in the middle of the night—to save the cost of a hotel room. Humphrey, Sr., loved poetry as well as music, and he expressed his passion with the same blend of the

I *have had many people ask me what is really what got you into public life—what is it that inspired you? And I said, first of all, my father. My Dad was my teacher—my best friend—I loved him dearly. Poor mother, she had to put up with all that argument that we had. We were always talking in our family—you know it came naturally—and we were discussing things. Dad was the mayor of this town. He was on the City Council. My Dad was one of those that fought for the municipal light plant up here—I remember that.*

HUBERT H. HUMPHREY
DOLAND SPEECH

Stay out of bed. Ninety percent of all people die in bed.

HUBERT HUMPHREY, SR.

The site of the original Humphrey drugstore in Doland

practical and the intellectual that characterized his other actions. During the period of his greatest enthusiasm, which came upon him when the family moved to Huron, he bought radio time in order to read poems to the puzzled burghers of that community. Not surprisingly, the radio spots didn't help sales at the drugstore, but they gave Humphrey an opportunity to share his interests with others.

Active in politics, at various times Humphrey served as town councilman, mayor, state legislator, and delegate to the Democratic Convention that nominated Al Smith for president in 1928. In addition to his busy public life, he was a proud father and a loving and protective husband. One time he told his sons, "Boys, your mother is a lovely woman, a fine faithful wife, and you treat her with respect every day of your life. There is only one thing I want you boys to remember, sometimes she is politically unreliable."[4] That year, she had voted for the Republican candidate for president, Warren G. Harding, and he had voted for James Cox, the Democrat.

The Humphrey drugstore in the 1920s

Three-year-old Hubert, Jr., with a favorite book

Humphrey, Sr., was not a formally educated man; the only schoolwork he completed beyond the twelfth grade was what was necessary for him to practice pharmacy. But the Humphrey household had the best library in Doland. Humphrey, Sr., was a voracious reader, particularly on the lives and works of his heroes, Jefferson, Lincoln, and Wilson. William Jennings Bryan was another favorite; at least twice a year Humphrey would recite Bryan's "Cross of Gold" speech to his family. He had a passion for hard work to match his enthusiasm for learning and self-improvement. Vacations for himself and his family were scorned: by the time he was thirteen, Hubert Humphrey, Jr., had only been out of South Dakota once, for a trip to Minneapolis.

Hubert, Jr., had a happy and in most ways a very typical childhood for the times, getting into the same scrapes as most kids. When he was just three years old and the family was still living in Wallace, he disappeared during a town celebration and turned up leading the town band down main street. Another family legend has him escaping from his mother after some mischief by hiding under the porch. When his father crawled under the porch to retrieve his son, Hubert called out, "Hi Dad, is Mom after you too?" Humphrey, Sr., began laughing so hard that he was unable to give Hubert the spanking he had come to deliver. Hubert got into more difficulties when, as a fifth grader, he played the lead in the school production of *Jack and the Beanstalk.* The beanstalk had been constructed with pegs behind the foliage to facilitate the ascent to the heavens. Going up was

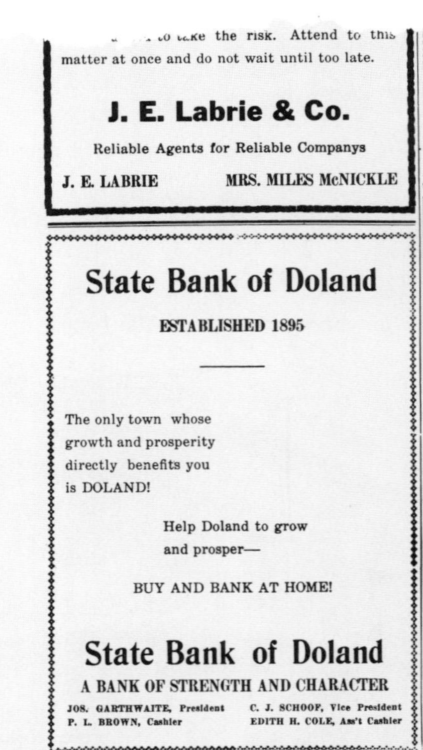

to take the risk. Attend to this matter at once and do not wait until too late.

J. E. Labrie & Co.

Reliable Agents for Reliable Companys

J. E. LABRIE MRS. MILES McNICKLE

State Bank of Doland

ESTABLISHED 1895

The only town whose growth and prosperity directly benefits you is DOLAND!

Help Doland to grow and prosper—

BUY AND BANK AT HOME!

State Bank of Doland

A BANK OF STRENGTH AND CHARACTER

JOS. GARTHWAITE, President C. J. SCHOOF, Vice President
P. L. BROWN, Cashier EDITH H. COLE, Ass't Cashier

Menu

Father and Son Banquet, Doland, South Dakota

February 12, 1926

MEAT LOAF — — MASHED POTATOES

ESCALLOPED CORN

COLD SLAW — — — PICKLES

JELLY — ROLLS

APPLE PIE — — CHEESE

COFFEE

PROGRAM

Toastmaster .... H. W. Sherwood

String Quartet—Miss Verna Brown Piano, Mr. and Mrs. A. I. Gillespie, Violinists, Miss Betty Gillespie Cello.

Introductory .... H. W. Sherwood

Abraham Lincoln—"The Man of The Age"— .... H. H. Humphrey

Male Quartet

"Keep On Keepin' On" .... Lewis Terpestra

String Quartet

"The Hard Game" .... Deschler Welch

Male Quartet

String Quartet

"Dreaming And Doing" .... Hubert Humphrey

Address—T. R. Harmon, Suptintendent of Public Instruction, Watertown.

String Quartet

Both Humphreys spoke at a Doland Father and Son Banquet in 1926.

Plankinton — Doland — Wessington Springs

You'll Be Money Ahead If You Paint This Fall

YOUR house should be painted this Fall. It needs protection from the Winter storms—and you'll be money ahead, for it's cheaper to paint than repair.

Winter is the season when the actual damage is done—damage that can be avoided by a good coat of

Lowe Brothers

HIGH STANDARD PAINT

We recommend High Standard for two reasons. First, because its tough, weather-resisting surface affords maximum protection for your house. Second, because the beautiful, clean colors of High Standard Paint are permanent and will keep their brilliance through the Winter. Spring will see your home quite bright and shining.

Come in and let us show you some color schemes. We might also have some suggestions on inside painting that would interest you.

H. H. Humphrey

Mr. and Mrs. Arthur James and son Berwyn and Buster Labrie were Huron visitors Monday.

Mrs. Fischer and children arrived Tuesday from Athol for a visit at the Herb Beltezore home.

fine, but during the descent, Hubert lost his hold and the pegs ripped out the bottom of his pants. His dramatics teacher, Olive Doty, safety-pinned the damage. Others might have been nonplussed by the disaster—Hubert was not. He spent the remainder of the performance facing the audience, and when the dramatics teacher broke her arm later that evening during the catastrophe-prone production, Hubert shepherded the grade school children through their roles and kept the show going.

Hubert was nicknamed Pinky during his boyhood because of his ruddy skin coloring. Delivering the *Minneapolis Tribune* and *St. Paul Dispatch* door-to-door after school, participating in football, basketball, and track in season, playing baritone horn in the band, and serving every day as a soda jerk and general helper at his Dad's drugstore left Hubert with a perpetually flushed appearance. He was working behind the soda fountain by the time he was eight; a special ramp was installed for him because he was too short to reach the spigots. There was little time for idleness during Hubert's boyhood. When a television producer came to town years later to recreate the story of his early life and included a scene in the local poolhall, the townsfolk got a bit indignant. Homer Krentz protested, "That wasn't Pinky. He just got to the front door of that poolhall to sell papers and that was it. He never went in and if he had they would of throwed him out anyway."[5]

Even if he did stay out of the poolhall, Hubert got into his share of mischief, and more often than not his companion was the minister's son Julian

Hubert (right) **and Julian Hartt**

Hartt. One of their most famous escapades was the time they filled an enormous trophy cup that sat outside the school assembly room with alarm clocks. The clocks were set to go off at two-minute intervals, disrupting the entire school. The prank worked but the boys got caught, and Hubert remembered later how the principal "shrieked" at him. On another occasion, Hubert was reprimanded by a teacher for flying up the steps of the school library three at a time. "Where are you going in such a hurry?" she asked. "To the library," he answered. "Why is it necessary to make such a wild dash to get to the library?" Hubert replied, "Well, there's a book I want and I'm afraid if I don't get it, somebody else will get it first."[6]

Though Hubert was an active participant in school sports, his athletic career is not the sort of

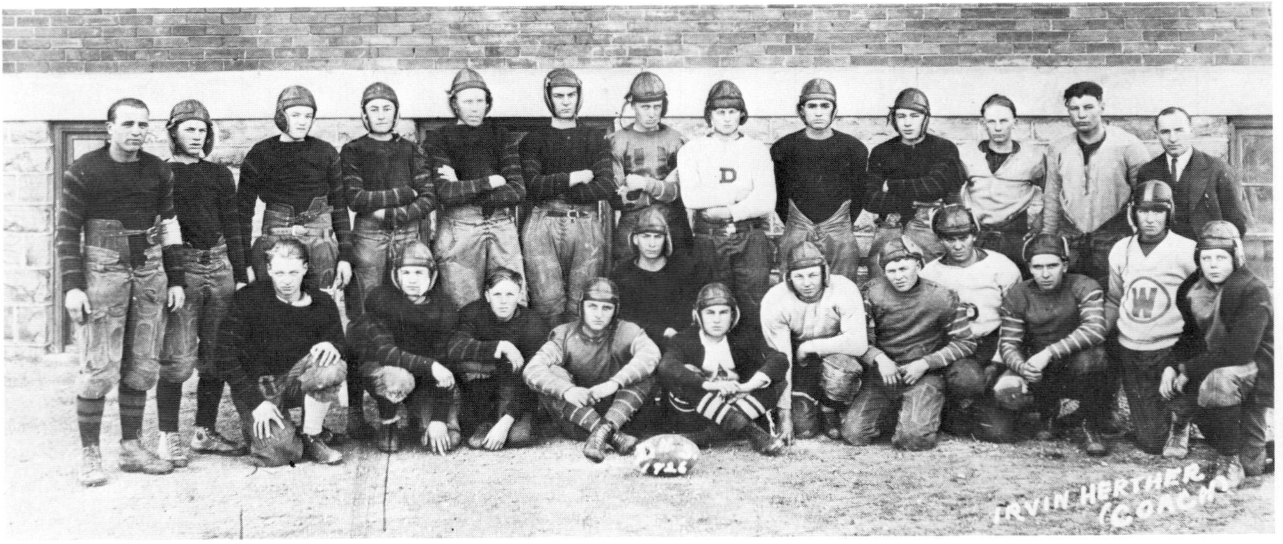

Hubert Humphrey, Jr. (standing, third from left), **was a guard on the Doland High School football team.**

He and I went out with my folks—my folks were from Maine and they loved to camp. We went with them once to Enemy Swim, which was a lake in the Northeast—well, it's still there. It was an Indian name and it was one of my father's favorite places to go camping. And I remember how chagrined we were in the middle of the night. We had put a pup tent alongside my folks' tent and since it was late at night, Hubert and I decided not to trench around the tent. Well, we had a cloudburst in the middle of the night, and Hubert and I were flooded out, where my folks were dry and snug. It was an object lesson of some sort, but there again, it was Hubert's response to these things, his indestructible good cheer, and his recognition that "well, maybe we should have listened to the words of wisdom rather than settling for what seemed to be a sure thing."

JULIAN HARTT

which legends are made; one-hundred-twenty-pound guards seldom achieve football immortality. His most memorable athletic quality was his enthusiasm. On one occasion, it was over-enthusiasm. He was sent in to substitute during the last few minutes of a close basketball game, and within five seconds of getting onto the court, over-eager to get the ball, he fouled an opponent, who was awarded two shots. Hubert was mortified. "I've lost the game!" he said to teammate Homer Krentz. But the enemy player missed both the free throws. To his great relief, Hubert managed to recover the rebound and pass the ball to Homer, who stalled out the clock to end the game.

Hubert's career as a student was more outstanding than his athletic achievements. In four years of high school he received only five B's amid more

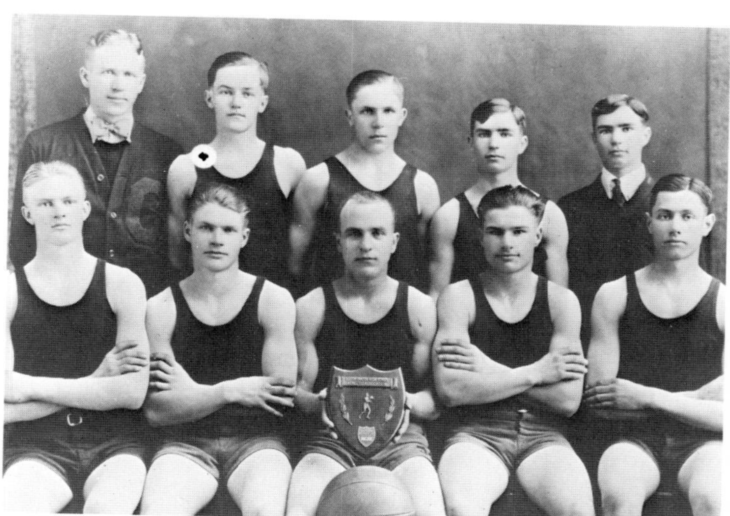

Hubert (standing, second from left) **and Homer Krentz** (seated, third from left) **with the Doland basketball team**

Doland High School

than sixty A's and A+'s, and he was the valedictorian of his graduating class. In his junior year, he took time off from his academic work to star in the class play, an opus titled *Nothing But the Truth,* which concerned two feuding business partners. As a senior, Humphrey had the leading role in *Captain Applejack,* a play about "as mild a man as ever scuttled a cup of coffee," who "changed into a bold bad buccaneer of the Spanish main, cussing

Name of Pupil	Date of birth	Name of Parents	Name of City
Hubert Horatio Humphrey	May 17, 1911	Hubert Humphrey Christine Humphrey	Doland - Spink County

Freshman 1925-1926	1 mo	2 mo	3 mo	4 mo	5 mo	6 mo	7 mo	8 mo	9 mo	
English I		A		A		A		A		
Algebra I		A		A		A		A-		
Gen Science		A		A		A		A		4½ credits
Latin		A		A		A		A-		
Debate ½ credit A-										
Sophomore 1926-1927										
English II		A		A		A		A		
Plane Geometry		B+		A		A		A		4 5/8 credits
Modern History		A		A+		A		A		
Caesar		B+		A		B+		A		
Debate								A		1 credit
Oratory								A		1/8 credit
Music										¼ credit
Junior 1927-1928										
English III		A		A+		A+		A+		
Am History		A+		A+						
Cicero		A		A		A		A		5½ credits
Solid Geom		A		A+						
Glee Club				A		A		B		¼ credit
Civics						A		A		
Sociology						A		A		
Debate								A		½ credit
Senior 1928-1929										
English IV		A		A		A+		A		
Physics		A-		A		A		A		5 credits
Virgil		A		A		A		A		
Alg II		A		A						
Musics		A		B+		A				¼ credit
Oratory										¼ credit
Debate										¼ credit
Extempore										¼ credit

Graduated May 1929

Certified as a correct copy of the original transcript

William McLeod
Superintendent of Dol nd School
May 24, 1968

H*e was popular but he didn't participate in things too much. That is, the fun that the kids had—he didn't have time for that because his father kept him so busy. He had to have help in the drugstore, and both of the boys worked there. Hubert did go out for every activity at school. He went out for football but wasn't the best player on the team. He was too slightly built. But he was an incessant talker when I was directing the play. He'd come, and when it came time to practice, I'd say, "For heaven sakes, Hubert, shut up. Keep still." But that was the nice thing about him, he was never insolent. If I told him to keep still, he'd try to keep still. He just bubbled.*

OLIVE DOTY

his crew, calling for his grog, dragging forth a comely wench, . . . and finally putting down a mutiny by cutting cards with its leader."[7]

During his years in school, Hubert Humphrey enjoyed many of the special benefits that growing up in a small town can afford a talented young person. Olive Doty, one of Humphrey's teachers, describes the advantages:

> There aren't thousands of other youngsters to compete with. Any youngster that can do something gets a chance to do it. And there's competition between towns. When you go out of town and win something, everybody in your town knows about it. It isn't like a big city where no one, even your next door neighbor, knows about your achievements. The school is the most important institution in town. The school holds a pep meeting

The graduating class of 1929. Class valedictorian Hubert Humphrey is third from the right in the back row.

> after you've won something and come back home. It recognizes the successful team or student. That student's self-esteem is raised, and he is motivated and continues to be motivated to accomplish more.[8]

Early in his school career, Hubert began to achieve this kind of recognition in debate. During his high school years, Doland debate teams began to win more and more of their contests with the

THIS IS THE FIRST PUBLISHED WRITING BY ERT H. HUMPHREY

"HI-SCO-PEP"

Helen Riddle
Editor-in-Charge

Doland High School added another triumph to its list of victories last Friday night. The Doland basketball team fought its way for a victory over the Ashton quint. Why did the boys of Doland High win? Mainly of course because of consistant and faithful practicing but yet there was another reason which prevails in all contests. This vital important reason was the loyal support of the Doland people and the school. The gymnasium was filled with Doland rooters and a few Ashton backers. All of these spectators were hoping that their team might win. The Doland fans were working for one aim, to beat Ashton. The aim was at last accomplished. The boys, of both teams, fought their way through four quarters of strenuous work. The spectators were rooting a still longer time for that one great aim.

Support is not only needed in basketball or any other activity of school life but it is needed in every person's daily work. We can not do half as well if we are being discouraged and laughed at by our friends and fellow citizens. We must have support. Be a "helper" not a discouragement. Thus it is with our school activities. We need your encouragement and support. Help us and we will equally help you. Give our school backing. Boost for our city and be proud of our enterprises. If we all pull together we can all win. One weak person or one knocker will hinder our success. The old proverb: "A chain is as strong as its weakest link," holds true in all work.

Come on folks be with us.
Back old D.H.S.

---Hubert Humphrey.

April 4, 1929

State Debate Tournament

On Monday, March 25, the Doland debaters, Hubert Humphrey, Earl Hansen, and Lewis Terpstra went to the state debate tournament which was held at Vermillion March 25, 26, and 27. Doland took part in the second debate of the tournament. The Doland affirmative consisting of Earl Hansen and Hubert Humphrey met the Watertown negative. The debate was held Tuesday morning at 9:00, and Doland won with a 2 to 1 decision. Dràwings were made for Dolands' next debate with Yankton. Again Doland drew an affirmative. This debate resulted in a 3 to 0 decision for Yankton. Earl Hansen and Hubert Humphrey again debated for Doland. Yankton and Rapid City met in the finals, and Rapid City won the tournement.

The debaters taking part in the decision contests were Hubert Humphrey, Myrtle Drayer, Earl Hansen, Lewis Terpstra and Margie Sheldon. In addition Frances Humphrey and Letitia Hahn took part in non-decision contests.

For the fourth time in five years Doland won the district championship and was represented at the state tournament: This is an enviable record and Miss Lois Crouch, the debate coach, is to be commended for the interest maintained and the success achieved in debate.

May 9, 1929

Hubert Humphrey and Myrtle Drayer
Win Scholastic Honors

At the close of school Wednesday afternoon Miss Jones announced the winners of scholastic honors for the class of 1929. First place, based upon scholast standing for the entire four years of high school, was won by Hubert Humphrey, while Myrtle Drayer placed second. Following closely were Mary Hill and Helen Riddle.

The winners for the class of 1929 have been very active in extra-school activities for their entire high school careers. For this reason they are to be especially commended that they were at the same time able to maintain a high standard of scholarship

---

Hubert's graduation picture

The great influence of my life in Doland was the Doland schools and the teachers that we had, and those teachers still today are a great influence in my life. And I think of the kind of community spirit that has characterized this community. There needs to be a sense of community for people to really belong and to feel that they are a part of a society. Or to put it another way, when you feel that you are a part of a society, there is a sense of community.

HUBERT H. HUMPHREY
DOLAND SPEECH

I think it was either at the District or at the State Debate Tournament, after we had won a 2-to-1 decision, that we were standing around in the corridor when this affable gentleman came up to us and indicated who he was and said, "Fellows, you really work great together. You've got a great attack . . ." and so on and so on. And then he said, "If I were you, I wouldn't worry so much about the facts." The fellow who made the comment was Karl Mundt, who later became a United States senator from South Dakota. He was a Republican, and he and Hubert served many years together.

JULIAN HARTT

I remember one funny thing. We were coming home one night from one of these junkets out somewhere and stopped at what we used to call a greasy spoon to get something to eat. It was fairly late at night, and we asked about this thing and that thing on the menu, and the proprietor of the place kept saying, "Sorry fellows but we are all out of that." Finally, Hubert said, "How about the tomato soup I see on the menu?" And the fellow said, "There's no problem there as long as the ketchup and hot water hold out."

JULIAN HARTT

schools in the surrounding districts. By the time Humphrey became a high school senior in 1928, the Doland debaters had won four district championships in five years and had come in second the year they didn't win. Hubert had become one of the four H's, a formidable debate team made up of Earl Hansen, Julian Hartt, Alvin Hahn, and Hubert Humphrey. One of the debate judges was Karl Mundt, a teacher in nearby Bryant and a Republican who later served in the United States Senate with Humphrey.

In 1928 a principal issue debated by the Doland teams was the McNary-Haugen Farm Relief Act, a measure designed to provide for government purchase of agriculture surpluses, twice vetoed by Calvin Coolidge as "socialistic." By the following year, Farm Relief was no longer just a question for debate—it was an imperative.

The Great Depression had come early to Doland; by 1926, farm prices had long passed their wartime peak, and both banks in town had failed. From 1926 onward, Humphrey's teachers were among the few people in Doland who could count on a steady income, though they were being paid in a kind of scrip called "warrants," which complicated things a bit. The salary—$1,500 a year—wasn't bad for the times, but there were no banks to cash the warrants. So the teachers took them to the only place in town where they could be redeemed, the local grain elevator. In order to encourage holders of warrants not to demand their money too promptly, 10 percent interest was paid on them from the time of issuance until a later date when they were "called" by the district. Not many teachers were able to hold out that long, so the warrants passed quickly into the hands of the elevator operators, who were better able to wait out the call.

Everyone in Doland suffered financial hardship during these years. In 1920, wheat had brought $2.76 a bushel. The price was less than half that in 1929, and it continued to drop. A local millionaire watched his fortune crumble when the price of the wheat he held dropped to 11¢ a bushel while the cost of storage on it reached 26¢ a bushel. Tip Miles, a Doland resident, recalls how his Dad wanted to load up some corn and trade it to the elevator man for coal. He was told that in order to take the corn in trade, he'd have to pay the elevator man 6¢ a bushel just to be rid of it. He didn't get his coal that day.

Tumbling farm prices were bad enough, but there were other problems. During the boom period of the First World War, farmers had expanded their holdings, and the postwar drop in prices left them unable to pay off their debts. While farms were being foreclosed and banks were failing as a result of the bad loans, a plague of almost Biblical proportions descended upon the Great Plains. From 1927 to 1937 there was not a single year of good crops. In 1932 the dust storms began; clouds of silt-like material were so enormous that they blotted out the sun. As the fine particles worked into the smallest openings, people held wet handkerchiefs over their faces so they could breathe. The dust storms were followed by the grasshoppers, which ate every particle of vegetable matter they could find and then, still hungry, ate the paint

Dust storms and plagues of grasshoppers devastated South Dakota during the 1930s.

off the houses and barns. They went away only when there was nothing left to eat.

Faced with such multiple disasters, farmers found it difficult to pay their taxes. "Taxes were only $35 a year on this quarter section [160 acres] of land," recalls Homer Krentz, "but you couldn't pay on that. The government had a wheat loan program and you'd go out and borrow on that. Before you got your loan though, they'd deduct your taxes and that's the way you could get your taxes paid."[9]

Things were no easier for small businessmen. Humphrey, Sr., was carrying over 500 accounts ranging from 50¢ on up and was continually being squeezed between his debtors in Doland and the creditors at Minneapolis Drug who furnished his merchandise. The Minneapolis wholesalers carried Humphrey, though somewhat reluctantly at times, and he never forgot their faith in him. All through his life he reminded his boys to keep them as their suppliers even when they could find the same goods cheaper elsewhere.

By 1927, the depression had begun to overwhelm the Humphreys. The pleasant two-story home that Hubert had grown up in, one of the handsomest in Doland, was sold to pay the family's bills. Hubert always remembered his boyhood home with fondness. "It wasn't a building that would be a showplace in a big city, but it was a pretty good house, as good as any in Doland. It was a large, squarish place, with white siding and a porch. Beautiful shade trees on the front lawn, and a plum and apple orchard in the back. Mother loved that house—it had hardwood floors, a big

Hubert Humphrey's boyhood home

basement, and two bathrooms. Dad loved it. And for the children—my older brother, Ralph, my two younger sisters, Frances and Fern, and me—it was as taken for granted and as beautiful as the sky or trees."[10]

The day the sale papers were signed, Hubert came home to see his father and mother standing in the yard in despair, unable to bring themselves to go back inside the house. It was the first time young Hubert had ever seen his father weep. In an article written many years later for the *Atlantic Monthly,* Humphrey described his feelings: "Dad told me we simply had to sell the house. This was the only way he could cover and pay the bills. And I seemed to learn then, no matter how competent my father may have been, or how good my mother, or how fine my community, that it could be destroyed and wrecked by forces over which we had no control." The Humphreys moved to a smaller house a block away, which they rented for the remainder of their days in Doland.

> This event was probably the most profound experience of my early years. It was the moment when I ceased being a child, when I began to have an adult's awareness of the pain and tragedy in life. . . . But through the years, I carried with me from that scene not just the picture of this masterful man in tears, but the fact that after this terrible loss, he carried not an ounce of bitterness, apology or defeatism. He continued to do what he had always done—to plunge into life without protecting himself with suspicion, reserve, or emotional caution. People like that enjoy the sunshine of life to the full. But many of them are unprepared for the storms, and when they are shocked or hurt,

The Humphrey family moved to this smaller house in 1927.

they withdraw and cover up. Not Dad. The same sensitivity to things he cared for that made him weep carried him beyond this wound into the future. Right up to the time he died.[11]

Losing the house did not bring an end to the Humphreys' troubles. As the months passed, customers of the drugstore ran up accounts that became tougher and tougher to collect. The notice reproduced here contains more than a hint of the exasperation that Humphrey, Sr., must have felt in

H. H. HUMPHREY
REXALL AND NYAL
DRUGGIST
DOLAND, S. D.,

DEAR SIR:

On November 1st we mailed to each one of our customers owing us on that date a statement of their account. On this statement was stamped the information that on the 15th of the month following the account would become due and that any additional credit would be discontinued until the account was paid.

This undoubtedly did not attract your attention, as being busy and the account being small, you let it slip your mind.

Now thats just the situation; you are busy and my account against you is small, but if you will take into consideration the fact that I have on my books 500 accounts ranging in amounts from 50 cents to $100 you will then realize why it is that I have set a limit on the time an account can run, it isn't that I want to be small and limit your particular credit; this rule applies to everybody, no one is exempted, on the last of each month we close our books and every one owing us is sent a statement, showing the amount due. This amount is due and payable before the 15th of month following date of statement mailed you.

On the 30th of last month we sent you a statement of your account. You undoubtedly received it. According to our books it has not been paid. Now I do not wish to be insistent, but to be fair I must ask that you give this your attention. The amount you are owing is notated below.

Thanking you in advance I beg to remain,

Yours very truly,

H. H. HUMPHREY.

....................Amount Due.

trying to prod his debtors into payment without offending them. When Humphrey finally gave up, closed down the store, and moved to Huron, South Dakota, in 1931, he tore up $13,000 in unpaid bills in Doland, rationalizing that at least a debtor would never have to be embarrassed about coming into a Humphrey store again once the bill was cancelled. Ralph Humphrey, now dead, and his wife, Harriet, who still runs Humphrey's Drugstore in Huron, later told Tip Miles, "God bless you people in Doland. You kept us going and never forgot us all during the early years in Huron." The elder Humphrey had been right. The people in Doland still traded with Humphrey when they did their shopping in Huron.

When the Humphreys were forced to close the drugstore in 1931, they joined the large numbers of Doland citizens who had already been overwhelmed by economic disaster. Yet even at the beginning of the new decade, when signs of financial chaos were everywhere, it had not been too late for the *Doland Times Record* to run the cheerful economic forecast of "Charles M. Schwab, Steel Magnate." Under the heading "Business Outlook All Right," Mr. Schwab wrote, "I have never felt more optimistic than I do today about the future of business. The recent speculative wave that has hit the country has brought losses only to those people who thought they were rich. We of the factories lost nothing, for we still have wealth in the bricks and mortar and machines of our factories. Business in the United States is going to grow just as surely and just as fast in the future as it has in the past. . . ."[12]

One of the great tragedies of the great urban centers today is that their people don't feel they belong. They live there, but they are not really involved. It isn't their life—it's their residence—it is a place they work, or a place they sleep. Or a place that they play, but it isn't their life. Doland was like one great big family—lots of times troubles, but don't we have that in families? Some times bitter arguments, but we've had that in families. People are very different, but that's true in families, but there was a sense of being and a sense of belonging and a sense of caring. Everybody knew everybody. There was really no place to hide. There was always a place to be—and you had the feeling that you were one.

HUBERT H. HUMPHREY
DOLAND SPEECH

Well, it used to be quite a business center. We used to have two doctors and a dentist, we had implement stores (a couple of them), we had garages there. Now we don't even have garages. We don't have a drugstore, a doctor, or a dentist, or nothing. It's just gone backwards completely. We don't have the trade center we used to have. All our people are gone. We used to have two or three times as many people in the area as we have now. That made a difference right there. Of course, there's never been much opportunity for a young man in this country, except maybe if you wanted to farm.

HOMER KRENTZ

Had the "steel magnate" had the opportunity to visit Doland, South Dakota, on the day he wrote those words, he might have found that the people there being ground down by the weight of the depression were not merely those who had recently indulged in a speculative binge. They were small farmers and business people like the Humphreys, whose economic problems were not of their own making. By 1932, people all over the country would feel what Doland had been feeling for six years.

Main Street, Doland, South Dakota

chapter 2

TO MINNESOTA

"I learned more about economics from one South Dakota dust storm than I did from all my years in college."

Hubert H. Humphrey, Jr.

My brother, Ralph, is no longer with us. He graduated from this high school in the class of 1926. And I remember full well that he went down to Dakota Wesleyan and I figured—boy, is he living it up now, going down there to one of those wicked colleges where you can smoke and really have some fun. I used to go down and see Ralph at Dakota Wesleyan. Mother and Dad let me drive the old Model T sedan we had down there. Mom thought it was just wonderful for a younger brother to want to go down to see the older brother. Mom never knew that the older brother told me, "Get that car down here. I need it for the weekend." I never saw hide nor hair of him after I got down there, but it always seemed to me that Mitchell was just about as far away as you could ever get.

HUBERT H. HUMPHREY
DOLAND SPEECH

It took Hubert Humphrey about 11 years, from 1929 to 1940, to complete the transition from South Dakota to Minnesota, to finish his education, and to set his life firmly on its course.

The first step came in the fall of 1929, when he left Doland for the University of Minnesota. There had been some family discussion to the effect that Hubert should join brother Ralph at Dakota Wesleyan, a small Methodist school in Mitchell, South Dakota, which later became George McGovern's alma mater. It was a choice that would have pleased Hubert's mother as well as the Doland athletic coach, Irven Herther, a Dakota Wesleyan alumnus. Herther's old school was well known to Doland residents because the coach had systematically reincarnated castoff Wesleyan athletic uniforms into those of Doland High. It was probably no accident that the nickname of the school teams, the Doland "Wheelers," coincided nicely with the "D" and/or "W" initials that occasionally appeared on Dakota Wesleyan uniforms.

Humphrey, Sr., eventually decided against Dakota Wesleyan because he wanted to give Hubert the broader exposure of a nondenominational school in a more cosmopolitan setting. In September 1929, he set Hubert down on the campus of the University of Minnesota in Minneapolis, then and now a school with one of the three largest student bodies on a single campus anywhere in the world. Humphrey, Sr., let Hubert out into a line of students winding in front of the administration building—"a line with more people in it than the whole population of my home county." "What will I do?" Hubert asked him. Humphrey, Sr., said,

"Just follow the line. You'll find out." And then with his parting advice to Hubert—"Goodby, good luck, grow up"—he left his son to his own devices, barely able to find his way from his rooming house to his classes and back.[1]

Hubert's early efforts at higher education produced mixed results. His freshman grades didn't compare with his record at Doland High, but a little academic slippage was understandable. He was a bit homesick and somewhat overwhelmed by the institution he was attending, which in itself had over 20 times more people than Doland, but he enjoyed the excitement of being on his own in a big city for the first time in his life. He frequently hitchhiked the 250 miles back home on weekends.

After only one quarter at the university, Hubert's father had to withdraw any financial help, and Hubert took on a part-time job at Swoboda's Drugstore near his rooming house in Minneapolis. When he returned home that summer to help his Dad in the drugstore, the family's financial circumstances had taken still another turn for the worse. Since Ralph had stayed out of school the previous year to help Humphrey, Sr., while Hubert studied, it was time for Hubert to return the favor. So Ralph took off for Minneapolis to continue his education at the University of Minnesota, and Hubert remained behind in Doland. After working through the fall quarter of 1930 (Minnesota being one of the few universities to operate on a quarter rather than a semester system), Hubert was temporarily rescued from the drugstore by a minor miracle. A $50 check arrived from Uncle Harry, Hubert, Sr.'s brother and a close and loving rela-

Frosh Week at the University of Minnesota in the 1930s

tive who worked as a plant pathologist in the Department of Agriculture in Washington. Hubert returned to Minneapolis for another quarter of school, though Ralph had by this time inherited his younger brother's job at Swoboda's. Hubert resumed employment under the supervision of Ralph, both quite aware that it was Hubert who had helped Ralph get work there in the first place. It was a bit of a strain.

During that quarter, Hubert's Dad showed up at Swoboda's Drugstore late one evening and broke the news to his son that the family would have to move to Huron, a city of about 14,000 forty miles south of Doland. "If we are going to go broke, we might as well do it in a big town,"[2] Humphrey, Sr., said. One major element of the move had yet to be resolved. Humphrey's creditors at Minneapolis Drug—George Doerr and Sewall Andrews—had to agree to an additional extension of credit. Humphrey, Sr., using his life insurance as backing and all his powers of persuasion, convinced his creditors to stake him in a new store in Huron. Both Doerr and Andrews personally "went on the note" to their supplier, McKesson and Robbins, and Humphrey got a chance to start over in a new town.

In March 1931, Hubert completed another quarter at the university and returned to South Dakota, this time to Huron and, by all indications, to a lifetime in the drugstore business. As the likelihood of this career choice increased in the months following, Hubert enrolled in a pharmacy school—the Capital College of Pharmacy in Denver. The $200 enrollment fee was financed by a

Hubert (left) and two friends in Denver, Colorado, 1933

loan from the local ice cream company, which was repaid 25¢ at a time from the profits for each five-gallon carton of ice cream the Humphreys sold. The pharmacy course was supposed to take four years. Hubert completed it in six months and finished second in the class on the final exam, after memorizing great gobs of English and Latin medicinal descriptions and dosages from the *Pharmacopoeia.*

In 1933, Humphrey was back in Huron and on his way to becoming a model of small town respectability. He was a member of the Methodist Church, scoutmaster of the church troop, and a member of the Young Democrats. It was because of his political activities that Humphrey got the chance to shake hands with FDR when the president made his dust bowl tour after taking office in March 1933. One minute Humphrey was standing

Scoutmaster Humphrey and his troop

He became a kind of second Roosevelt, operating from the weaker end of the avenue. He showed more imagination and originality in the uses of government on behalf of ordinary people than anyone to hit town since Roosevelt.

ERIC SEVAREID

at the back of the crowd, and the next minute someone appeared and told him he was wanted on the presidential train. Whisked on and off in two minutes, he had the only meeting in his life with the man whose program he perpetuated more effectively than anyone else ever associated with the New Deal except perhaps Roosevelt himself.

Hubert's political activities and his other interests kept him busy, but most of his time in Huron was spent in the family drugstore. To supplement their business, the Humphreys had become manufacturers and purveyors of patent medicines for both hogs and humans. A sign featuring an ugly wooden pig was hung over the drugstore to tell the public about this unusual service. Farmers got the message, and it was Humphrey's that became known as the farmers' drugstore in Huron. While Hubert, Jr., minded the store and stirred the con-

Hubert takes time off from work in the Humphrey drugstore.

coctions in the basement, Hubert, Sr., went on the road with "Humphrey's BTV" (Body Tone Veterinary), a mineral supplement and dewormer for hogs, and "Humphrey's Chest Oil" and "Humphrey's Sniffles" for two-legged sufferers. Though the magic elixir qualities claimed for most patent medicines in those days were absent from the various Humphrey cures, they worked well enough and constituted an important part of the family income. The farmers that bought the medicines were good customers, even if their methods of payment were somewhat unusual. Often lacking cash, "farm customers would pay for their prescriptions with chickens and eggs, which then became the next day's bill of fare for the lunch counter."[3] There were other customers to please as well. During the first two years he spent working at the drugstore, Humphrey slept in the store basement, waking up at 5:30 A.M. to be ready with breakfast for the truck drivers who arrived in town at the crack of dawn.

The Humphrey drugstore did not lack for business, but the move to Huron had not solved the family's financial plight. Though Huron was much larger than Doland, Humphrey was now competing with five other stores. Moreover, the depression had continued to deepen, and South Dakota remained among the most sorely pressed areas in the United States. The annual personal income in the state dropped throughout the thirties, falling from $417 in 1929 to $360 in 1940. The value of farm products sold in South Dakota dropped from $212 million in 1930 to $96 million in 1940. The value of the farmlands and buildings in the state fell

I've had such a wonderful good fortune in my life—to go to school in Doland, to live here in the formative years of my life, to go to the great university and receive a real inspiration for learning, and then to have learned hard lessons of sacrifice and trouble in the depression.

HUBERT H. HUMPHREY
DOLAND SPEECH

from $1.285 billion in 1930 to $692 million in 1935 and further still to $505 million in 1940. Neighboring Minnesota, always a much more prosperous state, had begun to recover as the thirties wore on; farmland and buildings there, worth $2.125 billion in 1930, had dropped to $1.383 billion in 1935, but by 1940 had edged up to $1.443 billion.

South Dakota was also plagued by bad weather during these years. Rainfall, always a problem in the semi-arid region that ran north and south through Doland and Huron, averaged less than 10 inches during several years in the 1930s. On Armistice Day, 1932, the first dust storm hit Huron. Humphrey was hunting pheasants at the time: "The sun was blacked out and all you could see

was a little shining disk. I didn't know what it was; it looked like a terrible smoke cloud. Debris—thistles and tumbleweeds—came before the storm. I thought it was the end of the world. Then a terrible, fine silt engulfed everything."[4] The dust storms increased in savagery. In the period from 1933 to 1934, there were over ninety in the Huron area. Two children were caught in one storm on their way home from school, and their bodies were found the next day, half buried in the dust. Layers of dust, two inches thick, covered everything, both indoors and out. It wasn't possible to plant crops; sometimes it wasn't even possible to drive a car, and it barely seemed possible to breathe.

When Humphrey, Sr., wasn't on the road selling patent medicines, he sat in his empty store by the hour, staring into the deepening chasm of disaster that were his ledgers—a scene as dramatic and wrenching as the moment Hubert found his father weeping in the front yard when they'd lost their home in Doland. Hubert and his Dad traveled to Minneapolis to attempt to persuade their creditors not to take the store away. It was more a matter of pride than anything else. Both Humphrey, Sr., and Jr., could have found jobs somewhere as pharmacists, but they had believed in the American dream for a long time. Humphrey had always owned his own business, and to lose it and go to work for someone else was more than he could bear. Somehow the debts would be paid, somehow he would manage to give his creditors every nickel he owed them, if only they would not take the store away—if only they would let him keep title to it and continue to call it the Humphrey Drugstore. The

I can still see him at his desk, his hands wringing, wondering how he could ever pay the bills, pay the taxes, take care of the family. I could see the sorrow, the burden on his life.

HUBERT H. HUMPHREY
ST. PAUL PIONEER PRESS
OCTOBER 2, 1977

creditors finally shrugged and agreed. Humphrey, Sr., had won—but what?

Hubert was growing increasingly unhappy under the pressures of both the depression and the drugstore. His year and a half at the university had shown him not only that things were better in Minnesota, but also that he could be a part of them. He had tasted the freedom of university life. He yearned to be rid of the staggering debts and the restrictions of small-town life and to be an actor on a bigger and more hopeful stage. But family and business pressure continued to interfere. He planned a trip to Chicago for the World's Fair in 1934, but Humphrey, Sr., objected, and a quarrel ensued, climaxed by a grand and melodra-

In 1933, a Minneapolis newspaper featured this picture of Minnesotans "singing away the Depression." Hubert Humphrey, Jr., hoped that life would be brighter for him across the Minnesota border.

matic scene in the drugstore complete with smashed glassware and angry shouts. He didn't go. Time dragged on. The store took most of it, but there was still a bit to be spared for the Young Democrats and the Epworth League and his role as scoutmaster for the church troop. And then, too, he had met a girl.

Her name was Muriel Buck. She was pert and attractive, and Hubert found her very appealing. Muriel was not the first girl in his life. He had been engaged to a young woman in Huron, but she had broken the engagement and had gone to Minneapolis to study music, taking Hubert's engagement ring with her. After that experience, Hubert vowed never to fall in love again, but meeting Muriel Buck made him change his mind.

Muriel Buck

> I met her first at a college dance and I enjoyed her very much. Then she came to the drugstore a couple of times. We had a soda fountain and she had a Coke. I remember she came in with another young lady. I always kid her about this and she doesn't like to have me mention it, but when she walked through that door, it was kind of like an x-ray, because the sunlight would come through and she was wearing a little light blue dress. I remember very well—I remember her hairstyle at the time, kind of a Dutch bob. . . . I thought, "Boy, that's a cute girl." She had big blue eyes. I can also remember—I can literally, shall I say this, I could see through that dress and I said, "Boy, what a shape that gal has—what a fine looking woman." I remember going to the dances with her. We used to have a dancehall about a mile west of the town. Wednesday night, we would have our Wednesday night dances. I loved to dance and so did she.[5]

At the Wednesday night dances, held at Lampe's Pavilion, Muriel and Hubert took to the floor to the music of the Hotsy-Totsy Boys (later known as Lawrence Welk and his orchestra) and Wayne King. It did not take long for Muriel to discover that Hubert was the best dancer in Huron. At first she found him too talkative, but the more she saw of him, the more she realized what a talented and serious person he really was.

The Buck family, with Muriel on her father's lap

Before the depression, Muriel's father, Andrew Buck, had been a prosperous produce wholesaler in Huron—a big butter and egg man, as well as a church deacon and a bank director. Muriel had graduated from Huron High and attended Huron College for two years, with hopes of someday

Muriel and Hubert receive honorary degrees from Huron College in 1966.

becoming a concert pianist. But the depression finally caught up with the Bucks. Andrew Buck sold the produce business and built some cabins on Big Stone Lake, running the operation as a vacation resort while Muriel took a job as a bookkeeper.

Soon after meeting Muriel, Hubert got a glimpse of a wider future that might someday be his. In the fall of 1935, he went to Washington, D.C. to see his sister Frances graduate from George Washington University and to take his boy scout troop on a tour of the nation's capital. The impression the visit made on him was considerable. He visited the Senate galleries and heard Huey Long, then at the height of his power. Humphrey wrote to Muriel:

> Maybe I seem foolish to have such vain hopes and plans, but, Bucky, I can see how someday, if you and I just apply ourselves and make up our minds to work for bigger things, how we can someday live here in Washington and probably be in government politics or service. I intend to set my aim at Congress. Don't laugh at me, Muriel. Maybe it does sound rather egotistical and beyond reason, but, Muriel, I do know others have succeeded. Why haven't I a chance? You'll help me, I know.[6]

They became engaged in December 1935, and after Hubert could finally extract sufficient time off from his father for a respectable honeymoon, he set the wedding date for early September 1936. There was almost a last-minute postponement to accommodate a vacation that Humphrey, Sr., absentmindedly promised one of his clerks for that same week, but Andrew Buck made it clear that there would be no further trifling with his daughter's affections, and Hubert and Muriel marched to the altar on September 3, 1936.

Their honeymoon started off as a threesome. Sister Frances, already in Hubert's bad graces that day for having caused him to be late to the wedding by mislaying her garter, hitched a ride with the couple as far as Watertown, South Dakota. With Frances disposed of, they headed for Duluth, Minnesota, and the North Shore of Lake Superior, determined to make the most of their five-day honeymoon. The honeymoon was a success, but on the way home, disaster struck; just ten miles away from Huron, their car hit a cow. Neither the cow nor the car survived the encounter, and after paying an irate farmer for one and a somewhat more understanding father for the other, Hubert found himself back at the drugstore in Huron.

Marriage strengthened Humphrey's resolution to leave the drugstore and pursue his own life. Muriel was not only supportive of his ambitions, but she also saved enough money during the next year from her job as a bookkeeper to make them believe that a move was possible. Her nest egg was all of $675, leading Humphrey to say in later years that he had married Muriel for her money. In August 1937, Hubert told his father he wanted to leave Huron and return to the University of Minnesota to complete his education. Humphrey, Sr., countered by offering his son a full partnership in the drugstore. In 1936, Humphrey, Sr., had been elected to the South Dakota State Legislature. Now there was starting to be some talk of his

When I had a chance to go to the University of Minnesota, which was my dream as a young man, for years I felt I was locked up in the South Dakota dust bowl, I felt that I would never get out, that I was in prison. Then I got married. My wife, Muriel, helped me. She said, "We're going to get out of here—we're going to give you a chance to become what you want to be."

HUBERT H. HUMPHREY
ST. PAUL PIONEER PRESS
OCTOBER 2, 1977

Hubert had great admiration for his father, who had a great influence on his political thinking. He spoke of his father as being the only Democrat in the South Dakota Legislature in the depression years. I was in Hubert's home for dinner a number of times when his father was there, and he was in deed a remarkable man. Both had great enthusiasm for Franklin D. Roosevelt.

C. DONALD PETERSON
ASSOCIATE JUSTICE
MINNESOTA SUPREME COURT

Muriel and Hubert shortly after their marriage in 1936

running for governor or for the United States Senate. But no such dream was in prospect if his son wouldn't be there to run the family business.

Hubert and his father talked of the dust storms in South Dakota and the growing economic resurgence in Minnesota, of Hubert's unfinished education, of his love for Muriel, and his desire to give her more than the drugstore could offer. Finally, the elder Humphrey put his dream aside, and the younger man picked up his. He and his young wife took that dream with them out of South Dakota and on to Minnesota.

chapter 3

BECOMING SOMEONE

"I didn't have time for four years in the university because I wanted to get my degree, so I did it in three. And Muriel worked day and night to make that possible."

Hubert H. Humphrey

The political atmosphere at the University of Minnesota was supercharged at the time of Hubert Humphrey's second arrival in the fall of 1937. Political radicals of various persuasions, although relatively few in number, were conspicuous on the campus. In good weather it was rare not to find a soapboxer holding forth in front of the new Student Union; it was difficult to cross campus without inheriting a pamphlet or two from some enthusiastic dispenser of new politics or old religion. The

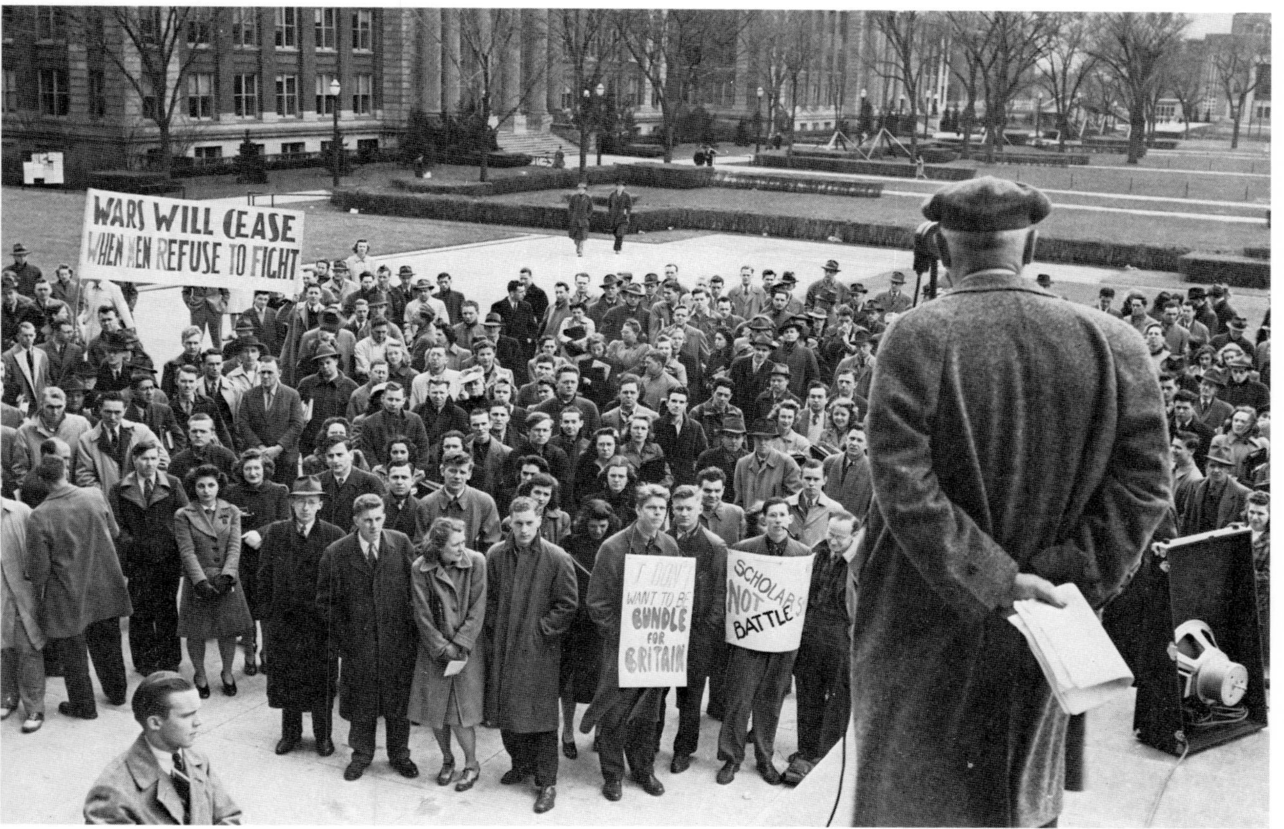

A war protest on the University of Minnesota campus in the 1930s

principal issues dividing the Minnesota students were the coming war and the continuing depression, and opposing sides in these controversies freely labeled each other "Communists" or "Fascists." The parallel to the student protest on campuses of the mid-sixties is irresistible, but the ultimate difference is that the campuses of the thirties never exploded into violence. "In those days," said Ben Lippincott, one of Humphrey's professors, "there were gentlemen."[1] There was also unrest, confrontation, name-calling, and even some minor fracases, but the fuse of campus revolt remained unlit.

The majority of students at the university regarded the name-callers, the lapel-clutchers, and the other political fanatics primarily as interesting crackpots. Students from wealthy families were more or less isolated from campus radicalism by the cocoon of fraternity and sorority life. Most students, Humphrey included, were associated with neither wealth nor fanaticism; they formed into small groups that were devoted to their own special interests. The artists, the farm boys, the urban sophisticates, all thrust into the potpourri of the huge state institution and without immediate prospects for employment or recognition, turned to like-minded people for identity and amusement. In a community of 18,000, there were enough different activities available to satisfy almost any interest.

Many students shared an intense interest in the exploits of the university football team. The late thirties were the days of the great Minnesota teams, when the Gopher coach was said to pick his

The funeral of a worker killed during the 1934 strike

The Minnesota National Guard was called out during the truckers' strike in 1934.

line by going out into the country and looking for the biggest boy he could find behind a plow. He would ask the boy for directions to the next farm, and if the boy simply answered, the coach passed him by and went on down the road. But if he picked up his plow with one hand to point the right direction, the coach saw to it that he was on his way to the University of Minnesota.

Athletics and other campus activities kept the students busy and absorbed, but no matter how much they might try, they could not isolate themselves completely from the world outside the university. The Minnesota campus was not exactly a bucolic grove of academe; there were no classes in the woods, no gentle professors chewing on blades of grass while cows mooed in the background to the sounds of Socratic discourse. Instead, there were 18,000 middle-class kids, two-thirds of whom had to work at least some of the time to help pay their way through school. The campus itself was set down firmly in the midst of a city of half a million. It was a knowledge factory, and the real world intruded on all sides.

Students at the university were well aware of the bloody truckers' strike that took place in Minneapolis in 1934. Organized by the Trotskyite Dunne brothers, the strike lasted off and on throughout the summer, and several blue-collar workers were killed or filled with buckshot during the riots. It wasn't until one of the local bluebloods, who had organized themselves into a "Citizens' Alliance" to break the strike, died in the "Battle of Deputies' Run" that the local establishment became outraged. Eric Sevareid, a student at the University of

Minnesota at that time, recalls seeing his father holding the newspaper with trembling hands and announcing "This is revolution" as he read accounts of the carnage.[2]

The war issue also captured more attention on campus as the threat of war itself escalated in Europe and the students were threatened by personal involvement in the conflict. Male students at the land-grant, state-controlled University of Minnesota were required to participate in military training classes. When a student named Kaplan skipped some military classes and was expelled, another brouhaha developed. The wildly popular and controversial governor of the state, Floyd B. Olson, finally persuaded the University Board of Regents to abolish military training before the issue was settled. Olson claimed that he himself had dropped out of the university briefly as a student in protest over military drill.

In the thirties, many students at the University of Minnesota joined the international student pacifist movement and took the so-called Oxford pledge: "I will not bear arms for flag or country." Among them was Dick Scammon, who later wrote the best-selling book *The Real Majority* with Ben Wattenberg. When war broke out, however, Scammon was one of the first volunteers for active duty. Another pledge-taker was Lee Loevinger, a close friend of Humphrey's; he became a warrant officer with the first United States naval mission to England. Student activists like Scammon, Loevinger, Eric Sevareid, and Ken Peterson were part of a campus political party called the Progressives and active in the Progressives' inner circle, the Jaco-

President Coffman was a College of Education kind of person, a professional administrator. In addition to that, he was a Republican and a Baptist rolled into one. So he was a pretty tough hombre. . . . He used to blue pencil the raises that Professor William Anderson, the head of the political science department, recommended for me because I was a Socialist. Anderson proposed two or three thousand dollar raises, and each time Coffman would blue pencil them. Coffman went over every person on the budget. One day I was asked to come to his office. He said, "Young man, do you realize that you're interfering with my budget?" and I said, "No sir, I don't realize that, sir." And he said, "Rumor has it that you're a Communist. Is that true?" I said, "No, sir, I'm really a Democratic Socialist." Coffman wasn't a smoker in those days. There was a wastepaper basket under his desk between his legs, and I knelt down and flicked my ashes in and he got grimmer and grimmer. He said, "Would you sign an affidavit to that effect?" I said, "Yes sir, on one condition, that this doesn't interfere with my academic freedom. Pass me the slip, sir."

BEN LIPPINCOTT

bins. The Jacobins managed to make life hell for university president Lotus Coffman. They invited the Dunne brothers to speak on campus, an act that did not generate admiration in high administration circles. Nor did the appearance on campus of Governor Olson, who despised the university officials. He had been denied the right to speak by the university, but he came anyway.

In addition to lively political groups like the Jacobins, there was a flourishing literary cult at the University of Minnesota during the late thirties. Among the campus literary figures was Tom Heggen, who was to write *Mister Roberts,* a novel about World War II that eventually became a long-running play and a popular movie. Heggen was a close friend of Max Shulman, later the author of such best-selling books as *Barefoot Boy with Cheek* and *Rally Round the Flag, Boys.* During his years at the university, Shulman had a column in the campus newspaper, the *Minnesota Daily.* Other members of the *Daily* crowd were Dorothy Lebedoff, now a story editor in Hollywood, and Norman Katkov, author of *A Little Sleep, A Little Slumber.* (Hubert Humphrey tried out for a position on the *Daily* staff but had been turned down.) When Shulman was later asked why so many of his friends from the university became professional writers, he explained, "I was the first guy to get a book published, and when I did it, they all said to themselves, 'If that dumb S.O.B. can do it, so can I.' And they did."[3]

Tom Heggen

The early writings of Shulman and company were far removed from their later professional works. Long before Shulman learned that he was

A picture of one of Hubert's heroes hung on the wall of the Humphrey apartment in Minneapolis.

funny, he and Heggen wrote stories of martyred youth and oppressed workers for the campus *Literary Review,* a magazine whose unofficial slogan was "Oh, God, the pain!" A sample of Heggen's work from 1940 reflects their concerns:

> The air raid alarm sounded in London at midnight sharp. It was the first one in nearly 8 hours and the people were more excited than usual. . . . Many of them, women and children, stood at the entrance to the bomb shelter and watched the fingers of the search lights pivot across the sky and the flare of the bombs. They were very close this time. "That's right up by the cathedral," the men cried. And a child turned to her mother and said: "Is that right, mother? Did they get us?" But the mother was watching the great flares and didn't answer.
>
> In America girls primped for dates and the boys talked loudly to one another. The couples danced close together and young people talked about the future and the things they wanted. And in the distance, almost inaudible, but becoming louder, was the sound of something strange coming to America; something very different and all the time growing.[4]

All the time growing and part of the time corny, Heggen's work still expresses both the idealism and the horror of war that America's youth felt as the country neared the precipice of World War II.

Like the literary circle at the university, Humphrey and his friends lived and breathed politics, although most of them were not numbered among the campus activists. Those close to Humphrey at this time included many men who went on to careers in politics and public life: Don Peterson, who was a debating partner of Humphrey and

The main thing I remember about Hubert is that he was not one of the better known liberals of that time; he wasn't that much of a campus activist; he was too busy working his way through college. But occasionally I'd see him, and he and I used to meet at the old Brown Drugstore. It would be late at night. He'd sweep out the store, while I had a Coke and we'd talk politics.

DICK SCAMMON

later an associate justice on the Minnesota Supreme Court; Arthur Naftalin, who served as Humphrey's assistant when he was mayor of Minneapolis and subsequently became a four-time mayor of the city himself; Max Kampelman, part of Humphrey's original Washington staff and later a partner in one of Washington's most successful law firms; and Orville Freeman, who babysat for the Humphreys and later became governor of Minnesota and U.S. Secretary of Agriculture.

Members of the university debate team in 1938: (from left to right) **Harold Margulies, Newton Margulies, Donald Peterson, and Hubert Humphrey**

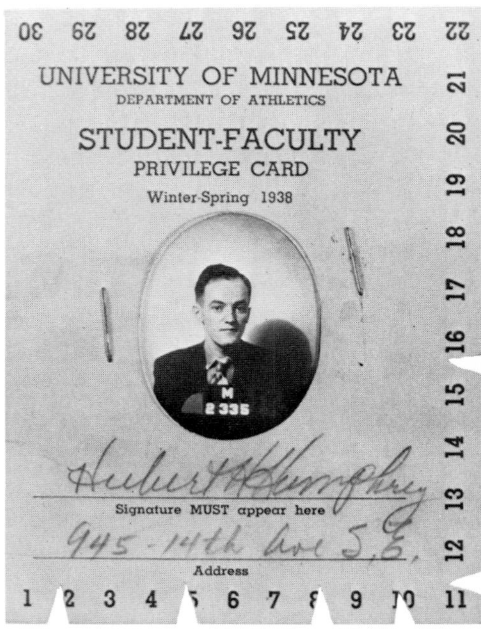

Freeman first met Humphrey in a political science class taught by Evron Kirkpatrick:

> We were on different sides in a discussion—not a hot one, but a vigorous one—in which I was proven to be completely wrong. As we left the class, talking and jabbering at each other, we got a few hundred yards away from the campus and somehow or other, we shifted and got into football. I was playing football then, on one of Bierman's teams, and Humphrey was an avid football guy—he just loved football, always did until the day he died, and so he started talking to me about football. He wanted to know all about this person and that person, this game, that game, who did what, where and how. He just loved to play football, but then I think he weighed 120 pounds. A strong wind would have blown him away.[5]

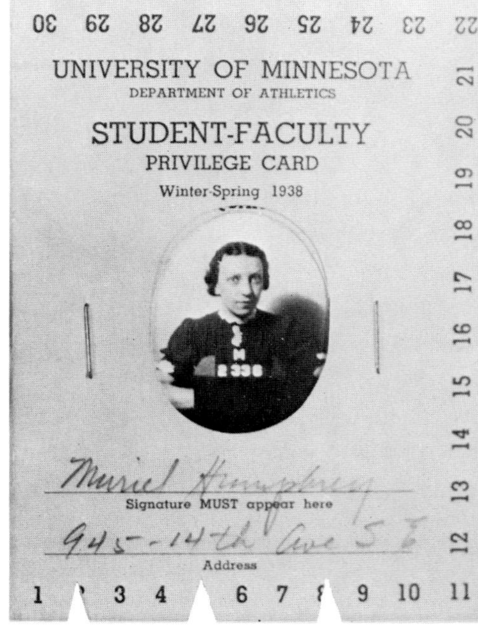

Freeman and Humphrey soon discovered that they shared as intense an interest in politics as they did in football. Unlike the Jacobins, however, they and their friends found an outlet for their political interests in debating rather than in campus politics. As members of the university debate team, Humphrey and Freeman visited other Minnesota campuses to debate the issue "Resolved: That the expenditure of federal funds to stimulate the economy should cease." The Humphrey-Freeman team took the negative—and usually won.

In one debate broadcast over a local radio station, thirty minutes were scheduled for a discussion of the 1940 presidential contest. Humphrey won the coin toss and led off with twenty-eight minutes of praise for his hero Franklin Roosevelt, leaving a full two minutes for his opponent, later University

He was naturally quick to take part in discussions. In my classes, discussion was conducted on a Socratic basis. No one was marked or demerited on the basis of agreeing or disagreeing with me. But he was very voluble and enthusiastic and full of ideas and he liked to argue ad nauseam. So at one time I had to say, "Humphrey, if there are going to be any five minute speeches made in this class, I'm going to make them. I've got to remind you that in this class I'm both pitcher and umpire. Now I appreciate your contribution—keep it up—but moderate it a bit." He laughed—he always took everything beautifully—full of humor and good will. A delight to have him in class.

BEN LIPPINCOTT

Hubert, Muriel, and Muriel's father

of Minnesota president Malcolm Moos, to extol the virtues of Wendell Wilkie.

Hubert Humphrey's duties as a member of the debate team and the demands of his school work—he maintained a straight-A average—occupied most of his time. He also had heavy family responsibilities as a husband, a prospective father, and a bread winner. Another force impelling him to action was the feeling that he was years behind everyone else: back in school after six years working in the Huron drugstore, with most of his classmates far younger than he, Hubert felt that he had a lot of catching up to do just to stay even. This feeling, coupled with his own natural energy, produced a life lived at an extraordinary pace.

While Hubert was at the university, he and Muriel made their home in a series of small apartments near the campus. In the first place they lived, the Humphreys shared a third floor—and a bathroom—with another married couple. "Our landlady left a lot of cats around the house," Muriel recalled. "Of course they weren't as bad as the cockroaches they also kept."[6] Later the Humphreys moved to an attic apartment in another rickety building, which prompted Muriel's cautious father to furnish his daughter and son-in-law with a stout rope to be kept handy at all times as an emergency fire escape. Hubert worked as a janitor in their apartment building, in addition to his parttime job as a pharmacist at Brown's Drugstore. Muriel also looked for work and was conscious of the prejudice against hiring married women; "I could never go without that ring, but I did wear a glove."[7] She finally found a clerical job at 50¢ an hour with Investors Syndicate (now known as Investors Diversified Services).

Humphrey's economic situation did not allow him to linger over the business of getting a degree. He compressed nearly three years of school work into two and graduated Magna Cum Laude and Phi Beta Kappa in June 1939. Among the awards he had won were a Forensic Medal, a prize for writing the best political science essay, and a fellowship to Louisiana State University for the 1939-40 academic year.

Hubert made the trip to Baton Rouge alone in the summer of 1939. Muriel, with their infant daughter, Nancy, born that year, had to return to South Dakota to help her father out. When she arrived in Baton Rouge in the fall, Muriel again helped Hubert to supplement their almost nonexistent income. She got a job typing for the university and, as she had at the University of Minnesota, made ham-salad sandwiches for Hubert to sell to fellow students for a dime apiece. Hubert's Uncle Harry in Washington once again offered assistance to his nephew. He sent the Humphreys $10 a month, without which "they couldn't have made it,"[8] said Hubert's sister Frances.

Though the move to Louisiana had left Humphrey's economic circumstances unchanged, he found the political atmosphere of his new school dramatically different. Or rather, undramatically different. For, despite the upheavals of the past decade, the student body in Baton Rouge was not gripped by the same moral fervor that inflamed hearts and aroused passions in the Midwest. The

Hubert in front of his apartment near the University of Minnesota

Hubert liked to recount that when his first child, Nancy, was born, I broke the silence of the library to announce to everyone that "Hubert had a baby." He did not own an automobile then, so I borrowed the family automobile to bring Nancy and her parents home from the hospital.

C. DONALD PETERSON

students, mostly Southerners, many of French origin, were light-hearted and not just a little cynical, perhaps with good cause. They were citizens of a state that had been ruled by the dictatorial Huey Long for almost twenty years. Even the "Kingfish's" assassination in 1935 had not put an end to the control of his political machine. When Hubert Humphrey arrived at Louisiana State in 1939, Huey Long's son Russell was a student there. The previous year, Russell Long had run for the presidency of the LSU student body on a platform calling for a five-cent laundry for shirts; it was a winning campaign. Hubert and Russell Long were on the university debating team in 1940, when the Long-sponsored candidate for student body president bolstered his claim for the position by securing the presence of a popular bandleader, Ted Lewis, for a political rally. That was another winning strategy. By Minnesota standards, the inanity of the student elections was surpassed only by the corruption and vituperation of the real thing, politics as practiced by the professionals in the statehouse at Baton Rouge.

An even more shocking experience for Humphrey was to see for the first time the circumstances of the Southern black. He had been born and grown up in a state with the second lowest percentage of blacks in the union, and his contacts with black people had been almost non-existent. Humphrey did remember one encounter from his early years.

> Once there was a big road construction job on the edge of town. A lot of the workmen were blacks. I

used to sell newspapers to the townspeople and also the black workmen. Pretty soon they let me ride the mule teams with them and sit beside them in the dump truck. When they would come into town, people would stare at them since most of the folks didn't know them. But the men would call me by name as they went by and I would get up on the wagon seat with them. It horrified my Mother, but my Father was pleased.[9]

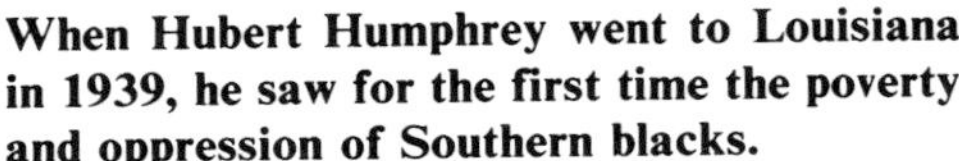

When Hubert Humphrey went to Louisiana in 1939, he saw for the first time the poverty and oppression of Southern blacks.

I was supposed to go down to New Orleans to talk to a Women's Club about tax conditions in Louisiana, but something came up in the family and I couldn't make the trip. I couldn't find anybody else to take the job off my hands so about three days before the meeting date I called Hubert in and told him that there would be $50 in it or some such amount and asked him if he thought he could read up and interview two or three people, and learn enough about the Louisiana tax system to go down and talk to those women. Well, he could sure try— and he did. And you know, the president of the outfit called me up and said that it was the best speech they had ever had, that they understood the Louisiana tax system for the first time in their lives, and could I arrange for him to come again and straighten them out on something else.

CHARLES S. HYNEMAN
PROFESSOR
LOUISIANA STATE UNIVERSITY

Even after Humphrey left his home state, his contacts with black people had not increased. He had gotten his first college degree in a state with scarcely more blacks than South Dakota. But in Louisiana he came to see blacks for the first time not as mere abstractions but as a people living in almost unrelieved misery. Their situation was every bit as bad as it had been pictured up north, and it was a matter of almost total indifference to the white ruling class. And yet the whites in Louisiana, rather than being snarling Simon Legrees, were human beings like people anywhere. Humphrey could see that white Louisianans were unaware that their racial policies were doing nearly as much to keep themselves poor and miserable as they were to oppress and restrict the blacks. While he was at LSU, Humphrey did not hesitate to express his opinion on the South's racial problems, but this did not prevent him from forming friendships with Southerners like Russell Long, friendships that would endure through a lifetime of political struggle and deep differences on issues.

By the spring of 1940, Humphrey had finished his Masters' thesis, "The Political Philosophy of the New Deal," an unabashed panegyric to his hero, Franklin D. Roosevelt. After a little good-natured bantering with the members of the examination committee, who threatened to flunk him so he could run for the Senate back home instead of becoming a professor, he was passed. He was on his way back to the University of Minnesota to get a Ph.D. and become a full-fledged professor.

Near the close of the academic year at LSU, Hubert came into my office looking for help. The dissertation for the Masters degree was finished but his faculty advisor said it wasn't objective; it would have to be written over from start to finish and Hubert's need to get on a payroll would make that impossible for any foreseeable future. What could be done?

I asked him a few questions and was assured by Hubert that he would defend his judgments and conclusions before any committee; they were based on solid evidence, soundly reasoned, and stripped bare of exaggeration. It wasn't hard for me to decide to bail Hubert out, being then (as I am now) of firm opinion that no professor attentive to his obligations lets a youngster get very far along with a research job without making sure from time to time that teacher and student have a common understanding about what is being done and what ought to be done. So I said: "Well, Professor X is going off to Harvard in a week or so to finish up his own work for a Ph.D., and by the time you can complete any necessary revision he won't be available to sit on the committee that decides whether you have earned an A.M. degree. Are you willing to go over your manuscript once more, making every concession to your advisor's demands that you think you honestly can make? Could you do that and be ready for an examination a month from now?" He answered, "I can if I can manage to live that long." Being also of strong opinion that occasional intake of food nourishes the intellect as well as the body, I scraped up enough money to pay him for a small research job.

After four or five weeks Hubert was ready to face his committee. If any of them found anything to com-

Russell Long (right) **and Hubert Humphrey eventually became colleagues in the United States Senate after attending Louisiana State together in 1940.**

plain about in the job he had done, I do not recall that he mentioned it. Most of the talk went to what Hubert intended to do in the future and came to a head with a declaration by one of the committee members which the Senator mentioned in his autobiography. In effect: "Hubert, either you promise that you will get out of this academic racket and go up to Minnesota and run for the U.S. Senate or I will flunk you out of school here and now." I do not remember what Hubert promised, but he carried his LSU diploma with him when he dusted Baton Rouge off his feet and headed North for whatever Minnesota had in store for an enterprising young man.

CHARLES HYNEMAN

Humphrey with two of his college professors, Charles Hyneman (right) **and Evron Kirkpatrick** (left)

chapter 4

PARTY POLITICS

Hubert Humphrey came back to Minnesota in 1940 determined to continue his education and to become a member of the academic community. But despite his intentions, he would soon find himself drawn away from the relative calm of academia and into the exciting world of Minnesota politics.

Ignatius Donnelly, a Minnesota politician who was one of the founders of the Populist Party

From its earliest days, politics in Minnesota had been closely associated with the spirit of protest and reform that manifested itself periodically in American political life. Ten years from the time that Minnesota achieved statehood in 1858, an agrarian protest movement had begun in earnest in the state. It took shape with the formation of the National Grange in the 1860s. During the next decade, the protest spirit was embodied in the Anti-Monopoly and Greenback parties; then followed the Farmer's Alliance of the 1880s, the Peoples' Party and Populism in the 1890s, and finally the Non-Partisan League, which served as the foundation of the Farmer-Labor Party in the 1920s. This independent political party was destined to play an important role in Minnesota politics.

Economic conditions in agriculture kept the protest spirit and the Farmer-Labor Party alive during the early twenties. The prosperity of the war years had vanished; mortgage foreclosures, bank failures, and low prices for farm products all provided fuel for the protest movement. In 1922, the first Farmer-Laborite senator, Henrik Shipstead, was elected to the United States Congress. That year, reform candidates emerged in other rural states: Wheeler in Montana, Howell in Nebraska, Brookhart in Iowa. In 1923, with the death of incumbent Knute Nelson, Minnesota's second Farmer-Laborite was elected to the Senate. He was a colorful rustic named Magnus Johnson, whose proud claim was that he had the loudest voice in Minnesota, thanks to a career as a glass-blower during his youth in Sweden. Senator George H. Moses of New Hampshire said, "If Magnus Johnson goes to

Magnus Johnson and his family down on the farm

Magnus Johnson, Farmer-Laborite senator from Minnesota

There's a famous story in Minnesota politics about Magnus Johnson, who was a great opponent of the Muscle Shoals Dam in Alabama. During debate in the House, an attempt was made to persuade him to support the project because the power it would generate would aid in the development of low cost fertilizer, which in turn would benefit the Minnesota farmer. No slouch when it came to discussing fertilizer, Johnson began to discourse at length on the merits and demerits of the various types—cow manure, sheep manure, and so on. A colleague finally gained the floor and asked him which he preferred. "It's all a matter of taste," replied Johnson.

KEN PETERSON

the Senate, there will be another vacancy in it. When Lodge [Henry Cabot Lodge, the prototypical Boston Brahmin] hears him speak, he'll drop dead."[1]

During the years of its early success, the Farmer-Labor Party captured the attention of the fledgling Communist movement. The party line during that period called for the formation of a national party that would be friendly to the Soviet Union and would fight for its recognition by the United States government. To achieve this goal, party members would try to infiltrate and capture control of the progressive movement. The Minnesota Farmer-Labor Party was a prime target for their efforts, and the problems this created over the years for Farmer-Laborites were monumental. Enemies of the Farmer-Labor Party freely labeled all Farmer-Laborites as Communists, and because the presence of Communists within Farmer-Labor ranks was undeniable, the Party was constantly on the defensive.

Between 1924 and 1930, the relative prosperity of the Minnesota farmer withered the protest spirit, and the Farmer-Labor Party found itself in the doldrums. But 1924 also marked the first time that an important political figure, Floyd B. Olson, sought state-wide office; it was Olson who was to dominate the Farmer-Labor Party in the 1930s and in many ways to foreshadow the emergence of Hubert Humphrey in the 1940s. Olson's family background—he had a Norwegian father and a Swedish mother—was made to order for the Minnesota electorate. He had been brought up in the rough and tumble of Minneapolis's near Northside and as a youth had knocked around as a farmhand and a railroad worker. Olson was the first Minnesota politician to combine a Scandinavian background with the sharp tongue and the streetwise tactics of the tough city kid. He was the first truly modern urban politician the state had seen, and the first Minnesotan to emerge as a truly national figure. For that reason, Olson bears a closer look.

Floyd Olson began his public life as a special assistant to the Hennepin County (Minneapolis)

Floyd Olson's birthplace in North Minneapolis

Olson was elected governor of Minnesota in 1930

Floyd Olson was brought up in what amounted to a Jewish ghetto on Minneapolis' Northside; he was probably the first and only governor of the state of Minnesota who could speak Yiddish. The Olson family home was located near an Orthodox synagogue. Orthodox Jews don't do work of any kind on the Sabbath, which runs from Friday at sundown to Saturday at sundown. When Olson was a kid, his Jewish neighbors used to pay him to turn the lights on and off and to keep the furnaces going in their homes on the Sabbath. He was what some called a "Shabbas goy"—a Sabbath gentile.

FRANK E. WEISBERG
MINNEAPOLIS ATTORNEY

attorney. When the attorney suddenly died, the District Court judges unanimously selected Olson to fill the unexpired term. During his career as county attorney, he was seldom out of the headlines, whether sending a passel of crooked aldermen off to jail or investigating the Ku Klux Klan.

In 1924, at the age of 33, Olson ran for governor and was defeated. Re-elected county attorney in 1926, Olson rejected the Farmer-Labor nomination for governor two years later, during the party's period of decline. With the economic collapse of 1929, however, the protest spirit began to revive, and Olson decided to enter the race for governor again in 1930. This time the Communists were busy elsewhere, engaged in an internal conflict, and the Republican ticket was weak and on the defensive. The Republican candidate for governor, Ray P. Chase, had for years been squabbling with the senatorial candidate, the incumbent Thomas Schall, whose two most memorable characteristics were his blindness and his penchant for telling dirty stories. Schall survived the election, but Olson buried Chase—473,000 to 290,000.

Olson's program as governor included a number of measures to save Minnesota's embattled farmers, the principles of which Franklin Roosevelt later incorporated into the New Deal. He called for public works, unemployment compensation, an old age pension plan, and a state income tax and increased corporate and "chain-store" taxes to pay for these measures. His farm program included mortgage moratoriums, rural credit plans, reduced interest, and government support of agricultural prices. Many of Olson's programs, together with later Humphrey programs like Food for Peace, today form the basis of the nation's farm policy.

Olson won re-election in 1932 and 1934 against inept Republican competition, in campaigns memorable mostly for the wounds inflicted by the sharp-tongued governor. Referring to a slate of his opponents, he said, "I will call the roll of the leading scandal mongers." Of one member of the opposition, Olson remarked, "He fits to any party and will always be found where there are the most pork chops." Another he described as "the errand boy for Northern States Power."[2] One campaign ploy that the Olson troops used in 1932 was to place a loud-voiced man in the front row during the rallies of his Republican opponent Earle Brown. "Mr. Brown, are you supporting President Hoover for re-election?" the man would say over and over again, in a louder and louder voice, until the hapless Brown was finally forced to answer "Yes." When he did, the ringer would stand up, announce "That's all I wanted to know," pick up his hat and coat, and leave.[3]

During Olson's second and third terms in office, the economic situation in Minnesota steadily worsened. Unemployed veterans from the state took part in the Bonus Expeditionary Force that marched on Washington in 1932, demanding payment of their World War I bonuses. Before the Minnestota contingent left, Governor Olson told its members that if capitalism wasn't able to deal with the nation's problems, "I hope the present system of government goes right to hell where it belongs."[4] Continuing his attack on capitalism, he later stated, "The only way the assurance of steady

Unemployed workers storm the Minnesota state capitol in 1933.

jobs can be obtained is by socialization of at least the key industries of the nation."[5] The governor's remarks made national headlines, and as the tone of his speeches became more and more radical, agitation grew for the formation of a third national party. Olson did not convincingly discourage it. The newly elected president Franklin Roosevelt, uneasy about the political potential of a third party movement that would draw a disproportionate amount of its strength from the Democrats, was anxious to maintain cordial relations with Olson and at the same time to appropriate as much of his program as the nation could digest in order to preempt any potential opposition.

In 1934, the platform of the Farmer-Labor Party announced the failure of capitalism and the need for immediate steps to abolish it. Olson all but disowned the most strident language of the platform, but it remained the principal issue in the campaign. Olson was re-elected but his margin of victory shrank from 198,000 to 72,000, in part because of the controversy surrounding the Farmer-Labor platform, but also because the unpopular Mr. Hoover was no longer around to drag down the rest of the Republican ticket.

Olson thrived on crisis, and his tenure continued to provide an ample supply. In 1934, the bloody Minneapolis truckers' strike smoldered through most of the summer with the governor in the thick of it, attempting to negotiate some fair settlement. He finally succeeded, only to have one side renege and the hostilities resume. Another truce was called, and at last a real settlement achieved. Both sides left the battlefield with dead and wounded, though it was generally felt the truckers had gained the most from the final contract. A second strike, this one at the Hormel plant in Austin, involved 2,700 workers and threatened another outbreak of violence. Olson negotiated a settlement. Disruptions over military training at the University of Minnesota also claimed the governor's attention; he resolved the matter unilaterally, and this decision was later confirmed by the Board of Regents.

By 1936, Olson was ready to run for the United States Senate. He received the Farmer-Labor nomination, but by July, Olson was at the Mayo Clinic in Rochester. He had suffered from a recurring stomach problem for several years, and in late 1935 had entered the Mayo Clinic for what had been called an exploratory operation. The problem could not be treated surgically, so X-ray therapy was used. Some seeming improvement took place, but new complications eventually developed. By the time Olson returned to Rochester in July 1936, the true nature of his illness had become distressingly clear. In a month's time, he would be dead of stomach cancer at the age of 45.

As the end drew near, the nation became aware that Olson was dying, and a dozen reporters hovered in the street outside his third floor hospital room, waiting for the final moment to come. Jack Mackay, a reporter for the Associated Press, had bribed a nurse to signal with a windowshade when the end finally came. She did, and Mackay ran off toward a grocery store a couple of blocks away where the only pay phone in the area was being held open for his benefit, thanks to another bribe

Floyd Olson (left) **with his physician, Dr. Arthur Hoaglund, in 1933**

given to one of the neighborhood kids. But as Mackay dashed wildly across the street, he was hit by a car. Somehow, he managed to get up, limp the rest of the way to the phone, and call in the story. He had scooped the country. Then Mackay limped back to the hospital and checked himself in.

Olson's successor, Elmer Benson, was a Farmer-Laborite and a former Commissioner of Banks who lacked none of Olson's fiercely held contempt for the established order and all of Olson's personal charm and political skill. Elected in 1936 in an outpouring of sympathy for the fallen governor, Benson rolled up the largest vote and the highest percentage of the vote in the state's history. Within

One of the last pictures of Olson taken before his death in 1936

two years, he had lost all of his support and was defeated by Republican Harold Stassen. Benson was stiff-necked and argumentative, constantly at odds not only with his opponents but also with members of his own party. What was worse, he permitted the Communist problem, which had plagued the Farmer-Laborites in the past, to divide and destroy the party. Unlike Olson, who was contemptuous of the Communists and constantly under attack by them, Benson refused to make even a token gesture against infiltration. He surrounded his administration with associates open to charges of Communist sympathies and cloaked himself in the mantle of righteousness; his enemies

Governor Benson addresses the Farmer-Labor Convention in 1938.

Elmer Benson

Governor Elmer A. Benson ran for re-election in 1938 and was defeated by Harold Stassen. A man who was active in the university radio station at the time . . . organized a youth rally for Benson in what was then the CIO Hall at the corner of 8th Street and 4th Avenue South. He collected a group of liberal students who had a willingness to speak on almost any occasion. I recall that I presided at the rally. Among the other participants were Hubert H. Humphrey, Orville Freeman, Arthur Naftalin, and John Mariucci. Mariucci was billed as speaking for athletes for Benson. He read his speech from a card that had been prepared for him.

C. DONALD PETERSON

were simply "Red baiters."[6]

In the 1938 primary for governor, Benson was challenged by Hjalmer Peterson, Olson's lieutenant governor, for the Farmer-Labor nomination. Though Benson narrowly won the primary, Harold Stassen overwhelmed him in the general election: the 250,000-vote victory of 1936 became a 291,000-vote defeat in 1938. The Farmer-Labor Party never recovered and never elected another governor or United States senator.

If the Farmer-Labor Party declined after 1938, the Democratic Party in Minnesota was in not much better shape. Though free of Communist influence, it existed as little more than a vehicle for patronage from the national Democratic Party. The Democratic candidate for governor of Minnesota got only 5.6 percent of the vote in 1938; 11.1 percent in 1940 (with Franklin Roosevelt heading the ticket); and 9.5 percent in 1942. The solution to the problems of the Democrats and the Farmer-Laborites was obvious: merger of the two parties. But in the early 1940's, there was no one who seemed able to bring about that solution.

chapter 5

ELECTED

Let me tell you of the last time I saw him in his student days. It was the fall of 1940. Hubert had graduated with highest honors in 1939 and had gone south to teach political science and earn a Masters Degree at the University of Louisiana. When he had reached this goal, we induced him to come back to Minnesota in the fall of 1940 to be an instructor in the Political Science Department and to continue his studies for a Doctors Degree in the field. He enrolled in a course offered for graduate students who were planning to make their careers in the study and teaching of government and politics. At the third meeting of this class, Hubert arrived on time, but fairly shaking with excitement. "Prof Anderson," I think he said, because he did professor me in those days, "I can't go through with this course." Then he explained that he had just accepted an administrative position with the WPA at a salary which, though not high, was so much better than the income that he had been able to make previously that, in fairness to his family, he could not refuse the offer. I thanked him for telling me and was going to offer him my best wishes, but I just wasn't quick enough. He was already on his way, as people used to say, "with his coattails flying."

WILLIAM ANDERSON

When he returned to the University of Minnesota in the fall of 1940, Hubert Humphrey set out to get his Ph.D. and become a university professor. He had spent the summer on a Works Progress Administration job in Duluth but was still plagued (as usual) with money problems. In Minneapolis, Evron Kirkpatrick got him a $1,800-a-year post as director of the WPA Worker's Education Program in the Twin Cities area, a position that would provide funds while Humphrey continued his education at the university. Hubert needed a car for his new job, but he couldn't afford one. So he borrowed the money from his old college friend Orville Freeman, who was flush with earnings from a summer job.

A May Day Parade in Minneapolis in the late 1930s

The WPA assignment provided valuable experience for Humphrey. It took him into Minneapolis union halls and not only led him into friendships with labor leaders that later proved useful politically but also gave him his first real exposure to the Communist activities that had become so firmly rooted in Minnesota political life. The instructors working under him in the WPA education program included a number of Communists, both Trotskyites and Stalinites. When Humphrey discovered that the two Communist factions were more interested in debating ideological niceties with each other than putting in the requisite number of hours teaching, he canned them, much to the amazement of the state WPA director, who never thought he'd find anyone with the courage to fire an employee of the WPA for loafing.

As Humphrey advanced to the position of state director of WPA Adult Education, his job began to take him throughout Minnesota and further and further away from his studies at the university. Despite his prodigious energy, he was never quite able to juggle his academic work with the need to make a living. His thesis remained unwritten, the requirements for his doctorate unmet. But he did manage to bring a novel twist to the adult education program. In order to give people who took the course some feeling of accomplishment, Humphrey designed a diploma in recognition of their efforts, which he then signed. By the time he first ran for office, 30,000 of the diplomas bearing his name had been sent out and were being proudly displayed on living room walls throughout Minnesota.

When the United States entered World War II

In the early '40s before Hubert became mayor and while he was still living over in University Village, he and Muriel came over to one of the union meetings of the Laundry Workers and Dry Cleaners Union. My Dad used to be the business representative for this union, and after the business meeting, they held a Bingo game. The Humphreys were in very shaky financial circumstances during those days, living in University Village, and I remember that they didn't have the $2.00 to play Bingo at the union hall. After the meeting, we had to follow them home in our car because Hubert didn't have enough gas in the gas tank to make sure that he would be able to make it home and, it was past the time when the gas stations were open. So I remember we trailed the Humphreys all the way back out to the campus to where they lived in University Village to make sure that they didn't get stuck on the road and out of gas.

ROBERT LATZ

Humphrey with George Phillips (standing, right) **and Governor Ed Thye**

in 1941, Humphrey helped to liquidate the WPA and then moved into a series of wartime agency jobs, among them state director of the War Production Administration, Training and Re-employment Division, and assistant regional director of the War Manpower Progress Commission. Humphrey's work with these agencies required his active participation in the endless rounds of service club and civic group meetings that Minnesotans seem to adore. Soon his man-in-motion image, speaking at one meeting after another, began to attract attention in political circles, particularly among labor leaders who had gotten their first working knowledge of Humphrey during his WPA years. Another political type who had taken early notice of him was Judge Vince Day, well connected at City Hall and an old-time lieutenant of the late Governor Floyd Olson. Humphrey's political career was given additional impetus by a chance meeting with two acquaintances in April 1943. In his autobiography, Humphrey described how, during a casual Sunday walk downtown, "two men I'd met through the WPA Worker's Education Program, George Phillips, President of the Minneapolis Central Labor Union, and George Murk, President of the Musicians' Union, stopped me outside of the Nicollet Hotel and we began talking about the mayoralty contest. . . . I really believe that had I not accidentally met Phillips and Murk that Sunday, I would not have run for mayor of Minneapolis in 1943."[1]

Votes in a Minneapolis city election were cast on a nonpartisan ballot, so Humphrey may have felt that he was being invited to enter a race somewhat removed from the wrangling that normally divided Farmer-Laborites and Democrats. The incumbent mayor, Marvin L. Kline, was a nominal Republican who had become vulnerable on charges of corruption, which, by the standards of Minneapolis in 1943, meant that he'd been none too vigorous in closing down the dice games and after-hour joints that flourished throughout the city.

Humphrey toyed a while with the notion of running, then checked with Art Naftalin, whose knowledge of the city gained through his experience as a local newspaper reporter led him to encourage his friend to make the race. Finally Humphrey plunked down the ten-dollar filing fee

On our debate trips together, and at other times, Hubert had forecast what his political plans were to be, which is almost what they turned out to be: He would run for mayor and quite possibly would be defeated in his first effort but would run a second time; he would run for governor or senator: and ultimately, for president. The qualities of intellect, vigor, and winsomeness that he exhibited in his political career were no different from those which we observed in school.

C. DONALD PETERSON

Marvin Kline

Right at the start of '43, here was this daring young candidate, but he had a worn hat with a very narrow brim and it looked terrible. It was important for him to have a new hat. So he marched into Maurice L. Rothschild's. Leo Pflaum was the owner and he waited on us. We paid $5.50 for that hat. Then we took the hat off his head and threw it into the street to baptize him as a candidate for political office. That brand new hat! He reminded me of that in 1964 when he was Vice-President, and I was running for re-election as mayor. I had him as a guest on a TV show I was running as part of my re-election campaign, and early in the show, he said, "I've still got this score to settle with you," and that had to do with the hat.

ARTHUR NAFTALIN

just nineteen days before the primary. Nine other candidates had filed for the primary, and though Humphrey did get some of the labor support he was counting on for his campaign, several left-wing unions, still nursing grudges from Humphrey's WPA days, sat on their hands. The Teamsters, with new leadership certified by a state labor conciliator in the service of the administration of Republican Governor Harold Stassen, endorsed Kline. Despite these defections, Humphrey ran like a dervish, speaking, shaking hands, distributing literature in the hallways of apartment buildings at three in the morning. He somehow managed to survive the primary, 13,604 votes behind Kline but still in the race for the general election six weeks away. During his campaign, Humphrey took advantage of the nonpartisan character of the race by making an appeal to Republican voters with a piece of campaign literature that showed him with his nose buried in a copy of Wendell Willkie's book *One World.*

As Humphrey began to close in on Kline, the mayor decided to try to wriggle free of the crime issue by pinning it back on his opponent. Kline charged that Humphrey's candidacy was being supported by "racketeers" and that "some of these racketeers introduced my opponent to the labor movement and helped foist him upon the honest working people of this city as a standard bearer."[2] The mayor's accusation set the scene for what the *Minneapolis Times* described as "the most dramatic meeting that Minneapolis politics has produced in many a year." On May 26, Humphrey, reporters and photographers in tow, charged into

The Minneapolis papers had promised to endorse Humphrey when he first ran in 1943 and when they didn't, needless to say, he was pretty disappointed. One of his strongest supporters, Judge Vince Day, finally asked the editor who had made the promise why they backed off. "When the big boys on Nicollet Avenue heard we wanted to endorse Humphrey for mayor, they went right through the roof. He was just too radical for their taste. They didn't want him using the mayor's office for a stepping stone for governor or the Senate."

GENE O'BRIEN
COLUMNIST FOR THE SUN NEWSPAPERS AND LONGTIME DFL ACTIVIST

Kline's office and demanded that he "name the racketeers." Kline, completely taken by surprise, hedged a bit, indicating that the racketeers he had referred to were backing Humphrey whether he knew it or not. But Humphrey was not to be put off and continued to press Kline to "name one." Kline finally answered: "George Murk." Humphrey retorted, "I knew you would use that name. I never knew Mr. Murk. He hasn't any part in my campaign." Murk, as well as being president of the Musicians' Union, was the reputed operator of the Musicians' Club, twice raided by police during Kline's administration. Humphrey questioned the mayor: "Why didn't you keep his place closed up? Why did you let it keep opening and closing? Why didn't you run him out of town?" Kline hemmed and hawed. He replied that he was powerless to do as Humphrey suggested and that these matters were up to the court. Then he shifted to the counterattack. Wasn't it true that if Humphrey were elected, he'd name Murk as Chief of Police? Humphrey replied that Murk had "as much chance [of becoming Chief of Police] as Mahatma Ghandi has of becoming President." The exchange finally wound down and the two men shook hands. But that night, in a radio speech, Kline defended himself, saying that Humphrey had "attempted to embarrass my administration by spreading rumors, by paying 'fly by nights' to open up sneak joints and the like. But we have met them at every turn. We'll continue to battle against them."[3]

When the election was held in November 1943, Kline won, but his margin had shrunk to 5,725 votes. It was apparent that Hubert Humphrey,

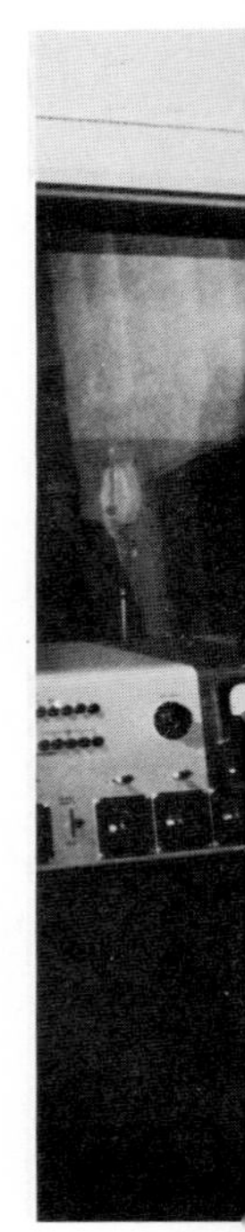

who had come from nowhere to nearly defeat an incumbent mayor, had a future in politics. Marvin Kline and, much later, Richard Nixon were the only people ever to defeat Humphrey in an election for public office. They share another common bond: both finished their public careers in disgrace. Nixon's troubles are well known; Kline went to jail as the result of financial manipulation involving the Sister Kenny Institute.

Humphrey's defeat left him, as usual, broke; he had $9 in cash and $1,300 in debts. In order to pay his debts off, he had to find another job in addition to managing the apartment building where he lived. So he took parttime work as a radio commentator on station WMIN. Muriel helped out by mowing the lawn at the apartment building. Recalling this period in later years, Muriel said, "We learned early that we could survive under the poorest of circumstances—no matter what setbacks we had. What better way is there to prepare for an elective public life?"[4]

Humphrey as a radio commentator at station WMIN

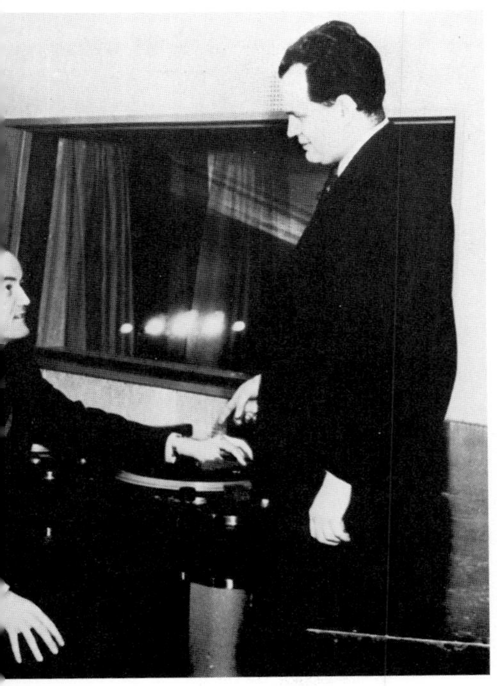

In addition to his other jobs, Humphrey went into business for himself. With Arthur Naftalin, he formed a public relations firm called Hubert Humphrey & Associates, a firm that, according to Naftalin's recollection, "mainly was a front for efforts to organize for the next mayor's race."[5] Humphrey's life became even more complicated when he was appointed as an instructor of political science within the Army Air Force Training Program at Macalester College in St. Paul. Teaching at Macalester was more than just a way of earning money and marking time until the next election. Humphrey brought the same enthusiasm to the classroom that he had shown as a campaigner. Macalester students remember a discussion of John Ray Carlson's *Undercover,* an enormously popular book in its day, that turned into a marathon session, beginning in mid-afternoon and still going strong past the 5 P.M. bell, when Humphrey recessed the class for dinner. After dinner they went at it again and kept going until 10 P.M., finally concluding with Humphrey's admonition to his students, "Get into politics. . . . Don't just be jeering from the bleachers"—advice not unlike that found in Theodore Roosevelt's famous "Man in the Arena" speech, which Richard Nixon was fond of quoting in his darkest hours.

Humphrey spent much of his free time at Macalester hanging around with the student staff of

Old Main at Macalester College

At a luncheon held to celebrate the seventy-fifth birthday of my father-in-law, Brad Mintener, Hubert told this story. When he was teaching at Macalester in the early days, a young student kept appearing in every class he taught. He couldn't figure out why this same face kept appearing and he felt pretty good about it. "Here's one kid I'm really turning on," he thought. Finally, well into the semester, the student came forward and said, "Mr. Humphrey, I want to apologize, I feel terribly guilty. The faculty has asked me to monitor all your classes because they were concerned you might be some kind of radical or pinko and they weren't quite sure what they were getting. So I've been trying to monitor your classes and make sure to get the feedback to the faculty!" Humphrey's response was, "Listen here, young fellow, don't you worry at all. You've got your job to do and I've got my job to do. Let's keep doing it and we'll get along fine." The amazing thing was that 25 years later, during the 1968 campaign, the fellow that was heading up Humphrey's effort in Texas called and said, "We have a friend of yours out here heading up the whole western section of Texas for you and he knew you back at Macalester." Sure enough, it was the same fellow that kept appearing in every class. He went on to become a minister in west Texas. That's just another example of how the old Humphrey warmth paid off and brought in big dividends.

PETER HEEGAARD

the college paper, the *Macalester Weekly.* Once while in the newspaper office, he leaped impulsively onto an old sink and from there to a table in order to retrieve some item from the rear of the darkroom, which had just had its floor painted. Another professor who had observed the acrobatics of his fellow faculty member bawled Humphrey out for his undignified conduct.

Although Humphrey may not have impressed all of the Macalester faculty, he proved to be a very popular teacher, as indicated by this letter from a student who was better at expressing his feelings than spelling them out: "Those of us who are taking your course would want to tell you we feel you zeal personality and subject matter cannot be surpassed. We are exceedingly greatful for it and feel proud of the college in having such an outstanding faculty member."[6]

While Humphrey was teaching at Macalester, he never stopped thinking about his political future. Although he had not yet been elected mayor, he was confident of his future success and had begun to look beyond the next mayoral election. No matter what satisfaction might come to him in that office, he would still be in a dead-end job unless the Democrats and the Farmer-Laborites, the two warring non-Republican factions, could be brought together. The mayor's job was nonpartisan, but every other important political position in the state was partisan, and Farmer-Laborites and Democrats continued to split the non-Republican vote and to lose elections that could be won. Humphrey felt that it was time to bring the two groups together.

One of the great myths that has always surrounded the merger of the Democratic party and the Farmer-Labor party was that FDR sent out some high-powered type from Washington who through his great skill and character and what they now call charisma was able to put the whole thing together. Nothing could be further from the truth. The guy they sent out was one of these striped-pants, cutaway-jacket types. He even wore a pince-nez. He had about as much rapport with us Midwesterners as George Wallace would at an NAACP meeting. Nobody paid any attention to him during the whole merger period. When

To begin his campaign, Humphrey wrote a twelve-page letter to Frank Walker, chairman of the Democratic National Committee, outlining the need for merger and the role that the national party could play in helping to bring it off. Dissatisfied with the form letter he got in reply, he set off for Washington to state his case in person. After a few days spent cooling his heels in Walker's waiting room, he was fed up and ready to go back to Minnesota. It was a "political operation on crutches,"[7] he wrote home. On his way to the bus depot, he stopped at the Willard Hotel to make a courtesy phone call to a family friend, W. W. ("Cecil") Howes, an assistant postmaster under Jim Farley and, unknown to Humphrey, still an effective political operative. Humphrey unburdened himself on the phone to Howes, who told him to wait at the bar of the Willard. A few minutes later Howes showed up, marched over to a pay phone, and in a flash, had the elusive Frank Walker on the other end of the line. Howes bluntly stated Humphrey's case, and within ten minutes, a limousine as long as the Willard Bar showed up to whisk the Minnesotan away to an audience with Frank Walker. Humphrey chewed mints on the ride up Pennsylvania Avenue to kill any trace of the scotch and soda he'd been drinking.

Walker listened carefully to Humphrey's account of the political situation in Minnesota. It was clear that the feud between Democrats and Farmer-Laborites would not help the national party's chances of carrying the state for Roosevelt in 1944. Finally, Walker dispatched an assistant national chairman, Oscar Ewing, to Minnesota to help

Humphrey participated in many meetings between Democrats and Farmer-Laborites in 1943.

the thing finally did get put together, we all decided to try to get him drunk to see if he was any different drunk than he was sober. Well, we got him drunk all right. But he wasn't any different. He passed out stiff as a board and I just laid him on the bed looking exactly as if he had been embalmed.

GENE O'BRIEN

We were all a little paranoid about the so-called Communist influence in the party at the time of the merger. It got so bad that some of us were almost afraid to go into a room with them. We thought that Communism was some kind of infectious brain disease.

GENE O'BRIEN

Humphrey organize the merger.

Over a hundred meetings between the two groups were held through 1943 and into 1944. They began with "balanced" committees of half Farmer-Laborites and half Democrats; Humphrey was the swing man, helping to chip away at the distrust that surfaced whenever members of the two parties faced each other. At the meetings, all the old wounds were laid open: there was the traditional distrust between the urban, largely Catholic Democrats and the Lutheran Farmer-Laborites, and there were feuds within feuds, with the Farmer-Labor Party itself divided between urban, often Marxist elements and rural Populist types.

Despite such divisions, there was support for the merger. The Minnesota Communists favored it for their own reasons. The current party line was to do whatever necessary to keep the United States war effort flowing smoothly, and the policies of the Democratic president, Franklin Roosevelt, suited their purposes at the moment. Ex-Governor Elmer Benson put his seal of approval on the fusion, albeit in his usual caustic fashion, at the same time denouncing Humphrey and State Democratic Chairman Elmer Kelm: "Kelm is a fascist. So is Humphrey. This is absolutely no good, but we must unite."[8] Others opposed merger not just on religious or ethnic grounds but as a matter of principle, feeling that neither major party gave sufficient voice to the underdog and that only a third party could "keep 'em both honest."

Finally, in April 1944, the two parties met in state conventions, approved the merger, and the

Democratic-Farmer-Labor Party was born. It was certainly not the end of the reform movement in Minnesota, but it was the end of seventy-six years of effort to merge an independent third party movement with the mainstream of American two-party politics. Humphrey's role in bringing about the merger was significant, but perhaps the finest tribute to the success of the effort was paid thirty-one years later by Minnesota Republicans, who in 1975 legally changed their name to Independent-Republicans. The Minnesota Democratic Party, the only Democrats in the United States not legally known as Democrats, were now joined in the sincerest form of flattery by the only state Republican Party in the country whose members are not Republicans, but Independent-Republicans.

As the newly born Democratic-Farmer-Labor Party emerged in 1944, Humphrey's own life was undergoing some major changes. On the very day of the first DFL State Convention, Muriel had to travel alone to South Dakota to bury her father, just fourteen days after the birth of the Humphreys' third child, Robert. (Their second child, Hubert Horatio III, had been born in 1942.) Humphrey was forced to stay behind to preside over another birth, a new political party. He gave the keynote speech at the convention.

During the convention, the DFL Party turned to Humphrey as their first candidate for governor. In a dramatic speech, he refused the nomination. He described the scene in a letter written in April 1944 to his friend and professor at Louisiana State, Charles Hyneman:

> There was no difficulty with resolutions and plat-

As for taking Democrats into the Farmer Labor Party I didn't approve of it at the time and I still don't. Who elected Roosevelt? It was the Farmer-Labor Party in Minnesota. It was the LaFollette Progressives in Wisconsin, and it was the non-partisans in North Dakota and the Norris organization in Nebraska. What I want to say is that from these parties grew his support and advice, and the question is where are you going to find a Roosevelt or a liberal today? That was the role that the Farmer-Labor Party played. The problem today is that under a two-party system, where are you going to find a Roosevelt? Liberal-thinking people had an organization then to support.

ERIC HOYER
MAYOR OF MINNEAPOLIS, 1949-1957

form, but when it came to candidates, that's where the trouble began. Early in April, I said that I was not a candidate for any office. It was my intention to go into the Armed Services. I made this decision plain to the Nominating Committee and the Democratic - Farmer-Labor Party. Again and again leaders of the Party came to me and asked me to run, and as many times I refused. Finally, at about 8:00 a.m., with over eight hundred delegates present, someone took the floor and in a rousing speech, nominated me for the office of Governor. Then all hell broke loose. There was one seconding speech after another. . . . They stomped their feet and shouted, "We want Humphrey!" until I felt it necessary to leave the hall and at least have a moment of thought. The demonstration lasted for over an hour. Finally I was informed that the delegates had drafted me for the office and I had to give them my decision. Well, as I've said, I definitely planned on going into the Armed Services. . . . I cannot help but believe that if a fellow is going to have any political future, he had better be in the Armed Services. Anyway, once having decided that it was my intention to join up, I just couldn't force myself to play political tricks by double-talk about desiring to be in the Navy, so my pal, I am not a candidate. Never in my life did I feel quite so emotionally upset as I did during that Convention. I don't suppose I'll ever have such a unanimous support again, but then, maybe I'm just a little bit upset about all of this, knowing that I had to turn down a big offer. In the long run, I believe my judgment will be right. What is your opinion? . . . Now here's something I want you to do for me. My application for commission will be in Washington this week. Is there anything that you can do to see to it that I am given favorable consideration? I can assure you that I have no desire to be on one of those landing boats and do believe that my qualifications are such that the

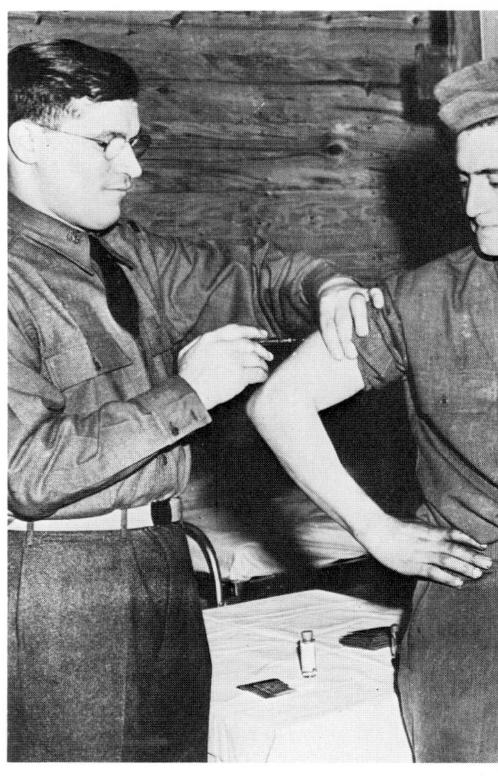

> Navy must have some place for a fellow like me. Of course, I would like to be in Naval Government, but I imagine that's impossible for a fellow my age. Anything that you can do will be greatly appreciated.[9]

All through his political life, Humphrey was dogged by the charge that he was a draft dodger during the Second World War. The facts are these: In 1940, Humphrey was first classified 3A, the category for a married man with children. Later he was reclassified 2A—essential civilian—while he was teaching Army Air Cadets at Macalester. Then in 1944, Humphrey made an attempt to get a commission in the Navy. The April letter to Charles Hyneman and another written in December, private letters to a friend, are not public displays of patriotism. They are contemporaneous with events as they occurred, not a subsequent attempt to color the facts. In these letters, Humphrey is quite candid about his motives, as he might not have been when speaking to the DFL delegates at the convention. He wants in, because "if a fellow is going to have any political future, he better be in the Armed Services." The basis for Humphrey's desire to be in the armed forces may be considered somewhat cynical, but that very fact gives the letter a believability that the unsubstantiated attempts to discredit Humphrey as a draft dodger simply don't have. Humphrey's asking for Hyneman's help in obtaining a commission is also difficult to construe as the act of a draft dodger.

After failing to get his Navy commission, Humphrey tried to volunteer as a Naval enlisted man and again was refused. Rollo Mudge, Chief of

Recruiting for the Navy in Minneapolis from 1942 to 1944, said, "Humphrey made at least twenty efforts to enlist in the Navy and was so persistent it was almost embarrassing."[10] In the spring of 1944, Humphrey was presented with a florist's box at the start of one of his Macalester classes. Inside was a bunch of carrots wrapped in blue ribbon. It had been discovered that part of the cause for Humphrey's rejection had been color blindness, and the gift was aimed at curing the deficiency (and raising the Prof's spirits). Finally, in September 1944, he tried the Army and was classified 1A. With newsmen in attendance, he was issued a uniform at the Fort Snelling center and informed that he had passed the physical. He spent five days at Fort Snelling, but instead of being inducted, he was told to return home because of a change in Selective Service policy limiting virtually all inductees to men under 26 who were physically fit for combat duty. So he hung up his uniform in the closet and waited for an induction notice. He was 1A, and he passed the physical, but the Selective Service simply was not calling up 33-year-old fathers of three.

Newspaper photographs from the 1940s showing members of "the great army of civilians . . . scheduled to be made into warriors for defense."

In December 1944, the Battle of the Bulge led to a new round of draft calls, and again Humphrey tramped down to Fort Snelling and again the papers showed pictures of doctors sticking wooden sticks down his throat. This time the call for 1As would have included Humphrey, but he flunked the physical—he was color blind and had a calcification of the lungs and a double hernia. But the Selective Service failed to reveal the reasons for its rejection at the time, making the whole thing even more confusing and mysterious. Each attempt by

Humphrey had been thoroughly attended by the press, and with every rejection, the sounds of his political opponents sharpening their knives for the spring mayoral election became more audible.

With no prospects for military service, Humphrey decided to run again for mayor. The rematch between Kline and Humphrey in 1945 was as brutal as any election the city had experienced. Kline knew he was in desperate trouble, and he attacked recklessly. Publicly, he tried to link Humphrey to the unpopular administration of Elmer Benson, and he hinted darkly of Communist influences that were about to take over the city.

A "Kline Veterans' Committee" took to the air to dwell at length on Humphrey's draft record, and a scandal sheet surfaced that turned Humphrey absolutely livid. He first became aware of it when a twelve-year-old boy he had been paying to distribute his literature turned up with a stack of four-page newspapers "with some really good cartoons." The cartoons made a few less-than-complimentary points about Humphrey's war record and source of campaign funds. "Where do you live, son?" Humphrey asked. "On the North Side," the boy answered. Humphrey hadn't asked, and the boy hadn't mentioned, that he had found the newspapers on the South Side, where he'd been delivering the Humphrey material. Humphrey hurriedly scheduled a Northside rally to combat the material. Pointing to stacks of newspapers laid out before his audience at Margolis' Garage, a traditional Northside political meeting place, Humphrey waved one of the offending sheets aloft, denouncing it as "the most dishonest, lying, scan-

During the campaign of 1945 we didn't have very much money. We used a kind of mimeographed, doublespaced handout in which we bragged that Humphrey was the son of Hubert H. Humphrey, Sr., who had served a term in the South Dakota State Legislature. I was looking at this one day and I thought it would be very funny if we had a few copies printed up that read "South Dakota State Penitentiary." So we developed this gag and went through a whole lot of manuevers to make sure that Humphrey would believe this had appeared in thousands of copies all over the city. We all gathered around his desk as he opened the correspondence that called attention to his mistake on page 3. There, circled in red, was the statement. "Hubert, why in the world did you put this in your biographical summary?" He idolized his father. He looked at it and he was just crushed. Then he looked at us and he could see I was the culprit and I was trying to suppress a smile. . . . I think this is the one time he came close to losing his temper. He was just infuriated. And then he began to lecture me about how we maltreated his father, this wonderful man about whom he felt so great, and how could we do that, and how could we be so insensitive, and what kind of a practical joke did we think that is, putting this out by thousands of copies throughout the city. We explained it was a joke and he had one of five copies. He was still incensed. He didn't see the humor at all. The end of the story is about a week or so later, at one of

INFORMATION FOR MINNEAPOLIS VOTERS

14 (NOT A NEWSPAPER)

If you want jobs in Minneapolis, don't elect Humphrey! His Communist supporters & Comrades scare industry!

His main ballyhooers are men in favor Russian System for United States of America

The voter must judge a candidate for office by the company he keeps and upon his past record.

Everybody is interested in jobs. You, who read this want to know if your main supporter will have a job. You want to know if the thousands of men and women in the service from Minneapolis will have jobs when mustered out of the service. Your future depends on jobs. Your family's future depends on whether or not your breadwinner can expect to make a living in the postwar years.

So—everybody in Minneapolis wants to know about jobs. Who is the right man to elect as mayor to make jobs for the thousands who will want them in the future?

Unless you again want WPA jobs raking leaves, or doing other menial tasks under government supervision, you must get decent jobs through the ability of certain men to run the businesses or industries that will create jobs.

You can talk all you want about state socialism and government jobs, but the American system, which has proved the best system, is where a man can find work with another man who has the vision, ability and money to build a business to give jobs.

Let us analyze this race for mayor in the terms of jobs.

The most noisy backer of Hubert Humphrey, Jr., for Mayor is the state CIO paper, "Minnesota Labor", adept in all of the tricks of European propaganda. Every issue is a propaganda blast for Humphrey and his promises, promises, promises.

Who runs this CIO sheet?

Well—it's business manager is Sam K. Davis. Does that name come back to you from the days when Governor Elmer Benson and his crowd were driving the state down the road to bankruptcy.

Sam K. Davis was COMMUNIST CANDIDATE for GOVERNOR ONCE. He led relief riots on the Minneapolis city hall—although he always was careful to be in the rear ranks when authorities were forced to intervene.

On the staff of the paper are several known Communist sympathizers. Of the thousands of known communists in Minnesota, virtually every one is a friend of this paper. It speaks as their bible—although they probably wouldn't like the allusion. Yes, it is their mouthpiece, but officially the organ of the CIO.

Another of Humprhey's most ardent supporters is Nat Ross, the state chairman of the Communist Political Association, 1218 Nicollet Avenue, formerly the Communist Party. Ross wrote the lead editorial extolling the run Humphrey made in the primary election and in the same paper is working up race hatred. His editorials make good reading for businessmen, conservative Labor union members, Democrats and Republicans.

Another ardent supporter of Humphrey's is John Gabriel Soltis, organizer for the Communist association.

Sure, Humphrey tries to keep these and others like them in the background. What promises does he make them for their ardent support, however? That is the question the voters must take into consideration. These folks don't work for their health. Everything is keyed to their long range program. How does Humphrey fit into that program, if he knows?

A special staff writer of "Minnesota Labor" is Roger Rutchick, former secretary to Elmer Benson, when Benson was governor. A Saturday Evening Post story, printed in 1938, shows Rutchick's connections and his philosophy. Rutchick is in Minneapolis, although his home is in St. Paul, working in Humphrey's interest. Is he the watchdog for Elmer Benson, now national head of the powerful Political Action Committee (PAC), who is sending men and money into Minneapolis to insure Humphrey's success.

What is Benson's interest in this election?

There are thousands of "right wing" members of the Farmer-Labor party, now living in Minneapolis, who saw how ruthless these Communists are, who fell prey to their infiltration tactics and saw them destroy the constructive work of years.

They saw their organization taken over by them. They saw the rotten administration that Benson gave as governor, simply because he was spokesman for them over the nation. Never in MINNESOTA HISTORY HAS THERE BEEN AN ADMINISTRATION WHICH FOUND MORE MEN CONVICTED OF CRIME THAN THE BENSON ADMINISTRATION.

Benson was elected by 250,000 majority in 1936. Two years later—just 24 months later, the voters kicked him out of office by 290,000 majority when they elected Harold Stassen governor. The same crowd that backed Benson is backing Humphrey. The same noisy, militant, arrogant gang that voters of all parties, Farmer-Labor, Democrat, Republican, fired from the statehouse now is trying to take over Minneapolis.

Humphrey, himself, spent all summer and fall of 1944 campaigning up and down the state of Minnesota to defeat Governor Ed Thye, Secretary of State Mike Holm, and others who held office with Stassen.

Let us analyze these Minnesota—the United States Communists, in fact.

When war was declared in early September, 1939, Russia and Hitler signed a non-aggression pact. Russia moved in and took over Finland, Estonia, Latvia, Lithuania and part of Poland.

American Communists called those who would stop Hitler and Nazis "capitalists" and termed the war a "capitalistic" and "bankers" war. They bitterly opposed all efforts of President Roosevelt and others in opposing Nazism because Russia was marching with Hitler.

Now Ross, in his editorials in Minnesota Labor, has the supreme gall to pat Humphrey on the back for supporting the "noble principles of President Roosevelt." What do the honest labor members in the CIO think about turning control of their paper over to this treacherous clique of avowed communists—Humphrey's most ardent supporters!

Then came June 22, 1941 when Hitler made his great mistake and attacked Russia.

Overnight those same United States Communists, who decried the war, and who abused those who wanted to fight Hitler, became pro-war. Their Russia was being attacked. So the war became popular with them and since that time, they have been vociferous in their backing of America.

This article is not meant to belittle Russia's splendid part in whipping Hitler. She was backed up clear to Moscow, Stalingrad and Leningrad and suffered incredibly. But she came back and gave the Nazis a pounding they will not recover from in decades.

All honor to her for her part in this war and the important part she played in winning it.

BUT — REGARDLESS OF HER GREAT FIGHT —DO AMERICANS WANT THE RUSSIAN SYSTEM OF GOVERNMENT FOR THEIR OWN. THESE AMERICAN COMMUNISTS WOULD HAVE THE RUSSIAN SYSTEM IN THIS COUNTRY — AND THEY'LL BE BACK AGITATING FOR IT AS SOON AS THEY FEEL THE TIME IS OPPORTUNE ONCE MORE.

These United States Communists are ceaseless workers. There never has been too many of them, but they are disciplined and THEY CONSTANTLY BORE FROM WITHIN.

By gaining control in Minneapolis, they hope to get back into power in the state.

To whom will Humphrey owe his election—if he is elected mayor? It won't be the Republicans or the Democrats. With their true interest in American institutions and way of life, they can't, in good conscience, vote for him.

True, he will get some Democratic votes, because there are some in that party who regard him as one of them. But, really, those to whom he will owe his election are the militant, CIO leaders, who carry the burden of his campaign.

It is they who have organized, collected money, and carried on a clever publicity campaign in the daily Minneapolis and St. Paul papers.

This handful of men have induced a few AFL and Railroad Brotherhood men to go along with them to indorse Humphrey for mayor.

THESE MEN FROM THE OLD-TIME, CONSERVATIVE LABOR UNIONS, THINK THEY ARE HELPING THEIR CAUSE. BUT ONE DAY, THEY WILL WAKE UP AND FIND THAT A HANDFUL OF RADICALS HAVE THE REINS, THAT THE CIO WILL BE IN A POSITION TO PUSH THE AFL AND THE RAILROAD BROTHERHOODS AROUND, AND THAT THEY HAVE CARRIED THE BALL FOR REAL ENEMIES OF GENUINE BENEFICIAL ORGANIZED LABOR.

What industry is going to put money into a business or factory in Minneapolis, knowing that men like Sam K. Davis and Nat Ross are in authority behind the scenes?

Why it is ridiculous to suppose that Minneapolis will have new industries with that setup. The city will be lucky if a number of factories and businesses already here do not move away to free themselves of such influence and power.

So—if you believe in jobs; if you believe in building Minneapolis; if you believe in honest labor unions that apply themselves to wages, hours and working conditions; if you believe that these are the functions of a union—then vote against Humphrey. If his crowd of backers get control of Minneapolis there will be nothing but agitation and trouble.

THIS IS IMPORTANT TO YOU JOB HOLDERS!

GENTLEMEN, I INVITE YOU TO MOVE THOSE FACTORIES AND BUSINESSES OF YOURS TO MINNEAPOLIS. WE NEED INDUSTRY THERE TO CREATE JOBS FOR OUR THOUSANDS OF WORKERS!
IF YOU ARE ELECTED YOU WILL BE DOMINATED BY THE MINNESOTA COMMUNIST LEADERS. NAT ROSS AND SAM DAVIS AND THEIR COMRADES ARE YOUR MOST ENERGETIC SUPPORTERS. WE CAN'T HAVE A HANDFUL OF RADICAL COMMUNIST LABOR LEADERS KNIFING US ALL THE TIME!
WE LIKE MINNEAPOLIS, MR. HUMPHREY, BUT DO NOT DARE TO ESTABLISH THERE. I COULD FURNISH 1,000 JOBS BUT THEY WILL HAVE TO GO ELSEWHERE IF YOU ARE MAYOR!
I HEARTILY APPROVE OF COLLECTIVE BARGAINING AS PRACTICED BY THE AFL AND RAILROAD BROTHERHOODS, THE OLD ESTABLISHED UNIONS. BUT I CANNOT PERMIT THE RADICAL LEADERSHIP OF THE MINNESOTA CIO TO DOMINATE MY BUSINESS. I, TOO, COULD FURNISH HUNDREDS OF JOBS BUT DO NOT DARE MOVE THIS BUSINESS TO MINNEAPOLIS IF YOUR GROUP IS IN CONTROL!

WELL, HERE IT IS! I JUST GOT MY CERTIFICATE AS A REGISTERED DRUGGIST!
NICE GOING, HUMPHREY! NOW YOU CAN HELP THE SICK AND INJURED!

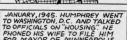

APRIL 15, 1944 DEMOCRATIC-FARMER-LABOR CONVENTION. HUMPHREY SAID-

"I WANT TO GO INTO THE ARMED FORCES---I WANT TO BE WITH THOSE OTHER YOUNG MEN AND WOMEN IN THE ARMED FORCES AND YOU CAN'T DENY ME THAT PRIVILEGE. I CANNOT BE YOUR CANDIDATE FOR GOVERNOR"

IN THE SPRING OF 1944 HUMPHREY'S DRAFT BOARD NO. 2 PLACED HIM IN 2-A BECAUSE HE TAUGHT POLITICS AT MACALESTER COLLEGE. HE LOST THIS JOB EARLY IN JUNE, 1944

YOU'VE GOT A GOOD TICKER THERE, YOUNG FELLOW!

IN THE SUMMER AND FALL OF 1944 HUMPHREY TRAVELED WITH BARNEY ALLEN TRYING TO DEFEAT GOVERNOR ED. THYE, MIKE HOLM AND OTHERS. THIS PROVED TO BE A NON-ESSENTIAL JOB IN MORE WAYS THAN ONE.

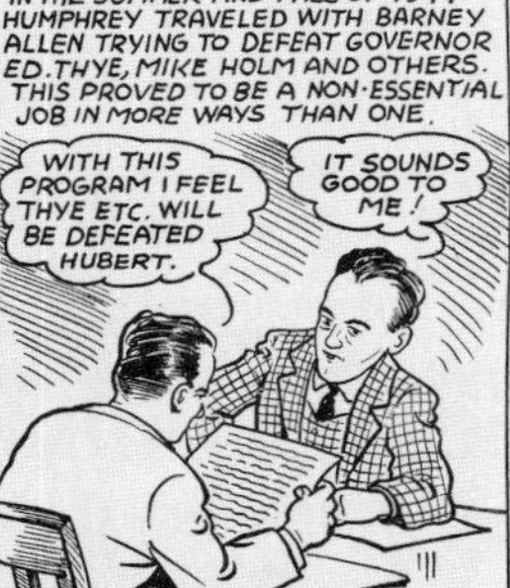

WITH THIS PROGRAM I FEEL THYE ETC. WILL BE DEFEATED HUBERT.
IT SOUNDS GOOD TO ME!

AND IN THAT SAME SUMMER AND FALL OF 1944---

THANK GOD FOR THE DOCTORS AND DRUGGISTS IN THE ARMED FORCES-WE CAN USE MORE.

JANUARY, 1945. HUMPHREY WENT TO WASHINGTON, D.C. AND TALKED TO OFFICIALS ON "HOUSING". HE PHONED HIS WIFE TO FILE HIM FOR MAYOR OF MINNEAPOLIS.

FILE ME FOR MAYOR, DEAR. I MIGHT BE ABLE TO MAKE SOMETHING OUT OF THIS "HOUSING" THING.

SPRING 1945 - EIGHTEEN MEN MADE THEMSELVES INTO A SO-CALLED POLITICAL COMMITTEE AND TOLD "LABOR" TO ENDORSE HUMPHREY AND AT THE SAME TIME DEMANDED $12,000 FOR CAMPAIGN FUNDS.

HEY, LET ME IN ON SOME OF THIS.
B-Z-Z-Z-Z

"THESE 18 MEN CLAIMED THIS WAS A "LABOR ENDORSEMENT." DID YOUR UNION VOTE ON IT??

THE RANK AND FILE OF LABOR HAD NO SAY IN THE ENDORSEMENT OF HUMPHREY!
LABOR

dalous piece of trash he'd ever seen."[11] That description, of course, piqued the curiosity of the audience, few of whom had any idea of what he was talking about. Humphrey probably gave the paper a lot more currency that it would have had otherwise, but Kline didn't benefit much from the assistance. His campaign was far too vicious and discomforting for the Minneapolis electorate, which genuinely preferred (and still prefers) an issues-oriented contest to the cut-and-slash tactics that characterized most municipal politics. Humphrey defeated Kline by the largest percentage the city had yet seen in a mayoral contest: 86,377 to 55,263. Thirty-four-year-old Hubert H. Humphrey was mayor of Minneapolis.

THE PUBLIC PRESS

Volume VII — MINNEAPOLIS, MINN., DECEMBER, 1944 — Serial Number 1

KLINE ADMINISTRATION MOST CORRUPT REGIME IN HISTORY OF THE CITY

MAYOR KLINE is A HYPOCRITE AND A LIAR!

Kline Regime Most Ruthless, Most Vicious, and Most Corrupt of Any Administration Within Memory of Present Generation! City Wide Open! Racketeers in Complete Control of City Government. Police Department Used as Tool by Mobsters! Unholy Alliance Evident as Dives Run Wide Open!

these campaign fund-raisers, Hubert, Sr., came to town. He was a lovely man. I could see out of the corner of my eye Hubert Humphrey, Jr., taking Hubert Humphrey, Sr., to one side. He said, making his voice sound very troubled, "Dad, a terrible thing has happened."

ARTHUR NAFTALIN

My dad owned a grocery store on Nicollet Island. The neighborhood grocery in those days was also the social club and community center, and a principal leisure time activity among the customers was talking politics. Every election our place was filled with political brochures and flyers. There were posters in the windows and arguments in the aisles. My dad let every candidate leave his literature, but the preferred spot, the one next to the cash register, that was for Hubert Humphrey. So taken was my dad with Humphrey that he asked me to take a stack of his campaign cards downtown to pass out on the street—he figured it was good experience for a 12-year-old.

There I was, passing out cards on the sidewalk on 5th and Hennepin when a man came charging up to me. I thought I was going to be arrested for doing something wrong. He grabbed me by the arm and led me to the center of the street where people lined up for the streetcars and said, "This is where you should be. Make sure each person has one to read on the streetcar." The traffic was whizzing by, and I was scared to death. Then he gave me a big smile, and we introduced ourselves. It was Hubert Humphrey! He reached into his pocket and gave me a quarter. Calling me by my nickname, he said, "Koochy, I want you to visit me when I get elected mayor." Now convinced I wouldn't get run over, I went out and passed out the cards.

Later that week he spotted me in a crowd of grown-ups at the Labor Lyceum in north Minneapolis. He took me aside and handed me a huge stack of cards to pass out as people left the building. Again he gave me a quarter and repeated his invitation to visit him in office.

Corny as it sounds, I still have those quarters.

HARRY J. LERNER

"D*o you know how I became mayor of Minneapolis?"—Hubert Humphrey twinkled the technique a generation ago to a former fellow graduate student at a cocktail party. "He spoke delightedly on the subject," my professor-friend recalls, without any trace of irritation, let alone condescension. He quoted Humphrey. "Well, I spoke every Saturday, and every Sunday, at the parks in Minneapolis—there are lots of parks in Minneapolis, you know. And, after the crowd would gather, I would pick up the microphone, and I'd begin to talk. Then—suddenly—I'd stop. And I'd say: 'Wait a minute. Wait a minute, I want to see the kids here up front. They're the future of the nation, folks, let's face it, your kids. Now come up here. Don't be shy! That's*

it . . . right up front, sit down and make yourselves comfortable. Right. Now, as I was saying . . . But I have to say something else first. You know, I've been around. I know the great state of Minnesota. But I know other states of the Union too, and let me tell you something, ladies and gentlemen: these kids here have got to be the most beautiful, the most wonderful-looking, the healthiest kids I have ever seen . . . anywhere!' Then you know what?"—he put his arm over the professor's back, "Later in the same afternoon, speaking to another audience, at another park, at another end of the city, I would say . . . exactly the same thing!" The miracle of the multiplication of the loaves!

WILLIAM F. BUCKLEY

Hubert Humphrey (left) **and other city officials being sworn into office after the election of 1945**

chapter 6

MAYOR

Naftalin: *"What do you remember about Humphrey as mayor?"*
Freeman: *"Action. Action. Peripatetic action. I can remember you saying your feet hurt. . . ."*

Mayor Hubert H. Humphrey

When Hubert Humphrey became mayor of Minneapolis, he assumed leadership of a city that had been in existence for almost one hundred years. Minneapolis had grown up along the banks of the Mississippi River at St. Anthony Falls, the northernmost point accessible to river traffic from New Orleans. The first settlers of the city, who came in the 1840s and 1850s, were New Englanders who used the falls to power their flour mills and who established a retail trade to sell goods to other settlers. Even today, many of the early Yankee families—among them the Crosbys, Pillsburys, and Daytons—are still very much the establishment in Minneapolis. The second wave of immigrants was made up of Scandinavians and Germans, often the second sons of rural families with slight chance of inheriting the family farm and making successful lives for themselves in the Old Country. They came to the Minneapolis area in the 1870s and 1880s to homestead or to work on the railroads. It was not until the very end of the 19th century that Jews began to settle in Minneapolis and well into the 20th century before significant numbers of southern blacks made their way to this far northern city. (Even in 1940, blacks made up less than 1 percent of the population.)

The pattern of immigration in Minneapolis was different from that in many other American cities. In eastern cities like Boston and Philadelphia, the second and third waves of immigrants came primarily from southern and eastern Europe; these newcomers were eager to wrest political control of the community from the flinty Yankee pioneers, whose cultural and political background was so different from theirs. In Minneapolis, however, the second wave of immigration was made up primarily of people from northern Europe who had much in common with their predecessors. The newcomers and the members of the establishment generally shared the same religious values and the same liberal democratic political tradition. Because of the homogeneity of its population, Minneapolis never experienced the corrosive ethnic friction that has characterized many eastern cities. This homogeneity has made for a somewhat bland atmosphere, but it has also led to the existence of a stable community that does not easily tolerate the petty graft and patronage that commonly infect municipal governments in the East.

Hubert Humphrey was the kind of politician well suited to assume the role of mayor of Minneapolis. His liberal political beliefs and his concern for reform and good government reflected the political attitudes of most of the city's citizens. When Humphrey took office on July 2, 1945, he wasted no time in putting his political ideals into action. One of the problems that cried out for the new mayor's attention was Minneapolis's lack of adequate housing. Humphrey himself was living in a $60-a-month, two-bedroom apartment that was too crowded for a family of five but all that he and Muriel could afford on the $6,000 a year that Minneapolis paid its mayor. The Humphreys' housing problem was minor, however, compared to that of others in the city. Minneapolis needed an additional 7,000 housing units due to shortages caused by the war and demand created by returning veterans. Even Marvin Kline recognized the

It was after the successful election of '45 and we had gone out to Big Stone where Muriel Humphrey's family had a cabin. This was to celebrate the victory. I remember that Bill Simms, who was his other administrative assistant, was there. We got into an argument—whether there was a God or not—but Hubert came on very firm and very strong insisting that there was a God. We demanded that he give us some evidence and he said, "The evidence is that all men are brothers, right? If all men are brothers, then they all must have a common father—and the common father is God." He was dead serious and he meant it all the way.

ARTHUR NAFTALIN

Humphrey with Orville Freeman (left) **and County Treasurer George Totten**

Arthur Naftalin

need. Conceding his defeat graciously, he stated, "In many ways, Humphrey can give direction and vigor to a housing program and it is reassuring that he has recognized it as a first item of business."[1]

Humphrey appointed Orville Freeman to serve as chairman of the administration's efforts to secure housing for the city's veterans. It was an appropriate assignment for Freeman, who had returned from the Marines an authentic war hero after being wounded at Bougainville and spending many months in the hospital. The housing programs that Freeman helped to plan were given nicknames such as "Shelter a Vet" and "House a Hero" by Arthur Naftalin, Humphrey's newly appointed secretary and a man with a flair for catchy phrases.

As part of his program to improve Minneapolis's housing situation, Humphrey spearheaded an attempt to secure a charter amendment that would give the city authority to receive federal housing subsidies and to engage in more urban develop-

When Hubert Humphrey was mayor he had three secretaries. Once we held a kind of informal contest to see who could take the most letters from him at one setting. I held the lead at 140 letters, and close behind me was June Hendrickson with 129. We never did know who really won because the third person on the stenographic staff, Lucille Achatz, used to take so many that she said "I haven't ever counted."

EVELYN LOVDJIEFF

ment. In a stormy meeting over the amendment, the mayor attacked the Minneapolis Property Owners' Association for their opposition to what was characterized as "socialized housing." The amendment lost: though it received 57 percent of the vote, the Minneapolis charter required a 60 percent majority in favor of a change. Humphrey chastised the state for failure to provide adequate help and then sought grass-roots support for a move to obtain housing legislation in Congress.

As a result of Humphrey's efforts, several emergency housing projects were eventually set up in Minneapolis. House trailers were hauled in; unused schools were used as apartments. One housing project for veterans with families was planned for an area in South Minneapolis near the university. There were 8,000 applications for the 500 dreary quonset huts that were finally built on a barren tract of land. Initially, the buildings weren't even distinguishable from army barracks in color, though some enterprising tenants painted over the olive drab with something a bit more cheerful and planted tiny flower gardens in front. Such housing might have been lacking in charm, but without it, many vets might never have been able to use their GI benefits.

Hubert Humphrey played an active role in providing postwar housing in Minneapolis, but his activities were severely limited in other areas of municipal life. Under Minneapolis' strong council–weak mayor form of municipal government, the only department of the city that truly lay under the mayor's control was the police. A new mayor's single most important official duty was to appoint

a chief of police and to set the tone for law enforcement in the city. Cynics watched Humphrey closely in the early days of his mayoralty to see if he was cut from the same mold as so many previous "reform" administrators: a lot of campaign oratory about cleaning up the town, and then business as usual once the election was over. But those members of the fringe element who were counting on a soft landing once the new mayor was safely installed were disappointed.

A rare picture of Hubert Humphrey with a cigarette. He gave up smoking in the 1950s.

At first Humphrey approached the problem of appointing a chief in a cautious fashion. He set up a blue ribbon advisory committee that included not only a number of the labor leaders who'd backed him against Kline but also a new element not usually prominent in DFL circles: several of the leading businessmen in the city. It was a shrewd decision for several reasons—not only because the mayor's office was officially nonpartisan and therefore Republican-versus-DFL games were somewhat less acceptable, nor just because it broadened Humphrey's own political base and helped him gain access to the business heavyweights who had so much to say about running the community, but also because it enabled him to select for chief the man he really wanted. That man was Ed Ryan, who Humphrey knew would be a controversial choice and would need all the support he could get.

Ryan already had some following in the community. When Humphrey asked Bradshaw Mintener, a vice-president of Pillsbury, to head the advisory committee, Mintener told him he'd serve only if an FBI-trained man were to be appointed chief. That could only be one man: Ed Ryan. In 1942, Ryan had been sent by Mayor Kline to the FBI Academy, the first member of the Minneapolis police department ever to attend. But there was labor opposition to Ryan (another reason why Humphrey's committee was balanced with nonlabor members) because of a statement made in 1943 in which he "urged labor to turn its back upon the policies of quick resort to force."[2]

It had been agreed that the committee would require a unanimous choice to make a selection, but after a marathon session, its members were locked into a twelve-to-one vote for Ryan. Humphrey tried to persuade the lone holdout, Bob Wishart, head of the CIO in Hennepin County, to go along with Ryan. "Too many mayors of Minneapolis have been crucified on the cross of law enforcement in Minneapolis," Humphrey reminded him, "and if I fail as mayor, the people of Minneapolis will treat it as labor's failure as well, for generations to come."[3] Wishart swallowed hard and went along. Humphrey had his chief, though it took him over a month to get him confirmed by the Council.

Ryan, 6-feet-four and well over 200 pounds, had built part of his formidable reputation as a police officer on having captured Matthew Nelson of the Roger Toughy gang and Tommy Gammon of the Dillinger gang. None of it was built on being the most tactful man in Minneapolis, nor did Ryan mellow with the years. He was always fiercely loyal to Humphrey, and on one occasion he took the opportunity to express that loyalty in no uncertain terms. During Humphrey's 1968 run for the

I was a friend of Humphrey's. I kind of laughed when he started out to run for mayor. I'm a Republican and Kline was a Republican. I was chief of police under Kline. Of course, Humphrey lost the first time he ran, but the second time he ran he ran on law and order. He called me up to his office and said, "Elmer, I'd like to keep you as Chief but you're in the wrong party." I said, "I understand. That's politics." He asked me to serve under him until he got someone else appointed, and so I did serve for about a month or so. He asked me if there was anything going on that he should know about. I laughed. "How could there be anything going on when you raised so much hell about it." He said, "Well, is there gambling or anything?" I said, "There's the old 14 game. You get 14 on so many throws of the dice and you get some chips. It's a business stimulator in coffee shops and so on. You get chips and you use it to buy merchandise." "By God, that's alright," he said. He said that in the morning. In the afternoon he calls me back into his office and asked how long it would take to close those places down. I said all I had to do is make one phone call, but I asked him what made him change his mind. "I called the Star *and* Tribune *and they said they'd crucify me if I let it run, so I have to close it down," he said.*

ELMER HILLNER

presidency, Ryan, retired from political life, was an invited guest at a Torske Club luncheon in Minneapolis. The speaker that noon, a rather partisan Republican, hoed a remarkable straight row over the political ground he was covering but finally couldn't resist the mildest of jibes at the "politics of joy," Humphrey's ill-chosen theme for his presidential campaign. In a moment, Ryan was on his feet proclaiming Humphrey the greatest mayor in the city's history and berating the speaker, who stumbled hastily through the rest of his speech to an embarrassed conclusion.

Ryan never forgot how he first came to know Humphrey:

> We were neighbors in Southeast Minneapolis.

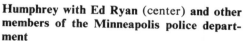

Humphrey with Ed Ryan (center) **and other members of the Minneapolis police department**

Our paths crossed frequently, especially during World War II. During the war, I headed the Internal Security Division of the Minneapolis Police Department and was a member of several speakers' bureaus. Hence, he and I appeared together at many functions.

Young Mr. Humphrey indicated an interest in local politics—especially the fact that Minneapolis was more or less in control of racketeers—and had been for years. Gambling joints, bookie parlors, slot machines, houses of prostitution, after-hour drinking places, etc., etc. One day he told me that he might run for office of mayor and if elected would "sure as hell" clean up the town. I'd heard that tune from so many candidates for that office down through the years that I wasn't much impressed—at first. However, he finally convinced me that he really meant business. In 1943 he did run and was defeated by about 5,000 votes. At a party the night of the election, he turned to me and said, "You don't know how close you came to being chief of police."

Ryan and Humphrey serve at a dinner honoring members of two high school football teams.

Came 1945. He again ran and was elected. . . . One day, after having been installed as mayor, he called me into his office. He said, "You've been yakking around here for years, telling all and sundry what you would do to the rackets if you were chief of the department. Don't look now, but you ARE chief!" He told me he wanted Minneapolis closed so tightly that even Kid Cann could not purchase a Coke after hours. He went on to tell me that he wanted the town closed NOW and not a month or a year from now.

Well, we DID close the town! However, we were astounded to hear moans and groans from certain highly respected businessmen. For example, at that time we had two telegraph companies—Postal and Western Union. The local head of one of these companies came to me one day and raised hell because we had closed the bookie and gambling joints. Seems as if his company had been receiving $18 a month rental for the ticker-tape machines which these people used in their operations—some having several in their joints. After hearing what I thought was enough, I told this fellow that if his livelihood depended on his income from those machines, he'd better find other employment. He left in a rage—informing me he'd see the mayor. About an hour later, the mayor called me and told me that this fellow had repeated what I had told him and the mayor told him that he couldn't have said it any better himself. I told the mayor, "Well, that's one vote we've lost." The mayor answered, "Eddie, you can't lose what you've never had!"

Hubert and Muriel with Ed Ryan and his family

> You see, the rackets were aided and abetted by the suppliers as well as by the labor unions, painters, plumbers, electricians, etc.—AS WELL AS BY ALL UTILITIES! Everybody gets into the act to make a buck. So cleaning up a large city like Minneapolis wasn't easy, nor was it safe![4]

With Ryan in his corner, Humphrey was able to fulfill his campaign pledge to clean up the town, the achievement for which he is perhaps best remembered as mayor. Actually, due to the peculiarities of the criminal organization in Minneapolis, it was easier than it looked, as Humphrey explained in a series of newspaper articles written after his first year as mayor:

> Our job of closing down the "town" and keeping it closed was facilitated by the very fact that illegal operations had been so well organized. The individual operator of an illegal device took his orders from the racket bosses, who in their own way, worked out a "policy" with their "connections" in the courthouse.
>
> When the "heat was on," all the gambling devices would go "down," by the single order of the racket bosses. When the "heat was off," up would come the boards, the dice, the after hours spots, the one-armed bandits, again by the single and mysterious order from the top.
>
> By the time we took office the operators had become so habituated to these up and down antics that a stern "down" word from the Police Department accomplished an overnight cleanup. The "down" order has remained in effect ever since—and there will be no change in that policy so long as the present administration is in office.[5]

Max Kampelman

Max Kampelman, a lifelong friend and associ-

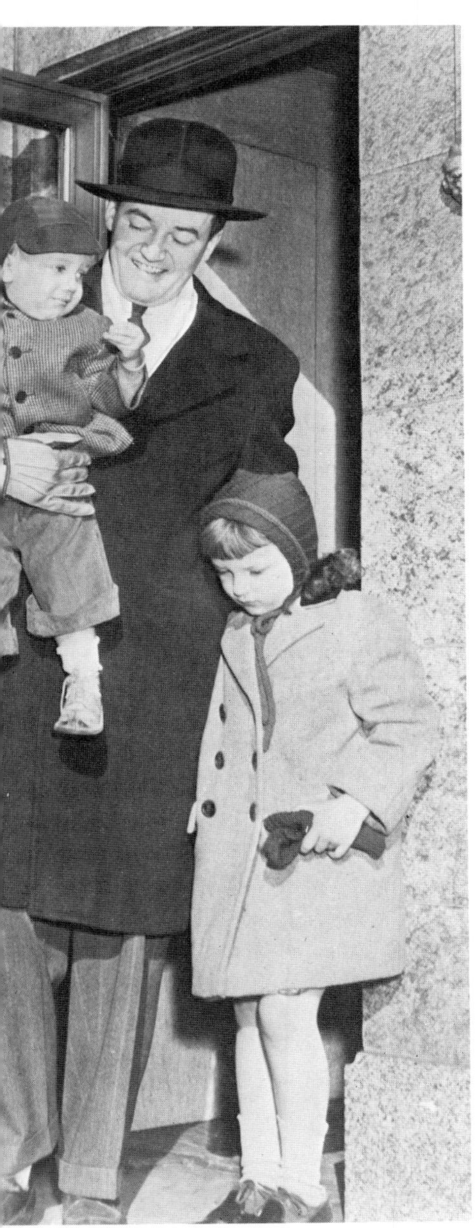

Mayor Humphrey with two of his three children, six-year-old Nancy and one-year-old Bobby

ate, recalls another phase of Humphrey's campaign to clean up the city:

> One day I came to City Hall to visit Art Naftalin, the mayor's secretary. Art was busy, as I recall. There was a meeting of all the tavern owners in the city and many of their wives. Hubert wanted them to go to the City Council and ask for pay increases for the police, the funds to come out of the increased license fees that they would pay. "I know you are paying off policemen now," he charged. "This must stop. Don't you wives want your husbands to be involved in a legitimate business that doesn't bribe policemen?" He promised to clean up the city and the police force. He promised he would end the police practice designed to entrap tavern owners into law violations. Miracle of miracles, they voted to cooperate.[6]

The only element that had been missing from the equation for a crime-free city had been a mayor who truly wanted one, and Humphrey was that mayor.

Probably the most permanent achievement that Humphrey made as mayor of Minneapolis was in the field of human relations. His early efforts to bring the city's small Jewish population into the mainstream of community life foreshadowed the role he played in bringing civil rights into the national political spotlight just three years later. Shortly after Humphrey became mayor, a Los Angeles attorney, Carey McWilliams, wrote an article for *Common Ground* in which he identified Minneapolis as the most anti-semitic city in the country. McWilliams pointed out that nowhere else in the United States were Jews so systematically excluded from service clubs and fraternal organizations. In fact, Jews couldn't even join the local automobile club; those who wanted or needed such services often became members of the club in Chicago. McWilliams attributed the problem to the fact that Jews hadn't settled in the city until after the first two waves of immigrants, the New Englanders and the Scandinavians. The ethnic homogeneity of the city had been firmly established before Jews arrived in a third wave during the 1890s and early 1900s. In cities like San Francisco and even St. Paul, where Jews had come with the earliest immigrants and all the founders of the community had sweated out their problems together, the atmosphere was much more open.[7]

Humphrey did not want to begin his political life as mayor of the nation's most anti-semitic city. Besides, the sort of attitude that fostered discrimination frankly puzzled him. He liked people, all kinds of people, and to be cut off from one group or another because of something as irrelevant as religion or skin color was totally alien to his nature. So he set to work. He outlined plans for a Human Relations Unit and gave the group the responsibility of developing anti-discrimination legislation. He called for the formation of a Fair Employment Practices Commission, the first in the nation. At a public hearing one alderman scoffed that "there is no need for it"; he was answered by a question from the audience—"Do you know of a negro teacher or clerk in our public schools?"[8] There were none. When the American Council on Race Relations established a consultation service for police training and race relations, Minneapolis

became the first city in the country to take advantage of the service. Another nationwide first was a survey conducted by Humphrey's new Council on Human Relations to determine the extent of racial and religious tensions in the city and to discover means of relieving them. "If they like what they see in the mirror when they compare it to their American ideals, fine," said Humphrey. "If not, they will want to bring about the change."[9] The Mayor's Council, headed by the Reverend Reuben Youngdahl, the brother of Minnesota's Republican governor, Luther K. Youngdahl, used the results of the survey not only to examine the city's attitude but also to appeal to the conscience of its citizens, from a level reflecting the highest religious, social, and economic achievement in Minneapolis.

The mayor celebrates his birthday.

Gradually much of the suspicion that divided Jew and Gentile, black and white, began to dissipate. Minneapolis had not become a heaven on earth, however. Passing almost unnoticed at the time of Humphrey's appointment of the Reverend Darsibe Kitagawa, Executive Secretary of the United Christian Ministry to Japanese Americans, to the Mayor's Council on Human Relations was another story that appeared in the *Minneapolis Times* on the opposite page; concerning a war crimes trial, it was titled "Jap to Hang."[10]

During his first term as mayor, Humphrey kept up a staggering pace. "He would come back to the office at 12:30 or 1:00 in the morning with a satchel full of stuff from meetings," remembers Naftalin. "All of it would end up in my basket, and all of it would be marked RUSH."[11] On one occasion, the mayor had the opportunity to use his skills as a negotiator in working out a settlement for a "telephone strike that had really gotten pretty nasty."[12] Humphrey's gift for diplomacy was also called into play during the polio epidemic of 1946, when the mayor attempted to ease the atmosphere of distrust and competition that existed between the National Foundation for Infantile Paralysis and the Sister Kenney Institute, which was headquartered in Minneapolis. Sister Kenney, an Australian nurse who had come to the United States in 1940 to introduce her methods of treating poliomyelitis, turned out to be quite a handful for Mayor Humphrey. Less than a week before the 1945 mayoral election, she had released a statement describing Marvin Kline as a "great humanitarian." Later, miffed by what she considered to be Humphrey's failure to carry out an assignment, she announced she would go back to Australia. "Very well, Sister," Humphrey said. "If you have made up your mind, I shall be glad to help with your travel arrangements. What day do you plan to leave?"[13] She stayed, and became friends with Humphrey.

Sister Elizabeth Kenney

Humphrey's first stint as mayor of Minneapolis wasn't all hard work—the mayor had some fun on the job as well. During the polio epidemic, when young people were quarantined in their homes, he put his own version of the Sunday comics on the radio for the kids who weren't allowed to get out. In the mayor's funnies, the locale of Bugs Bunny's adventures appeared to be Lake Calhoun in South Minneapolis, and the policeman who interrupted Blondie's shopping expedition resembled one of Minneapolis' finest. Humphrey's weekly reading of

Mayor Humphrey had the pleasant duty of throwing out the first ball at the opening of baseball season.

the Sunday comics over radio station WCCO helped ease some of the boredom and fear that accompanied the polio epidemic in Minneapolis.

Max Kampelman recalls other occasions when the mayor enjoyed the lighter side of his job, for instance,

> the frequent Saturday night "parties" of the university's political science department, which Hubert made a point of attending after his last mayoral function of the day, even though it might be midnight before he would appear. There was one night in Mitzie and Herb McCloskey's apartment. The street light in front of the house had gone out. When Humphrey appeared, Carrol Hawkins began an ideological attack on the mayor, claiming such reckless disregard for the public interest could not take place under socialism. That started it. Humphrey took the offensive, saying that even Norman Thomas knew better than that. Social democracy was fine; socialism was fraught with danger. The debate went on, with all its ramifications, into the wee hours. And then I remember, after we got to Washington, bringing Norman Thomas into the office to meet Humphrey. There was an immediate spark of mutual admiration and respect.[14]

Humphrey's first term in office was rewarded by the voters with a second. In 1947 he overwhelmed the hapless Frank J. Collins and carried every ward in the city. By this time, it was apparent to everybody that Humphrey's political future was not going to be limited to the boundaries of the city of Minneapolis. Humphrey had begun to cast his eye toward the United States Senate seat held by Republican Joe Ball.

It was the spring of 1946. I was a 14-year-old farmer's daughter, living in southeastern Minnesota. One Saturday the Fillmore County Farmer's Union held its annual convention in the Harmony, Minnesota, high school gymnasium. The main speaker was the then still youthful mayor of Minneapolis, Hubert Humphrey. He gave the most stimulating, exciting, and down-to-earth speech I had ever heard. After he finished speaking, I was standing out in the hallway next to the Coke machine. Humphrey was thirsty and came out for a Coke, only to discover he didn't have a nickel. I loaned him a nickel, and he asked my name and wanted to pay me back. I said, "I'll collect it from you when you get to the White House." For the next 30 years that nickel was my most exciting investment!

MARILYN HARSTAD MOYNAHAN

I first met Humphrey in 1947. I came out of the service and I was attending St. Olaf. Karl Rolvaag was a friend of mine, and I roomed at the Rolvaag home my sophomore year. I had met Eugenie Anderson who later became Ambassador to Denmark (also a DFL'er). So one evening, these people came to our apartment to talk politics. This was at a time when the Republican Party dominated the state of Minnesota. Humphrey was the up and coming leader of the DFL Party and the mayor of Minneapolis. He had a vision for his party, and he came and discussed it that night. He wanted me to join his team. What he was doing was going from campus to campus meeting with people he thought were likely candidates to help him in his political career. This was the way he built his team. He was able to convince a lot of these young veterans that had just come out of the service that they had a future in the country. They were starry-eyed, they had just won the war, they had saved the world, and they were ready to go back to school and do what they could. It was quite impressive. But by the time he had come, I was pledged to Luther Youngdahl, who was running for governor as a Republican. Down through the years, I considered myself a friend of Humphrey's and I think he considered me the same, even though we were on different sides of the fence.

ROBERT FORSYTHE
FORMER CHAIRMAN OF THE
MINNESOTA REPUBLICAN PARTY

Humphrey and Robert Forsythe

chapter 7

TO WASHINGTON

"There are those who say—this issue of civil rights is an infringement on states' rights. The time has arrived for the Democratic Party to get out of the shadow of states' rights and walk forthrightly into the bright sunshine of human rights."

Hubert H. Humphrey
1948 Democratic National Convention

In 1948, Minnesota was one of the most Republican states in the nation. Republicans held the governorship, both United States Senate seats, eight of the state's nine congressional seats, and control of both houses of the state legislature. In addition, the fall elections held the promise of still more honors for Minnesota Republicans. The former boy wonder of Minnesota politics, ex-Governor Harold Stassen—whose youth, brilliant war record as flag officer to Admiral "Bull" Halsey, and leading role in the formation of the United Nations had thrust him onto the national stage—would be contending for the Republican presiden-

Harold Stassen (left) **and Joseph Ball**

tial nomination. In the light of Harry Truman's waning popularity, it appeared certain that the Republican nominee would become the next president. On the DFL side of state politics, however, things were as muddled as ever. Hubert Humphrey's star seemed to be rising, but the Minneapolis mayor had done nothing to enhance his national standing when he lent himself to a dump Truman movement by suggesting that William O. Douglas or General Dwight D. Eisenhower might make stronger nominees for the Democrats. Other than Humphrey, the DFL had little to offer the electorate by way of attractive candidates. To make matters worse, the Communist-dominated radical wing had been a major force in the DFL party since the 1946 state convention.

With the breakup of the Soviet-American alliance at the end of World War II, the period of cooperation between Communists and non-Communist liberals in the United States had come to an end and the Communists had openly moved to take over the machinery of the DFL party. They had laid the groundwork for such a move in 1944. Although the radical wing had not commanded an absolute majority of the delegates to the 1944 state convention in St. Paul, its members had been disciplined, organized, and fanatically dedicated, as those opposing them were not. By 1946, the Communists had achieved their goal. As the principal architect of the effort that forged the DFL party in 1944, Hubert Humphrey had returned to deliver the keynote address at the 1946 convention, but this time he was greeted with boos and catcalls. "What a convention!" Max Kampelman remem-

Well, that 1946 convention was a catastrophe. When we went to the DFL state convention in St. Paul, the Humphrey forces had no idea of the disaster that lay ahead. They had expected that they would be able to elect their slate and carry the convention. Instead, they lost. We were simply slaughtered by the left-wingers.

EUGENIE ANDERSON
AMBASSADOR TO DENMARK, 1949-1953

bered. "At one point, I was bodily lifted by a big tough and carried out, only to have Hubert, from the dais, grab the microphone and yell 'Leave that man alone!' Humphrey was the most popular elected official the party had and they could not afford to alienate him. But they did."[1] Never terribly interested in the nuts and bolts of organizational politics, Humphrey did not heed the warnings of Naftalin, Freeman, and a few others who saw the disaster coming. He left the St. Paul convention in 1946 all but locked out of his own party, but he soon realized the seriousness of his situation. The first order of business in 1948 would be to take back control of the DFL.

The struggle for control between the Humphrey forces and the radical wing of the DFL, dominated by ex-Governor Benson, centered on two major points: Communist influence in some of the unions in the Twin Cities area and the third-party candidacy of former vice president Henry Wallace. The Wallace candidacy was the crucial issue. Overall Communist strategy in 1948 was intended to weaken President Truman's already fading chance at retaining the presidency by supporting the Wallace third-party movement in the hope that it could attract enough liberals to defeat Truman. The Democratic Party would shatter, and the Communists would be there to pick up the pieces. Humphrey was faced with the need to defeat this strategy in Minnesota and to recapture his party if he was ever to have a political base again.

One element in Humphrey's plan was built upon the formation of a Minnesota chapter of the Americans for Democratic Action. This non-Communist liberal group, established in various parts of the United States in 1947, was made up of individuals who took a liberal position on issues such as housing and discrimination, while at the same time maintaining a strong stand against the Communist line. When Humphrey and his friends established a Minnesota chapter of the ADA, they acquired valuable allies in their struggle against the Communist influence in the DFL. "We enlisted the aid of the Americans for Democratic Action," Naftalin said. "They brought in speakers and helped get union support."[2] Another effort made by Humphrey was to persuade the national labor movement to help rid the Minnesota unions of Communist influence. Phil Murray, head of the CIO, dispatched two of his best organizers to the state. One of them was Smaile Chatek, an ex-coal miner whose broken English communicated the kind of common sense that appealed to the working people of Minnesota.

But the most important effort was organizational. In 1948, the "right-wingers" (an unlikely but accurate designation for a Humphrey group) would not be undermanned or unprepared, nor would the farmer delegates leave the convention early to go home and milk the cows. Humphrey marshalled formidable forces in the struggle: Humphrey regulars Arthur Naftalin, Orville Freeman, Evron Kirkpatrick, Herbert McCloskey, and George Matthews were joined by some new faces, among them a young sociology professor from St. Paul named Eugene McCarthy and Eugenie Anderson of Red Wing, who had recently made the move from the League of Women Voters to the rough-and-tumble world of partisan politics. As a part of their effort, the DFL regulars mastered parliamentary law, a device that had been a most effective tool in the hands of their opponents, whose use of parliamentary tactics had won them victories at earlier conventions even when they were in the minority. At the same time, a group of young Humphrey supporters, led by Doug Kelm, later-to-be congressman Donald Fraser, and Jo-

Eugenie Anderson (center) **receives her appointment as ambassador to Denmark in 1949.**

seph Dillon, a future mayor of St. Paul, organized a parallel effort to take over the Young DFL Party.

The 1948 DFL precinct caucuses began on April 30, and as the results of the meetings began to appear, it became apparent that the DFL regulars, who had been weakest in the Twin Cities area in 1946, were staging a comeback. The state convention in Brainerd put the "right-wingers" back in control of the party. Benson and his followers stormed out and held a rump convention of their own, but their attempt to put Wallace's name on

Humphrey at the state DFL convention in Brainerd, 1948

One time I sat beside Muriel at a dinner in the White House and I talked to her about a comparison between Harold Stassen in Minnesota and Hubert Humphrey. She said, "Well, we came up the hard way, and he sort of came in at the top and that was some of the difficulty that he had."

LEVERETT SALTONSTALL
U.S. SENATOR FROM
MASSACHUSETTS, 1945-1967

the DFL ballot in Minnesota failed in a court test.

With the recapture of the party accomplished, Humphrey had a decision to make: should he run for the Senate against Joe Ball or for the governorship against Luther Youngdahl? Max Kampelman recalls that "the wise political people told him that if he ever wanted to be president, he had to run for governor, because no senator would be chosen as a presidential candidate. 'Hell,' he responded, 'you fellows also told me that no one ever moves any place after being mayor.' And so he ran for the Senate."[3] But before Humphrey's campaign for the Senate began, he would head the Minnesota delegation to the Democratic National Convention in Philadelphia in July.

The Republican Convention was also held in Philadelphia that year; it began on June 21, about three weeks before the Democrats were scheduled to arrive. Harold Stassen had started his campaign for the presidency months earlier by announcing in January that he would enter several primaries, including the Ohio Republican primary against Senator Robert Taft. "Mr. Stassen made a great mistake," said Taft, "but if a primary battleground must be chosen, I am delighted he has selected Ohio where he has no chance of success."[4]

Stassen's early efforts went well. He finished first in the Wisconsin and Nebraska primaries and headed the write-in poll in Pennsylvania. He lost some ground in New Hampshire, but his downfall came in Ohio, where he won only nine delegates, having contested Taft in eleven of the state's twenty-two districts. The coup de grace was delivered by Thomas E. Dewey in Oregon, where Stassen and the New York governor met in a face-to-face debate. Both the debate and the Oregon primary went to Dewey. At the convention in Philadelphia, Stassen finished a distant third on the first ballot with 157 votes, just two more than his floor manager, a young lawyer from St. Paul named Warren Burger, had predicted before the counting began. On the third ballot the Republicans gave the nomination to Dewey.

By July, Stassen had accepted the presidency of the University of Pennsylvania, and though he remained a factor in Republican politics through the 1952 convention, from 1948 onward it was all downhill. Stassen had been an important figure in Minnesota public life for many years. Even after he had left the governorship of the state in 1943, Minnesota newspapers had been filled with his exploits. On the day that Humphrey was sworn into office as mayor, a picture of Stassen in his Navy Commander's uniform appeared on the front page of the Minneapolis papers in connection with a story on the United Nations. While Humphrey was occupied with mill levies and liquor licenses, Minneapolis read of Stassen's views on the great issues of the day. But in 1948, unbeknown to either man, Stassen had begun the descent to political oblivion while Humphrey's star had begun to rise.

Harold Stassen in his Navy uniform

In July came the Democrats' turn in Philadelphia. The Minnesota delegation that Humphrey had been selected to lead to the national convention was uninstructed in deference to Humphrey's earlier support of William O. Douglas or Dwight Eisenhower, which had been an ADA-inspired strategy to stop the nomination of Truman. Not until three days before the convention opened did Humphrey announce his support for the president.

By the time the delegates reached Philadelphia, the controversy surrounding the convention had shifted from the nomination of a presidential candidate, now almost certain to be President Truman, to the issue of civil rights. Many observers thought that the Democrats were in enough trouble as it was without still further lessening their chances by antagonizing the Southern states over civil rights. But just as Republicans never seem to enjoy a convention that involves much controversy, Democrats don't seem to enjoy one without it. And in 1948, Hubert Horatio Humphrey would be at the heart of the controversy because of his position as a member of the Platform Committee.

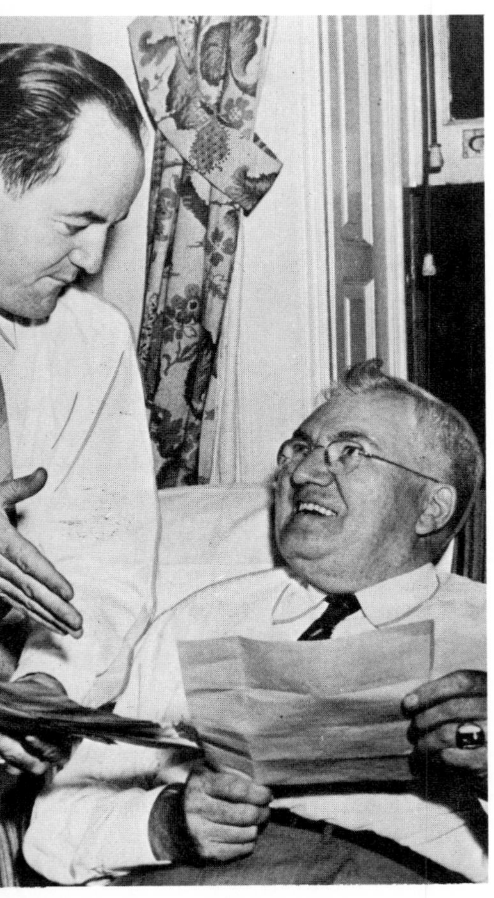

Humphrey, Sr., and Humphrey, Jr., at the Democratic National Convention, 1948

The civil rights issue in Philadelphia focused on a single paragraph in the platform pledging the party to support enactment of a National Fair Employment Practices program. The measure was central to Truman's civil rights program, though the president hardly wanted the convention to become embroiled in a fracas over the kind of hard-line approach embodied in the draft of the plank that Humphrey proposed. In defending his position, Humphrey berated administration spokesmen for what he considered a wishy-washy and generalized statement on civil rights. Here was a lowly mayor of a bush-league midwestern city not only defying the wishes of the president of the United States, but possibly also causing the walkout of the crucial Southern delegations and the loss of the national elections if he succeeded in getting his plan to the floor of the convention. With the

Wallace third-party progressives already drawing away Democratic votes, a fourth-party candidacy of the Democratic solid south was sure to be fatal. The platform committee voted overwhelmingly against the Humphrey position and sent the administration plank to the floor of the convention.

Humphrey's draft of the plank, which caused so much controversy, read,

> We call upon Congress to support our President in guaranteeing these basic and fundamental rights: 1) the right of full and equal political participation; 2) the right to equal opportunity of employment; 3) the right of security of person; and 4) the right of equal treatment in the service and defense of our nation.[5]

While today such language seems tame enough, it was heady stuff for 1948, six years before the Supreme Court ordered the desegregation of public schools. Cross currents of pressure swirled around Humphrey as he tried to decide whether to take the fight to the floor of the convention. Big city political bosses like Ed Flynn of New York encouraged Humphrey to fight. These representatives of the urban, Catholic wing of the Democratic Party were eager to repay the Protestant Southerners for turning their backs on the candidacy of Al Smith twenty years earlier. The administration also made its feelings clear to the young senatorial candidate: If the civil rights plank split the convention and if Thomas Dewey were elected president, a major share of the blame for destroying the Democratic Party would fall on Hubert Humphrey. There would be no future for him in politics.

I first met Hubert Humphrey when he keynoted an Americans for Democratic Action conference in Chicago in March, 1947. It was the best civil rights speech I had ever heard and seemed all the more remarkable being delivered by a young mayor (aspiring to be senator) from a state with no significant number of blacks. Precisely because Hubert Humphrey was speaking for civil rights from his heart rather than for political advantage, he remained steadfast throughout his long political career to the course he set for himself that day. The test of Humphrey's devotion to civil rights was not long in coming. The fledgling ADA decided to make a fight for a strong civil rights platform plan at the 1948 Democratic National Convention in Philadelphia, and by common consent Humphrey became the leader of that effort. On the Tuesday evening of the convention he lost the struggle against the meaningless majority civil rights plank in the platform committee by a large vote, and the faint-hearted within his ranks urged against carrying the issue to the convention floor the following day. All Tuesday night the battle raged—with the ADA group assembled in a University of Pennsylvania fraternity house urging floor action and the politically more significant leadership of the party telling Humphrey he had already gone quite far enough with so divisive an issue. Truman, Barkley, Democratic national chairman McGrath, all the party bigwigs, favored the weak majority plank. David Niles, Truman's civil rights assistant, told me that a Humphrey floor fight would

"ruin the chances of the best political talent to come along in years." But around 5 A.M. Wednesday morning, Humphrey added to the draft minority plank the words "We highly commend President Harry Truman for his courageous stand on the issue of civil rights" and announced he would speak for the plank on the convention floor that afternoon. The cheer at the fraternity house could have been heard at Convention Hall blocks away.

JOSEPH L. RAUH
FORMER PRESIDENT OF THE
AMERICANS FOR DEMOCRATIC ACTION

The Minnesota delegation wanted to take the civil rights fight to the floor, despite the risks that were involved. Hubert Humphrey, Sr., attending the convention as a delegate from South Dakota, advised his son to do what he felt was right but not to do anything that would hurt the party.

The Humphrey group wrestled with the issue until 5 A.M. on the day that the platform report was to be presented. Finally, Eugenie Anderson suggested adding a sentence praising Truman for his stand on civil rights. Her suggestion crystallized Humphrey's decision—he would take the issue to the floor.

When his turn came, Humphrey mounted the platform of the tension-filled auditorium and began speaking, first paying his respects to those who

As soon as Humphrey had made the final decision, that he was going to go ahead with this, he told us to get busy and start contacting delegates at an early hour of the morning. We started calling up people, wakening them up and telling them that they must be there and vote for this minority resolution. Humphrey felt at the time that it was doubtful we could win, but he wanted to be sure that we would at least make a good showing—a respectable showing—so that we wouldn't look ridiculous. We and our supporters worked very hard on the friendly delegates. In the end, the Humphrey plank won by a comfortable margin. We won by a much better margin than what we had really expected. But I think it was very important that Humphrey himself made the final decision—not because he thought he would win it, but because he had really wrestled with it and come to the conclusion that he would do it because it was the right *thing to do. We hoped that he was not making a political mistake which many of his friends said would be the end of him nationally. It was a very courageous decision on his part.*

EUGENIE ANDERSON

disagreed with his position and then swiftly building his case until he came to the payoff:

> There are those who say—this issue of civil rights is an infringement on the states' rights. The time has arrived for the Democratic Party to get out of the shadow of states' rights and walk forthrightly into the bright sunshine of human rights. . . .
>
> For all of us here, for the millions who have sent us, for the whole two billion members of the human family—our land is now, more than ever, the last best hope on earth. I know that we can—I know that we shall begin here the full realization of that hope—that promise of a land where all men are free and equal, and each man uses his freedom wisely and well.[6]

There are not many moments in American political history when a stirring speech or a memorable event has swayed a national party convention. The "We Want Willkie" demonstration at the Republican convention in 1940 was one such moment. This was another. When the dust had finally settled, Humphrey's liberal plan had won 651½ votes to 582½. (Hubert Humphrey, Sr., had proudly reported that South Dakota's eight votes were to be recorded "Aye.") Within hours, the Southern delegates had bolted from the convention; it was not long before they had nominated Strom Thurmond as their candidate on a States' Rights ticket. Humphrey had brought his party into the bright sunlight of civil rights, but many thought he had also brought it to the brink of disaster.

Back in Minnesota after his victory at the Philadelphia convention, Humphrey was ready to begin

A campaign button from 1948

the campaign for the Senate against Joe Ball. Ball was a most unlikely senator. He had been appointed by Harold Stassen in 1940 to fill out the unexpired term of Ernest Lundeen, who had been killed in a plane crash. His selection had come as a surprise to nearly everyone, Ball included. Ball had been a political reporter for the St. Paul papers; his newspaper work was principally remembered for the relish with which he had described some of the more unsavory characteristics of the Benson administration. There were many who felt that Stassen chose Ball merely to keep the seat warm for himself should he decide to run for the Senate in 1948, but it eventually became apparent that Stassen had other things on his mind that year. Ball might not have been willing to step aside in any

Humphrey is welcomed back to Minneapolis after the Democratic Convention.

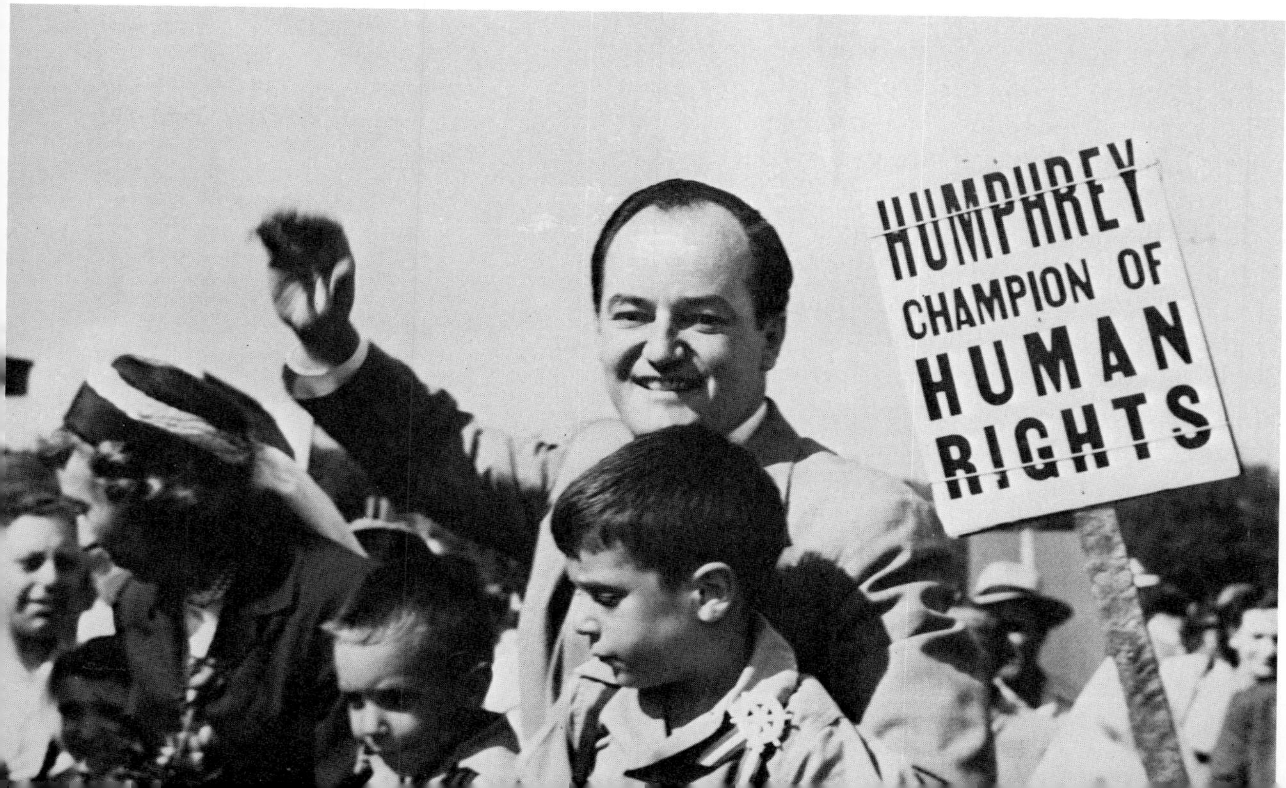

case. As a senator, he had begun his career as something of a maverick and an internationalist, going so far as to support Roosevelt over his own party's candidate in 1944. But by 1948, he was regarded as a conservative, having voted in favor of Taft-Hartley and against the Marshall Plan for European Recovery. "If American policy had been decided by the vote of the Senior Senator from Minnesota," said Humphrey, "we might be negotiating with the Russians now in London instead of Berlin."[7]

Ball finished the primary 60,000 votes ahead of Humphrey, yet he had polled 30,000 fewer votes than Republican Governor Luther Youngdahl. Humphrey was not discouraged by the primary results. He took his campaign on the road, speaking eight to twelve times a day. He went to every one of Minnesota's 87 counties at least twice, and he spoke in at least two-thirds of the state's 723 municipalities. During the course of the campaign he attended 500 meetings and lost 19 pounds. For once, the war records of the two opponents were not an issue. As Humphrey pointed out, "Neither Senator Ball nor I can go around talking about how many miles we marched in the war. Neither of us was in it."[8] Humphrey's campaign was helped in part by a speech Stassen gave in Detroit in which he spoke out against 90 percent of parity. Stassen's speech would cost most Republican candidates, including Dewey, a substantial part of the farm vote.

Humphrey wound up his campaign with a half-hour radio show complete with music and skits, dramatizing the high points of his political career.

I worked on Joe Ball's campaign and Humphrey annihilated us. We got into a buzzsaw. Humphrey was ready—he was vigorous, on the way up, and he had a leg up on Ball before Joe came back to campaign. Part of the problem was that Senator Ball underestimated Humphrey. I think his supporters did. I think Joe was afflicted with the disease that a lot of Republicans have; that is, if you do your job and stay quiet and don't say anything, people will appreciate a job well done, hard work and effort, and they'll reward. I don't subscribe to that theory—I think you have to work for it, and Humphrey was working hard. He just walked away with the 1948 election.

ROBERT FORSYTHE

The program was carried in Minneapolis on WLOL and KSTP and rebroadcast across the state. On election day, he got a haircut, bought a new suit, and went to Tuttle School to vote. He spent the evening listening to the radio: "There was some sweet music on the radio," Humphrey said.

There was indeed. Humphrey walloped Ball 729,494 to 485,801 and became Minnesota's first DFL senator.

Humphrey campaigning with President Truman

Muriel and Hubert receive the news of the election victory.

Senator Humphrey with his parents

chapter 8

FRESHMAN

"The man who was the most articulate spokesman of the Fair Deal among the newcomers was Minnesota's brash, bustling Senator Hubert H. (for Horatio) Humphrey Jr., 37, a hard-working, fast-talking fireball from the Midwest."

Time, *January 17, 1949*

There were no welcoming parties or throngs of well-wishers to greet Hubert Humphrey when he arrived in Washington to take up his duties as a United States senator in 1948. His debut in the nation's capital had a particularly inauspicious character. Broke, as usual, the Humphreys did not have enough money to pay the company that had transferred their belongings to Washington, so the furniture sat on the van for two days until they could get help from Hubert's Dad. Help came, and the movers unloaded the furniture they had been holding for ransom and carried it into the tract house Humphrey had bought at 3216 Coquelin Terrace in Chevy Chase. The down payment for

The Humphreys' 1948 Christmas card

the house had taken all the money Humphrey had and, of course, had also required a loan from Humphrey, Sr. For years after his election to the Senate, Humphrey was unable to sustain the financial burden of another residence in his home district; his legal address in Minnesota was a room in the Nicollet Hotel in downtown Minneapolis.

But at least the salary of a United States senator was a marked improvement over that of the mayor of Minneapolis. Humphrey's pay leaped from

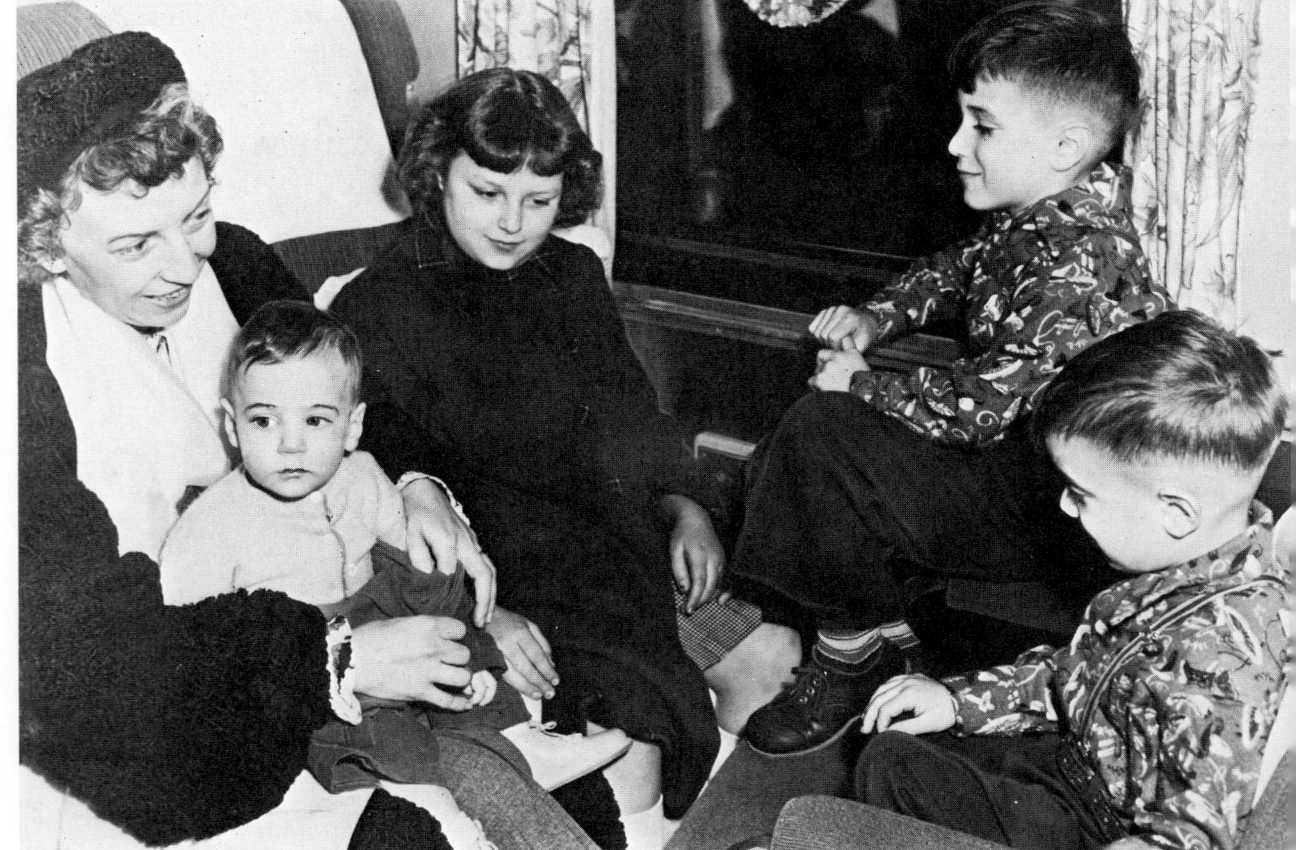

Muriel and the children make the trip to Washington.

$6,000 to $12,500 a year. Another financial benefit that flowed from his election to the Senate was that his fees as a speaker, which had plateaued at the standard $5 paid a Minneapolis mayor, now skyrocketed to $50 a performance. For years, whenever there was another dental bill to be paid or new carpeting needed for the family room, Hubert went out on the road to speak to still another trade association or national convention. As might be expected, he was much in demand by

The Humphreys' new home in Chevy Chase

his fellow druggists; there is probably not a pharmacist alive in the United States over the age of thirty-five who has not heard Humphrey speak at least once.

The reception Humphrey found in the Senate was no friendlier than the one given him by the rest of Washington. While the senior senators of other states brought the other freshmen senators to the floor to be introduced to their new colleagues during the recess session, Humphrey sat glumly in the gallery, cold-shouldered by Ed Thye of Minnesota. Finally Lister Hill of Alabama brought him to the floor, and he shook hands with the men he would be serving with over the next six years. Alone among all the freshmen, Humphrey was not provided office space until he was sworn in. He spent his first month in the Capitol working out of an office loaned him by Washington lawyer Paul Porter.

Humphrey's first task as a senator was to assemble a staff. Max Kampelman recalls his role in that project:

> By December 1948, I was teaching at Bennington College in Vermont. Maggie and I were in Chicago visiting friends during Christmas week. A phone call from Bill Shore in Washington brought news that Humphrey had not yet selected his complete staff. He knew I had a three month vacation from teaching and would I come down and help him open and staff the offices? Yes, I would. I obviously was not going to consider going to work for him, because it is difficult to work for a friend, but it would be interesting for a few weeks. It ended up with my hiring myself.[1]

After he became a Senator in 1948, I went down to say "hello" and offer congratulations. His secretary said he was on the floor, and she would take me around and show me all the offices, which she did. At the end of the tour, she couldn't contain herself any longer and looked up at me and said, "Mr. Lippincott, you're the only professor who gave our Senator a B." I said, "Miss, is that so? I can hardly believe that. I'll go back and check." I said, "If so, it must have been a 'Creative B' because he's gotten a straight A ever since." And so I went back, went through all the blue books and, lo and behold, it was a B and on the outside of the cover was the comment "TOO GLIB."

BEN LIPPINCOTT

Bill Simms, a member of Humphrey's staff at the Minneapolis mayor's office, also came to Washington. One of his first assignments was to find out "when in hell do we get paid?" "Every two weeks. In cash," was the answer.[2]

When Humphrey was sworn into the Senate in January 1949, his father and mother came from South Dakota for the ceremony. One of Humphrey's few pleasant recollections from those early Senate days was the courtesy shown his family by President Truman, who, despite all predictions, was still occupying the White House in 1949. Humphrey had asked Truman's appointments secretary if his parents might perhaps be able to meet the president for a few moments when they came to Washington. What could have been a perfunc-

Humphrey with President Harry S Truman and Eugenie Anderson

tory visit became a grand tour of the White House, led by the president of the United States. Truman let the speechless Humphreys peek into the president's private living quarters. These were the parents of the same young man who Truman believed had defied the party and had threatened his own chances for re-election at the Philadelphia convention in July. No matter—Truman heaped praise on Hubert and assured the parents that their son would make an important contribution to the country.

As Humphrey, Sr., watched his son being sworn into the United States Senate, he dabbed at his eyes. "He's going to be a great Senator—maybe he's going to be something else too."[3] But the Humphreys' visit ended on a somber note. Humphrey, Sr., the lifetime optimist, took his son aside before he left for home and told him he did not think he'd live to see the end of the year. It was time for Hubert to begin making arrangements to provide for his mother. By November 25, 1949, Humphrey, Sr., had died of a cerebral hemorrhage, with Hubert, Ralph, Frances, and Fern all at his bedside in Huron.

Humphrey, deeply unhappy with both the Senate and Washington at the time of his father's death, was thoroughly unsettled by the loss. He talked to Max Kampelman about the role that his father had played in his life: "I could really never go seriously wrong because if I did and it appeared in the newspapers, Dad would be on the phone giving me hell. He was always watching what I was doing." "What concerned him," Kampelman writes, "was whether he would still be as true to his

His assets are character, intelligence, energy, and an informed sense of public service—a man of probity and integrity. He threw his political lot and future with the little fellow—the farmer, the worker—and the everyday people who work for a livelihood. I salute him as a man truly of the people and for the people.

HARRY TRUMAN

Senator Humphrey in Washington with his parents and his sister Frances

ideals now that his father was not looking over his shoulder. About a year or two later I reminded him of that conversation and asked him what he had found. 'Dad is still looking over my shoulder,' "[4] he responded.

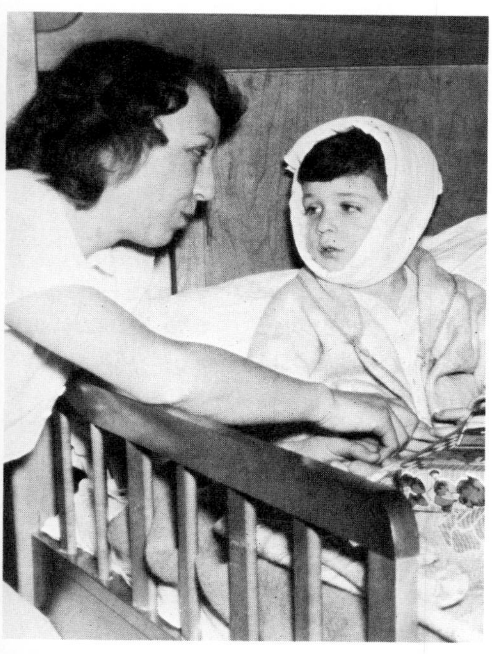

Muriel Humphrey comforts Hubert III, ailing with the mumps.

Muriel Humphrey's early days in Washington were no happier than her husband's. She had come to the city uncertain as to how to cope with the superficial sophistication and the social climbing that were part of the local scene. Absorbed by the care of her four young children—including baby Douglas, born in 1948—Muriel found little appeal in Washington party giving and protocol. She soon came to the conclusion that "you can't be a social butterfly and a good mother."[5]

Hubert also found it difficult to adjust to the demands of his new life. His early attempts to transplant to Washington the speaking style that had wowed the crowd at country fairs and had won him oratorical contests were notable failures. A get-acquainted dinner at an exclusive Washington club with a group of influential Minnesota businessmen turned into an embarrassment when Humphrey lectured his audience for over an hour and a half on an occasion intended for casual conversation. Another informal luncheon produced the same result. Humphrey's reputation as a talker and know-it-all was fast growing.

To make matters worse, a cover article about Humphrey appeared in *Time* magazine a week after he was sworn into the Senate. The portrait on the cover showed an intense young firebrand staring back at the viewer with a tornado whirling madly through the landscape in the background.

Describing Humphrey as "brash," "glib," "cocky," "slick," and "shallow," with "the cyclonic attack of an advertising salesman,"[6] the article did nothing to improve the initial impression he had made on his fellow senators.

Humphrey had also brought with him to the Senate the black marks earned by his performance at the Democratic convention. Resentment against him lingered, kept alive by an article in the *Saturday Evening Post* that had been especially biting in reminding readers of Humphrey's effrontery. Its author, Rufus Jarman, wrote, "Like many other orators of fame, Humphrey is at his most eloquent when debating issues which are less relevant to the problems of his own constituency than to the constituency of others." Jarman went on to suggest that civil rights was of as much concern to the citizens of Minnesota as the "threat of the tse tse fly to the inhabitants of Spitsbergen."[7] Few had yet recognized that Humphrey's Philadelphia speech had not endangered Truman's re-election but, on the contrary, had probably done much to elect him by turning out black and big city voters who had been indifferent to the Democrats' cause until Humphrey thrust the party into the struggle for civil rights.

Humphrey's Senate colleagues did not see much to praise in any of the Minnesota senator's actions. In fact, they had nothing good to say about him at all. One day as Humphrey walked through the Senate corridors, he heard Georgia's Richard Russell, one of the Senate establishment, speaking loudly enough so the passing Humphrey would be sure to hear: "Can you imagine the people of

I vividly remember the first time I met Hubert Humphrey. It was at an AF of L Convention in Cincinnati a few days after election day in November 1948. I was then stationed in Paris in charge of the European operations of the Marshall Plan and had returned for a brief visit to the United States. I had addressed the convention in the morning to thank the members for all their help with the European non-communist labor unions to make the Marshall Plan a success and to encourage them to continue and increase their effective work.

I was asked to stay over for lunch and to hear the newly elected youthful senator from Minnesota speak in the afternoon. Hubert was given the floor after lunch, and he held it for a good two hours or more. He gave every speech he had made during the campaign, and they loved it! I can still hear the ringing applause throughout the speech and see the standing ovation he was given when he finally finished. It was a unique experience for me that I valued highly, because in that one afternoon I learned everything that Hubert thought on every subject of national importance. This laid the foundation for my profound admiration for him.

W. AVERELL HARRIMAN

Minnesota sending that damn fool down here to represent them?"[8] The vice-president of the United States, Alben Barkley, had his own little Humphrey joke. "That Minnesota is a great state. First they send us their Ball, then they send us their Thye, and now they send us their hind-quarters."[9]

'Veep" Alben Barkley wielded a bigger gavel than the junior senator from Minnesota.

The United States Senate, the body of which Hubert Humphrey found himself an unhappy member, is an institution with its own peculiar traditions and mores. While each senator is theoretically the equal of every other member of the Senate, a 200-year tradition and the nature of relationships between one hundred humans of differing interests and abilities have made some senators more equal than others. Most Southern senators seem to become members of the Inner Club—a club without rules or officers—that truly runs the Senate. In many ways the Senate is a Southern institution: deliberate, conservative, parochial, sentimental, deeply concerned with tradition, deeply committed to the principle of compromise.

The story is told about a group of senators who, making a gesture toward modernity, attempted to have the individual snuff boxes that are placed on each senator's desk removed from the Chamber. As they pointed out, there hadn't been a snuff dipper in the Senate for decades. But the Old Guard resented such a radical break with tradition, and the issue was finally resolved in typical Senate fashion. Two lacquered snuff boxes that are never used are now affixed to the Chamber's north wall: a symbol of the spirit of compromise that rules every decision made there. In the Senate, the

When I went to the United States Senate in January 1941, I joined forces with Senator Robert LaFollette of Wisconsin in promoting the St. Lawrence Seaway, the Food Stamp program . . . and other programs designed to provide better foods for children and poor families and better markets for farmers. Bob LaFollette lost his seat in the Senate in 1946. . . . In 1948, however, Hubert Humphrey was elected to the U.S. Senate from Minnesota and I promptly latched on to him to

common failings of the flesh are noted without much disapproval, but those actions that bring discredit on, or violate the tradition of, the United States Senate as an institution are not so readily tolerated. The offender is placed in a kind of exile; he may remain in the Senate, attending committee meetings, introducing bills, casting votes, but he is without real influence. He tries to speak, and pointed disorder and inattention greet his remarks. His bills, no matter how well conceived, are not acted upon; he is in coventry.

It did not take long before Freshman Senator Hubert Humphrey found himself in coventry for having violated one of the Senate's most sacred traditions. For three months after coming to the Senate, Humphrey played it safe. He did not try to speak on the Senate floor, wisely keeping in mind both his own reputation for long-windedness and the Senate tradition that freshmen were to guard their tongues. He gave his maiden speech—a brief one—on behalf of a bill to establish a Missouri Valley Authority similar to the TVA.

Humphrey didn't wait long after his first speech to deliver another, and soon he was on the Senate floor day after day, carrying the debate on foreign policy to Republican conservatives who wanted to ease the nation's commitment to European recovery. "What have the British got that we don't have?" fumed Homer Capehart, a tyrannosaurus rex among the dinosaurs of the Republican right. "Westminster Abbey," responded Humphrey, who won some respect from both sides of the aisle for his quick put down.[10]

But Humphrey soon overreached himself again

The Senate Chamber

help on the projects which Bob and I had worked for. Hubert was a good partner. I tried to hold him down on speaking too much (without too much success), but as members of both the Foreign Relations and Agriculture committees, we were quite successful in seeing to it that people—both here and abroad—had enough to eat and a far better living than they had been used to.

GEORGE D. AIKEN

and, in February 1950, made what he later regarded as the worst mistake of his legislative career. Working from materials prepared for him by a liberal academic lobby, he launched into an attack on the Joint Committee on Reduction of Non-Essential Federal Expenditures, a Senate appendage that served mainly as a patronage vehicle and publicity mill for Senate patriarch Harry F. Byrd of Virginia. By the peculiar standards of the Senate, it didn't matter much that Humphrey's criticism was basically well founded. What did matter was that he had challenged one of the Senate's most respected and powerful members—a senator whose political machine dominated every corner of his state, in whose person were embodied the manner and bearing of a Southern gentleman. Here was a true Senate establishment type being challenged from within his own party by one of the Senate's most junior members, a penniless midwestern liberal nicknamed the "Voice." Worse yet, Humphrey had unknowingly violated tradition by making his charge against Byrd's committee when the senator was not on the floor, but attending the bedside of his sick mother.

Byrd waited six days for the horror of Humphrey's deed to soak thoroughly into the atmosphere of the Chamber. Then, addressing a Senate filled with his cronies, with Humphrey seated at his desk, he began his response. Speaking softly, he first expressed his regret at being unable to be present for Senator Humphrey's remarks and recounted in detail the reasons for his absence, to a chorus of sympathetic clucking from his friends. Humphrey slouched at his desk. Describing the many accomplishments of the committee now under attack, he recalled how the original motion for its establishment had come from one of President Roosevelt's own New Deal brain trusters. Humphrey seemed to drop a few more inches. Discussing at length the "nine misstatements" that Humphrey had made in his speech, Byrd noted that "I have mentioned nine misstatements in two thousand words. This is an average of one misstatement in every two hundred and fifty words and the Senator speaks like the wind."[11] Finally, he concluded with the poignant thought that he was ready to resign if his fellow members so desired. Humphrey had all but vanished beneath his desk, but the members of Byrd's claque leaped to their feet to defend their embattled leader. Of course, he could not resign—the senator and his committee were "doing a magnificent job." The chorus continued its chant.

Harry F. Byrd

Humphrey quickly recovered his aplomb and decided that the best defense was a counterattack. But his response only made matters worse. The chair at first refused to recognize him, and when it did, he made a little speech about being "no shrinking violet," but it was all bravado. In the most dramatic moment of the entire four hours it took to play out the scene, a dozen senators walked over to Humphrey, "stood around him as if to isolate his figure, and then turned their backs on him and walked silently out of the Chamber."[12] The action couldn't have been more brutal if it had been performed by a firing squad.

Only one senator, Millard Tydings of Maryland, rose to Humphrey's defense, although Paul Douglas of Illinois, another freshman liberal who never did make it into the Senate Inner Club, maintained a sort of silent vigil in support of Humphrey during the ordeal.

When it was all over, Humphrey dragged himself out of the Senate Chamber and back toward his office. He gave three rings for the elevator, the signal that a senator was awaiting service. And when the door opened, there was Senator Byrd. "Senator, I know when I've been licked,"[13] said Humphrey, and he extended his hand. That gesture hardly wiped the slate clean, but at least it demonstrated that Humphrey was capable of learning the hard lessons that could be taught in the United States Senate.

Homer Capehart

Several other unpleasant incidents marked Humphrey's early years in the Senate, which Humphrey later called "the toughest years"[14] and "the most miserable period of my life."[15] In April 1951, there was an actual scuffle with the erratic Homer Capehart after a radio talk show. Capehart had taken offense at some hard tongue by Humphrey while they were on the air, and as they were leaving the studio, the 220-pound senator from Indiana grabbed the 165-pound Humphrey by the lapels, forced him against the wall, and raised his fist. Humphrey had not called Homer "the famous White House S.O.B. without the initials,"[16] as Capehart charged. Humphrey's version of the incident was backed by Herbert Lehman, Robert Taft, and Lee Loevinger, who were all there, but there were still plenty of snickers around the Senate when the scene was described. By that time, Humphrey's Senate career had reached its lowest point.

chapter 9

RECOVERY

Despite his problems in Washington, Humphrey's stature in Minnesota still remained relatively high. But even though Humphrey was the DFL's highest office holder, he was in no position to dictate his party's fortunes as Harold Stassen once had to the Republicans. In 1949 the Humphrey organization had supported John C. Simmons for mayor over the incumbent Eric Hoyer, an old time Farmer-Laborite who had succeeded Humphrey when he went to the Senate. Hoyer won. Humphrey wanted York Langton as the

Minneapolis mayor Eric Hoyer at the wheel of a car with three distinguished passengers—President Harry Truman (left), **Senator Hubert Humphrey, and Governor Luther Youngdahl**

Humphrey saw Youngdahl as a big threat. Youngdahl at the time may have been even more dramatic than Humphrey—really handsome, really big guy, great Scandinavian name.

ROBERT FORSYTHE

candidate for Congress in the legislative district that included Minneapolis. The candidate was Marcella Killen. That same year, the Humphrey organization supported Orville Freeman for the DFL nomination for governor. Instead they got Harry Peterson. In the election, Peterson was overwhelmingly defeated by Governor Luther Youngdahl, who won a third term. "Muriel Humphrey, wife of Senator Humphrey, called me on the day after the election," Governor Youngdahl reported, "and told me she had violated party lines and had voted for me as governor."[1]

That news might have pleased Youngdahl, but anything that increased Youngdahl's margin could hardly have had the same effect on Humphrey. With Stassen now safely out of the way in Pennsylvania—when he wasn't chasing the will-o'-the-wisp of the presidency—the Minnesota Republican whom Humphrey had to fear most was Luther Youngdahl. A big, husky, enormously handsome man, he had been elected to a third term by his largest margin yet, 60.7 percent of the vote. The son of Swedish immigrants, fluent in both Swedish and Norwegian (not the least of political assets in Minnesota), Youngdahl had had a distinguished career of service as a judge on both the District Court and the Supreme Court of Minnesota. His record as governor had been in the best tradition of Minnesota reform politics. He closed down the illegal gambling and slot machines that were operating in the resort areas in the northern part of the state, integrated blacks into the National Guard, contrary to national policy,[2] and totally overhauled and modernized the state's archaic program for

treating mental illness. Youngdahl's achievements were not lost on the voters. Even though Minnesota was carried by Truman in 1948 and Humphrey defeated Ball by a large margin, Republican Youngdahl had cut through the national trend to re-election.

Later, Youngdahl recalled the subsequent course of his political career:

Governor Youngdahl and Senator Humphrey

> After my third term election in November of 1950, there was continual talk among Republicans about my running for the fourth term as governor and then to run against Senator Humphrey for the Senate as he sought reelection for a second term. From intimates of both the Senator and myself, I learned that Senator Humphrey was aware of this possibility and wanted to avoid it if possible. He felt that I could beat him and he liked his job so he became aware of the fact that I might be interested in a Federal Judgeship. Ray Ewald, a mutual friend who was head of the Ewald Dairy, had spoken with Senator Humphrey about my appointment to the United States Supreme Court and Senator Humphrey had given him encouragment. However, when a vacancy occurred in the United States District Court for the District of Columbia, created by the death of T. Allen Goldsborough, Senator Humphrey went to President Truman who indicated he was willing to appoint me to the vacancy. Senator Humphrey called Mrs. Youngdahl at our Lake Minnetonka home and informed her of this and indicated that he didn't want me to come to Washington on a wild goose chase. I didn't have to make any promises but if I was interested to let him know and he would set up the appointment. So the appointment was set up with President Truman on July 5, 1951, at 8 A.M.
>
> Ray Ewald made the trip to Washington with

Ray Ewald (left), Hubert Humphrey, and Dr. Reuben Youngdahl, the governor's brother

me on July 4, 1951. My staff in the Governor's Office didn't even know about this appointment. We were met at the plane by Senator Humphrey and his aide and went to the Statler Hotel where a reservation had been made for us to discuss the 8 o'clock appointment the next morning. Shortly before 8 A.M. on July 5, Senator Humphrey and I went into the White House and entered the President's Office by a narrow hidden stairway so that the President's secretary didn't even know about the appointment.

It had always been my ambition to scoop the newspapers and I surely did this on this occasion. President Truman told me that if there had been a vacancy on the Supreme Court, I would have been appointed but I could have the job of United States District Judge if I wanted it. He recalled for me, which I had forgotten, that shortly after he had fired General Douglas MacArthur I was the only governor in the country, and a Republican governor at that, who came out with the statement that we had to stand by our Commander-in-Chief regardless of the issue involved and we could not tolerate insubordination. President Truman had been to Minnesota in 1949 to help us celebrate the Territorial Centennial and I had become acquainted with him at that time. When we came out of the President's office, we came out to face about 20 newspapermen. Among them was Wilbur Elston who later became vice-president of the *Minneapolis Tribune*. When informed of the appointment, he stood speechless. I had succeeded finally in scooping the press.[8]

The Humphrey family in the early 1950s

Humphrey might never have been alerted to Youngdahl's willingness to forego the Senate race if Ray Ewald had not been accepted as a go-between by both men. Humphrey's good judgment as mayor in retaining Republican Ewald on the

At a time when no one, but no one, challenged the Titans of the Senate like senators George and Millikin on their own turf, the junior senator from Minnesota took them on in a David-and-Goliath battle on tax loopholes. Let me give you just a few quotes . . . from the Congressional Record, starting with a colloquy between Senator Humphrey and Senator Paul Douglas of Illinois—"MR. DOUGLAS: Is there not a case in which a leading accountant made his one-year-old son a partner in his accounting business and then divided the income of his business between himself and his one-year-old son as his partner? MR. HUMPHREY: That is correct; that case is well known. MR. DOUGLAS: Is it not true that the same accountant would have been grievously offended if it had been said that the profession of accountancy was so simple that a one-year-old child could master it? MR. HUMPHREY: I'm sure that it is a wise observation by the Senator from Illinois. Nevertheless, for tax purposes, one-year-old Charlie became a member of that firm. MR. DOUGLAS: I do not know that he had a certificate as a CPA but certainly he shared in the emoluments of the firm. MR. HUMPHREY:

City Planning Commission may have raised a few eyebrows in the DFL at the time, but it had certainly paid off later.

As for Youngdahl, it is popularly believed that he could have beaten Humphrey in 1954. Not so enthralled by politics as Harold Stassen, whose thirst for office overshadowed his great abilities to perform once elected, Luther Youngdahl had more modest goals. "My ambition was to end my career in the Federal Judiciary,"[4] he said. And he achieved his ambition.

As Humphrey's political future in Minnesota began to brighten with the Youngdahl appointment, he began to pull himself out of the hole he'd dug for himself in Washington. From the Byrd affair Humphrey had not only learned the value of Senate tradition but had also been forcefully taught that while grandstand plays might sit well with the public, they were fatal when attempted at the expense of another United States senator. Describing the qualities required in the Senate, he later said, "It isn't enough to be intelligent, clever, or even political. You simply have to work."[5]

As a sort of repentance for his earlier mistakes, Humphrey began to master tax legislation, a complex field that does not lend itself to crowd-pleasing speeches, despite its formidable impact on social concerns. In the Senate debate over the 1950 tax bill, Humphrey introduced twelve amendments, all of them aimed at closing tax loopholes. They were all defeated, but he argued them well and with some humility, before his fellow senators graciously shot the legs out from under him. When the 1951 tax bill was introduced he offered twenty amendments. This time he had done his homework even more thoroughly, and though he was gunned down again, he responded with dignity and restraint. Eugene Millikin, who led the Republican opposition to the Humphrey proposals, was sufficiently impressed to congratulate him on the thoroughness of his presentation. Gradually, the atmosphere began to thaw. Having learned that the Senate is "a good forum, but a poor audience,"[6] Humphrey continued to go about his Senate work conscientiously and with proper deference shown to the Senate establishment.

As his position in the Senate became more assured, Humphrey began carrying the administration program in labor and civil rights. His first major legislative accomplishment was a program that provided emergency shipments of wheat for India made available at very liberal terms, an achievement that literally averted starvation for millions. By 1954 this program had evolved into Public Law 480, which allowed the sale of surplus farm commodities for foreign currencies; by 1959 it had become the Food for Peace program. Other Humphrey measures had equally long but successful histories. The very first bill he had introduced in 1949, Post Hospital Care for the Aged under Social Security, didn't go far his first term, but it finally passed in 1965 as Medicare.

During his first term in the Senate, Hubert Humphrey involved himself in a great variety of legislative concerns. Three of his early committee assignments, Agriculture, Labor, and Small Business, just about covered the spectrum of interests and issues in Minnesota. Humphrey got an amend-

Senator Paul Douglas (right) **with Humphrey and Adlai Stevenson**

Yes. Not only did the one-year-old child realize the great pleasure and honor of sharing in his father's firm, and the prestige which came from knowing he was associated with his distinguished father, but he did not have a single worry about what would happen to his money because his father took care of that and took control of the entire business. The advantage the father obtained by making such an arrangement was that he did not have to pay as large a tax as he would have to pay if he had waited until his son became old enough actually to perform work for the firm, before taking his son into the firm as a partner. MR. DOUGLAS: By means of that arrangement the father reduced the taxes he had to pay although he remained in control of the business. MR. HUMPHREY: That is the point I've been making."

This particular tax loophole was later closed.

WALTER W. HELLER

He once said to me, "It isn't that I'm smarter than other senators, or that I'm more creative than other senators. I work an extra eight hours every day."

NORMAN SHERMAN
FORMER HUMPHREY AIDE

Early in the 1950s, a subcommittee of the Senate Small Business Committee conducted hearings on a newsprint shortage, and I worked as counsel for the subcommittee for about one day or so a month for the ten months it was in session. When it became known that Humphrey would chair it, an editorial appeared in Editor and Publisher *to the effect that the newspapers of America were about to be socialized by this wild-eyed radical, etc. By the time Humphrey and the subcommittee finished,* Editor and Publisher *finally made a grudging admission that perhaps Humphrey hadn't done any harm and perhaps had done some good.*

LEE LOEVINGER

ment passed requiring the Secretary of Defense to appoint a special assistant on small business, and he co-sponsored a bill that created the Small Defense Plants Administration. An investigative subcommittee that he served on looked into the scandal of the Reconstruction Finance Organization; another investigated the grain storage program. His successful legislative accomplishments included amending the displaced persons bill to permit 15,000 orphans to be admitted to the United States, compelling the armed services to accept greater racial integration, and acting as floor leader when the Hoover Commission plans on reorganization of the federal government were adopted by the Senate.

A lesser accomplishment, but one that certainly didn't hurt Humphrey's re-election chances, was his sponsorship of the Communist Control Act of 1954. Introduced on August 11, the measure was passed by August 25. Considering that it took seven years to get the test ban treaty and sixteen years to enact Medicare, the speed with which this bill was passed speaks eloquently of the hysteria gripping the nation—and its lawmakers—at the height of the McCarthy era. The bill itself, of questionable constitutionality, required Communists to register with the government and prevented them from appearing on the ballot in elections. Said Humphrey later, "It wasn't one of the things Humphrey [he often referred to himself in the third person] is proudest of. It grew out of my frustration and anger over the way the Republicans were using the Communist issue. I just decided to do something about it. It got the issue out of

Joseph McCarthy earned a reputation as "Tail-gunner Joe" before he became famous for his anti-Communist activities in the Senate.

the Congressional Committees and into the Courts. And it saved the life of at least two Democratic Senators."[7]

While the motivation may have been largely political, Humphrey's hard-nosed and uncompromising reaction to the Communist issue of the 1950s was in character with his response to the Communist infiltration of the DFL Party back in the '40s. He was severely criticized then for the tactics he had employed to regain control of the DFL, for while mayor, he had used FBI files to help identify Communist infiltrators in the party. Years later, when opposition to his Viet Nam position began to swell, there was a long period, perhaps far too long, when Humphrey analogized his situation to those earlier struggles, hoping that by taking a hawkish approach he would succeed much as he had in the past.

As his first term in the Senate moved toward its close, new prospects began to open for Humphrey. They came by way of his connection with a Texan named Lyndon Johnson, who had entered the Sen-

Lyndon Johnson (right) **and Speaker of the House Sam Rayburn**

ate with him in 1948 and who had been elected minority leader in 1952. Johnson's Senate credentials were impeccable: a Southerner and a conservative with moderate leanings, he first had been a protegé of Franklin Roosevelt as a young man in the House, and then of House speaker Sam Rayburn. Moving on to the Senate, he fit comfortably into the circle of Senate types like Walter George and Richard Russell of Georgia, Harry Byrd of Virginia, and Russell Long of Louisiana. Long, who had known Humphrey at LSU and was now his next door neighbor in Chevy Chase, introduced the Minnesota senator to Johnson. Recognizing in Humphrey a worthy subject for reclamation as well as a natural leader of the liberal wing of the party ("my link to the bomb-throwers," Johnson was to call him), Johnson began to give him more responsibility in Senate affairs.

Johnson's reliance on Humphrey was not a reward for political support. In fact, Humphrey had opposed Johnson for the Senate minority leadership and had backed the hopeless cause of fellow liberal James Murray of Montana. When Johnson learned that the liberals were going to run a candidate to oppose him, he summoned Humphrey, who was the manager of Murray's effort. As was always the case, Johnson was obsessed with obtaining as large a majority as possible, perhaps in hopes of banishing the image of "Landslide Lyndon" that had stuck with him since he won his Senate seat with an 87-vote majority during a highly questionable election in which nearly 1 million votes were cast. Johnson was unable to understand why Humphrey would willingly continue to fight for Murray's losing cause. When he asked Humphrey how many votes he expected for his candidate, Humphrey responded "twenty." Johnson asked him how he arrived at his count, and every time Humphrey named a senator who would be supporting Murray, Johnson would respond, "No, you don't have him. I do."[8] When the vote was taken in the caucus, Jim Murray had won just three votes—his own, Humphrey's, and one other. This latest embarrassment had taught Humphrey another lesson about the Senate: the votes flow to where the power lies, or in Johnson's words, "Quit fooling around with people you can't depend on."[9]

This episode had made Johnson respect Humphrey's candor, if not his ability to count votes. Johnson also understood that his success as minority leader depended in part on his ability to develop a working relationship with the liberals. In order to do that, he needed a lieutenant he could trust. And Humphrey was that man. Humphrey could introduce him to liberal labor and political leaders like Walter Reuther of the UAW, David Dubinsky of the Garment Workers, and Alex Rose of New York's Liberal Party.

As for Humphrey, it wasn't difficult to see why he was both flattered by Johnson's attention and eager to play a more important role in Senate affairs. His years in the cold had taught him where the levers of power were; Johnson was his vehicle for the chance to lay a hand on them. He performed a variety of legislative chores for the minority leader, and in return Johnson fixed on Humphrey as the only senator through whom he

In a conversation with James Markham, editor of the Hennepin County Review, *Humphrey said, "Well, you know, my objective is that Foreign Relations committee," but he said to get on there, "I have to make my peace with Lyndon Johnson." And Markham responded in these very words: "Don't you cut, shuffle, or deal with that son of a bitch. He's no good. He's owned lock, stock, and barrel by the Texas oil and gas interests. I'd rather see you on the District of Columbia Committee than have anything to do with that bastard." And Humphrey said, "That's the way it goes here, Jim. If you're going to get anywhere, you've got to play ball." And Jim said, "Don't do it. Stick to your principles. Don't sell out to that guy." So anyway, Humphrey did. That was the beginning of his eventual downfall, because that damn Johnson never had the same loyalty toward him that he had toward Johnson.*

GENE O'BRIEN

Humphrey with fellow members of the Senate

would deal with the liberals' requests for committee assignments and the like. Far from being captured by the right wing of his party, Humphrey became an articulate spokesman for the liberal senators.

Johnson rewarded Humphrey for his diligence by giving him a seat on the Senate Foreign Relations Committee, with the consent of committee chairman Walter George of Georgia. This choice assignment would have been undreamed of a few years earlier in Humphrey's Senate career. Service on Agriculture was the meat and potatoes of political life, but Foreign Relations, with its opportunities for travel, was the dessert. Humphrey had not just begun to arrive in the Senate; he had arrived. His importance was acknowledged by the Senate as a whole when, on one occasion, that august body spent several hours manufacturing a delay in the midst of a roll call so that Humphrey's plane, late on arrival from Minneapolis, could land and his vote be recorded. By the time Humphrey's first term ended in 1954, the irascible Senator George (his wife referred to him as "Mr. George"—*always*), who had scorned the upstart Humphrey upon his arrival in the Senate, was writing letters to the somewhat puzzled voters of Minnesota on behalf of his re-election.

In Minnesota campaigning for his second term in the Senate, Humphrey attempted to repair the damage that Ike had inflicted on the DFL in the Republican sweep of 1952. Orville Freeman, who had been defeated for attorney general in 1950 and again for governor in 1952, had said in a moment

One thing about Humphrey was that he could always learn a lesson from his defeats and the defeats that his party suffered. He just learned to pick up the pieces and go on from there. In 1952, in the Eisenhower landslide, the DFL got wiped out. Freeman ran for governor in 1952, and he got clobbered. He was so disconsolate he made the statement that he just wasn't going to run anymore. Nobody can beat Republicans in this state, he

thought. Well, in 1954 Humphrey came back and led the team, and Freeman got elected governor and they controlled the legislature. Humphrey just helped them pick themselves up off the floor, and all of a sudden, they were a factor to be reckoned with. . . . They were down in the dumps in 1952, but he was able to pick them up and carry them.

ROBERT FORSYTHE

of dejection that he would not run for office again. Largely because of Humphrey's urging, he did run again, was elected governor, and went on to serve three terms in that office before becoming John Kennedy's Secretary of Agriculture.

Humphrey's own re-election in 1954 seemed to be a shoo-in, but nevertheless his campaign proceeded at a frantic pace. A fixture in every Humphrey campaign was his driver and factotum Freddie Gates, a roly-poly Lebanese who owned a coin-operated machine business in Minneapolis and who had cast himself in the role of Sancho Panza since Humphrey's mayoral days. Gates kept a

Humphrey on the campaign trail

month's supply of crackers and cheese odorously ripening in his Buick so that the senator wouldn't have to stop for such time-consuming rituals as eating during his journeys around the state. Another candidate campaigning with Humphrey in 1954 described a typical day on the road:

> After a refreshing sleep of two or three hours, we got up at 6 A.M. and showed up at 7 for a breakfast with party officials from the area. We made speeches and listened to them. We shook hands all around. Then Humphrey made a speech on the sidewalk outside the hotel. More handshaking. Our driver whizzed us down the highway to three more towns, more sidewalks, more speeches, more handshaking. . . . In the afternoon we stopped at four industrial plants and several more towns for handshaking and literature distribution. We were late for dinner because Humphrey stopped after one sidewalk talk to tell some school kids all about the

In 1954, Humphrey ran against Val Bjornson. All during that campaign, he had nothing but praise for Bjornson. I remember one time they made a joint appearance. Usually, it is the incumbent that speaks last in this kind of situation because it's considered an advantage to be able to speak last and be in a position to answer any charges that the challenger makes. But Humphrey chose to speak first, and what did he say? He told a story about how he had come home from campaigning one night, and his little boy had come up and sat in his lap and said, "Daddy, what are we going to do if you get beat in this election?" And he said, "Son, don't you worry

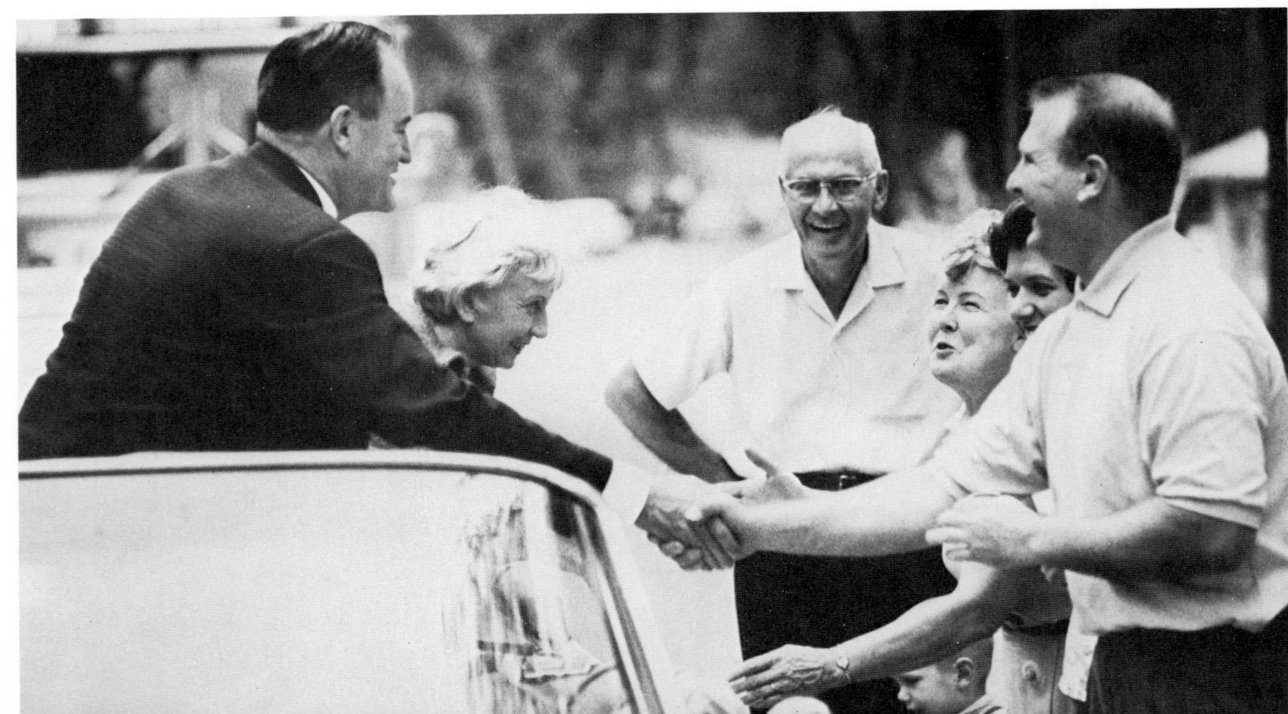

about that. If I get defeated, I'll be defeated by one of the greatest Americans who ever lived—Val Bjornson. And if Val Bjornson is elected to the U.S. Senate, you and I can go to sleep at night and not have to worry about government, or peace, or the economy, or whatever." Well, after he had finished, it was now Val Bjornson's turn, and what's Bjornson going to say? Attack Humphrey? Praise him? What do you do? Well, all you can do, I suppose, is just stumble around as gracefully as possible. Just a beautiful technique—Hubert just loved him to death.

ROBERT FORSYTHE

latest developments in guided missiles. For once no dinner meeting had been arranged. By this time I had made so many speeches and shaken so many hands I wanted to march off into a secluded corner of a dark cafe and make believe people just did not exist. Humphrey? He insisted on sitting at a table near the entrance so he could chat and handshake with everybody who came in. You know what I think? . . . He loves it.[10]

On election day Humphrey led the DFL ticket with 642,193 votes, gaining a 162,000-vote margin over Republican Val Bjornson. His coattails had been long enough to carry into office Orville Freeman as governor, Karl Rolvaag as lieutenant governor, and Miles Lord as attorney general. The day after Humphrey led the DFL landslide, the *Minneapolis Tribune* wrote: "This state is his, as much as it was Harold Stassen's back in the days when Stassen's bids for the presidency were news."[11]

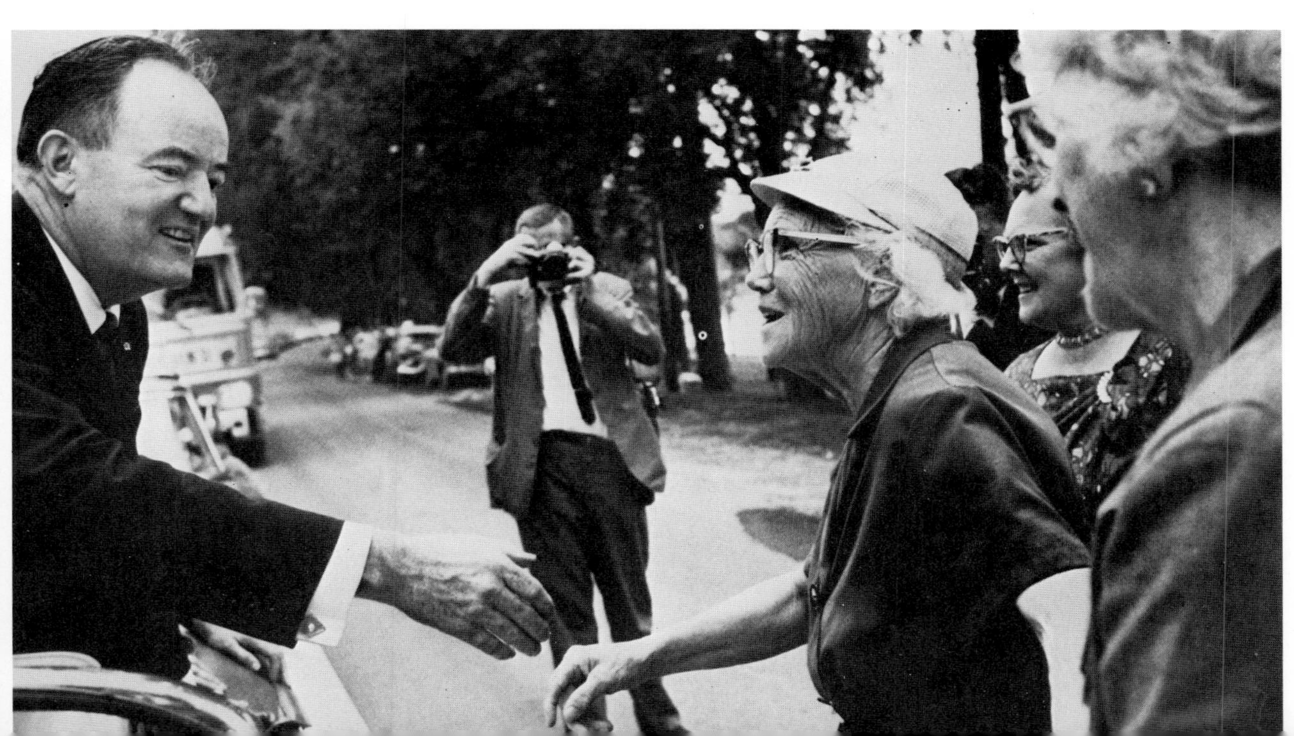

chapter 10

RECOGNITION

". . . My life as a public official has been an exciting one in many ways. Muriel and I have traveled the world over. We've dined with kings and emperors, and we have been with the poorest of the poor. We've been with people of every walk of life, every race, creed, and nationality."

Hubert H. Humphrey

Even though Lyndon Johnson was eager for a Democratic majority to elevate him to Senate Majority Leader, he made only one campaign trip to a northern state during the 1954 elections. He toured Minnesota for his friend Hubert Humphrey. The visit probably did more for Johnson than Humphrey, who was in an easy race. Johnson was given to dark moments, brooding over his belief that Northerners made fun of his Southern accent and his "Landslide Lyndon" election and looked down their noses at his less-than-impressive education at Southwest Texas State Teachers' College. While some Northerners did do these things, the farms of western Minnesota harbored no Harvard-educated elitists determined to snub the Texan. Johnson's reception in Minnesota was cordial and deepened his regard and affection for Humphrey. Before he left the state, he hinted broadly that Humphrey most likely would be appointed to fill a vacancy on the Democratic Policy Committee left by the retirement of Senator Edwin Johnson.

By late 1954, the McCarthy era had drawn to a close with the Senate censure of Senator Joseph McCarthy by a vote of 67 to 22. In keeping with the institutional character of the Senate, the bill of particulars laid much stress on McCarthy's having "failed to cooperate with the Subcommittee on Privileges and Elections of the Senate Committee on Rules and Administration . . . and acted contrary to Senatorial ethics and tended to bring the Senate into dishonor. . . ."[1] No mention of the people outside the Senate who were abused, some even ruined, by McCarthy's witch-hunts. Never mind the fear and hysteria that McCarthyism had provoked across the country for the last five years. What mattered in the Senate was that McCarthy had broken Senate rules; for those infractions and those alone, he was censured. When last seen, McCarthy was careening through the corridors of the Capitol, his arm in a sling from some mysterious accident. He quickly slipped away and by 1957 was dead.

Before his career ended, McCarthy had become

Senator Joseph McCarthy conducting a hearing in the Senate

indirectly involved in Humphrey's 1954 senatorial campaign. A rumor had circulated that he was investigating a favorable tax ruling that Humphrey was alleged to have obtained for a Minneapolis businessman. Humphrey was also supposed to have spent a summer living on this same businessman's farm. Humphrey denied ever having been involved in the tax ruling but agreed that he had lived on the farm for several months. He produced his cancelled check for $500 and the businessman's deposit slip to his own bank account to show that it had been an arm's length transaction, and that was the last ever heard of the affair.

When the 84th Congress convened in early 1955, there were substantial Democratic majorities in both houses. Lyndon Johnson was elected Senate Majority Leader, and Humphrey was given his post on the Policy Committee. In this position, he would play a part in determining much of what the Senate would and would not do over the next five years.

Humphrey's misgivings about the relatively minor role he had played in combating McCarthyism surfaced early in his second term in the Senate. In 1955, he was responsible for a unanimously adopted Senate resolution that provided for an in-depth study of the federal government's loyalty security program, long an object of liberal criticism. Humphrey made no attempt in this session to strengthen the Senate anti-filibuster rules, another liberal goal that was intended to prevent Southern senators from using the filibuster to thwart civil rights legislation. He knew that the anti-filibuster move didn't stand a chance in the Senate, but he did see the possibility of restraining the Southerners within the Democratic Party by developing a party loyalty provision that would keep the South from bolting the 1956 Democratic National Convention while still requiring delegates to pledge some minimal fidelity to the candidates and platforms of their party. When the convention was held that year in Chicago, Humphrey would refuse to be drawn into a rerun of the 1948 Philadelphia convention and another bitter struggle over a civil rights plank in the platform.

It wasn't the party platform that occupied Humphrey's attention at the Democratic National Convention in 1956, but the prospects of being his party's vice-presidential candidate. Since the 1952 convention, when he had been nominated for president by Congressman Eugene McCarthy as a favorite-son candidate and then had released his delegates to Stevenson, Humphrey had been developing a strategy that would land him on the ticket in 1956. The 1952 effort had been primarily for domestic consumption; Minnesota voters had been favorably impressed to see their junior senator, up for re-election in just two years, nominated for president of the United States before a national television audience. The 1956 effort had a bit of stagecraft about it too. Several Democrats, Hubert Humphrey and John Kennedy among them, realized that while the prospects of the Democrats defeating President Eisenhower were remote, there was much to be gained from the vice-presidential nomination. The party's vice-presidential candidate would receive national exposure, an opportunity to become acquainted with the party structure

While Humphrey was Senator and I was DFL Chairman, the flow of correspondence between our two offices in Washington and New York ran into hundreds of letters a month, requests for appointments, whatever. Humphrey had won his reputation for being effective in part because he always answered constituent requests promptly, usually getting off some sort of reply in less than a week. . . . It was common knowledge in Minnesota that when you wanted something down in Washington, Republican or Democrat, you went to Humphrey's office. To maintain that reputation, Hubert would occasionally shake up his staff. At one time there had apparently been some slip up, and henceforth every letter had to be answered right away. Whether the action requested was taken or not, at least the letter would be ac-

knowledged. So one day I received a form letter from Humphrey's office addressed "Dear Mr. Farr," acknowledging the receipt of my letter and wanting me to know they were working on the problem. What problem? The letter was meaningless since I'd probably made 100 requests of one kind or another that week. So I chose the logical response—I devised a form letter, cut a stencil, and sent it off to Washington. "Dear Senator Humphrey, the problem you've been working on has been resolved. You need not look into it any further. Sincerely, George Farr, DFL State Party Chairman."

I'm sure he never saw my letter. And if he did, he wouldn't know what the hell I was talking about, because I sure didn't know what the hell he was talking about.

GEORGE FARR

and organization in nearly every state, and, unless some terrible gaffe were made, none of the blame for the inevitable defeat. Best of all, the vice-presidential nominee would have a leg-up for the Democratic presidential nomination in 1960. Then the Republican candidate would not be the grinning General but most likely the dark-visaged Richard Nixon, a much more inviting target.

Humphrey's first move in his effort to be named

Humphrey and Richard Nixon

to the ticket was to take the field early for Adlai Stevenson, judging correctly that Stevenson would be the Democratic presidential nominee. With the Minnesota DFL Party on record as endorsing Stevenson for the presidency as early as November 1955, the next step was to persuade Stevenson to enter the Minnesota presidential preference primary to be held in March 1956. Stevenson consented. The issue was joined when a maverick group of DFLers led by Robert Short, a trucking and hotel executive, and two state legislators, Donald Wozniak and Peter Popovich, entered Estes Kefauver of Tennessee in the primary as well. Kefauver had come to the Senate with Humphrey in 1948. Even though he was a Southerner, he was regarded as a lightweight by his colleagues. He was well known nationally, his reputation built on headline-grabbing investigations of organized crime and fine-sounding but rather empty proposals for an Atlantic Union. But Kefauver was basically a showhorse in an organization that respects a workhorse.

When Kefauver and Stevenson came to Minnesota for the primary campaign, the differences in their political styles were painfully apparent. Stevenson was at his least attractive during the Minnesota campaign. Impossibly correct and ill at ease, he lurched about among the casual and matter-of-fact voters of Minnesota, while Kefauver coonskin-capped his way through the state, radiating warmth and folksiness. Stevenson's failure to come out for high price supports did nothing to aid his cause in rural areas. On election day, state Republicans took advantage of the fact that Minnesota laws do not require registration by party

and stampeded to the polls for Kefauver, delighted at the prospect of embarrassing their celebrated tormentor, Hubert Humphrey. Kefauver won by 60,000 votes. Neither Humphrey nor Gene McCarthy, whose names appeared on the ballot, were elected as delegates to the national convention, though their congressional standing—McCarthy had been elected to the House in 1948—would permit them to go anyway. Humphrey spent the last few days of the campaign in Washington, working on the farm bill, so he was unaware of the extent of the disaster. The morning after the primary, he called Stevenson and said, "Hello, Adlai,

Estes Kefauver

I think the Republicans took an awful licking in Minnesota yesterday."[2] Stevenson's response is unrecorded, which is probably all for the best. Humphrey wisely decided that his best course would be to lie low for a while and let the Kefauver fever run its course in Minnesota. Humphrey even ducked the Jefferson-Jackson Day dinner, an annual spring event from which DFL officeholders did not normally absent themselves. "If I went out there and people started arguing, we'd have a fist fight before we got through,"[3] he said.

Max Kampelman recalls what happened in Washington later that spring:

> We were at the Mayflower Hotel at a Congressional dinner. Hubert, as I recall, was Chairman, and Adlai Stevenson was the speaker. A quiet whisper between the two. At the end of the dinner, a signal from Hubert to join him upstairs. There we were, the two of us together in a room with an exhausted Adlai Stevenson changing into bedclothes. His trusted friend, Bill Blair, and Jim Finnegan, his political manager, were in the room. "Whom do you think I should have as my running mate?" was Adlai's question. Down the list we went, analyzing each name. Finally, we came to the point, with Stevenson asserting that he wanted to choose a Vice President who was qualified to step in as President as well as a man who could help him politically. And Hubert Humphrey, he unequivocably said, was that man. What he wanted us to do was arrange for some of the Southerners to tell him that Hubert would be acceptable. The task was easy. The revered Walter George of Georgia had already told Humphrey he favored him. Lyndon Johnson had offered to help. So had Sam Rayburn, John Sparkman, and Brooks Hays.

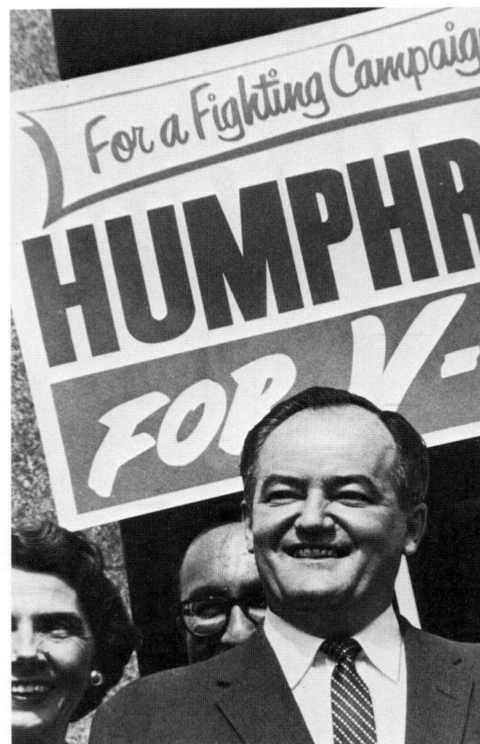

> We left the hotel with stars in both the skies and in our eyes.[4]

When Humphrey left Stevenson's room at 5 A.M., he was certain he had what amounted to a commitment. In July, Humphrey sent out a letter openly seeking support for the post, and Gene McCarthy was dispatched on a cross-country tour to try to drum up interest for his colleague. Since Stevenson had clearly stated that Kefauver was unacceptable to him, Humphrey perceived John Kennedy as his principal opposition. He therefore sought support in the farm states, hoping to capitalize on Kennedy's vote against high price supports, an understandable position for a senator from Massachusetts but a vulnerable point for a national candidate.

At the national convention, with Stevenson duly nominated, Humphrey was busy writing an accep-

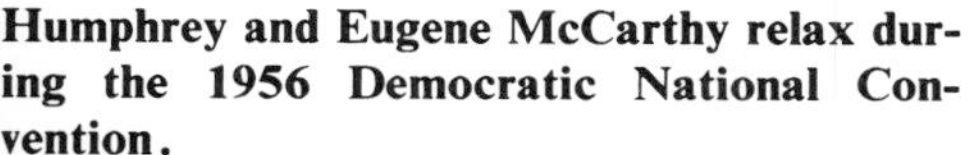

Humphrey and Eugene McCarthy relax during the 1956 Democratic National Convention.

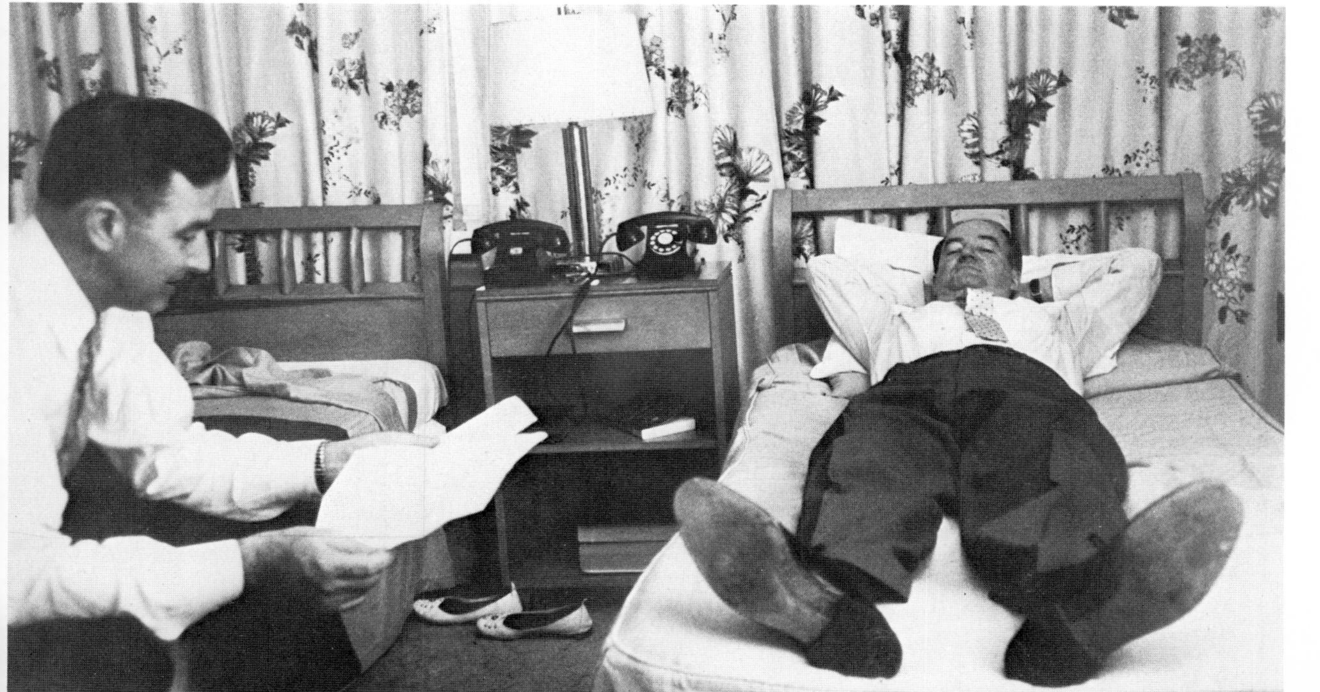

tance speech when he learned from television coverage that Stevenson had decided to throw the nomination open and let the delegates pick the vice-presidential candidate. It was tantamount to handing the spot to Kefauver, who had a disciplined cadre of delegates and a nationwide organization still in place from his presidential effort. There would be no problem switching them to a whirlwind vice-presidential nominating campaign. The cruelest blow was dealt by the Kefauver forces that dominated Humphrey's own Minnesota delegation; they patronizingly announced they were supporting Humphrey on the first ballot at the request of Senator Kefauver. The result of the balloting was that Humphrey finished fifth behind Kefauver, Kennedy, Albert Gore of Tennessee, and Robert Wagner of New York. "Humphrey and I, in the bitterness of the night, recalled the intense negative feelings about Kefauver and his qualifications that had been expressed by Stevenson in the secrecy of the Mayflower suite,"[5] remembers Kampelman.

One lesson learned from the 1956 debacle was that seeking a place on the national ticket required a national constituency as well as a regional one. Humphrey never neglected his responsibilities as a Minnesota senator. "Go home on weekends. That's the difference between winning and losing elections,"[6] he later told a group of freshman lawmakers. But Humphrey realized that while he had to keep his political home base secure, it wasn't enough simply to be known as a farm state or a regional senator. Besides, he hadn't gotten elected to the United States Senate "to become the great-

This campaign button featuring Humphrey as Stevenson's running mate turned out to be premature.

If I had to put my finger on the one thing that made Hubert Humphrey tick, that drew people to him, it is that he had an enormous love of people. He loved being in a crowd, he liked it there. Watching him walk into a large room with a lot of people around was just a joy. It was not a duty for him. I've watched all kinds do the same thing, and it's hard work. Gene McCarthy—it was difficult for Gene to do that kind of thing. Humphrey loved it.
GEORGE FARR

A dejected Humphrey at the end of the convention

est living expert on the boll weevil."[7]

Participation in the leadership operation of the Senate, while important to his status within the Senate itself, was not of sufficient interest outside of Washington to develop the kind of national constituency that a presidential or vice-presidential candidate needed if he were to be taken seriously. Kefauver had proved that a senator could still capture national attention if he chose the right issues, despite the quality of his congressional work. John Kennedy, regarded as a barely adequate senator by his colleagues, had also finished ahead of Humphrey in the vice-presidential balloting at the 1956 convention.

But for Humphrey it was something of a problem to focus on the "right issues" in his legislative career. His range of interests was incorrigibly broad; during his first two terms in the Senate, Humphrey sponsored 1,044 bills and joint resolutions. "Good God, Hubert, please don't shoot at every rabbit that sticks his head up," urged Jim Webb, a friend of his. "I can't help it, I'm interested in everything," replied Humphrey.[8] When Humphrey had taken his seat on the Senate Foreign Relations Committee in 1952, however, he had found an area of particular interest to him. He had given up his seat on Agriculture at the same time, a rather risky decision for a Minnesota senator facing election in two years. (Fortunately he was able to regain the seat on Agriculture just before the 1954 election.) But it was a chance worth taking, for in Foreign Relations, Humphrey recognized an area where he could not only make a contribution but also gain the kind of national

The Humphreys during their tour of the Middle East in 1957

stature that could help dissolve an image that usually cast him in the role of a prairie populist.

In 1951, Humphrey had taken his first overseas trip as a senator and observed that "if there is to be a European unity, it would have to be based on trade and economics and not a political federation."[9] The establishment of a European Common Market several years later confirmed his forecast. Humphrey's interest in foreign affairs also involved him in the issue of international disarmament. Despite widespread apathy on the part of both Congress and the people, in 1955 he secured passage of Senate Resolution 93, which called for the establishment of a subcommittee on disarmament. At one of the first meetings of the subcommittee, Thomas Murray of the Atomic Energy Commission, discussing the risks of unlimited nuclear fallout, provided the basis for Adlai Stevenson's call for a nuclear test ban treaty in his 1956 campaign. After the election, Humphrey kept up the pressure for disarmament in a series of letters to Secretary of State John Foster Dulles and raised the collateral issue of the need for effective on-site inspection.

Humphrey made his first extensive trip abroad in 1957, as Chairman of a Middle East subcommittee on Foreign Relations. He toured the countries of the Middle East and southern Europe and visited with Ben-Gurion of Israel and Nasser of Egypt. In the Arab countries, "Humphrey conquered suspicion by listening attentively, answering Arab complaints by clear-cut definitions of U.S. aims, letting his hosts have the last word. The Arabs came to accept him as no Zionist, but a man

Humphrey met David Ben-Gurion, prime minister of Israel, during his 1957 trip.

of understanding and sympathy."[10] Humphrey advised Nasser, "If you would concentrate your talents and energies on the political and economic development of Egypt, you would be making a real contribution to the world, but your fishing in international waters will lead to nothing but trouble. Why dabble in international matters when you have so many economic troubles at home that need your attention?"[11] Nasser shrugged.

Humphrey returned home to praise from John Foster Dulles. He had ably defended United States policy, had gotten firsthand knowledge of Turkey, Greece, Italy, Spain, and other areas of southern Europe, where he observed the utilization of United States farm surpluses. From a personal standpoint, he had gained self-confidence in his ability to deal with foreign leaders, a skill he would have occasion to call upon during his next trip.

Humphrey's success in the Middle East quickly bore fruit. After his return, he got a long distance call in Minnesota from the Syrian foreign minister. Would Humphrey come to New York to discuss a matter with him? No one else seemed willing to help. Humphrey came and not only heard the diplomat out but also made sure that the State Department became aware of its responsibility for listening to the representatives of friendly Middle Eastern nations.

In 1958, Humphrey again went abroad, and this time his assignment was much more impressive. As a member of the Foreign Relations Committee and a delegate to the General Assembly of the United Nations (a post to which he had been appointed by President Eisenhower in 1956) and the world health organization UNESCO, he was officially attached to the American negotiating team in the Geneva disarmament talks. Accompanied by Muriel, he began his 1958 trip as a UNESCO delegate, going first to Paris, then to Geneva as an official observer at East-West discussions of suspension of nuclear testing. His next stop was West Berlin, where he met with Mayor Willy Brandt. Then, wearing two hats, a Russian fur and his chairman-

During Humphrey's 1958 trip to Europe, he and Willy Brandt had concluded their private talks and were holding a press conference at the American headquarters on Clay Avenue in Zehlendorf. Suddenly Humphrey grabbed a microphone from one of the reporters who had accompanied him on his trip, held it under the nose of the Mayor, and said, "To my listeners at home in Minnesota! The Mayor of Berlin will now speak to you in English." Brandt spoke. Humphrey said, "And now in German." Brandt fulfilled that request. "And in conclusion, in Scandinavian." Brandt did it in perfect Norwegian. After the Mayor had spoken in English, German, and Norwegian for the listeners in Minnesota, Humphrey thanked him, saying, "You did that handsomely. But now I want you to promise me one thing—never come to Minnesota and campaign for a seat in the Senate—you would be elected in my place."

DR. THOMAS MIROW
PRESS REPRESENTATIVE
FOR WILLY BRANDT

Humphrey and Nikita Khrushchev

ship of a subcommittee on national health that had been established by a Humphrey resolution, he was in Moscow. He appeared on Moscow television, went sightseeing, wrote several articles and even attended church services, joining the pastor at the door to shake hands with the departing congregation.

Humphrey's official business—rounds of meetings with Soviet officials—was interrupted at 2:30 P.M. on the afternoon of December 1, when he was asked to present himself immediately at the Soviet Cultural Society office. "I asked what was up. I had asked for an interview with Khrushchev, but I expected to be turned down," said Humphrey. When he reached the office, he was told that the premier would see him. "When?" "Right now."[12] Taken to a waiting limousine, he was driven to the Kremlin, led through a labyrinth of lobbies, stairs, and corridors, and ushered into Nikita Khrushchev's office. A half dozen ears of corn, the gift of Iowa farmer Roswell Garst, were the only decoration. The premier, seated behind his desk, rose and shook hands; photographers took a few pictures, then left, and, except for an interpreter, the two men were alone.

While today Russian and American leaders seem to be in constant communication, this meeting came in the midst of an era when the Cold War was the everyday reality of United States foreign policy. The McCarthy period, though officially ended, was more than just a memory for McCarthy's sympathizers, many of whom still held public office. Humphrey's very last meeting before seeing Khrushchev had been a Cold War gesture

The famous meeting in Khrushchev's office

of United States solidarity with the citizens of West Berlin against the threat of Soviet aggression. Given this atmosphere, for the premier of the Soviet Union to undertake an unscheduled, wholly extemporaneous discussion with an obscure American senator—a discussion that eventually touched on every outstanding dispute and controversy that lay between his nation and its principal adversary—was extraordinary and sensationally newsworthy.

The two men spoke for eight hours. Humphrey offered to leave on three separate occasions, fearing that he was taking up too much of the premier's time, but Khrushchev gestured to him to sit down and stay. After five hours, a dinner of banquet proportions was brought in, and soon after appeared First Deputy Premier Anastas Mikoyan, who served primarily as an echo chamber for Khrushchev during the final hours of the meeting. While Humphrey asked questions, Khrushchev did most of the talking. With the premier's permission, Humphrey took over twenty pages of notes. They covered the Berlin crisis, Soviet weapons, developments in the field of rocketry, Soviet nuclear advances, East-West trade (a Khrushchev favorite), the suspension of nuclear testing, and the relations between Russia and China (a Khrushchev non-favorite, and the first hard evidence of the growing estrangement between the two Communist superpowers).

Humphrey returned to his hotel room at 11 P.M. "Tired?" Muriel asked. "Oh no," said Humphrey. Later she told reporters, "He was just bubbling."[13]

. . . Khrushchev had a bottle of Armenian brandy brought in, and I already had one drink, but I was scared to death to drink much of anything because I thought he might want to get me loaded and I didn't want that to happen. . . .

The very first thing Mikoyan did was to pour a brandy for me. I said, "No. I've had mine."

"No, no," Mikoyan insisted, but I repeated that I didn't care for another and finally Khrushchev interrupted and he poured out three glasses of brandy and told Mikoyan, "You drink all three. My friend's from Minnesota, my glass and yours—you drink all three." By God, he did drink all three.

HUBERT H. HUMPHREY
ST. PAUL PIONEER PRESS
JANUARY 21, 1973

I said I wanted to ask him about China . . . no military questions, I ust wanted to ask you about Chi-ese communes. Khrushchev said, 'We tried those. They won't work."

Then he leaned back and said, 'My friend, do you know what rinciple those communes are based n? They are based on the principle, ach according to his ability, to ach according to his need."

Then with a dramatic pause of a reat actor, Khrushchev said, "You now that won't work." He said it akes incentive to get production.

I said, "Mr. Chairman, that ounds like capitalism to me." He aid, "Call it what you will. It's ue isn't it?" I said, "Well, that's he way we think."

HUBERT H. HUMPHREY
ST. PAUL PIONEER PRESS
JANUARY 21, 1973

At 7 p.m., four hours after we started, I figured now this is really too long. I asked him if there was any chance that I might use your bathroom. He said, indeed and showed me where it was, and I went back there. When I got back to the bathroom, I opened his medicine cabinet and saw medications he had been taking. He had told me during the visit that he had been to the doctor and that he wasn't drinking anymore.

HUBERT H. HUMPHREY
ST. PAUL PIONEER PRESS
JANUARY 21, 1973

Muriel and Hubert come home from Russia.

chapter 11

SETBACK

"I'm gonna vote for Hubert Humphrey,
I'm gonna vote for Hubert Humphrey,
I'm gonna vote for Hubert Humphrey.
He's the man for you and me.

He makes everybody happy,
He makes everybody happy,
He makes everybody happy.
He's the man for you and me."

1960 campaign song by Jimmy Wolford
(Sung to the tune of "That Old Time Religion")

Humphrey greets his son Douglas after returning from Russia in 1958.

Muriel's first reaction to the Khrushchev interview had been "Here we go again,"[1] and she was right. When the Humphreys returned to the United States, one of the first things that they saw was a color picture of Hubert in his new Russian fur hat on the cover of *Life* Magazine. Humphrey knew that such public notice of his meeting with Khrushchev could provide the stroke of good luck that his career needed. The day he got back to Washington, he held a press conference attended by 200 reporters. Squeezing every last ounce of publicity out of the meeting, Humphrey told the press corps that he was taking a personal message from Khrushchev to President Eisenhower, that it contained "two secrets," and that "you couldn't pry them out of me with a crowbar."[2] Several days later he confirmed reports that the secrets had been that Russia had an 8,700-mile intercontinental ballistic missile and a five-megaton hydrogen bomb. The CIA later declared haughtily that it already had that information.

The publicity that Humphrey received didn't ignore the impact that the Khrushchev interview could have on his presidential hopes. James Reston of the *New York Times* observed that Humphrey "is beginning to get the political breaks."[3] Arthur Krock, also a *New York Times* columnist, said, "Humphrey got more publicity mileage out of eight hours with Khrushchev than Lincoln did in weeks of debate with Douglas."[4] Another columnist, Doris Fleeson, said, "It's a very Merry Christmas for Hubert Humphrey,"[5] and a reporter for *U.S. News and World Report* suggested that Humphrey had "managed to start a Presidential boom from the steps of the Kremlin itself."[6] There was no finer tribute given than the one by the vice-president of the United States: "[Humphrey] has a good mind, he's fast on his feet, a fine organizer, and a terrific worker. He probably has gained more in the respect of his colleagues than any other Senator I've known," said Richard Nixon.[7] The *Minneapolis Star,* attempting to add to the excitement by getting a story from Khrushchev himself, put in a telephone call to the Kremlin, but

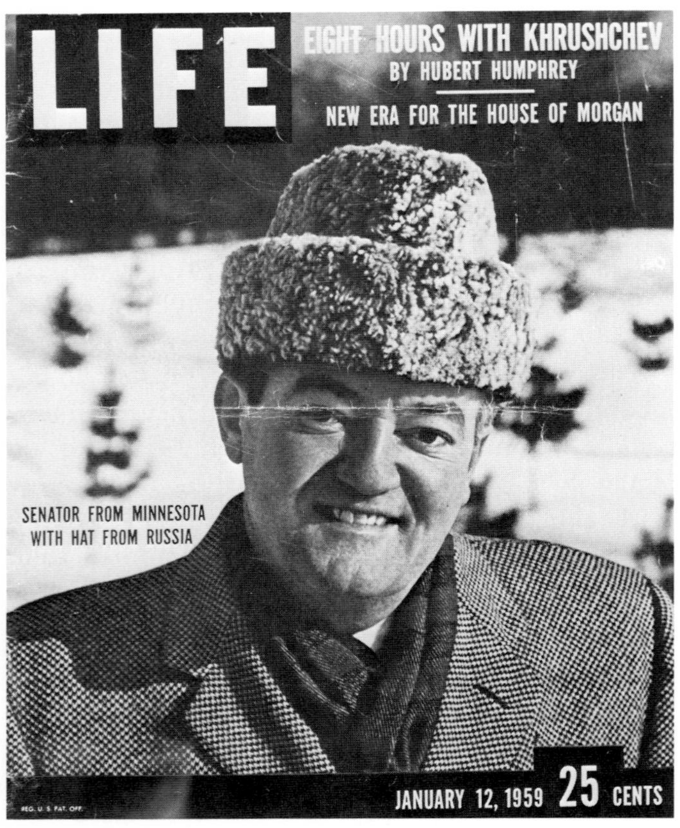

Of course, I knew Humphrey quite well over the years. . . . One of the things people didn't realize about him was his sense of historical perspective. I remember a conversation we once had, and he asked me to name the two people who I thought had been the most significant political figures in the world since the Second World War. Well, I didn't come up with anything very startling but when I asked him the same question, he made a couple of choices I thought were very unusual and very interesting. He named Nikita Khrushchev and Pope John XXIII. Both of them started life as poor peasants, both were seminary trained, and both rose above their origins and changed the entire sense of direction of the institutions they led. Khrushchev had the power to go to war with the United States. In fact, he was strongly urged to do that. But he saw the world through the eyes of an international statesman and not a rough Communist partisan. Pope John did very much the same thing when he opened the Church up at the very moment when the challenge to modernity was the greatest. Humphrey really understood these things and could explain them in a way that no other man of his era could.

AL HOFSTEDE
MAYOR OF MINNEAPOLIS

He told a reporter once how he used to go over his speeches with Muriel. "If you have about an hour and a half I'm going to sit here and do something that helps me pull my speeches together more tightly. Muriel usually helps me with this but she isn't here. When you are particularly interested your eyes will light up. When you aren't they will cloud. I'll leave those parts out. That's how I will know how to cut my speech to size."

JOHN KNOBLE
NEW HAVEN REGISTER

the Moscow operator informed the reporter, "Your party does not talk with anyone in the States."[8]

Humphrey himself wasted no time capitalizing on his coup, but he was careful not to make the same mistakes as in the past. This time he would build a solid campaign structure and not depend upon a single individual to decide his fate as he had in 1956. To begin the campaign, a small luncheon was arranged in a private dining room at New York's "21" Club. About sixty of the nation's largest contributors to liberal causes heard Humphrey give a brief talk on his trip. It was no long-winded tirade; Humphrey had come a long way from the days when he had turned off a Minneapolis business crowd with a storm of bombast. The people attending the luncheon were not so naive as to believe they had been invited for their good fellowship, but no appeal for funds was made. That would come later and would be handled quietly.

One of the hosts for the "21" luncheon was Lansdell Christie, a mining company executive who had been the largest single contributor to the 1956 campaign of Adlai Stevenson. He was gradually drawn into the Humphrey camp while Stevenson, who refused to shut the door completely to a third try, continued to vacillate, to the growing irritation of his old supporters. Humphrey's claim as the rightful heir to the support of the party liberals was strengthened by the regard with which he was held by Eleanor Roosevelt, who felt that, of Humphrey, Stevenson, and Kennedy, Humphrey alone had "the spark of greatness."[9]

Early in 1959, Humphrey began to hire additional staffers to help in his presidential effort.

In 1959 Senator Humphrey was lining up support for his 1960 presidency bid. I was then active in the Democratic Party in Nassau County, a pivotal suburban county in New York State. At the request of a mutual friend, I had arranged a breakfast meeting so the senator could meet the then Nassau County Democratic leader.

The meeting was held in the senator's room at what is now the Park Sheraton Hotel in New York City. The assemblage consisted of Senator Humphrey, the county leader, a lawyer from Washington who was active with the senator, the mutual friend, and me. I was seated immediately to the senator's left. As the conversation continued, breakfast was served and a soft-boiled egg was placed in front of me. Being on my best behavior in such august company, I was most careful in approaching my food. But to my horror, as I dipped my spoon into my egg (of which I had carefully broken the shell), the whole inside of the egg popped up and out into my lap. After a momentary hesitation enshrouded in mortification, I took a large spoon, scooped the morass off my lap, and put it on the

There was a full-time foreign policy researcher, a full-time farm researcher, a legislative assistant, and a chief of staff. Another early recruit was Jim Rowe, who had once served as FDR's executive assistant and had become an intimate of Lyndon Johnson. He was to be Humphrey's principal advisor on strategy, and it appeared increasingly likely that he would be giving advice on a strategy of blocking the candidacy of John Kennedy.

So far Kennedy and Humphrey were the only contestants to have taken the field. Already out of the running were G. Mennen "Soapy" Williams of Michigan, who had been narrowly re-elected governor of his state, and Averell Harriman of New York, who hadn't. The players who were still

Eleanor Roosevelt with Humphrey and Adlai Stevenson

plate. However, a large wet yellow and white stain remained. At this moment, Senator Humphrey jumped up and said, "Come with me." I said, "Oh no, it will dry," and furtively dabbed the mess with my napkin. But the senator was not to be denied. He grabbed my arm, literally pulled me up, and dragged me to the bathroom where we stood alone. He took a washcloth, turned on the faucet, and immersed the cloth. Then to my consternation, he immediately fell to scrubbing the full front of my pants until every visible fragment of the egg and stain was either gone or soaked through. After he was done, he patted me on the back, saying something to the effect that "that ought to do it." We marched back into the breakfast area and completed breakfast without batting an eye or saying a word.

After the meeting, I kept hoping that he would be elected president, not simply because I was such an admirer of his but because it would have been a great story to tell about an encounter with someone who was the President of the United States.

BERTRAM HARTNETT

waiting on the sidelines—Stuart Symington, Adlai Stevenson, and Lyndon Johnson—were pleased to see Humphrey in the race, hoping that he would keep Kennedy from running away with the nomination before the game had even started.

On July 11, 1959, at the dedication of the St. Lawrence Seaway in Duluth, Humphrey met with a group of his closest political advisors in an aging hotel to discuss his prospects for the Democratic presidential nomination. At the meeting were Muriel, Gene McCarthy (who was now a senator, having defeated Ed Thye in 1958), Governor Orville Freeman, congressmen John Blatnik and Joe Karth, DFL leaders Gerald Heaney, Ray Hemenway, and William Kubicek, and Herb Waters, a Humphrey aide. Before them was a memo from Jim Rowe setting forth his plan for the campaign. "In politics, your strategy is never based on choice—it is forced on you,"[10] said Rowe. For Humphrey this principle meant that he would have to enter the primaries. With no demonstrated voter appeal outside his own state and no powerful allies among the bosses who could broker the nomination for him in back room dealings, he had to take his case to the people. Only by demonstrating his ability to win contested primaries could he overcome the "too lib–too glib" image that had been hung on him. With a base of several hundred delegates and proven vote-getting power, he would have the tools to convince the hard-eyed bosses of the controlled delegations to back him. But because his resources were bound to be meager, Humphrey would have to pick his spots carefully. He would not be able to enter all sixteen primaries.

A full year had passed since the Khrushchev interview before Humphrey formally announced his candidacy on December 30, 1959, in the Senate Chamber. In the chaos surrounding the exact timing of the announcement, Humphrey had forgotten to advise Muriel of his final plans. He got a sharp reminder when a telegram from her arrived in Washington—collect: "Congratulations on your decision. Let me know if I can be of some help."[11] Help was something that Humphrey would need plenty of; he was well aware that his candidacy was an uphill fight. Even the Minneapolis papers, which had long been supporters of nearly every Humphrey project, recognized that he was not the front runner for the presidency. The *Minneapolis Tribune* questioned whether Humphrey's plans "may be longer-ranged than 1960, and he may also be shooting for the vice presidency."[12]

John Kennedy announces that he is a presidential candidate.

Three days after Humphrey's announcement, John Kennedy formally announced his own candidacy in the Senate caucus room. Like Humphrey, Kennedy was forced by circumstances to take the primary route to a presidential nomination. Kennedy's problem was to persuade the delegates at the Democratic convention that a Catholic could be elected president. In 1928, Al Smith, a Catholic, had been nominated by the Democrats and had lost the election to Herbert Hoover. No amount of charm or persuasion—only hard evidence of voter appeal gleaned from winning primary elections—could convince the Democratic Party to take another chance on a Catholic candidate.

For both Kennedy and Humphrey, the easy primary wins wouldn't count. New Hampshire, lying in Massachusett's backyard, was a gimme for Kennedy, and therefore uncontested. The same results obtained for Humphrey in the District of Columbia, with its large black population, and in South Dakota, Humphrey's home state. The first real test between the two men would come in the Wisconsin primary on April 5.

Wisconsin was a state with a political history similar to Minnesota's. A third party, the Wisconsin Progressives, led by Robert LaFollette, had been a major instrument for political reform in the state during the 1930s, just as the Farmer-Labor Party had been in Minnesota. But by the mid forties, most of the Progressives' strength had melted away, and in 1946, the party formally merged with the Republican Party from which it had originally sprung. By this time, however, the Republican Party of Robert LaFollette had become the party of Joe McCarthy, and most of the Progressive rank and file eventually found a political home with the Wisconsin Democrats, who, like their neighbors in Minnesota, were primarily urban and Catholic, their party serving mainly as a vehicle for federal patronage. With the influx of new blood came a resurgence of the Democratic Party in Wisconsin. In 1957, Democrat William Proxmire was elected to succeed Joe McCarthy in the Senate, and in the following year, Gaylord Nelson became governor of Wisconsin. Each was only the second member of the Wisconsin Democratic Party to hold a Senate seat or the governorship in the twentieth century.

There were several reasons why Humphrey had chosen Wisconsin for his first real primary effort.

Wisconsin's similarities to Minnesota both in its political history and in the mix of agriculture and industry in its economy would seem to make its voters receptive to Humphrey's appeal. Then, too, Humphrey had developed close contacts in Wisconsin during the years that Joe McCarthy had represented the state in the United States Senate. He had been known as Wisconsin's third senator, handling a number of routine constituent requests and legislative chores while McCarthy was busy chasing the Commies. Finally, because the state bordered on Minnesota, a campaign theoretically could be run more cheaply there, with travel and phone calls at minimum cost and weekend volunteers from Minnesota providing much of the man-

Someone once told me that Wisconsin is the Gateway of Paradise, and I told him that that's right—Minnesota is just across the border.
HUBERT H. HUMPHREY

Humphrey addresses a gathering in Wisconsin.

I worked in 1959 and 1960 as Humphrey's Wisconsin campaign coordinator, and I saw Hubert at very close range in those days. One thing I'll never forget. We had a meeting called for a Sunday morning at the Jewish Community Center in Milwaukee—just two days before the election. The national press was streaming into Wisconsin to catch the last few days of the campaign. The crowd was very thin. It was early in the morning on a Sunday. And there was a lot of ice and snow on the streets.

But Humphrey rose to the occasion in ways that completely turned that meeting around. "They say the Humphrey campaign is disorganized—but I want you to know that the most organized thing that ever happened almost destroyed civilization." Those cutting remarks were not lost on a meeting in the Jewish Community Center.

FRANKLIN WALLICK
UAW WASHINGTON REPORT
JANUARY 16, 1978

power. There was also a negative reason for Humphrey's decision: to permit Kennedy to take an election from him in his own backyard would be fatal.

As the two men began slogging through the snows of Wisconsin early in 1960, significant differences in their campaigns soon became apparent. Humphrey's home-team advantage never materialized, and he was beset by organizational problems. The liberal faction of his staff, headed by Joseph Rauh, and the conservative faction, led by Jim Rowe, were not well coordinated, and the campaign became disorganized and disjointed, with the candidate constantly behind schedule. Inadequate financing, always a problem, permitted Humphrey to fully staff offices in only two of the state's ten districts, while Kennedy, who had no money problems, maintained offices in eight. Lack of funds continually hampered the efforts of Humphrey workers, among them Forrest Harris, a University of Minnesota professor who was given the responsibility of organizing seven key Wisconsin counties with a total campaign chest of $100.

One of the major differences between the Humphrey and Kennedy campaigns was the amount of time that the two candidates spent campaigning. Humphrey spread himself very thin, in Washington one day "chewing out a bureaucrat because a Minnesota company has not been allowed to bid on a contract,"[13] back in Minnesota the next day. His time and energy were divided among three different jobs—campaigning as a candidate for president, raising money so he could continue to be a candidate for president, and attending to his senatorial responsibilities. Since Humphrey was up for re-election in 1960, he simply couldn't afford to abandon his fallback position as a senator from Minnesota. Kennedy, who had no Senate election to worry about until 1964, was able to give his full attention to the matter at hand, aided by a collection of relatives so glamorous as to seem almost regal to unsophisticated midwesterners. Flying in a private jet from one stop to another, Kennedy was able to look fresh, to be prompt, and to invest his time in meeting voters, not in traveling to and fro. Far too much of Humphrey's time was spent in his campaign bus, sliding into snowbanks between one town and the next.

The Wisconsin campaign was further complicated by confusion over the issues that divided the two candidates. To most observers, the overt issues, farm policy and the necessity of economic stimulation, were subordinated to the question of Kennedy's Catholicism. Humphrey doggedly stuck with his New Deal programs and stayed away from religion. "If you have a campaign based on bigotry, innuendo, and smear, you can have your politics—I don't want any part of it,"[14] he said. But Humphrey's refusal to use the religious issue did not prevent its use by others. A vicious anti-Catholic tract was anonymously mailed to Catholic households in the state, presumably in an attempt to confirm the allegiance of Catholic voters to John Kennedy. Humphrey suspected that the Kennedys themselves might have been behind the maneuver, but he felt that it could not be attributed to them "with the same absolute assurance"[15] as could the spreading of the story that Jimmy Hoffa,

Working as a senator and as a candidate for president kept Humphrey constantly busy.

nobody's shining model of clean living, was behind the Humphrey candidacy as a way of getting even with the Kennedys for their vigorous attacks on labor racketeering. Unfortunately, these tactics were only the beginning; the dirty tricks that would be used by Humphrey's opponents in West Virginia would make Wisconsin look like a pink lemonade party. Although the Kennedys were not overly scrupulous about their own tactics, they were always quick to complain if Humphrey's criticism drew blood, even when it was fair and accurate. At one point, Kennedy sent a message through Gene McCarthy: "Tell Humphrey to lay off my farm voting record." McCarthy refused. "Jack, you've got looks, money, and personality, and all Hubert's got is your voting record,"[16] he said.

Campaigning in Wisconsin

When the Wisconsin primary finally took place on April 5, the results did not solve the riddle of whether a Catholic could be elected president. Kennedy carried the state with 56 percent of the vote to Humphrey's 43.5 percent, but the vote distribution complicated things. Humphrey carried the western part of the state, which was closest to Minnesota and also heavily rural and Protestant. Kennedy did best in Wisconsin's industrial districts, which were also those most heavily Catholic. (About 31 percent of the state's total population was Catholic.) To confuse matters further, the votes cast in the Democratic primary outnumbered

Humphrey and Kennedy on the night of the Wisconsin primary

the votes cast in the Republican primary by two to one, suggesting to Humphrey that a number of Catholic Republicans (more numerous in Wisconsin than in the eastern states) had taken advantage of the state law permitting crossover voting in a presidential primary and had voted for Kennedy.

After the Wisconsin primary was over, someone asked John Kennedy to interpret the outcome—"What does it mean?" "It means," said Kennedy, "that we have to do it all over again."[17]

But Humphrey was elated by the results from Wisconsin. He felt that the Kennedy victory had been achieved only by Republican crossovers, the same bugaboo that had scrambled the results of the 1956 primary in Minnesota. The next primary in West Virginia, he felt, would be another matter. Here primary voting was strictly by party registration. With no Republicans to muddy the waters, it would be a contest between Democrats to be decided by Democrats. Campaigning in West Virginia, Humphrey would stress his impeccable labor credentials and strong identification with the New Deal philosophy and programs of Franklin Roosevelt, who remained the state's greatest political hero for his part in John L. Lewis' organization of the state's dominant labor force, the coal miners. In West Virginia, Humphrey's own humble beginnings would generate understanding and support among a population that was overwhelmingly poor.

I guess that really was why so many people loved him. He made politics fun. He cared deeply about the issues—and he always wanted to win—but he wanted to win in such a way that nobody went away mad.

FRANKLIN WALLICK
UAW WASHINGTON REPORT
JANUARY 16, 1978

Looking forward to the challenge of West Virginia after the preliminaries in Wisconsin, Humphrey said to his staff, "I always told you fellows politics could be fun, didn't I."[18] But Jim Rowe was sceptical. "What the hell are you going to do for money?"[19] Rowe was not only unimpressed with the Wisconsin outcome, but he was also well aware that the Humphrey campaign was entering West Virginia already $17,000 in debt. Rowe's scepticism was shared by many political professionals. In their eyes, Humphrey had already lost the nomination. If he could not carry a state adjoining his own, so very like Minnesota in its economic and political outlook, then what could he carry?

By the time the Humphrey campaign reached West Virginia, Humphrey's money faucet, which

On to West Virginia

had always been slow-running, was reduced to a thin dribble. Labor, a principal source of Humphrey financial support over the years, was urging him to get out of the race. To make sure that Humphrey's other major source of funds was dried up, Governor Abraham Ribicoff of Connecticut, a Kennedy operative, was dispatched to deliver a message to Stevenson liberals: if they continued to contribute to Humphrey, Adlai would not even be *considered* for Secretary of State in a Kennedy administration. John Bailey, the Democratic National Chairman, also delivered a threat of reprisal to Senator William Benton, the wealthy publisher of Encyclopaedia Britannica and a long-time Humphrey backer. There were others eager to get Humphrey out of the game. Governor Pat Brown of California implored Orville Freeman to use his influence to persuade Humphrey to withdraw. The benchwarmers—Symington, Stevenson, and Johnson—were no longer on Humphrey's side since they had nothing further to gain from his candidacy. If Humphrey lost in West Virginia, it would be clear that Kennedy would win the nomination. On the other hand, if Humphrey were to pull out, then a West Virginia victory for Kennedy, against no opposition, would be meaningless and there wouldn't be a chance for a convention deadlock. Faced with such discouraging lack of support, Humphrey stubbornly refused to quit. The pressure had made him more determined than ever to take his chances in West Virginia.

Kennedy was able to use the religious issue to great advantage in West Virginia, a state 95 percent Protestant, with a reputation of anti-Catholicism so fierce that a former Ku Klux Klan member, repentant of his youthful indiscretions, could be elected to the United States Senate. The Kennedy forces recognized that the religious issue could only be met head on, so they arranged for a paid television broadcast during which Jack Kennedy, gazing directly into the eye of the camera and into the consciences of the people of West Virginia, said, "I refuse to believe that I was denied the right to be President on the day I was baptized."[20] Kennedy answered every question that the broadcast moderator, Franklin D. Roosevelt, Jr., posed for him on the religious issue by pledging unwavering allegiance to the separation of church and state.

Humphrey had no device for dealing with the issue of Kennedy's Catholicism in West Virginia. He was certainly not going to mount an appeal to the bigots. The best course was simply to call for tolerance, and that is what he did. The people of West Virginia, with the eyes of the nation focused on them as they never had been before, had too much pride and decency to add to their reputation for extreme poverty the shame of being known as a pesthole of hate as well. Many a proud mountaineer whose distrust of the "Papists" had been inbred for generations would swallow hard when election day came and pull the lever for John Kennedy.

There were other factors in the West Virginia situation that worked to Kennedy's advantage and against Humphrey. One was the role of Franklin D. Roosevelt, Jr., who performed more chores for the Kennedys than just playing straight man on TV. Carrying a name almost worshipped in West

Humphrey and Kennedy during a television debate in West Virginia. Kennedy's skillful use of the medium's visual impact gave him a decided edge over Humphrey.

Virginia, Roosevelt used it to lend credibility to a campaign of unrestrained libel directed at Humphrey's war record, a potent tactic in a state that had the highest percentage of Medal of Honor winners of any state in the Union. Proof of the inaccuracy of the charges was presented to the Kennedys, but that didn't shut Roosevelt off during the campaign. He apologized for his actions—later.

Another peculiarity of West Virginia politics that played a role in the outcome of the election was the quaint and expensive practice of "slating" the candidates, a euphemism for paying off local officials for the privilege of having the candidate's name appear on a recommended slate in each county. There was a germ of good sense behind the practice, because the laws of West Virginia had created a primary ballot so long and complicated that voters did almost require a road map to make an intelligent selection. Of course, the confusing ballot may have also existed, at least in part, for the purpose of promoting the slating scam in the first place. Whatever the reason, election time in West Virginia found the candidates darting from office to office, county to county, carrying their West Virginia campaign kits: black briefcase, checkbook, long manila envelopes, and plenty of cash. In such a competition, there were few contestants who could match the Kennedys. Though Humphrey, not to his credit, made a half-hearted stab at it, he was out of his league from the start. After having the practice explained to him, Humphrey was told that his staff members had let "the appropriate people" know that they "were prepared to put up twenty-five thousand dollars." "What was the response?" asked Humphrey. "I was laughed out of the office," said one of his aides.[21]

Towards the end of the West Virginia campaign, Humphrey, now more in debt than ever, dug deep into his own pockets and made one last throw of the dice with a poorly produced television call-in show that seemed to generate nothing but cranks and droners. It was a disaster. Humphrey felt in his gut that he was facing another defeat, and he was right.

When the election was held on May 10, Kennedy carried over 60 percent of the vote and all but seven of West Virginia's fifty-five counties. Humphrey even lost in the black districts, usually an area of his greatest voting strength. In part, this surprising outcome may have been the result of some rather well-timed Kennedy charitable contributions to black Protestant churches throughout the state. The contributions were made in an effort to help stamp out prejudice in the voting booth, or so it was explained years later to Humphrey, with a wink, by Cardinal Cushing, a Kennedy confidant who had participated in the scheme. Humphrey discovered that day he could still be shocked by what went on in politics.

The final scenes of Humphrey's 1960 presidential effort were played out in his rooms in the Ruffner Hotel in Charleston, West Virginia. As the outcome of the primary became clear, Humphrey called his supporters and thanked them for their help, sent a telegram to Jack Kennedy conceding the election, and looked out over a sea of

Watching the early returns in West Virginia

coffee cups and cigarette butts, all that was left of his presidential campaign. There was bitterness and there were tears that evening. When Bobby Kennedy came over to pay his respects, Muriel, who had swallowed every political insult thrown at her husband since he began his career, stiffened and turned away angrily at his touch. Humphrey manfully decided to go back with Bobby to the Kennedy headquarters. On their way through the rainy streets of Charleston, Humphrey made one last stop at his own headquarters on Capitol Street. It was past one in the morning, but a death watch of Humphrey stalwarts still held vigil there, among them Jimmy Wolford, a country singer who had traveled with Humphrey during the campaign and who had composed a theme song that had been sung at every whistle stop. When Humphrey arrived, Wolford tried a last chorus of "Vote for Hubert Humphrey. He's your man and mine," but the familiar words did not provide any cheer. Even Bobby Kennedy had tears in his eyes as he watched Humphrey's efforts to relieve the gloom. His dreams dashed, aching for a few words of comfort himself, but always giving more than he was getting, Humphrey went over to Jimmy Wolford and put his arm around him, told him it would be all right. Then, drawing strength from his own words, he went to the Kennedy headquarters to offer his congratulations to the proud victors.

Jimmy Wolford

chapter 12

"Oh, he is the most professional of professionals. This political life is meat and drink for Hubert."
Everett Dirksen

Humphrey's West Virginia experience ended with one last twist of the knife. The morning after the election, he woke to find that his campaign bus, left outside the hotel overnight, had been tagged for illegal parking.

That same afternoon Humphrey was back on the floor of the Senate. Sensing that it would be "painless as long as [Hubert] kept moving,"[1] Lyndon Johnson had arranged a therapeutic scrap with the Republicans involving an obscure measure to provide federal payments to state and local governments in lieu of taxes. With the West Virginia primary over but not forgotten, Humphrey spent the next few days locked in sour combat with Karl Mundt, his old debate judge, now a Republican senator from South Dakota.

It was not long, however, before presidential politics was back on Humphrey's mind. The Democratic National Convention was scheduled for July, and the Minnesota delegation would be playing a central role in its deliberations. When the convention opened on July 11 in Los Angeles, the fate of Minnesota's thirty-one delegate votes would be one of the few unknowns left to the Kennedy ballot-counters, and Humphrey meant to keep it that way as long as possible. The suspense would generate national media exposure, which would help both his and Orville Freeman's re-election campaigns, and it would also inconvenience Kennedy: West Virginia had left Humphrey in no mood to shorten Kennedy's march to the nomination. For Freeman, it was a different story. Unlike Humphrey, he was operating from an increasingly shaky political base—after three terms as governor of Minnesota, his re-election was by no means a certainty. Jack Kennedy had been dangling the vice-presidency in front of him, but there was no hope of achieving that plum if Freeman couldn't deliver his own delegation. Not surprisingly, he pleaded with Humphrey to come out for Kennedy.

The friendship between the two Minnesotans had gone back to their college days, when often the only hot meal Freeman ate all week was Sunday waffles at the Humphreys. Together they had been through many political trials, each trying to ease the other over the rough spots, but now the friendship was beginning to strain. "I did everything you wanted," said Freeman. "Now it's my turn."[2] Despite Freeman's urgings, Humphrey couldn't

Once when I was working for Governor Freeman, I contracted ambulatory pneumonia and stayed home for some time trying to recover. At the time I was working on a highway problem of some kind. I recall that my wife received a call for me. She answered the phone and asked who it was, and the caller said "Orv." She said, "Who?" and the caller once again said "Orv." My wife, still not realizing who it was, asked again, "Who?" The caller finally said, "Oh hell, this is the Governor." Of course I was very flattered that he would call me when I was lying home sick and was deeply touched by his thoughtfulness. That was the first time he called. He called the second time later that day and asked me if I was feeling any better, and I began to get a little curious about the depth of his concern. Finally, he called me a third time, and after once more inquiring about my health, he finally got to the point. "How are you coming on that highway material?" I said, "Governor, I've got it right here on my bed," and I did. And if I hadn't been actually dying, I know that's exactly what he would have expected of me.

GEORGE FARR

Orville Freeman and John Kennedy

bring himself to support Kennedy's nomination. He realized that by crossing the Kennedys, he was risking serious consequences both to himself and to Freeman. But Humphrey believed that he had good reason for his refusal. It wasn't just West Virginia, or Bobby Kennedy jabbing his finger into Humphrey's chest at the convention and threatening, "Hubert, we want your announcement and the pledge of the Minnesota delegation today—or else."[3] He felt that he owed both his conscience and his party the best choice he could make for president, and that choice was Adlai Stevenson, the man he had supported twice previously.

I was made an honorary Minnesota delegate [at the Democratic Convention] with a floor pass and lots of parties to sing at. I met Lyndon Johnson, Adlai Stevenson, Mrs. Eleanor Roosevelt, Bobby Kennedy, Eugene McCarthy. But my biggest thrill was meeting my boyhood hero, Gene Autry.

JIMMY WOLFORD
THE WEST VIRGINIA HILLBILLY
FEBRUARY 4, 1978

Working on Freeman's behalf, Humphrey helped strike a bargain with the Kennedys that gave Freeman the national prestige of making Kennedy's nominating speech in exchange for Humphrey's promise not to nominate Stevenson himself. When that deal was cut, Humphrey persuaded the Stevenson forces to have Gene McCarthy put Stevenson's name in nomination. McCarthy's speech, a moving tribute to Stevenson, turned out to be the high point of the convention. As was expected, John Kennedy was the convention's final choice, with Lyndon Johnson as his running mate, but on the first ballot the Minnesota delegates cast their votes for Hubert Humphrey. "You can never count that old Hubert out," said John Stennis of Mississippi. "Here he is, a defeated Presidential candidate without a bit of power and the first thing you know, one of his boys nominates the winning candidate, another of his boys gives the best speech of the convention, and his delegation still votes for Hubert!"[4]

Humphrey's re-election campaign for the Senate that fall was run against his old classmate and debating partner at the University of Minnesota, former Minneapolis mayor Ken Peterson. The campaign featured the reappearance of that old favorite, the war record issue, but this time Humphrey had had enough. "I'm not about to be called a draft dodger," he said. "I'm ready to meet head on those who accuse me." At a bean feed, Humphrey invited "those who want to take a potshot at me to come to the Speakers' platform. I've two attorneys in the audience and if the charges are false, I'm ready to take appropriate action."[5] That was the end of the battle of World War II, at least for that election.

Humphrey got a brief scare a week before the election when the polls showed Peterson within striking distance, but he wound up winning with 884,168 votes—57.8 percent of the total. Humphrey's 235,582-vote margin over his Republican opponent helped Kennedy to squeak through Minnesota by 22,000 and to carry the state's ten electoral votes in the closest presidential election in history. Orville Freeman did not share in the Democratic victory in Minnesota, but his loss of the governorship would soon be compensated by his appointment as Secretary of Agriculture in the new Kennedy administration.

On the night of the 1960 election, the Humphreys' first grandchild was born to their daughter, Nancy, and her husband, Bruce Solomonson. The first hint that something might be wrong came when the obstetrician asked Muriel, "What do you know about mongolism?" "It isn't easy no matter

I remember one campaign where someone got the bright idea that they were going to charge Humphrey with being one of the founders of the ADA—the Americans for Democratic Action, which is considered in some quarters to be quite a liberal group. At that time, the argument that it was wrong to be associated with it may have been considered somewhat persuasive. Well, the charge came out just prior to Turkey Day down at Worthington, and Humphrey was very big at Turkey Day. He got on the platform, and you know, he never tried to hide the charges against him. He just took that newspaper up on stage with him, and he waved it around, and he said "Now look what they're charging me with, they say here that I am a member of and a founder of the ADA. And I just want you good people to know that I am a member of the ADA, and I am a founder of the ADA. And I am proud of my membership in the American Dairy Association." Well, that was the last anyone heard of that charge.

ROBERT FORSYTHE

Freeman became Secretary of Agriculture during the Kennedy administration.

how you're told," said Muriel later. "Between the unparalleled joy of the night before—and now this—it was probably the biggest drop that one could experience in life."[6]

All the medical advice was that the child should be institutionalized immediately. "You don't take these babies home,"[7] the nurses said. But the Solomonsons and the Humphreys fought the pressure to give up the child. "I said to myself this child has four grandparents, two parents, a room that is waiting for her at home. . . . What foster parents, what institution can do more for her?"[8]

The family's determination to keep and cherish the baby, named Vicky (actually Victoria, for the election victory that marked her birthdate), became more than a commitment to a single child. Muriel's personal concern eventually turned into a crusade for the retarded. Appointed to the President's Committee on Retardation during the Johnson administration, she worked to establish better programs for the retarded and to bring the problems of retarded people and their families out into the open. "I hope by talking about Vicky, I can help other families with retarded children who might feel embarrassed or ashamed,"[9] she said.

Vicky (left) **and Amy Solomonson with their grandfather**

Senator Humphrey takes time out for lunch.

The birth of his granddaughter and the recognition of her problem brought significant changes in Hubert Humphrey's life. When Humphrey returned to the Senate after the 1960 election, he found that important changes were taking place there as well. Lyndon Johnson had gone to the vice-president's office, and his position as Majority Leader would be filled by Mike Mansfield, formerly Majority Whip. Now Humphrey had to consider the possibility of assuming the duties of Majority Whip himself. It would be a heavy workload, added to his already burdensome responsibilities as chairman of five different subcommittees: Disarmament, General Farm Legislation, International Medical Research, Hoover Committee Reorganization, Small Business Wholesaling, and Retailing Distribution. With the Democrats holding the presidency, the Whip would be responsible not just for rounding up support for the passage of the administration's programs but also for scheduling votes, calling up bills, and keeping track of Senate business. Humphrey realized that part of the job involved working in the political trenches for his

We went to a rather no-account nearby restaurant that night where Humphrey had never been; but the headwaiter, overcome by a rare encounter with celebrity, boomed out in a voice no diner (for two blocks around) could miss: "Your usual table, senator?" Humphrey loved it, and did everything he could to help. "Oh my, yes," he said, not knowing which way we were going to be led. When he had pondered the menu and placed his order, he remembered to add after whatever it was: "You know, my usual . . ."

MEG GREENFIELD
COLUMNIST IN THE
WASHINGTON POST

ex-rival, John Kennedy, but he decided that the advantages outweighed the disadvantages. "I knew it would mean sacrifice, but it also gave me an opportunity of seeing the President at least once a week, and I don't mean just socially."[10] When Humphrey accepted the position of Majority Whip, his days as a "free-lancer and political guerilla warfare artist"[11] came to an end, but his career as a legislator was about to show its greatest results.

Within two years, Humphrey was being described as "the President's most valuable ally on Capitol Hill."[12] He was not only an ally but also an idea factory for the Kennedy administration; one of his most memorable ideas led to the creation of the Peace Corps. Inspired by the thinking of a Minneapolis newspaper reporter, Humphrey had proposed the establishment of such an agency during the Wisconsin and West Virginia primaries. The concept, which Humphrey traced back to the American philosopher William James, called for a group of young people who would be sent abroad to fight poverty, ignorance, and disease armed, not with weapons, but with idealism. On June 15, 1960, Humphrey introduced Senate Bill 3675, calling for the establishment of the Peace Corps. With Kennedy pushing it, the bill passed and the agency came into being in 1961 under the direction of the president's brother-in-law, Sargent Shriver. The Youth Employment Bill, which Humphrey had introduced during the Eisenhower years, also became law during the Kennedy administration. Two other measures originally conceived by Humphrey, the Wilderness Bill and the Youth Opportu-

John Kennedy and his "most valuable ally on Capitol Hill"

I'm also enclosing a letter from Peter Grothe of Senator Humphrey's office relating to his proposal for a "Peace Corps" and for bringing more cultural groups to the country from under-developed areas. Perhaps this should go in your lesser ideas files.

ADLAI STEVENSON
IN A LETTER TO GEORGE BALL

As a junior high school student in 1962 I was active in an organization called High School Students for Better Education. We were fighting for better funding for the public schools in Washington, D.C., which were being shortchanged because they were overwhelmingly black and all funding had to be approved by Congressional Committees dominated by Southern whites. Humphrey was one of the few senators who really seemed to care about the problem. He took the time to listen to us, and a few weeks later made a speech on the Senate floor about conditions in the D.C. schools. He read from one of the textbooks used in the schools. Remember, this was 1962. "Yes, Lindbergh's flight across the Atlantic was a wonderful event and soon there will be large clipper ships flying passengers across the Atlantic in fifteen hours or less." The day before Humphrey's speech, John Glenn had spun around the earth two and a half times in six hours. The story made the front pages in the Washington Post *the next day, and with Senator Humphrey's help, $135,000 in additional funds was appropriated for the replacement of obsolete textbooks in D.C. schools. Need I add—the world needs more Hubert Humphreys.*

ARIEL DOUGHERTY

nities Bill, were passed as well. Humphrey even managed to get Leif Erickson Day approved, not his greatest triumph but an idea that had been kicking around for twelve years.

Humphrey's legislative efforts included measures in behalf of the business community as well as young people and the unemployed. "I am for a tax credit to industry for capital investments," he said. "After all, following the war we helped European countries to build up their new plants. Why can't we do a little for our industries?"[13] His call for a personal and corporate tax cut came when Kennedy was still undecided on the question. The president postponed the decision for a year, and the tax cut wasn't passed until Johnson became president in 1963.

Since the passage of Senate Resolution 93 in 1955, establishing the Senate Disarmament subcommittee, Humphrey had been pushing for the

President Kennedy signs a bill while Humphrey and Attorney General Robert Kennedy (right) **look on.**

creation of a permanent disarmament agency in the State Department. With the Berlin crisis hot and military reserves being called up in 1960, it appeared there would be no chance for congressional approval. When Humphrey introduced the bill in the Senate, it went nowhere. Keeping the pressure up, Humphrey emphasized to President Kennedy that a strong response to Communism was compatible with the strong support of disarmament. Finally, during a swim with Kennedy in the White House pool, Humphrey persuaded the president to support the bill. In July 1961, Humphrey addressed a ten-nation conference on arms control and foreign policy in Geneva, stressing the need for international controls under United Nations supervision. In the fall of 1961, the disarmament agency was established. A year later, convinced that technology had progressed to the point where tests in the atmosphere could be detected, Humphrey began seeking a limited test ban. During this period, President Kennedy accepted Humphrey's position but the Russians were not willing to cooperate.

After Kennedy delivered a speech at American University and thirty-two senators sponsored a resolution calling for negotiations in support of a limited test ban, the Russians finally agreed, and the negotiations took place in Moscow. In July 1963, after the test ban act was signed, President Kennedy presented the pen to Humphrey and said, "Hubert, this is your treaty."[14] The Senate ratified it on September 26, 1963, less than two months before President Kennedy's assassination.

Humphrey was attending a luncheon at the

We both concerned ourselves with foreign affairs, and in August 1963, President Kennedy placed us on a committee of six to go to Moscow for the last meeting and signing of the Test Ban Treaty. We concluded our final meeting about 9 p.m. Moscow time, and I went to bed. Hubert acquired a good interpreter, went out onto the Red Square, gathered an audience, and made a speech. But then that was Hubert.

GEORGE D. AIKEN

He had the greatest capacity for forgiveness in the political wars that he fought of any man I've ever met. For this reason alone he commanded the admiration of many who were his colleagues and co-workers in the body of politics for many years.

HAROLD E. HUGHES
FORMER GOVERNOR OF IOWA

Chilean Embassy on November 23 when he first learned that the president had been shot in Dallas. As rumors swept through the room and as confirmation began to follow, the shock and incomprehension turned to tears. Humphrey, as upset as anyone there, dashed out of the Embassy and "was the first person outside of the President's staff to be admitted to the White House."[15] Humphrey's association with President Kennedy had long since erased any residual bitterness from the 1960 primary campaign. An ineffective hater as politicians went, Humphrey never held grudges. He and Kennedy had worked too closely together during the three years of Kennedy's presidency and had been too professional to permit past campaigns to interfere with their responsibilities or their new relationship.

Lyndon Johnson, thrust into the presidency by Kennedy's assassination, immediately reached out

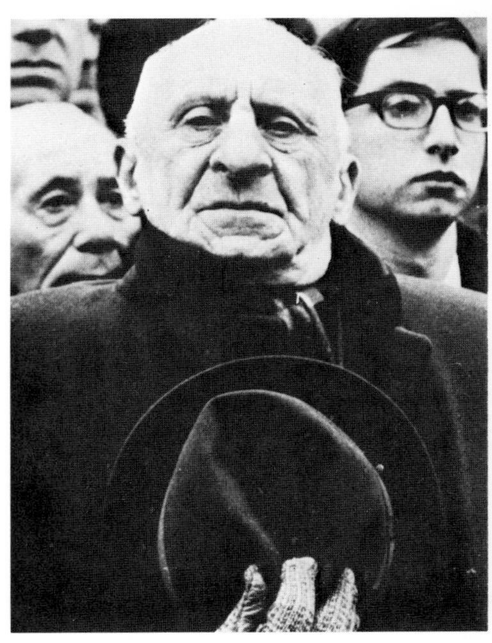

for Humphrey, his old Senate colleague. The very night that Johnson assumed power, he summoned Humphrey to his home and the two men talked until dawn, trying to come to grips both with their own unsettled emotions and the new demands that Johnson would face.

Humphrey strongly counseled Johnson to make clear to the American people that the immediate task of the Johnson presidency would be to continue the work of the Kennedy administration. The shock of the assassination required that the president reassure the American people that the policies of the United States government could not be changed by the work of a gunman.

On November 24, John Kennedy's flag-draped casket lay in state in the Capitol Rotunda while Americans throughout the nation mourned the president's death.

The great unfinished piece of business that lay before Congress and the president at the time of the assassination was the first comprehensive civil rights bill since Reconstruction. In 1954, the Supreme Court decision in *Brown vs. the Board of Education* had ended nearly a century of official neglect of minority rights and had begun a civil rights revolution. As a legislative leader, Johnson had helped pass some of the enactments in 1957 and 1960 that came in the wake of the Supreme Court's decision. These measures represented progress in the area of voting rights but left untouched a system of deprivation and second-class citizenship that gripped black Americans in much of the nation, particularly in the South.

In the early 1960s, an ever-escalating series of events began to dramatize the need for congressional action. Violence resulted when James Meredith tried to enroll at the University of Mississippi's law school in September 1962. More violence came when Bull Connor let loose his billy clubs and police dogs in Birmingham in May 1963. In June of that year, President Kennedy sent the Civil Rights Act to Congress, and in August, 200,000 Americans, black and white, gathered at the foot of the Lincoln Memorial to hear Martin Luther King, Jr., tell them, "I have a dream."

When President Kennedy was assassinated in November, a new president took office, determined to show the nation that the first Southerner to hold the presidency since before the Civil War could be a strong advocate of civil rights. The stage was now set for Hubert Humphrey to secure the passage of the Civil Rights Act.

"I have a dream."

Joseph Rauh, a former president of the Americans for Democratic Action and a friend of Humphrey's since his days as mayor, describes the dramatic events as they occurred:

> The bill the President sent to Congress in June 1963, while not as strong as Humphrey and the civil rights forces were urging, was a monumental step forward, outlawing discrimination in public accommodations, supporting school desegregation, and withholding federal funds from state or local agencies engaged in segregation or discrimination.
>
> The bill passed the House of Representatives by a wide margin on February 10, 1964. But much of the conventional wisdom in the Senate proclaimed that the filibuster would defeat the House-passed bill or gut it as had been done in 1957. That conventional wisdom reckoned without Hubert Humphrey, who, once again by common consent, became the floor leader for the bill in the Senate.
>
> On March 9, Majority Leader Mike Mansfield moved to take up the civil rights bill, and the three-month filibuster was on. But for once the filibusterers were out-organized and out-fought. Humphrey designated different senators to handle specific titles of the bill, and he arranged for a newsletter to be published early each morning reporting on the previous day's activities and giving the schedule for the day. He presided over regular semi-weekly meetings of the leading senators, their staffs, and the representatives of the Leadership Conference on Civil Rights led by NAACP lobbyist Clarence Mitchell. Humphrey also let everyone know that, with President Johnson's concurrence, the effort would go on as long as necessary to get the two-thirds vote needed to end the filibuster. He kept tabs on the Senate to assure a quorum at all times, bluntly reminding his colleagues one Saturday in April when some of them

His boy had cancer—it was Robert, I think—in 1964 at the time of the Civil Rights debate. I had a cancer operation back in 1947, so I recognized what you go through—it is a pretty difficult time in a person's life. So I dropped Humphrey a note. I didn't know his son, but I said, "I don't know whether it does you any good or not, but this thing isn't always necessarily as bad as it sounds. At least that's been my experience in life." I sent the letter off, and about a week or so later, I got a letter back from Hubert, saying that it was very thoughtful and appreciated and that all indications were that his son would be all right. It was a very nice letter, and of course his son was all right. It was almost a fetish with Hubert—letters had to be answered—they had to be answered quickly, responsively, and if possible, no form letters.

ROBERT FORSYTHE

failed to show up that "the only way we can lose the civil rights fight is not to have a quorum when we need it." As the filibuster droned on, the words "Let's try to close debate and see if we have the required two-thirds" began to be heard in the Senate halls. But Humphrey held fast—"No vote on cloture until we have 67 votes absolutely committed."

Early in May 1964, things slowly began going Humphrey's way. Senators noticed that the tenor of their mail was changing from opposition to support. The Harris poll reported that 70 percent of those questioned in their surveys supported the bill and an even larger group disapproved of the filibuster. Leaders of religious groups visiting Republican Senator Everett Dirksen of Illinois reported that his opposition was lessening. Against this background, Humphrey made his move—he began negotiations with Dirksen for changes in the bill that would bring the Illinois senator (and the needed additional Republicans with him) to vote for an end to the filibuster. Humphrey gave way on matters of form and allowed Dirksen to make change after change that had no real impact on the bill; he held fast on virtually all substantive changes. On May 14, he showed his tentative agreement with Dirksen to the representatives of the Leadership Conference. They read the changes with trepidation, but it soon became evident that Humphrey's patience, good humor, and courage had won the day. Cloture was voted, the bill passed the Senate, the House agreed to it, President Johnson signed it on July 2, and Humphrey had won his biggest civil rights victory.[16]

Humphrey was content to let much of the credit for passage of the bill go to Everett Dirksen, as the Illinois Republican's reward for finally agreeing to lend his support. It was not the first time that

Humphrey had shown his willingness to share the glory in order to achieve worthwhile objectives. In 1958, he had persuaded Clinton Anderson of New Mexico to introduce the Medicare Bill. Humphrey had been working on the measure since 1949, but he knew it might stand a better chance if the powerful Chairman of the Senate Finance Committee were to become the author. The bill's chances did improve, and Medicare came into existence in 1965.

The passage of the Civil Rights Act of 1964 was more than a major administration victory and a demonstration of Hubert Humphrey's mastery of the legislative process. It was the accomplishment of Humphrey's long-standing goal of providing a legislative basis for the dismantling of a system that had locked twenty million Americans into a generational cycle of misery. It was the greatest achievement of his legislative career.

chapter 13

WINNING

"Who can forget those storied names from our glorious past—Daniel Tomkins, William A. Wheeler, Garnet A. Hobart, Henry Wilson?"

Hubert H. Humphrey on the vice-presidency
Minneapolis Tribune, *January 23, 1965*

Hubert Humphrey and Robert Kennedy were the frontrunners in the 1964 vice-presidential contest.

Within weeks after Lyndon Johnson assumed the presidency in November 1963, speculation began about the person he would choose for the vice-presidential candidate in the 1964 election. Attention immediately focused on Attorney General Robert Kennedy and on Hubert Humphrey, and Humphrey began to develop a strategy to persuade Johnson to offer the job to him. Early polls showed Kennedy ahead of Humphrey in popular support, but Humphrey's years of campaigning for local Democratic candidates and the countless bean feeds and chicken dinners he had attended earned him an edge over Kennedy in a poll taken of Democratic county chairmen in January 1964.

But the choice of a Democratic vice-presidential candidate would be made neither by the public nor by the professional party politicians but by Lyndon Johnson himself. And President Johnson did not want Robert Kennedy to be his vice-president. When he himself had held that position, he had suffered too many indignities at the hands of the Kennedys to want to be locked into a political marriage with Bobby Kennedy. Johnson's first move to rid himself of Bobby was to try to float the name of Sargent Shriver—a Kennedy-in-law and the director of the Peace Corps—as a potential running mate, hoping to split the pro-Kennedy support. The result was a brief flutter for Shriver in the polls, but by June it had faded. The Kennedy forces would not be satisfied with an ersatz Kennedy; they wanted the real thing. Johnson tried another tactic that spring, hinting broadly that Secretary of Defense Robert McNamara was a leading possibility, but Humphrey supporters helped scuttle that choice by generating criticism from Democratic party officials that the selection of McNamara, a nominal Republican, would be unacceptable.

Lyndon Johnson was not a man to tolerate having a choice thrust on him. Fond as he was of Hubert Humphrey, the president was not about to be cornered into selecting Humphrey as his running mate by having him be the only candidate under consideration. Besides, Humphrey was not an unmixed blessing. He had support among blacks, liberals, farmers, and organized labor, but in the Southern wing of the party, his strong civil rights posture had made his appeal questionable, and the business community had long been suspicious of his liberal attitude on economic issues. Johnson made it clear that in order for Humphrey to establish a good case for his candidacy, he would have to round up support among both his natural allies in liberal and labor circles and his unnatural ones in the South and in the business community. It was not long before senators from Florida, Georgia, and North and South Carolina were calling on Johnson and advising him that he needed "a Northern liberal like Humphrey on the ticket to be elected President in 1964."[1] Business support for Humphrey was originally motivated in no small part by a dislike of Bobby Kennedy, but there had also come to be an awareness that several of the principal themes of Humphrey's legislative career, particularly civil rights and labor laws, had been of benefit to businessmen, contrary to their expectations.

As Johnson manipulated to "keep his options

When the annals of our time are written, I believe the name of HUBERT HUMPHREY will stand for all that was best in American society. Throughout this remarkable American's career, his clear calls to the national conscience have been a comfort to the afflicted and, occasionally, an affliction to the comfortable.

JAMES WRIGHT
REPRESENTATIVE FROM TEXAS

Humphrey underlines Johnson's strong points. McCarthy fills in the gaps. It depends on what kind of campaign the President wants to wage. If he chooses to slug it out on every issue, he is going to pick Hubert Humphrey. If he chooses more of a restrained high road, and not to counterattack every Republican charge, I think he will pick McCarthy.

NICK KOTZ QUOTING
A McCARTHY SUPPORTER
MINNEAPOLIS TRIBUNE,
AUGUST 14, 1964

open," a favorite theme of his presidency, another vice-presidential possibility began to surface. Eugene McCarthy, Minnesota's junior senator, had formidable qualities to enlist in support of his candidacy. A popular description of him, the source often attributed to McCarthy himself, though he denied it, was that he was "twice as smart as Symington, twice as Catholic as Kennedy, and twice as liberal as Humphrey." McCarthy had strong Southern backing, principally from John Connally, the Democratic governor of Johnson's home state of Texas. Another important McCarthy supporter who had the president's ear was Lady Bird Johnson. Mayor Richard Daley of Chicago had also indicated a preference for McCarthy, leading the Minnesota senator to observe that "for an Irishman to say he's partial to you is practically as though you are engaged."[2]

In addition to his varied supporters, McCarthy had other credentials to recommend him. His memorable nominating speech for Adlai Stevenson had been the high point of the 1960 Democratic Convention, and he had written a well-regarded book, *The Liberal Answer to the Conservative Challenge,* in response to Barry Goldwater's *The Conscience of a Conservative.* It was felt that anyone who could speak that well and write that well could be an important asset to the Democratic ticket. Not the least of McCarthy's attractions to Lyndon Johnson was that while there were many outward similarities between the handsome Irish Catholic liberal Gene McCarthy and the handsome Irish Catholic liberal Bobby Kennedy, McCarthy had a fierce dislike for the Kennedys and seemed to enjoy political warfare with them. Finally, McCarthy appeared to have the additional desirable quality of passivity. In a Johnson administration, there would be only one voice and one policy spokesman, and that would be Lyndon Johnson. Multiple-choice policy statements seemed much less likely in the kind of restrained intellectual atmosphere that Gene McCarthy would bring to the vice-presidency than they would from the ebullient and outspoken Hubert Humphrey.

As Johnson continued to dangle the prize before the two Minnesota senators, savoring the suspense he had injected into a convention whose results would otherwise have been a foregone conclusion, the Republicans were meeting in San Francisco to nominate Barry Goldwater, the conservative Arizona senator, as their candidate for president. Johnson's decision on a vice-presidential candidate would of course be affected by whom the Republicans chose and by the impact of their choice on the electorate. Johnson was a great fan of public opinion polls; after all, the figures seemed to show how popular he was, and he was not unsusceptible to flattery. His pockets bulged with Gallups and Quayles and Harrises, and opinion surveys and columns of figures were constantly being produced to illustrate this point or confirm that course of action. Therefore he was impressed by a poll taken by Lewis H. Bean, a Gallup affiliate, in early July showing that in trial heats with a Republican ticket headed by Barry Goldwater, a Johnson-Humphrey ticket would do 2 percent better than a Johnson-Kennedy ticket, swamping Goldwater with 70 percent of the vote. That poll gave Hum-

Every vice-president brings his own thoughts to the job. Mine would be that the role is to stay healthy and quiet.

EUGENE McCARTHY

In 1964 I exerted every effort as governor of Iowa to secure the vice-presidential nomination for Senator Humphrey. The primary effort was in taking ten governors to the White House for a conference with President Johnson in July of that year, prior to the convention, to convince him of the importance of having Hubert Humphrey on the ticket. All of us made a strenuous effort in his behalf, and the president was very open and receptive.

I do believe that it did have an effect on his selection of Hubert, though I am sure that there were many others who had equally important counsel and advice to give to the President.

HAROLD E. HUGHES

Barry Goldwater, Republican candidate for president, on the stump

phrey's chances a major boost. Now with Bobby Kennedy no longer the favorite in the public opinion polls, Johnson felt free to eliminate him from consideration and to exercise complete freedom of action in making his selection.

To get Bobby out of the running, Johnson hit upon the device of announcing that "no one who serves in the cabinet or meets regularly with the cabinet" would be invited to join the ticket. While this formula could be interpreted to include about a hundred people in addition to Attorney General Robert Kennedy, it fooled no one. Kennedy quipped that while of course he regretted that he had been eliminated as a vice-presidential choice, "I was sorry I had to take so many good men over the side with me." After the meeting at which he told Kennedy of his decision, Johnson called in the reporters to fill them in on what had happened. A master raconteur, Johnson delighted in performing

the "Telling of Bobby" for almost everyone who would listen, and he had a wide audience. Finally, Kennedy put out his own version of the event, and it helped blunt Johnson's somewhat—but not much.

Kennedy had been eliminated as a candidate, but an argument could still be made for Gene McCarthy. He might strengthen the ticket even more than Humphrey by bringing in some wavering Catholic support that might otherwise go to the

Gene McCarthy was another possibility as Johnson's running mate in 1964.

Republican slate, which had as its vice-presidential candidate a Catholic ex-congressman from New York, William Miller. But with a possible 70 percent of the vote as a cushion, Johnson could base his choice on something other than purely political considerations. The president could consider friendship and loyalty, and he could select the man who he felt was the best equipped to lead the nation if the presidency became vacant. With Kennedy jettisoned, Humphrey became the undisputed front-runner for the nomination. As a kind of harbinger of what he might expect if he were chosen, however, Johnson made the requirements on the issue of loyalty clear to Humphrey in no uncertain terms.

With the Democratic Convention in Atlantic City now less than a month away, Humphrey called in every IOU earned over years of promoting liberal and labor programs and of campaigning for local Democratic candidates across the country. Every senator, governor, labor leader, every spokesman for civil rights or Jewish causes, every administration official who might possibly have the ear of the president, was called upon to participate in a campaign to woo the one-man electorate of Lyndon Johnson. Johnson himself was in the habit of raising the question of the vice-presidential selection among his Cabinet members and top political advisers. At a meeting shortly before the convention attended by John Bailey, Richard Macguire, Walter Jenkins, Jim Rowe, Jack Valenti, Bill Moyers, Henry O'Donnell, and Larry O'Brien, Johnson referred to a private poll he had taken that purported to show him in trouble if he didn't have a Catholic on the ticket. Going around the room, he asked each person there if he agreed. Only one person did agree, and that was Jack Valenti, often regarded as Johnson's most unwavering "yes" man. "I think that killed McCarthy right there,"[3] said Rowe, later.

But Humphrey's nomination was still far from being a certainty. McCarthy had not been officially eliminated, and the convention itself could bring additional complications. Joseph Rauh explains:

> There was a cloud on the horizon hanging over his hopes that President Johnson would choose him as his running mate. That cloud was the challenge being prepared by the Mississippi Freedom Democratic Party to the regular Mississippi Democratic organization. The last thing Johnson wanted was a divisive black-against-white credentials fight at the convention. Johnson told Humphrey that he had seen on television that I was representing the MFDP and he told Humphrey in no uncertain terms that it was his job to make sure nothing got off the rails and that the matter was resolved without a bruising convention battle. So every time MFDP's preparation for the convention got into the media, Johnson would complain to Humphrey that he wasn't doing enough to damp down the conflict. Humphrey phoned one day in late July or early August to say, "Joe, the President is very concerned about this, and I've got to tell him something." When I asked him how he felt about the MFDP matter himself, he responded, "Well, Joe, you've got to do what your conscience dictates." Even with the vice presidency at stake, civil rights was still to Hubert Humphrey a matter of conscience.

The MFDP took their case to the convention. On the Saturday afternoon before the convention,

My wife and I were the only guests of President and Mrs. Johnson the weekend before the Democratic Convention in 1964, . . . and President Johnson had a list of possible Vice Presidential candidates. . . . He gave us the pros and cons of each one, including Senator Humphrey. Then he looked at me, and he said, "Billy, which one would you choose?" When he asked me that question, Ruth kicked me under the table. We'd known President and Mrs. Johnson for many years so I just looked at her and said, "Ruth, why did you kick me?" And the President looked at her, and he said, "Yes, Ruth, what did you kick Billy for?" And she said, "Mr. President, I think he ought to give you only spiritual counsel and not political counsel." And he said, "Ruth, you're right. I think that's right." So Ruth and Mrs. Johnson went on out into the private living room, and the President wouldn't let me go through the door. He closed the door, and he said, "All right," he said. "Tell me who you really think." And I'm going to tell you what I told him. I told him Hubert Humphrey. I think he'd already made up his mind.

BILLY GRAHAM

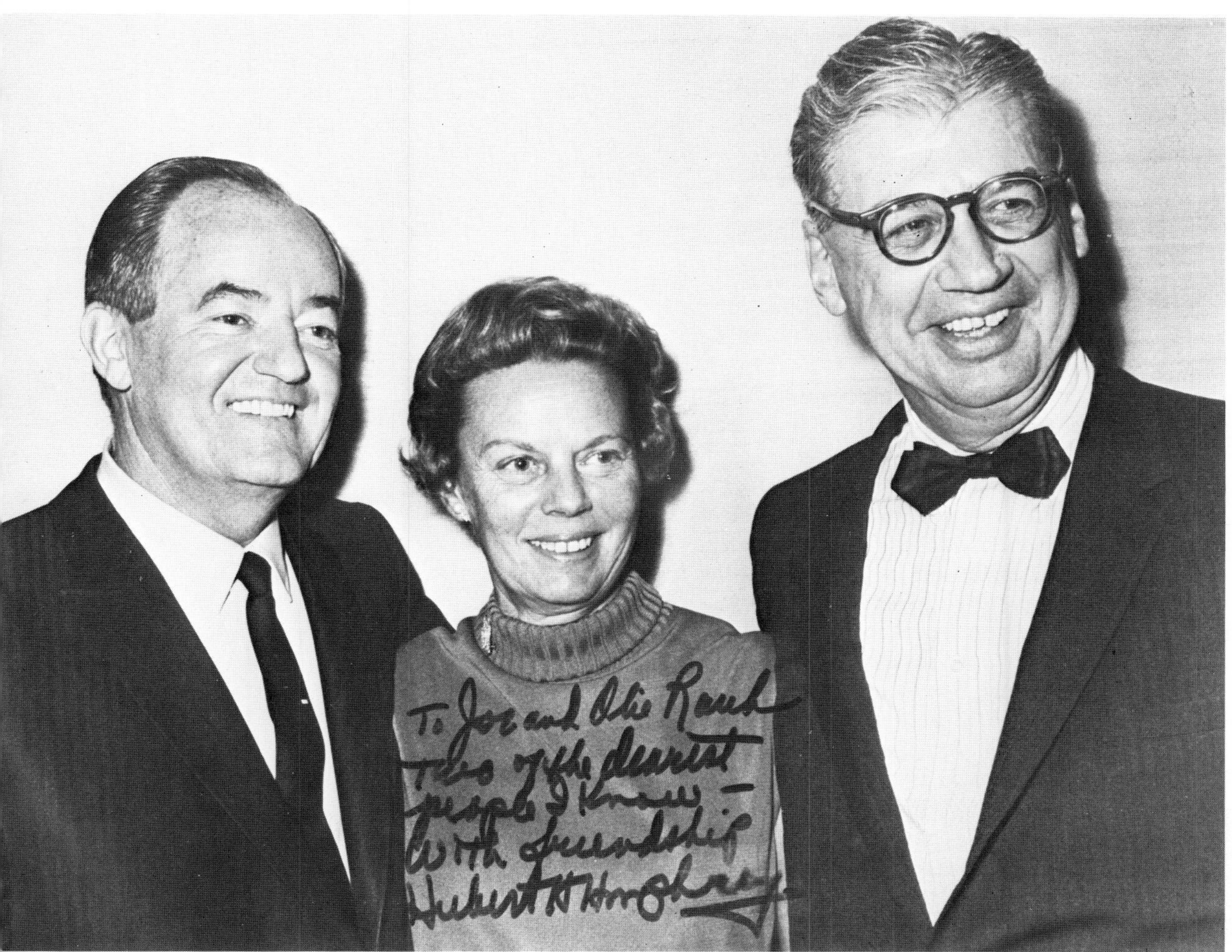

Iumphrey with Joseph Rauh and his wife, Olie

Aaron Henry and Fannie Lou Hamer, backed up by Martin Luther King and Roy Wilkins, made their famous presentation of Mississippi "horrors" to the Credentials Committee. Johnson saw the presentation on television and went right up the wall; he told Humphrey bluntly that he was doing a rotten job. MFDP's total rejection of the meaningless offer made to them on Sunday by the Johnson convention leadership only exacerbated the tension. A meeting in Humphrey's suite on Monday once again failed to resolve the conflict, and Johnson's pressure on Humphrey to get a settlement reached its crescendo. Finally, on Tuesday, under Humphrey's prodding, the Credentials Committee voted to exclude the lily-white Mississippi regulars and give the MFDP two at-large

> seats in the convention. They also promised a Special Civil Rights Committee to integrate the Democratic Party and agreed to seat the MFDP at the next convention if the regulars did not mend their ways. Although the MFDP rejected the Credentials Committee action, it was generally hailed as a civil rights victory. The full fruits of that victory were evident in 1968 when Aaron Henry and Fannie Lou Hamer walked on the floor of the Democratic Convention in Chicago as the leaders of the duly accredited delegation from Mississippi.
>
> Humphrey's performance at the 1964 Convention can only be described as beautifully sensitive. Every night before I went to bed, I would go by his suite in Atlantic City and try to extract some further concession for the MFDP. We would be alone at four o'clock in the morning negotiating. Never once, even with his vice presidency at stake, did he ever say, "Joe, please, for all the years we've worked together, accept this settlement to help me." To me that was the highest ethical standard, but it was also the deepest devotion to civil rights. That devotion never left him.[4]

As if he didn't have enough to do, Humphrey was given another assignment by the president on the Tuesday of convention week. Johnson had been explaining his thoughts on the requirements of the vice-presidency to reporters, and he wanted Humphrey to be aware of those remarks and to have no doubt as to their implications. He made it clear that the *Washington Star,* not the *Washington Post,* contained the most complete exposition of presidential thinking on the subject. Walter Jenkins, who conveyed Johnson's orders to Humphrey, made it seem as if Humphrey had to memorize the newspaper article and recite it back point by point

. . . Some of our close friends frankly begged me to urge Gene to withdraw from consideration for the vice presidency. They did not want him to dance "while that Texan shoots at his feet," as one of them put it.

ABIGAIL McCARTHY

before his candidacy would be considered further.

Meanwhile, another potential candidate had eliminated himself from the running: Gene McCarthy had decided that he had had enough. On Wednesday, August 26, with the convention underway, McCarthy first gave reporters the text of a telegram he had just sent to President Johnson and then phoned the White House to tell the president personally of his decision. The telegram began, not without a trace of bitterness, "I have, as you know, during this Convention and for several weeks, not been indifferent to the choice that you must make . . . ,"[5] and it went on to recommend to the president that he select Humphrey as his running mate. Angered at McCarthy's unwillingness to permit himself to be toyed with any longer, Johnson injected still another name into the running on Thursday afternoon, just hours before the vice-presidential candidate was to be announced to the convention. The president called Humphrey in Atlantic City and summoned him to Washington so that he could make a return trip to the convention accompanied by Johnson and by Senator Thomas Dodd of Connecticut, who was ostensibly a late entry in the vice-presidential derby. This time, though, the president took mercy on Humphrey. After warning him of the consequences that could result if he disclosed the presidential game plan, Johnson told Humphrey that Dodd was a ringer. He would be used to keep up the suspense until Johnson made the announcement, which apparently would come at the convention itself that evening.

When Humphrey finally arrived at the White

Humphrey arrives in Atlantic City for the Democratic National Convention.

House after his flight to Washington, he was so exhausted that Johnson had to rap on the car window to wake him. His appearance had been stalled for an hour while the limousine crawled around the capital's streets, delaying Humphrey's entrance so it wouldn't interfere with television coverage of another Johnson-orchestrated event, Lady Bird's arrival at Atlantic City.

Finally, the moment was at hand. First the president staged a Johnson-Dodd-Humphrey conference, which took the form of a little trot across the White House lawn. The next act was a Johnson-Dodd conference inside the White House while Humphrey sat cooling his heels outside, surrounded by reporters. Try as hard as he could to go along with Johnson's endless gag, Humphrey was coming to the end of his rope. He stood there with a kind of sappy smile on his face, and when it started to rain, he said, "It's raining? I thought we were just getting blessed."[6]

At last Dodd was ushered out of the White

House and Humphrey was led in. "How would you like to be my vice-president?"[7] Johnson asked. Humphrey replied that he would, and after once again outlining the demands of the offer and the need for loyalty with a capital "L," Johnson called the reporters in and introduced them to the next vice-president of the United States.

That night in Atlantic City, Humphrey was nominated by Gene McCarthy. When Humphrey himself took the podium, he gave the speech that set the tone for the campaign:

> Most Democrats and most Republicans in the United States Senate, for example, are for the nuclear test ban treaty—
> but not Senator Goldwater.
>
> Most Democrats and most Republicans in the United States Senate voted for an $11.5 billion tax cut for the American people—
> but not Senator Goldwater.
>
> Most Democrats and most Republicans in the United States Senate, in fact over ⅘ths of the members of his own party, voted for the civil rights act of 1964— but not Senator Goldwater.
>
> Most Democrats and most Republicans in the United States Senate voted for the establishment of the arms control and disarmament agency that seeks to slow the nuclear arms race among nations— but not Senator Goldwater.
>
> Most Democrats and most Republicans in the United States Senate voted last year for an expanded medical education program—
> but not Senator Goldwater.
>
> Most Democrats and most Republicans in the

I knew Hubert for over twenty-five years. I served with him in the Senate, I ran against him in campaigns, I debated with him, I argued with him, but I don't think I have ever enjoyed a friendship as much as the one that existed between the two of us. I know it may sound strange to people who see in Hubert a liberal, and who see in me a conservative, that the two of us could ever get together; but I enjoyed more good laughs, more good advice, more sound counsel from him than I have from most anyone I have been associated with in this business of trying to be a senator.

BARRY GOLDWATER

United States Senate voted for education legislation— but not Senator Goldwater.

Most Democrats and most Republicans in the United States Senate voted for the national defense education act— but not Senator Goldwater.

Most Democrats and most Republicans in the United States Senate voted to help the United Nations in its peace-keeping functions when it was in financial difficulty—
but not Senator Goldwater.[8]

Johnson and Humphrey at the podium in Atlantic City

Muriel shares her husband's triumph at the 1964 convention.

By the time Humphrey had said "but not . . ." for the third time, the delegates had begun to get the idea and were chanting "but not Senator Goldwater" right along with Humphrey. The device was such a success that during the early weeks of the campaign, all Humphrey's speeches had a chorus or two of "but not . . ." in them. The crowds loved to chime in and always made the refrain the high point of the speech.

After the convention, Johnson flew the principals in the campaign down to his ranch for a strategy session. Among those in attendance was Bob Short, who had led the Kefauver forces that embarrassed Humphrey in 1956 but had reemerged as national campaign coordinator for Humphrey's 1964 campaign. Short recalls:

> It was kind of cold all the time we were down there—a real Texas chill—and Humphrey and Johnson were dressed in hunting jackets. We had a planning and strategy meeting, and we started going around the room with each person explaining what he thought we should do and where we should go and how we should proceed. Johnson was being very quiet. Finally we got to him, and he said, "Well, boys, I'm going to tell you how it's going to be." And that's just what he did. "You've got to analyze the United States for those we've got, those we haven't, and those we probably can't get." By the time he got through with just the states we'd already got, it was clear you couldn't lose the election if you didn't do a thing except stand around with your foot in your mouth. . . . Now about the old man, I can tell you this, they can say whatever they want about Lyndon Johnson, but he knew politics.[9]

On the LBJ ranch

In a newspaper interview published after the election, Short described the plan that Johnson laid out:

> Our first decision was to get him into the 11 states we needed to win. Everything beyond that was insurance. We put Humphrey in Ohio seven times—almost equally spread over the whole campaign. He was in Pennsylvania at least six times. Other key states were New York, Texas, Florida, California, Wisconsin, Illinois, Massachusetts, New Jersey and Michigan.[10]

On the campaign trail, Humphrey for once had no money problems. It was a first class operation all the way. In the primaries just four years earlier, Humphrey had lumbered through the snows of Wisconsin and the mountains of West Virginia on a rickety bus while John Kennedy soared over him in his private campaign plane. Now Humphrey traveled in style in his own plane, which at Johnson's insistence was equipped with a bed and a masseur. Despite such comforts, Humphrey was subjected to a few hardships during the campaign. As he reached out to shake hands with the crowds, he was stripped of at least four watches and countless numbers of cufflinks.

The 1964 campaign was trying at times, but it was also fun, if for no other reason than it was a winner from wire to wire. Humphrey was in his element, taking potshots at his opponents whenever he had the chance. In a swing through the South, the single pocket of Goldwater strength in the country, a young man shouted out to Humphrey,

To visit the [LBJ] ranch was to be an actor on Lyndon Johnson's stage. You might be an extra, or have just a walk-on part. You were part of the audience as well. He would parade across that stage his friends, his relatives, his old cronies, and he would tell stories he had told a thousand times before of his mother and father, of his youth, of student days and teaching. He would talk of his aunts and uncles and he would talk about the land, his hill country, his Texas.

HUBERT H. HUMPHREY

Campaigning for the 1964 election

"I'm for Goldwater." Humphrey replied, "Son, it's all right to study ancient history but don't vote it."[11] Responding to William Miller's continual jibing at Humphrey's middle name, Hubert suggested, "If we get the votes of all the people who are trying to forget their middle names, we'll have the majority of the American voters."[12]

They did even better than that. The Johnson-Humphrey ticket carried all but five states; the only state the Democrats lost outside the Deep South was Barry Goldwater's native Arizona. The winning percentage of the vote—61.0 to Goldwater's 38.5—was the largest in the nation's history. And when it was all over, Hubert Horatio Humphrey was the thirty-eighth vice-president of the United States.

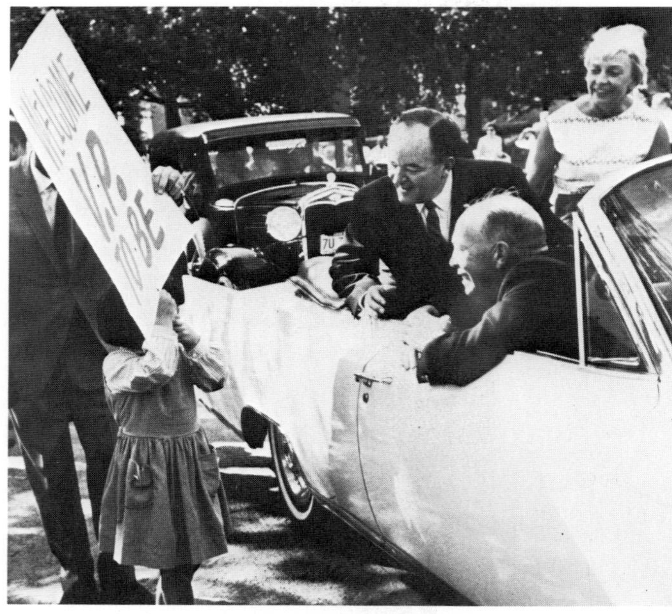

"Welcome V.P. To Be."

chapter 14

HAWK

Humphrey looked after that crowd as though they were among the crowned heads of Europe and he was delighted to have them come. He no more would have thought of apologizing and saying, "Well, I didn't ask them to come. They just climbed on the train and showed up here." It was clear that he was looking after them. He was proud to have them share in the moment.

JULIAN HARTT

The inauguration that celebrated the Johnson mandate cost over $2 million and attracted 75,000 visitors to the nation's capital. But the president gave strict instructions that his more colorful followers, particularly those whose somewhat uncommon manners or appearance might evoke snickers from the sophisticated Easterners, were to be discouraged from leaving Texas for the inaugural. Unlike Johnson, Humphrey was not embarrassed by his origins. If the friends and relatives from small-town South Dakota and Minnesota who swarmed to Washington for the celebration may have seemed less than chic to jaded eyes, Humphrey never gave a sign. His good fortune was theirs; his old friends were not forgotten. Freddie Gates, the rotund Minneapolis pinball machine owner, was there to hold the Bible for Humphrey's swearing-in; the Doland High School Band pa-

Freddie Gates (center) **holds the Bible as Hubert Humphrey takes the oath of office.**

raded past the reviewing stand; the guests at one of the inaugural balls included the wife of a life-long Humphrey supporter who was so overcome that she went pushing through the crowd shouting, "He kissed me. The Vice-President just kissed me."[1]

After all the celebrating was over, Humphrey settled down to the job of being vice-president. At first his assignments offered him enough substance to balance the purely ceremonial functions of the office. When voting rights legislation was being considered by Congress, Humphrey, who had been floor manager of every civil rights bill that had come before the Senate between 1949 and 1964, worked with administration supporters on getting the measure passed. He had been on the Hill long enough to know how sensitive legislators were to any interference from the executive branch, however, and he defined his task narrowly: "My job is not to design the legislation—my role is that of a magnet to bring people together."[2]

As vice-president, Humphrey had a variety of other jobs to perform. In the course of a typical working day, he might listen to a dozen influential Texans who were concerned about cotton legislation, hear another complaint, this time about freight rates, from some equally influential midwesterners, discuss farm legislation with the budget division, and attend a congressional dinner. In general, he saw his role as "easing the domestic burdens of the President."[3] Former vice-president Richard Nixon saw it differently and, as it turned out, somewhat more accurately. In May 1965, he told a Minneapolis reporter: "In the current administration, the Vice-President is more restricted

One of the easy jokes for years was the deriding of Hubert Humphrey over his zeal for talking—a joke that Humphrey himself enjoyed telling about himself. . . . But not nearly enough has been said about Humphrey's other great zeal. He was a magnificent listener. . . .

I will never forget one particularly memorable occasion. It was back in 1965, when I was serving both as assistant director of the Office of Economic Opportunity and as special assistant to the Vice President in connection with his responsibilities in the antipoverty effort. I had asked Mr. Humphrey to join us at a meeting of our Community Representatives Advisory Committee. This was a group of about 20 men and women, all of them very poor, who had been named from their respective antipoverty program boards around the country. We had been told that the Vice President's schedule was very rough that day but that he had himself insisted on at least "dropping in" for about five minutes.

When he arrived, the meeting was in progress. Chairing the meeting, I suggested we stop the discussion and hear some words from the Vice President. "No," he said, "please proceed. I want to hear what these folks have to say." We had been getting brief reports from each of the committee members. The reports continued: An Oklahoma Indian describing living conditions on his reservation. A black woman from a Chicago ghetto. A white woman from the Cleveland Hough area. An old man from a former textile town in New England. Mr.

Humphrey had placed his hands on a table and was leaning forward to hear every word. Occasionally he would ask questions. He wanted to know as much as possible about each of them; and they soon knew that he wanted to know.

After a half-hour, he motioned to his aide and then whispered in his ear. When I said I'd understand if he had to leave, he retorted, "Relax, I wouldn't miss this for anything. I just changed my schedule." He stayed for two hours. He was a mighty good listener. He had a third ear—his heart.

HYMAN BOOKBINDER
NEW YORK TIMES
JANUARY 29, 1978

than I was. In my case Dwight Eisenhower only wanted to conduct the Presidency, not the politics. He wanted to be the Chief Executive, not the politician, and therefore I could do a lot of freewheeling. But Lyndon Johnson is going to run both the Presidency and the politics, and he's not going to let Humphrey or anyone else do any pre-empting in either of those areas."[4]

The burden of Nixon's term in office had been that Dwight Eisenhower had given his vice-president plenty of rope—enough to hang himself. In-

Enjoying vice-presidential duties

stead of being able to use the office to erase the image of hatchet man that he had earned from his earlier campaigns for the House and Senate, Nixon found himself cast in the same role as vice-president. The burden of Humphrey's vice-presidency was the opposite of Nixon's: he was given no rope at all. The leash he was on was so short that soon even his cruises on the Potomac and his use of aircraft assigned to the executive branch had to be cleared through the president's office, which usually meant that Marvin Watson, a Johnson aide, controlled the comings and goings of the vice-president of the United States.

Even before Humphrey took office, Johnson had occasion to invoke the loyalty oath that he had exacted from him before the convention. In November 1964, after the election but before Humphrey had been sworn in, the vice-president-elect made some off-the-cuff remarks that suggested he would be shaping the education policies of the new administration. Johnson called Humphrey on the carpet and made it clear that policy-shaping was not one of his responsibilities. Then, just as he had done after telling Bobby Kennedy he would not be on the ticket, Johnson called reporters into his office to re-enact the "Telling of Hubert," complete with colorful references to Humphrey's emasculation. As in the Kennedy story, this tale of Johnsonian triumph once again focused on the sufferings of the victim—how he had been brought to his knees and debased by the president's power. Johnson delighted in such stories. Sadly, they say more about Johnson himself than they do about the objects of his cruelty.

American soldiers in Vietnam

In the early months of 1965, Lyndon Johnson and his administration found their attention focused increasingly on the situation in South Vietnam. During the early sixties, the American military presence in the Southeast Asian country had gradually expanded until by the time of President Kennedy's assassination in 1963, there were about 16,300 American "military advisers" in South Vietnam. In July 1964, a month before the Democratic National Convention, Congress had passed the Gulf of Tonkin resolution at President Johnson's request, granting to the president the power "to take all necessary measures to repel any armed attack against the forces of the United States and to prevent further aggression." Now, as Johnson's new term in office began, the president was faced with several critical decisions concerning the United States role in Vietnam.

On February 7, a mortar attack by Viet Cong on an American barracks at Pleiku had killed nine Americans and wounded over a hundred more. This was the first time that a Viet Cong attack had been directed unmistakably at American troops. The Pleiku raid came at a particularly sensitive time in the history of American involvement in Vietnam. The American military effort had not stabilized and had reached a point where it seemed to require either a withdrawal or an escalation that would include bombing targets in North Vietnam. McGeorge Bundy, Special Assistant for National Security Affairs, was on the scene at Pleiku soon after the Viet Cong attack. In an angry and emotional cable, he told President Johnson that retaliation was required—anything less would be inadequate. Bundy, an ex-Harvard dean, liberal Republican, and Kennedy holdover, was the very model of the Eastern Establishment respectability that Lyndon Johnson so loved, hated, and envied. Bundy had been a dove on Vietnam, but the sight of the wounded and dying at Pleiku had shattered his cool Establishment reserve. Together with Robert McNamara, the Secretary of Defense, and Dean Rusk, the Secretary of State, Bundy urged the president to mount a retaliatory bombing attack against North Vietnam.

At a series of meetings held in the White House, the president's advisers had the opportunity to argue their cases and to review all the administration's options. Hubert Humphrey was one of those heard. He had expressed his views on Vietnam as early as January 1950, when he had said, "If we lose the South part of Asia, we shall have lost every hope that we have ever had of being able to maintain free institutions in any part of the Eastern World."[5] Five years later Humphrey asserted, "If we abandon free Vietnam, we will have abandoned all Southeast Asia,"[6] and in March 1962, he had expressed the hope "that American participation in this area [Vietnam] can be limited to military assistance, to supplies, and to military training, and it is my view, I state so there will be no doubt about it, that it should be so limited."[7]

Now, in February 1965, while Humphrey still believed that Viet Cong success could result in the fall of all Southeast Asia to Communism, he counseled the president against the bombing, particularly as Soviet Premier Aleksei Kosygin would be in Hanoi, the capital of North Vietnam, during the

Humphrey at work in his office

proposed raids. His advice, given at a National Security Council Meeting on February 10 and again in a lengthy memo to Johnson dated February 15, 1965, was both wise and prophetic:

> People can't understand why we would run grave risks to support a country which is totally unable to put its own house in order. The chronic instability in Saigon directly undermines the impression that we are the prisoner of events in Vietnam. This blurs the Administration's leadership role and has spillover effects across the board. It also helps erode confidence and credibility in our policies. . . . If . . . we find ourselves leading from frustration to escalation and end up short of a war with China, but embroiled deeper in fighting in Vietnam over the next few months, political opposition will steadily mount. It will underwrite all the negativism and disillusionment which we already have about foreign involvement generally. . . . [8]

Humphrey's advice was not only ignored, but he was also punished for offering it. Word of his dovish stance had gotten out, and Johnson, a keeper of secrets in a city where there are none, was enraged at the leak and held Humphrey responsible. On the president's orders, the vice-president was systematically excluded from the war councils during the period between February and July 1965, when the critical decisions were made to escalate United States military involvement in Vietnam. From July on, war policy remained essentially unchanged throughout the Johnson administration.

Once such a course of action is determined by a government, it seems to have a life of its own. With the critical initial decisions made and reinforced by more and more secondary decisions, by additional costs, new adherents, and more hardware, the original basis for the policy, whether right or wrong, is no longer questioned. To do so, and then to discover that the initial premise was false, could destroy the whole apparatus, ruin reputations, and amount to an admission of failure. Thus it was with United States policy in Vietnam.

Humphrey made his way back on board Johnson's team late in 1965 by swallowing his doubts about the military buildup in Vietnam and trying to convince some of his old liberal colleagues in the Senate, and even on the board of the Americans for Democratic Action, to support the war. It didn't wash, nor did Humphrey's efforts heighten the liberals' regard for their old ally. By December, Johnson had decided that Humphrey had repented sufficiently to be sent on an inspection tour to South Vietnam. When word of the trip leaked out, the president characteristically exploded, and Humphrey's Far Eastern tour was limited to the Philippines, Formosa, Korea, and Japan. South Vietnam was not included. In an interview, Humphrey said that Vietnam "had never been considered or planned" and that the report of his going there was "erroneous" and "conjecture." Taking the administration's line on the war, he responded when asked about a halt to the bombing, "You can't ask one side to put down its arms while the other side continues to shoot."[9]

We Asians don't understand pulling punches in a war.

FERDINAND MARCOS
PRESIDENT OF THE PHILIPPINES

The overall purpose of Humphrey's Far Eastern trip had been interpreted as an attempt by the president to help Humphrey bolster his sagging popularity. His standing in the polls had slid during recent months to the point where 58 percent of those polled were saying that they did not want to see him become president. This interpretation was correct as far as it went, but Johnson had another motive. The trip was also intended to be a dry run testing Humphrey's ability to sell the administration's Vietnam policy to America's friends in Asia. Johnson sent Jack Valenti, a White House aide, along with Humphrey on the journey. The official explanation was that Humphrey wanted somebody from the White House to vouch for his performance in order to forestall any carping from the

In December 1965, Hubert and Muriel attended the inauguration of President Ferdinand Marcos of the Philippines. Marcos and his wife are standing on either side of the Humphreys in this picture.

State Department over his first diplomatic mission as vice-president. A more plausible explanation was that Valenti was there to shadow Humphrey as Johnson's eyes and ears.

Humphrey did his best to push the administration's Vietnam line on his tour, and Johnson, apparently satisfied with the reports of his watchdog, quickly decided to send Humphrey on a second trip. He had only been back in the United States for ten days before the president sent him to New Delhi to attend the funeral of Indian Prime Minister Lal Bahadur Shastri. This time Jack Valenti stayed home. When Humphrey returned, he was able to give Johnson a report on a two hour meeting he had had with Premier Aleksei Kosygin, who had attended the funeral as the representative of the Soviet Union.

By now Humphrey had been restored to favor, and in February 1966, Johnson was ready to send him out on the real thing—a nine-nation, 43,000-mile, two-week tour of Southeast Asia that would include South Vietnam. The purpose of the tour was to promote the administration's Vietnam policies among America's Asian allies and then come back home and do it again to the growing ranks of critics at home. Johnson instructed Humphrey to stress not only the military aspects of the American effort but also the economic assistance program that had been developed in part with one eye on Bobby Kennedy, who was rapidly appropriating Humphrey's old liberal constituency by calling for greater attention to humanitarian needs in Vietnam. According to the Honolulu Doctrine arrived at by Johnson and South Vietnam Premier

I remember going to India with Hubert to represent President Johnson at a funeral in 1966. He talked all night about the problems of Washington and being a vice-president. He told me that the most important thing and the thing he most frequently forgot was to greet LBJ by saying, "Good morning, Mr. President." If he said, "How are you, Mr. President," he always received a severe look.

JOHN KENNETH GALBRAITH

South Vietnamese Premier Ky with Humphrey in Saigon

The vice-president talks to an American soldier at Bien Hoa air base.

Nguyen Cao Ky, the Vietnam struggle was to be a two-front war, designed to achieve both military victory and social reform.

Given only twenty-four hours notice of his important assignment, Humphrey made frantic preparations. His first task was to pick up Nguyen Cao Ky, who had just finished meeting with Johnson in Honolulu, and to fly back with him to Asia to spread the gospel. The ebullient, energetic Humphrey plunged into the murky politics of Southeast Asia with the same enthusiasm he had shown at midwestern county fairs. "Humphrey set out deliberately, for example, to show South Vietnam Premier Ky how to politic and by the end of the first day, Ky had his sleeves rolled up and startled Vietnamese villagers and slum dwellers by talking man-to-man with them and asking them about their problems."[10] Ky's experiment in American political techniques made good copy, but it didn't take. He was far more interested in demonstrating his skills in fast-draw and gun-twirling techniques with his ever-present six shooters. The South Vietnamese premier once displayed these talents during a briefing by Averell Harriman, who viewed the demonstration with something less than enthusiasm.

After touring South Vietnam, Humphrey went on to visit other Asian countries. In Canberra he told the Australians that the United States would "pursue the enemy relentlessly" in Vietnam and, together with its allies, would "not let them win."[11] Prime Minister Harold Holt responded by telling Humphrey that "there was not a single member of the Australian Government who did not wholeheartedly support the American policy in Vietnam."[12] The Australian prime minister conveniently ignored the 150 demonstrators who had gathered outside the parliament building during Humphrey's speech. Other Asian leaders, publicly critical of American policy, privately told Humphrey that they were eager for the United States to remain in Vietnam since it was the only force capable of resisting Red China.

Humphrey returned to Washington to be greeted by live television coverage of his arrival and a welcoming bear hug from Johnson. In discussing his trip, he defined the enemy in the hard-line terms he had used twenty years before in Minneapolis when he had helped drive the Communists out of the Farmer-Labor Party: "I fought them then and I am going to fight them now. We licked them then and we can lick them now. They are not the forces of freedom, we are."[13] Humphrey told Johnson, "I return, Mr. President, with a deep sense of confidence in our cause—and its ultimate triumph. . . . The tide of battle in Vietnam has turned in our favor."[14]

Maybe history will say we were wrong, that we never should have been [in Vietnam]. But it is my view that we made the only decision that we could have made at the time, that it was a responsible decision in light of the evidence.

HUBERT H. HUMPHREY

While Humphrey's efforts had helped him win his way back into Johnson's circle, the strain on his relations with the liberal community were beginning to show. One of the first signs appeared among the members of the academy. A number of University of Minnesota professors, several of them old and valued friends of Humphrey, circulated a letter criticizing his "betrayal" of liberal values growing out of his position on Vietnam. A flap ensued, the letter was withdrawn, and a second letter surfaced, this one more subdued. It expressed "profound disappointment" with Humphrey's "uncritical support" of the administration's Vietnam policies, but softened its attack with a cover letter indicating that the professors understood the "difficulties" of Humphrey's current position. Humphrey responded in kind, describing liberals as "volatile. . . . If you do something to displease them, they become cynical. I want to be tolerant, but I can't see the difference between containment of communism in Europe and Asia. When the communists infiltrated Henry Wallace's Progressive Party in 1948, we fought them."[15]

An antiwar demonstration at North Dakota State University

While the breach between Humphrey and the liberal community was now out in the open, it was still tentative and capable of healing. Humphrey had too much political capital in reserve from a lifetime of working for liberal causes to dissipate it in a single stroke. But there were more losses to come. Humphrey undertook his assignment of selling the war on the home front with the same high energy level that always characterized his efforts, and as his own pace quickened, so did the criticism. The California Democratic Council, the liberal wing of that state's Democratic Party, denounced Humphrey at its convention while praising Robert Kennedy, the former aide of Senator Joseph McCarthy, for his support of a coalition government in Vietnam that would contain Communist elements. Yet despite the growing storm, long-time allies continued to defend Humphrey. "Frankly we believe Humphrey's prestige and popularity as a political leader has declined since he took office, but for reasons beyond Humphrey's control,"[16] said Max Kampelman. Even more to the point was Joseph Rauh's comment: "If criticism of Humphrey can be justified, it must be in the fact that he appears to endorse the president's program with even more vigor than the President does himself. . . . He couldn't campaign half-heartedly for anybody or anything if he tried."[17]

Humphrey's friends did not ignore the potential political consequences of his position on Vietnam. "Let's assume that Johnson decides not to run in 1968," speculated Max Kampelman, that prescient judgment coming in January 1967. "I don't see Bobby taking the nomination away from Hum-

I haven't changed my mind on Vietnam. I think that we made a commitment there. I think it is unfortunate the way we got into it. I don't see how we can get out of it unless we can, in some way, insure that this area is not going to fall over, one country after another, to the Communists. I can't see anything that changed my theory that, if they take Vietnam, they will keep going. They will take Laos, Cambodia, and they will be knocking at the doors.

GEORGE MEANY

phrey. I think all Johnson's political crowd would go behind Humphrey and so would the labor and business people."[18] On a political level, that appeared to be precisely the gamble that Humphrey was taking. Despite the mounting unpopularity of the war, he expected the issue to be behind him by the time that Johnson's presidency was completed. Then, be it 1968 or, more likely, 1972, those who had failed to back their country and their own party's leaders would have little to say about whom the Democratic presidential nominee might be. To back off now would only mean that Humphrey was certain to be dropped from the ticket if Johnson ran again in 1968, even if the president would have to replace him with Bobby Kennedy to get re-elected. There seemed to be no choice but to ride out the storm.

In February 1967, Humphrey told George Meany and other members of the AFL-CIO Executive Council that the Viet Cong could not win the war in Vietnam.

Humphrey's commitment to the administration's Vietnam war policy had become equally deep on a personal and emotional level. Humphrey could not forget the victories of his own past, when he had fought Communists successfully by taking a hard-line approach. What was so different now? What was different was that a growing number of the American people neither understood nor were committed to United States objectives in Vietnam. Polls still showed that a majority supported the war, but that support was lukewarm at best, and might even have existed for a while as a form of automatic patriotism if Johnson had decided to invade Canada or napalm Guatemala. American voters had rejected the escalation of the war in the 1964 presidential elections, only to find that the administration they had elected, as Humphrey had pointed out in his memo, had "bought the Goldwater position."[19]

Humphrey's personal commitment to a hard-line policy in Vietnam had been influenced not only by the lesson of the past but also by present experience. His first trip to Vietnam had much the same effect on him as the Pleiku raid had on another earlier convert to hawkdom, McGeorge Bundy. The sight of the dead and wounded American soldiers, and the suffering and poverty of the Vietnamese themselves, had stiffened his resolve to repay the Communists in kind. But overriding all other considerations was Humphrey's need to demonstrate his loyalty to Johnson. The relationship between the two men had not sprung up overnight. They had been friends for fifteen years before they had run together in the fall of 1964. It had been

Humphrey visits with American troops during his first trip to Vietnam.

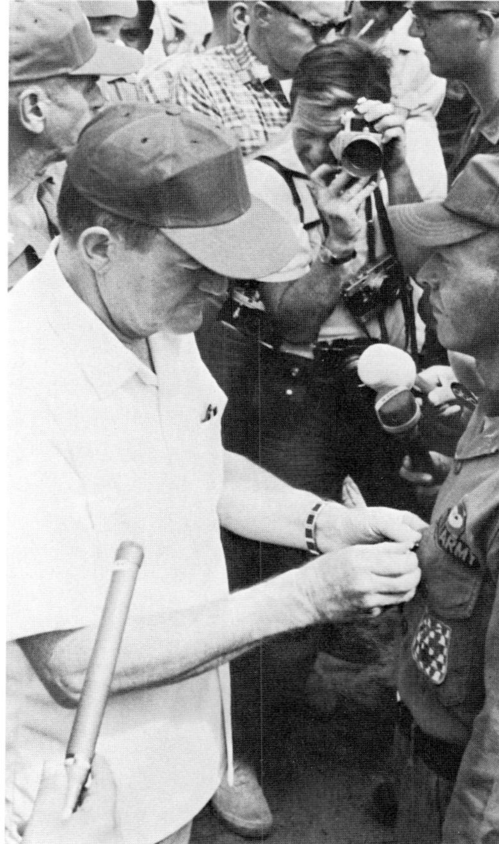

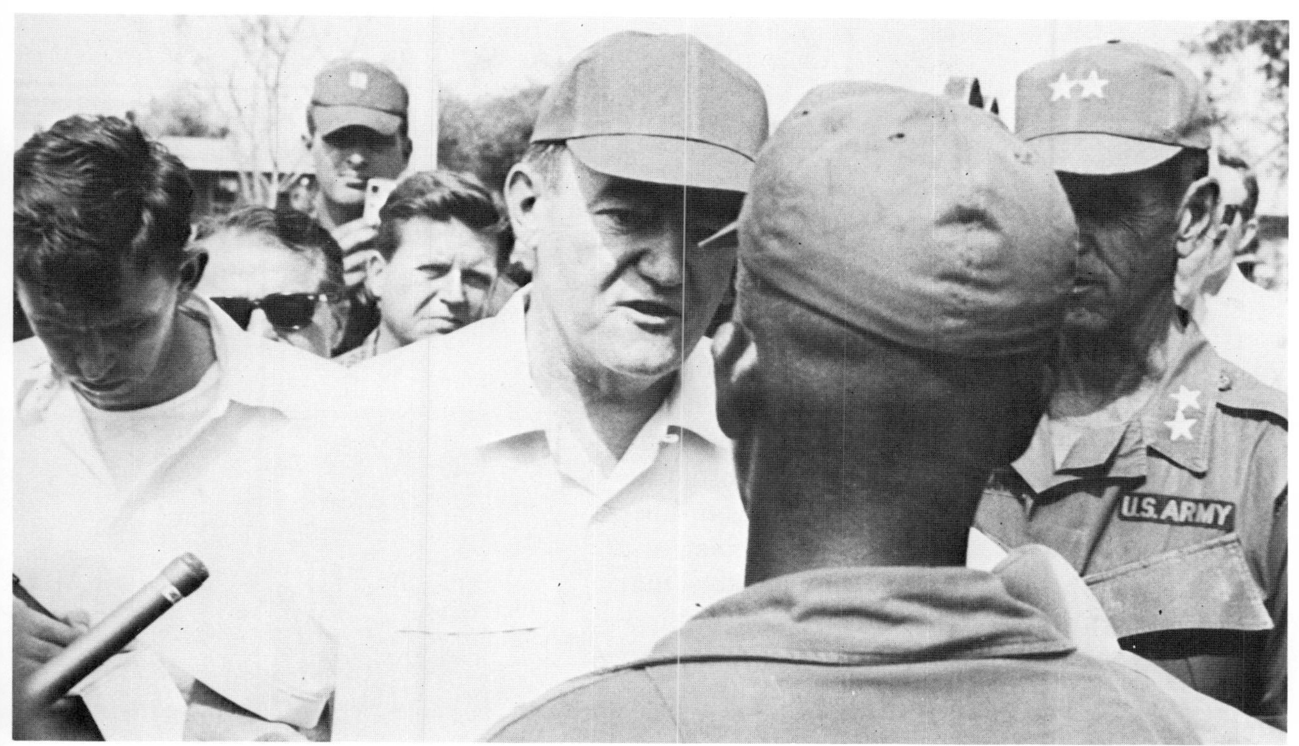

I had a President who was absolutely paranoid about the war—beyond his ego, which we all know about, which he certainly had, which any man does have who is President. But beyond that, you've got to remember he had two sons-in-law who were over there. Why, anybody who said the slightest thing to him about change in Vietnam—why, my Lord!

HUBERT H. HUMPHREY

Johnson who had taken Humphrey from the back benches of the Senate in the early fifties and helped guide him into the Senate's inner circle, who had made it possible for him to become Senate whip, and who had chosen him to be vice-president of the United States when he could have just about taken anyone he had wanted. And it was Humphrey who had promised, time and again, to maintain unwavering allegiance to Johnson's policies.

The dilemma of Humphrey's position, and the irony of it, can be seen in sharper perspective by bringing another figure into the picture: Bobby Kennedy. On February 18, 1962, Kennedy, then a member of his brother's cabinet, had said, "We are going to win in Vietnam. We will remain there until we win."[20] After John Kennedy's death, however, Robert Kennedy became one of the leading spokesmen against the war. (Reminded of his former position, Kennedy shrugged, "Past error is no excuse for its own perpetuation."[21]) Humphrey, no less a part of Johnson's administration now than Bobby had been part of his brother's administration then, could not indulge himself in the luxury of second-guessing and still fulfill his role as a nonpolicy-making spokesman in the Johnson administration. Had John Kennedy lived, his brother would probably have remained in the Cabinet, and Humphrey in the Senate. It is not unlikely that their roles would have been reversed: Humphrey still leading his natural constituency on the left as a critic of the war and Kennedy defending administration policy.

Of the more than forty vice-presidents who have held office in the United States, only one—the states rights champion John Calhoun—defied his president and resigned his position over policy differences. It was Humphrey's tragedy to maintain the almost unbroken tradition of vice-presidential subservience at a time in American history when the need to shatter that precedent was the greatest.

The war was Humphrey's primary burden, but there was little comfort for him on the home front. As a result of the mid-term elections in 1966, the Republicans achieved a dramatic recovery from the Goldwater disaster, electing three new senators, eight new governors, and forty-seven new house members. Taking a large share of the credit was that indefatigable Republican campaigner Richard Nixon, who was a likely candidate for the Republican nomination in 1968. In Minnesota, Humphrey had gotten himself embroiled in another internecine dispute within the DFL, as the party dumped the incumbent governor, Karl Rolvaag, and endorsed Lieutenant Governor A. M. "Sandy" Keith. Keith was a Kennedy-style politician, with John's haircut and Bobby's talent for knocking down people who stood in his way; his political enemies had nicknamed him the "Smiling Barracuda." But Rolvaag stubbornly refused to be shunted aside and ran in the primary, where the Republicans performed their time-honored ritual of doing their best to embarrass the DFL by supporting the weaker candidate, Rolvaag. Rolvaag won the primary, but lost the general election to Harold LeVander, the Republican candidate.

In 1966 and 1967, racial unrest and rioting in the nation's black ghettos intensified an already explosive political atmosphere. During the summer of 1966, House Republican leader Gerald Ford had criticized Humphrey for remarking that, if forced to live amid squalor, disease, and hunger, "I've got enough spark left in me to lead a mighty good revolt under those conditions."[22] In the summer of 1967, Humphrey's civil rights attitudes came under liberal attack. He had taken a Southern campaign swing and had been photographed arm-in-arm with Georgia's segregationist governor Lester Maddox. Forgotten in the uproar over the picture was that shortly after his meeting with Humphrey, Maddox refused to go along with Alabama governor Lurleen Wallace's call for unified Southern resistance to desegregation. John McKeithen of Louisiana, another governor whom Humphrey had visited, also rejected the call for Southern unanimity.

During the summer of 1967, the nation's racial problems increased when the city of Detroit expe-

This picture of Humphrey with Governor Lester Maddox of Georgia was the subject of a great deal of criticism.

rienced the worst racial violence in its history. Speaking in Detroit, Humphrey said that the nation must be willing to pay the price for a Marshall Plan to rebuild its cities and to provide a framework of social and economic justice for black Americans. This time he caught flak from Johnson, who was not about to embark on a Marshall Plan or a Humphrey Plan or any other damn plan until he, Lyndon Johnson, was ready to do so, at which time, he, Lyndon Johnson, would be happy to announce the program and describe it to the nation, that is, if Hubert Humphrey didn't object. Humphrey may have objected, but there was nothing he could do about it.

Even a liberal can find the truth if you give him enough time.

LESTER MADDOX
GOVERNOR OF GEORGIA

By this time, Humphrey's liberal friends had all but despaired of turning him around on the war. That spring a meeting with Joseph Rauh, an ADA associate, Clayton Fritchey, James Wechsler, and Gil Harrison, all influential journalists, and Harvard professors J. Kenneth Galbraith and Arthur Schlesinger, Jr. had turned into a bitter shouting match. The liberal leaders left thoroughly disillusioned with their old comrade and ready to look for someone else to lead the country out of war. Soon they would find him—in the unlikely person of Senator Eugene McCarthy.

Meanwhile, Humphrey tightened his grip on the Vietnam tar baby.

Eugene McCarthy, Humphrey's old friend and fellow Minnesotan, was destined to become the leader of the antiwar forces in the Democratic Party.

chapter 15

TO CHICAGO

After the 1964 convention, Eugene McCarthy had returned to relative obscurity as Minnesota's senior senator, nursing a deep hostility toward Lyndon Johnson, who had robbed him of the chance to be vice-president. McCarthy's re-election campaign in the fall of that year against a millionaire stockbroker had been a pushover.

Gene McCarthy with the Humphreys at the 1964 Democratic National Convention

When he returned to the Senate in 1965, McCarthy managed to trade his seat on the Agriculture Committee for one on Foreign Relations. It was a small sop for having lost the vice-presidential nomination, but the prize was sweetened by having been gained at the expense of the newly elected senator from New York, Robert Kennedy, who had also sought to fill the vacancy.

McCarthy's change of committee assignments in the Senate marked a new stage in his career. His departure from Agriculture signaled his abandonment of his old Minnesota constituency, which had begun to bore him anyway, while his move to Foreign Relations provided McCarthy with a new constituency, the Eastern-liberal-academic community. Throughout the remainder of his Senate career, McCarthy cultivated a following among this group; in fact, he was sometimes referred to as New York's third senator, just as Humphrey had once been known as Wisconsin's third senator.

When McCarthy assumed this new role, he found himself faced with new political opportunities and responsibilities. As a politician, McCarthy had some of the qualities of adolescent genius. So brilliant that he could get by without having to work much at anything he did, he spent long stretches of his career functioning at half speed. Then, energized by some event, he would work at capacity just long enough to demonstrate his brilliance, only to slow down again for no apparent reason. Such enigmatic behavior amused him and annoyed others, but the pattern disguised a deeper disturbance. During his productive periods, McCarthy's successes were often so enormous that

they frightened him. When his achievements forced him to act as a leader, and not just a protestor, he was unable to cope with the role. Therefore he frittered away his triumphs in irrelevancies and sarcasm, in strangely inept performances, in anything that would relieve him of having to assume permanent responsibilities.

When the parade had passed him by again, he would nurse deep grudges, resentful of those who had seized the initiative from him. McCarthy always appeared as an heroic failure, and this was not the least of his attractions. Eventually the nation's young people would come to identify with his weaknesses as well as his strengths.

The issue that would force Eugene McCarthy to assume the frightening responsibility of leadership was the war in Vietnam. McCarthy's seat on Foreign Relations gave him access to testimony and other evidence that caused him to conclude, far sooner than most, that the president had been subverting the constitutional responsibilities of the Senate, deceiving the American people, and leading the nation into catastrophe in Vietnam. Allard Lowenstein was one of a number of liberals who had reached that same conclusion and who were searching for a candidate who could challenge Lyndon Johnson on the war issue from within the Democratic Party. Lowenstein was an obscure choice to become history's catalyst for the toppling of a sitting United States president. Thirty-eight years old, seemingly a permanent student, Lowenstein had been president of the National Student Association during the organization's pre-CIA era and had once served on Hubert Humphrey's staff. He was in touch with a vast network of political activists on campuses throughout the country, and he planned to use them in an organized effort to embarrass Lyndon Johnson in the 1968 primaries. But Eugene McCarthy was not his first choice to lead the antiwar forces. Bobby Kennedy was.

Bobby Kennedy

Lowenstein had approached Kennedy in late

In a free society, the President does not have the unilateral authority to wage a war against the will of the majority, and the President better understand that.

ALLARD LOWENSTEIN

August 1967, but he had been turned down. His proposal had also been rejected by other possible candidates, including George McGovern, Kenneth Galbraith, James Gaven, and Gene McCarthy. McCarthy felt that only Bobby could lead the revolt within the party, but he had left the door open a crack. Lowenstein wanted to have a candidate by December 1967, when a conference of his fledgling group, Concerned Democrats, would be held in Chicago to call attention to the war issue. By the end of October, he had achieved his goal. Persuaded that Bobby Kennedy would not run and that Lyndon Johnson must be challenged, McCarthy agreed to head the antiwar forces.

On November 12, Vice-President Humphrey returned from his second trip to Vietnam, confident of eventual American victory: "I think we are winning the struggle. I don't say it has been won. I say we are winning it. . . . There has been genuine progress in every area. . . ." Progress on the military side "has been tremendous"; on the political side, "very significant."[1] To support his statement, Humphrey furnished figures for his three-day visit that showed a body count of 375 Viet Cong killed against 35 South Vietnamese losses. No American losses were reported.

Four weeks after Humphrey's return, Gene McCarthy announced his candidacy for the presidential election in 1968. His campaign would be directed at the war and would not attack Johnson personally, McCarthy stated at the outset. McCarthy's stance as a presidential candidate was so tentative that within a week he was announcing the conditions under which he would withdraw. At the conference of Concerned Democrats held in early December, he was visibly upset by Lowenstein's fire-eating denunciation of Johnson, and he disappointed the audience with a dry, low-key speech on the war. Despite his lack of enthusiasm, however, McCarthy had begun making plans for the upcoming primaries. He had originally thought that his initial effort would be in Massachusetts on April 30, but, feeling that the Kennedys would never give him a fair shake there, he had decided to make his first test of strength in the earlier New Hampshire primary. His opponent in New Hampshire on March 12 would be Lyndon Johnson.

The presidential year of 1968 began on an ominous note, setting the tone for a period that would bring the nation closer to anarchy than at any time since the Civil War. Assassinations, resignations, campus revolts at Berkeley and Columbia, rioting in the ghettos, rioting in the streets of Chicago, all would follow the first grim surprise—the Tet offensive. At the beginning of Tet, the Vietnamese New Year, on Monday, January 29, the Viet Cong unleashed a massive offensive against South Vietnam, involving a strike force of approximately 150,000 troops and attacks on twenty-six of the South's forty-four provincial capitals. By Wednesday, January 31, a Viet Cong suicide squad had managed to penetrate the grounds of the American Embassy in Saigon, the very heart of the American presence in South Vietnam, considered American soil under international law.

The Viet Cong attack in Saigon and elsewhere was rapidly deflected. Within a short time it was

U. S. Marines fighting in the streets of Hue after the Tet offensive

clear that the Tet offensive was an overwhelming military disaster for the Communists, who ultimately lost 42,000 troops—nearly a third of their attacking force—and failed to capture a single one of the provincial capitals. But the psychological impact of the Viet Cong effort, coming after years of assurances and reassurances of impending South Vietnamese victory, was enough to blow away the last shreds of confidence in the administration's ability to bring the war to a speedy conclusion. From Tet on, the Johnson administration was constantly on the defensive, holding its supporters through appeals to loyalty and patriotism. The light at the end of the tunnel had winked out.

Tet gave McCarthy's campaign in New Hampshire a mighty boost. Student volunteers, who formed nearly the entire McCarthy forces, were reinforced by still more students who feared that Tet signaled increased draft quotas drawn primarily from their ranks. Johnson's own inept campaign also helped McCarthy's cause. Organized from the top down with big-name New Hampshire Democrats, his campaign lacked both the workers and the enthusiasm of the McCarthy effort. When Johnson's people asked New Hampshire Democrats to sign pledge cards indicating their support of the president, McCarthy seized on the device as a crude attempt to exact a loyalty oath from the independent New Englanders.

Although Johnson's name did not actually appear on the New Hampshire ballot (he was represented instead by a slate of delegates), although he had run a poor campaign and had never made an appearance in the state, he won the primary with 49.6 percent of the Democratic vote (27,520) to McCarthy's 41.9 percent (23,263). The media, however, hailed the results as a great McCarthy victory, and not without reason. By foolishly predicting a much lower percentage of the vote for McCarthy, Johnson's leading supporters had helped to transform their candidate's victory into a humiliating defeat. McCarthy wasn't given very long to enjoy his New Hampshire triumph. As he was coming down the gangway from the airplane that had carried him back to Washington, he was told that Bobby Kennedy was "reassessing his position" on running for the presidency. Four days after New Hampshire, Kennedy announced his candidacy. McCarthy would later say, "The turning point in the quest for the 1968 Democratic nomination was the day before St. Patrick's Day, when Bobby Kennedy came into the race."[2]

McCarthy was bitter over Kennedy's decision, correctly foreseeing that the contest would no longer be a challenge to Lyndon Johnson's war policies but a battle of personalities between himself and Kennedy. But McCarthy did not claim that Kennedy's actions had been a breech of faith. Though Kennedy earlier had stated publicly that he would not run "under any foreseeable circumstances,"[3] he had been noncommittal in his private conversations with McCarthy: "I didn't ask him what he was going to do. I just said 'I'm not worried as to whether I'm a stalking horse for you,' meaning if Bobby were to enter later on, I would not say I'd been tricked."[4] Commenting ten years later on Kennedy's fateful decision, McCarthy

Campaigning in New Hampshire

McCarthy's whole operation is a carpetbag operation. You can import 10,000 people and end up with 5,000 votes.

BERNARD BOUTIN
MANAGER OF JOHNSON
CAMPAIGN IN NEW HAMPSHIRE

I would give a hell of a lot of credit to McCarthy. He's allowed the kids to work their way back into the system. Could Kennedy have done it without McCarthy? Could Kennedy have asked the kids to shave off their beards, to go to New Hampshire? I think Kennedy and all the other candidates can now capitalize on the student interest McCarthy aroused.

JOHN EVANS
MICHIGAN STUDENT

artfully avoided saying that Bobby promised him he wouldn't run, explaining instead that "Kennedy had stated publicly that he wasn't going to run, and he repeated the same reasoning to me in private."[5] "Repeated the same *reasoning,*" but no mention as to whether Kennedy had made the same disavowal as he had in public.

No matter what its antecedents, the decision that Kennedy had been weighing, conferring about with aides, and running polls on since October was finally made. For the next two and a half months, the two antiwar candidates would slug it out in the primaries.

Faced with two challengers, with the mandate of 1964 flapping in tatters around him, the Great Society an unfinished shell, the Vietnam war tearing the nation apart, Lyndon Johnson was doing some reassessing of his own. He was facing another political disaster in the Wisconsin primary on April 2, and this time there would be no way to blame the media for misinterpreting the figures. His political operatives had told him that McCarthy, the only other candidate on the ballot with him, would win a majority of the vote. Lyndon Johnson was well aware that no president of the United States had been denied the nomination of his own party since John Tyler in 1844. While Johnson believed that he could probably still command sufficient allegiance to win the nomination, there was a good chance that he might not and that the eventual showdown would be against Bobby Kennedy. Lyndon Johnson was determined not to leave the presidency of the United States feet first, remembered forever as the man who had been

Humphrey during his visit to Mexico City in March 1968

conquered and humiliated by his greatest political rival.

On the morning of March 31, 1968, Hubert and Muriel were packing for a trip to Mexico City, where Humphrey would serve as a United States representative at a treaty-signing. There was a knock on his door, and when Humphrey answered it, he found himself face to face with Lyndon Johnson. Taking Humphrey aside, Johnson showed him two drafts of the conclusion of a speech that he would be delivering that night. In one draft, he announced his withdrawal from the presidential race in order to take the issue of the war out of the election. Determined to re-establish his credibility, Johnson told Humphrey that he was willing to sacrifice his presidency and devote himself to ending the war. The president went on to say that he was not sure yet which ending of the speech he would use, but he urged Humphrey to listen to the broadcast that night in Mexico City and to keep quiet about the whole thing until then. Muriel's instinct told her that something was wrong, but Humphrey bit his tongue and went off to Mexico City, uncertain whether Johnson really intended to withdraw.

Endicott Peabody, a former governor of Massachusetts, was in Mexico with Humphrey when Johnson made his speech:

> We arrived in Mexico City on the evening that LBJ was supposed to give a fireside chat, and we were told that dinner would be at the U.S. Embassy, that the President of Mexico and his party were coming, and that there would be one cocktail and we would go in for dinner.

We arrived promptly in order to get that cocktail and to be there in time for President Díaz Ordaz. One cocktail went to two, two went to three, three went to four, and I guess we might have had as many as six cocktails waiting for the Vice-President and for the President to get together. What had happened was that President Johnson was giving his speech withdrawing from the presidency for the 1968 campaign, and Hubert was listening to the broadcast. I know Hubert was very much moved and there were tears in his eyes when he finally came in following the speech. The U.S. television team that was with us of course crowded around him and were all interested in his reactions, which he was not then prepared to give, at least insofar as his own plans were concerned.

We went in for dinner and I sat at the same table with the Vice-President. On his right was Mrs. Díaz Ordaz, and on his left was the wife of

President Johnson announces his withdrawal from the presidential race.

> the Foreign Minister, both charming ladies but both understanding the politics of the situation. Hubert carried on as though nothing at all had happened. He was perfectly charming and delightful to each of them and really was the life of the party. All of us meanwhile were biting our fingers because we knew this put a new look into the presidential campaign and that Hubert was the logical person to run if he wanted to do so, but he refused to budge. On the plane home there was much talk of it, and I had a conversation with the then Ambassador to the OAS, later one of our negotiators for the Panama Canal treaty. We felt that if Hubert announced soon that he would be able to pick up the Democratic nomination. When we arrived home on the first of April, however, Hubert was not ready to make any announcement, and it wasn't until about the 25th of April that he did finally decide to run for the presidency.[6]

Pressure on Humphrey to announce his candidacy was immediate, but the vice-president was not ready to make a decision. Of course, Johnson's resignation had not come as a complete surprise because of the warning that Humphrey had received. In fact, there had been speculation that the president might resign at least as early as January 1967, when Max Kampelman, a Humphrey confidant, had openly discussed the possibility with a reporter. But from the actual moment of Johnson's withdrawal, Humphrey was determined to give himself a chance to sort out the situation thoroughly before he made a commitment.

While Humphrey hesitated, others were acting on his behalf. In Washington, Bill Connell, Humphrey's long-time political operative, had been unable to reach his boss in Mexico City and had acted on his own to call over a hundred political leaders across the country, asking them to stay uncommitted. As Connell made his calls, he discovered that Bobby and Teddy Kennedy were making exactly the same rounds, with the same message.

The Wisconsin primary, which had weighed so heavily on Johnson's decision, was held on April 2, two days after the president's announcement. Gene McCarthy's victory—56.2 percent of the vote to Lyndon Johnson's 34.6 percent—had been rendered meaningless, as Johnson had intended it to be, by the president's withdrawal. McCarthy had beaten a political corpse, but waiting for him at the next bend of the road was a fresh combatant, Bobby Kennedy. As McCarthy and Kennedy prepared to square off, the nation's attention was diverted by another crisis. On April 4, two days after the Wisconsin primary, Martin Luther King, Jr., was assassinated in Memphis.

Humphrey and Martin Luther King, Jr.

King's assassination was the sequel to a long series of racial disturbances in American cities. Each summer since 1965 had been marked by new battlefields in the urban war: Watts was the first black ghetto to explode in 1965; 1966 led off with a minor racial disturbance in California (only two killed this time), followed by other incidents in Washington, Omaha, Des Moines, and Chicago, adding up to a total of forty-three riots before the year was over. In 1967, there had already been fifty riots before Newark burned on July 13, the worst disturbance to date. Newark stayed at the top of the list for only ten days, until Detroit erupted on July 23, leaving a total of forty-three dead and $45 million in property damage. It had

His death is a tragedy and sorrow to his family and our nation. The criminal act that took his life brings shame to our country. An apostle of non-violence has been the victim of violence.

HUBERT H. HUMPHREY

Detroit, July 23, 1967

Corretta King at a memorial service for her husband in Memphis

taken only nine dead Americans in Pleiku to precipitate the massive retaliation and bombing raids that led into the Vietnam quagmire and divided the nation bitterly between the people and their leaders. The war in the nation's cities touched an even more sensitive nerve, dividing black and white Americans and raising another dangerous and volatile political issue, with every bit as much potential for tearing the nation apart as Vietnam.

Martin Luther King's assassination on April 4, 1968, was the signal for an uprising that spread to more than 100 cities and left thirty-nine dead. The

A mule-drawn caisson bears the body of Martin Luther King through the streets of Atlanta.

Humphrey appeared on the cover of *Time* a week after he announced his candidacy.

next night, Washington, D.C., was set afire. Machine gun emplacements were positioned on the Capitol steps, and the looting and burning came within two blocks of the White House, which was outlined in the night sky against a sea of flames.

Against this background of upheaval and madness, Humphrey announced his candidacy for the Democratic nomination on April 27. In making his announcement, he tried to reverse the dark spirit that had come over the nation and to place his candidacy squarely within the framework of optimism that had been his political trademark. As a part of this attempt, Humphrey made an offhand reference to "the politics of joy," a phrase not in the written text released to the press. In the grim world of 1968, the call for joy marked Humphrey as a Pollyanna, blind to the realities of hate and pessimism that had seized the nation. The Declaration of Independence might speak of the pursuit of happiness, Gene McCarthy might call for the "pursuit of the public happiness," but for Humphrey, an associate of Lyndon Johnson and a defender of the war, to call for happiness and joy was impermissible according to the morality of the moment.

Soon after Humphrey made his announcement, a group called United Democrats for Humphrey was formed, under the leadership of senators Walter Mondale of Minnesota and Fred Harris of Oklahoma. The group's members included such assorted figures as former President Harry Truman, who was honorary chairman; governors Bufford Ellington of Tennessee, William Guy of North Dakota, and Terry Sanford of North Carolina; representatives Hale Boggs, James O'Hara, Clement Zablocki, Chet Holifield, and Henry Gonzalez; mayors Ivan Allen of Atlanta and A. J. Cervantes of St. Louis; George Meany, head of the AFL-CIO; Frank D. O'Connor, president of the New York City Council; George Weaver, Assistant Secretary of Labor; Robert Nathan, vice chairman of the ADA (which had endorsed McCarthy, by the way); Robert Partridge, general manager of the National Rural Electric Cooperative Association; and James Farley, James H. Rowe, Willard Wertz, William Benton, Patricia Harris, and Ben Heineman. Mondale and Harris, who were far more than front men for the group, did much of the delegate hunting themselves.

The strategy of the Humphrey campaign was based on the assumption that McCarthy and Kennedy would destroy each other in the primaries and that Humphrey's best hope would be to win the nomination in the nonprimary states, which included three-fourths of the nation's total. The first primary to pit McCarthy and Kennedy against each other was the Indiana primary, held on May 7, ten days after Humphrey announced his candidacy. (The Massachusetts primary on April 30 had been uncontested; McCarthy's was the only name on the ballot.) Kennedy won decisively in Indiana, with 328,118 votes (42.2 percent) to McCarthy's 209,695 (27 percent). In fact, McCarthy finished third to Indiana Governor Roger Branigan, a favorite-son candidate who polled 238,700 (30.7 percent). McCarthy later complained, "Indiana was a prime case of what happened. Between us, Kennedy and I had 70 percent of the primary vote. Yet at the convention, McGovern got a few votes, I got a few votes. The other 80 percent of Indiana went to Humphrey."[7] A week after the Indiana contest, Kennedy beat McCarthy again in Nebraska, 84,102 (51.7 percent) to 50,655 (31.2 percent). At this point, it appeared as if McCarthy might be all through. If he could not beat Kennedy in a predominantly rural state with a liberal tradition that dated back to Senator George Norris—a state with few minorities and blue-collar workers, the great

May 12, 1968—Eugene McCarthy campaigns for the Nebraska primary.

sources of Kennedy strength—then his candidacy seemed doomed.

But on May 28 in Oregon, McCarthy caught fire again and handed the Kennedy family its first defeat in twenty-eight elections. Between Nebraska and Oregon, there had been a major shake-up at the top in McCarthy's disorganized campaign forces. The resulting improvement in their efforts made a difference, but even more important was the feverish antiwar sentiment in Oregon, which

May 27, 1968—Students at Hamline University in St. Paul wish Hubert Humphrey a happy fifty-seventh birthday.

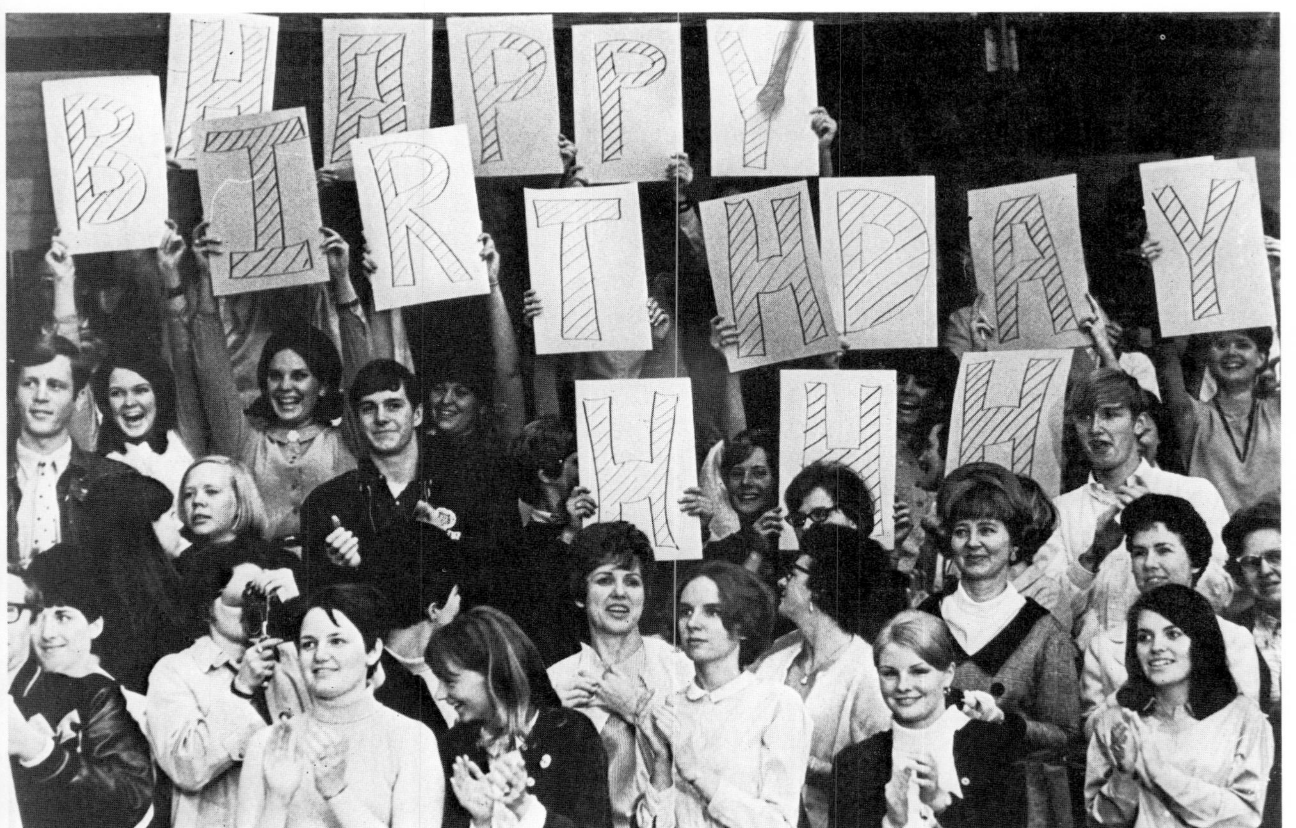

enabled McCarthy to concentrate his message on Vietnam instead of having to defend his overall voting record, as he had been forced to do earlier. McCarthy won Oregon 163,990 (43.9 percent) to Kennedy's 141,631 (37.9 percent). But his surprising victory and the sympathy that the media held for his views helped disguise the fundamental weakness of his candidacy. On the same day that McCarthy won in Oregon, George Smathers beat him in Florida, 236,242 (61.6 percent) to 147,216 (38.4 percent).

The showdown between Gene McCarthy and Bobby Kennedy was to come in California's winner-take-all primary on June 4, just a week after Oregon. Here Kennedy's charm and emotional appeal, plus the very diversity and sprawl of the enormous state, would add up to an immediate advantage over the dry, intellectual McCarthy. In California, Kennedy would not be confined to the war issue, which was somewhat less than a one-sided matter in a state that was the home of legions of retired servicemen and whose principal employer was the defense industry. Here Kennedy could expand on his civil rights theme. Campaigning in California, Kennedy toured the ghettos, and despite the rising divisiveness between black and white engendered by the riots, he sparked an enthusiasm that bordered on hysteria as crowds swarmed over his open car and reached out to touch him.

Three days before the election, a television debate took place between McCarthy and Kennedy. McCarthy, who had appeared relaxed and joking in the final moments before the crucial confronta-

Campaigning with Eugene J. McCarthy isn't like campaigning with LBJ or HHH or Barry Goldwater or Dick Nixon. It is perhaps more like campaigning for high office in Plato's Republic—except, of course, for the ineluctable vulgarities of raising money, conferring with professional pols, making the cocktail rounds and holding press conferences.

NEW YORK TIMES
JANUARY 14, 1968

The Democratic hierarchy out here [in California] is like that of the Presbyterian Church. It's pretty hard to find the hierarchy.
EUGENE McCARTHY

tion, gave one of his curiously flat, disinterested performances. When it was all over, he refused to discuss the matter: "I don't want to talk politics. I want to talk about Dante's Sixth Canto."[8] Later McCarthy came to ascribe his loss in California, not to his lackluster performance, but to the defection of some leading Democrats when Kennedy entered the race: ". . . I do think that if people like Schlesinger had said they were not going to go with Bobby—John Galbraith and Dick Goodwin, for example—then we might have won in California."[9]

When the California primary was held on June 4, the results showed Kennedy with 1,472,166 (46.2 percent), McCarthy with 1,329,301 (41.7 percent), and a no-preference slate headed by Attorney General Thomas Lynch with 380,286 (11.9 percent). The South Dakota primary, held the same day, gave Kennedy 31,826 votes (49.5 percent) and McCarthy 13,145 (20 percent). Johnson, whose name was still on the South Dakota ballot, did better than McCarthy, receiving 19,319 votes (30 percent of the total). So far, McCarthy had entered nine primaries: Massachusetts, New Hampshire, Wisconsin, Indiana, Nebraska, Oregon, Florida, California, and South Dakota. He had won only three—Massachusetts (uncontested), Wisconsin (uncontested when Johnson withdrew two days before the election), and Oregon—but in doing so he had changed the history of the country.

The night of the California primary, Humphrey had completed an exhausting day of campaigning that had begun on the East Coast and had ended in

Robert Kennedy gives his last speech.

Colorado Springs, where he was scheduled to deliver a commencement address at the Air Force Academy the next day. About one o'clock in the morning, D. J. Leary, a Humphrey aide who had been watching the California returns on television, rushed into the bedroom where Humphrey had just fallen asleep:

> He thought highly of me, he knew me, and he often had a nice word to say, but I was a long way from being able to burst into his bedroom in the night, and I just shook. "Mr. Vice President, Mr. Vice President, they hit Bobby, they hit Bobby," I shouted. He thought it was just some kind of terrible joke I was playing. I said, "They shot Senator Kennedy." And I got hold of his pajamas, and I'm leading him into the parlor out of his bedroom and turning the television set on at the same time so that it can say what I'm trying to say. "You know they shot Senator Kennedy." And he sits down there, and he's just like this, you know, "My God!"
>
> Behind me there come some Secret Service agents, and other people start to filter in. Most everyone had gone to bed, and now they're coming with more confirmation. "Ambulances on the way . . . Senator seen bleeding on the floor . . . six shots have been fired . . . they've captured the person who did it . . . Rosie Greer and Rafer Johnson were there, and they grabbed Sirhan Sirhan."
>
> It was one of the most unbelievable nights. David Gartner was there, handling the telephone, . . . and I was on occasion answering the calls. I remember one time picking up the phone and hearing the sobbing of Pierre Salinger. And I think the Vice-President talked to Pierre, and David talked to him and told him to calm down, that we'd do everything we could. . . .

The appeal of a Robert Kennedy, just as the appeal of John Lindsay, George Wallace, Eugene McCarthy or Ronald Reagan, lies not in the fact that they are Democrats or Republicans, liberals or conservatives, hawks or doves—many of their followers don't even know—but they appear as enemies of the established order, as non- or even anti-politicians who care deeply about the way things are and want to change them.

FRANK MANKIEWICZ
FORMER PRESS SECRETARY OF
ROBERT KENNEDY

In the meantime, there were two camps forming as to what Humphrey should do. Should he cancel his schedule and leave? Should he give his speech at the Air Force Academy? This is in the middle of the night, and graduation isn't until the next morning. And there's tension building, really building up. I sat down and I wrote the Vice-President a memo. My mind was kind of fuzzy, but there were some things clear to me then. "You're the Vice-President of the United States," I said, "but to the world you're a candidate for president first. You arrived not on a Vice-Presidential plane, you arrived on a campaign plane. Anything you do will be interpreted politically." I just felt this was a national tragedy, that anything could happen. . . .

Later I went up to Humphrey's room, and the Air Force men were around. Humphrey had gone back to bed for about an hour and then gotten up. He was in shaving and General McConnell had followed him into the bathroom, and he said something very close to this: "Now you're my Vice-President, and you may very well be my President, and I respect you, but I'm telling you you can't worry about a few of these people who are just going to be against you because you might go out there. These kids worked four years and they deserve to have the Vice-President of the United States give their commencement speech. They deserve this and you can't cheat them out of it. . . . You can't let those people get to you," McConnell said. "You ought to see some of the letters *I* get on Viet Nam," which was the wrong thing to say. Humphrey turned and put a steel-eyed look on him, and he said, "General, I get those letters too. I get one hell of a lot of letters." And he turned around and went into the shower. McConnell felt the intensity, and he turned around and went in the other room. Humphrey didn't give the speech.[10]

Humphrey returns to Washington after Kennedy's assassination.

Ethel and Ted Kennedy at Robert Kennedy's funeral

After Robert Kennedy was killed on the night of the California primary, the whole campaign took on a different aspect. With Kennedy dead and McCarthy no longer really caring what happened, the question was not whether Humphrey could get the nomination, but whether it would be worth anything when he did. There was one primary left, and it was held in New York state on June 18. McCarthy did better than expected, winning 62 of the state's 123 delegates, which were elected on a district-by-district basis, though the state convention later awarded the bulk of the remaining delegates to Humphrey. McCarthy's constituency had broadened and now included Kennedy supporters who saw him as the only alternative to Humphrey, still considered the embodiment of the Johnson war policies. Some of Kennedy's minority constituency also went over to McCarthy, and polls showed him leading Humphrey in a number of states. Yet McCarthy himself had gone into one of his blue funks. He had resumed campaigning June 12, after announcing that he would conduct a "limited campaign"[11] and that he would not ask for the support of delegates who had not decided between him and Humphrey. He had refused to campaign at all in the New York primary and had avoided contacting several governors who had let it be known they were considering supporting him. To make matters worse, McCarthy discussed publicly going to Paris to play a role in the Vietnam peace negotiations. Since the United States had negotiators in Paris, the added presence of a presidential candidate with his own set of proposals would have divided and weakened efforts to achieve peace. While McCarthy's behavior had become patently inconsistent with winning the nomination, it was perfectly consistent with the reactions of a man trying to escape the responsibilities of leadership. In yet another cry for help, he dismissed the Russian invasion of Czechoslovakia on August 20, a week before the Democratic Convention began, saying "I do not see this as a major world crisis"[12] and criticizing Johnson for calling a midnight meeting of the National Security Council. McCarthy was finally dragooned into issuing a statement that he regarded the invasion as "a cruel and violent action."[13]

"Once Bobby was killed, why it was bound to be Humphrey,"[14] insisted McCarthy, but he was obviously afraid that he might somehow be proved wrong.

After Kennedy's death, Humphrey, like McCarthy, had put a brief moratorium on his campaign. He returned to active campaigning on June 20 in an appearance before the National Press Club in Washington. Humphrey did not mention the war in his prepared remarks. A few days earlier he had been ready to make a speech on the war that would have called for a bombing halt and a cease-fire. Wanting to be certain his remarks would not harm the prospects for peace, Humphrey decided first to check with Averell Harriman and Cyrus Vance, the two chief United States negotiators in Paris. President Johnson's position was that to call for a bombing halt was to throw away a trump in the Paris negotiations. If Harriman and Vance concurred, then Humphrey was willing to drop the speech. The two negotiators could give Humphrey no encouragement, for though they, too, were in

I know that, as president, Hubert would have stopped the Vietnam War in 1969. He told me he would have appointed Clark Clifford as Secretary of State, and Clifford's views on ending the war were well known. Under Hubert's leadership, I feel sure we could have negotiated a responsible settlement at that time when we had 500,000 troops in Vietnam. His election would have avoided the extended tragedy of the Vietnam War as well as Watergate. In addition, I believe that period would have been a time of economic and social progress under an irresistibly optimistic, wise, and determined president.

AVERELL HARRIMAN

favor of a bombing halt, they were in no position to embarrass the president, and, knowing Johnson's mood, they feared that Humphrey's proposed speech might make him all the more belligerent. Their hope was to persuade Johnson privately to accept a bombing halt. Humphrey, faced with the knowledge that his action might harm his nation's chance for peace, withdrew the speech. Speaking later of the incident, Chester Cooper, a special assistant to Harriman at the Paris talks, said of Humphrey, "America has been blessed with few statesmen during the last several decades, but on occasion, a politician makes a genuinely statesman-like move."[15]

In the speech that Humphrey did make to the National Press Club, he tried to put some daylight between himself and Johnson by emphasizing that if he were elected president, he would be his own man: "One does not repudiate his family in order to establish his own identity. . . . I have not asked my son to live my life, but to live his own life. The President has not asked me to live his Administration if I have a Humphrey Administration. . . . If I'm permitted to be president, I'll be president. . . . Every conductor makes his own music, even from the same score and with the same musicians. . . . Hubert Humphrey as Vice-President is a member of a team; Hubert Humphrey as President is captain of a team. There's a lot of difference."[16]

The task of drawing away from Johnson's position was made more ticklish as a result of a minor flap that had emerged a few days before Humphrey's National Press Club speech. Bill Moyers, a former presidential press secretary-turned-newspa-

Most of us believe we are now following the policy that would have been followed if Barry Goldwater had been elected. In fact, we are carrying out not the policy of Barry Goldwater but the policy the Republicans have tried to put forth for 20 years. Really, the dead hand of John Foster Dulles is writing the history of tomorrow.
EUGENE McCARTHY

perman, had said Humphrey was taking two positions on Vietnam, one publicly and another privately. Humphrey had denied the charge, saying, "I can stand people opposing me because they think I am wrong, even stupid, but I will not have anyone oppose me because I am a hypocrite."[17]

Humphrey's attempts to stress his willingness to change the course of Vietnam policy if he were elected were too subtle and finely drawn to distinguish his position from Johnson's. Polls continued to show McCarthy as the stronger candidate, and Humphrey was finally persuaded that only by making a major break with the administration would he be able to pull the party together. With the convention only two weeks away and Richard Nixon newly selected as the Republican nominee, Humphrey flew down to Texas on August 9 to show Johnson the draft of a speech that called for an immediate bombing halt in North Vietnam.

Though Lyndon Johnson had not been a candidate for over four months and was now a lame-duck president, he was still a powerful force in the Democratic Party. Johnson controlled every important facet of the convention that would begin in Chicago on August 26. The site for the convention had been selected by the president. Humphrey's support in the vital Southern delegations came only with Johnson's approval. The podium at the convention would be controlled by men selected by Johnson, and they would be able to shut off any speech from the floor with the flick of a switch. Access to the visitors' galleries would be in the hands of Johnson's operatives; to get tickets for the Humphrey family, Humphrey's son-in-law had to

A social interlude during Humphrey's visit to the LBJ ranch on August 9, 1968

stand in line each morning at the headquarters of the Johnson ticket man. Lyndon Johnson might not be coming to the convention, but he wouldn't be absent either.

When Humphrey presented the draft of his speech to the president, Johnson made it clear that the speech was unacceptable and that, were Humphrey to give it, Johnson not only would have to oppose him publicly but would also have to label him as disrupting the negotiations for peace in Paris, where, he claimed, a breakthrough was imminent. An additional threat hanging over Humphrey's head was a rumor gathering force among leading Democrats that Johnson might just decide to get back in the race after all and to accept a draft from the Democratic Convention. This might be the only way he could prevent the nomination from being fought over by two candidates both of whom rejected the policies that Johnson had sacrificed the presidency to preserve.

Humphrey left the Johnson ranch knowing that there was no way he could give the speech calling for an immediate bombing halt and win the nomination. And only if he could win the nomination could he unite the party and defeat Richard Nixon.

chapter 16

CHICAGO

"If I had kids of my own, I wouldn't know how to explain it. We nominated a man for president with the Army in the middle of Michigan Avenue."

Demonstrator at the Chicago Convention

Richard Daley

The 5,611 delegates who came to the 1968 Democratic Convention in Chicago were asked to travel from their downtown hotels to the International Amphitheatre, the convention site, along a four-mile "approved route" that was festooned by banners reading "Welcome Delegates, Richard J. Daley, Mayor." Also on hand to welcome the delegates were the 11,900 members of the Chicago police force, who would work in twelve-hour shifts throughout the convention, 4,649 members of the Illinois National Guard called up by Governor Sam Shapiro ("an ounce of prevention is worth a pound of cure," said Mayor Daley[1]), and 2,000 plainclothesmen, federal marshals, and FBI men flown in from around the country. Augmenting these forces were 5,000 combat-ready troops from Fort Hood who had recently undergone intensive riot-control training in an exercise called "Operation Jackson Park," named after the troop bivouac during the riots in Chicago that had followed the assassination of Martin Luther King in April. Flying into the city on Sunday, August 25, in their C-141 transports, the soldiers unloaded their jeeps and quarter-ton cargo carriers and trucks. Looking around, some of them noticed that Hubert Humphrey's plane had landed at the airport about the same time. "It's kind of funny all the troops coming in over here and Humphrey landing over there,"[2] one soldier said.

In addition to the soldiers, police, and guardsmen, there were other security measures, including a contingent of 200 firemen with fire-fighting equipment stationed in and around the amphitheatre area and a special portico constructed at the building's delegate entrance to protect against sniper fire. As a final precaution, all the manhole covers near the amphitheatre had been sealed off with tar to deny the use of the sewers to potential evildoers.

All these preparations, the most elaborate for any convention in the Democratic Party's history, were undertaken in order to counteract the efforts that the antiwar forces would make to disrupt the gathering in Chicago. The National Mobilization Committee to End the War in Vietnam, under the leadership of Dave Dellinger, Tom Hayden, and Rennie Davis, had arranged antiwar demonstrations the previous year in Washington and New York that had involved hundreds of thousands of dissenters. The demonstration planned for Chicago was to be the biggest protest yet, attracting not only antiwar activists but also hippies, new leftists, Yippies, and other hangers-on. No one had a really sound estimate of how many demonstrators there would be in all, but the organizers hoped the total would come to well over 100,000. It didn't. There were only about 25,000 protesters in all. But that proved to be enough.

Demonstrators and delegates were converging on a city that had been chosen as the convention site by President Lyndon Johnson. Johnson had selected Chicago at the urging of Mayor Daley, who wanted to show the nation the progress that the city had made under his leadership since the last Democratic Convention held there in 1956, a year after Daley's first election as mayor. The time of the convention had been scheduled long before Johnson had announced his withdrawal. Because a

Some of the 25,000 protesters at the Democratic National Convention

short campaign is thought to work to the advantage of an incumbent, the dates selected were the closest to the election of any Democratic Convention in history. The Republican candidate, Richard Nixon, would have five extra weeks to organize his presidential campaign and unify his own party—time that would not be available to the Democratic nominee.

Hubert Humphrey had wanted the convention to be held in Miami, where logistics made the inevitable demonstrations easier to control and

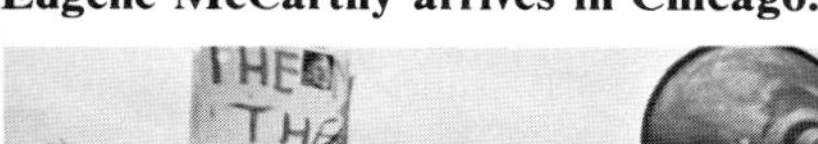

Eugene McCarthy arrives in Chicago.

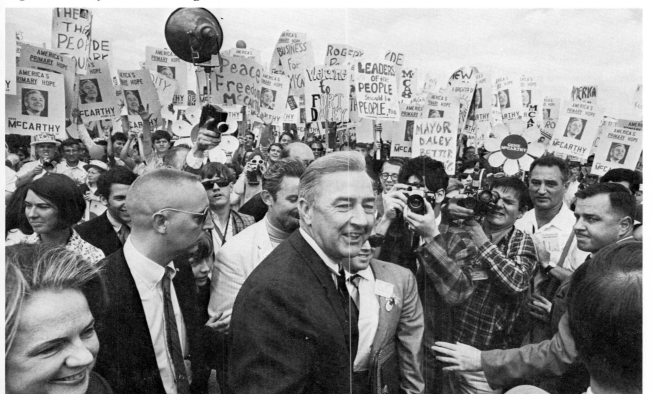

where television equipment and other media apparatus would already be in place from the Republican Convention held earlier in the month. But Johnson refused to change. He was not about to break his word to Daley in order to switch the convention to a site in a state controlled by a Republican governor. Accepting the inevitable, Humphrey wrote Daley trying to persuade him to set aside a special area where the demonstrations could take place. Daley never answered—he would run his own city without any help from Hubert Humphrey. But the mayor's elaborate security measures made it clear that he did not expect a peaceful convention.

By the time of the convention, there were other factors adding to the potential for chaos: Chicago was experiencing transit, telephone, and electricians' strikes; the Russians had precipitated an international crisis by invading Czechoslovakia; the *Chicago Tribune* had reported a plot to assassinate Humphrey and Eugene McCarthy, which it attributed to black extremists; a former president of the United States, Dwight Eisenhower, appeared to be dying, which, if it happened during the convention, would add a further element of uncertainty; and the current president of the United States not only had refused to say whether he would attend his party's convention but also seemed to be having a last minute change of heart about withdrawing from the race. Or so it seemed to many of the delegates and alternates who had been sent a copy of "To Heal and to Build," a collection of Johnson's speeches and statements, shortly before the convention.

There had already been some late entries in the presidential contest. Georgia Governor Lester Maddox had announced his candidacy a few days before the convention and seemed to be enjoying the Secret Service protection that his new status conferred. A more serious effort to secure the Democratic nomination had been launched two weeks earlier by Senator George McGovern. McGovern's candidacy had attracted some members

George McGovern (right) **joins the other presidential candidates.**

of the old Kennedy phalanx, who had not forgiven Gene McCarthy for his harsh remarks during Bobby Kennedy's last campaign. Humphrey hoped that McGovern might provide a bridge to the antiwar elements once the convention was over, but there was a possibility that the McGovern candidacy might be nothing more than a holding action for Edward Kennedy, who was sitting out the convention in mourning for his brother but who would possibly be available for a draft.

The chance of a last-minute Kennedy candidacy sweeping the convention on a wave of sympathy for Edward Kennedy's two martyred brothers was a genuine threat to Humphrey's nomination. Yet if Humphrey were to try to appease the Kennedy constituency with the only appeal that might work, breaking publicly with Johnson on the war, it was a certainty that the president would retaliate by destroying Humphrey's candidacy. Without the support of the Johnson-controlled delegations in Texas and the South and with Mayor Daley and the Illinois delegation still uncommitted, Humphrey would not have the votes to ensure the nomination.

The convention seemed to be headed for a fierce struggle over the presidential nomination, but before the Democrats could get down to the business of selecting their national ticket, two crucial issues had to be dealt with: the seating of delegates and the party platform on the Vietnam War. The issue of seating and delegate selection was tackled first, and significant changes were made in the traditional procedures; the unit rule, the method by which the majority of a delegation controls the

In the years that I knew Hubert Humphrey, it was difficult at times to reconcile my views on national policy with his. But somehow Hubert was different from others who advocate a broader role for the federal government. I think it was because of his concept of political power. It was his eternal hope that federal action should not mean the

On the floor of the convention

expansion of power for the sake of power itself. He believed in government with a heart. This is his legacy to America after a lifetime devoted to public service. A partisan without venom and an advocate without arrogance, he gave all he had to the American political system. Our country is the better for it.

JOHN CONNALLY

vote of the whole delegation, was abolished not only for future conventions but for the 1968 convention as well. The issue was fiercely contested, with Texas Governor John Connally leading the Southern opposition and hinting that his delegation might draft Lyndon Johnson if the unit rule were abolished. Opposition was quelled, however, when both the Humphrey and the McCarthy forces united to force the change. In another credentials fight, Mississippi's regular delegation to the convention was barred, and a bi-racial delegation, including many blacks who had struggled for years to take their places as delegates, was seated. Even more importantly, a procedure was agreed upon for establishing guidelines to insure the representation of minorities and women at future Democratic conventions. Out of that process came the Reform Commission, later placed in the hands of Senator George McGovern, who would use it to great advantage in winning delegates in 1972.

As expected, the Vietnam plank in the platform became the major issue of the Democratic Convention. The moral dilemma created by the war came close to destroying the Democratic Party as the delegates attempted to decide whether it was more immoral to jeopardize American troops and abandon traditional support of the nation's leaders in wartime or to continue to contribute to the deaths of innocent people by supporting a war that the United States had no business fighting. It was a dilemma that seemingly gripped many other Americans. Polls taken at the time of the convention showed that while 53 percent of the American people felt that the United States had made a

Vietnam—the major issue of the Democratic Convention

mistake in sending troops to fight in Vietnam, 61 percent opposed a bombing halt. The majority of America seemed to be saying, "Vietnam was a mistake, but keep on bombing anyway," an attitude shared by many delegates at the Democratic Convention.

Even before the convention had gotten underway, the committee responsible for drawing up the platform had begun wrestling with the Vietnam issue. Its members had heard testimony from Gene McCarthy, Edmund Muskie, Edward Kennedy, Clark Kerr, and other Democratic doves, who proposed a plank that would call for an unconditional bombing halt, de-escalation, and mutual withdrawal by both sides. Rather than demanding a coalition government, the plank required that the South Vietnamese negotiate with the National Liberation Front concerning the makeup of the government. There seemed to be considerable support for such a plank, but any real possibility of its acceptance was summarily quashed on August 19, when Lyndon Johnson, speaking at a Veterans of Foreign Wars Convention, announced that he would make no further move toward de-escalating the war until the North Vietnamese began de-escalation. Hale Boggs, Johnson's hand-picked Platform Committee chairman, got the message; he recessed the hearings and called a special committee session for the next evening that would be addressed by Secretary of State Dean Rusk.

By adhering to the Johnson line, Boggs gave Hubert Humphrey little opportunity to achieve his goal of forging a compromise with the antiwar delegates. Humphrey had prepared a draft of his

I have always felt myself that the chances were about 50-50 as between a negotiated settlement and a simple withering away of the violence.

DEAN RUSK

own, which he hoped would be the basis for a compromise plank. It called for a bombing halt and included a provision that such a step should take into account the potential risk to American troops but that the absence of any risk should not be required as a precondition. Humphrey's draft also proposed that South Vietnam negotiate with Hanoi and its allies for withdrawal of troops. The phrase "and its allies," which could be construed to include the National Liberation Front, met with administration disapproval, as did some other refinements designed to bridge the dispute between the administration and its critics.

Despite having cleared his draft with Dean Rusk and Walt Rostow, a Johnson advisor, Humphrey soon learned that his attempt at a compromise had left Johnson himself unmoved. The president continued to press for his version of the plank, summoning Boggs to Washington, ostensibly for a

Those who disagree with the conduct of the Vietnam war include persons who are not iconoclasts, fuzzy theorists or summer patriots, but men of talent, who want to change our national policies in order to preserve our country's future.
HAROLD E. HUGHES

Hale Boggs

briefing on the crisis in Czechoslovakia but in reality to be instructed by General William Westmoreland that an unconditional bombing halt was a "sophisticated fiction." Johnson also dispatched Charles Murphy, a former chairman of the Civil Aeronautics Board, to Chicago to see that his wishes were carried out. Establishing himself in Suite 1221A of the Conrad Hilton, twelve floors below Humphrey's headquarters, Murphy asked to see Humphrey's draft and made it clear that the compromise plank had to be replaced by the administration version.

Finally, responding to Johnson's demands, the Platform Committee rejected all conflicting positions and produced a plank that stated unequivocally, "We reject as unacceptable a unilateral withdrawal" and added, "We strongly support the Paris talks and applaud the initiative of President Johnson which brought Vietnam to the peace table." The administration plank called for a bombing halt "when this action would not endanger our troops in the field" and specified that any cessation of bombing "should take into account the response from Hanoi."

On Monday afternoon, August 26, the members of the Platform Committee obediently affirmed the administration proposal by a two-to-one margin. The Vietnam plank was ready to go to the floor.

The day after the Vietnam plank was finished, an interview appeared in the *New York Times* in which Lyndon Johnson stated publicly for the first time that he hoped the nomination would go to Humphrey because he had supported the adminis-

One of Humphrey's closest friends was Freddie Gates. I loved that guy, but he could be quite a pain at times. He kept track of every penny for Humphrey. During the Democratic convention in 1968, I remember being at the Conrad Hilton in Humphrey's room. I had already contributed about a million dollars to the campaign, but every time I wanted to make a telephone call out of the room, Freddie Gates would say, "Put a quarter in the dish, put a quarter in the dish." Well, I did it three or four times, but finally I said to Freddie, "You just go to—" Well, you know what I said, and that was the end of my having to put a quarter in the dish. But when I stopped to think about it, not only had I given Humphrey a million bucks, but the calls from the room didn't even cost a quarter.

JENO PAULUCCI

tration's Vietnam policy. Johnson strongly suggested that those who would offer more concessions to North Vietnam—meaning Kennedy, McGovern, and McCarthy—were only prolonging the war by reinforcing Viet Cong intransigence at the bargaining table. In another effort to help Humphrey, Johnson put pressure on the Southern delegates, who were still smarting over the abolition of the unit rule and were ready to climb on a "Draft Teddy Kennedy" bandwagon that had been formed by Jesse Unruh of California and encouraged by Mayor Daley. With the Southerners back in line and with Johnson now openly supporting him, Humphrey was finally sure that the nomination would be his.

As the time for the nomination drew closer, the tempo in the streets of Chicago began to quicken.

Some confrontations and incidents had already taken place. On Saturday the 24th, before the convention had begun, the dissidents had heard speeches from the Reverend Jesse Jackson and Harry Belafonte protesting the use of federal troops. Belafonte said the troops were in Chicago to intimidate and provoke blacks. On Sunday there had been some violence when the police made a sweep of Lincoln Park and arrested Tom Hayden. Monday, August 26, there were demonstrations for the release of Hayden; the police used tear gas and broke through the protesters' barricades. Forty people were injured and fifty-five arrested. Among the estimated 3,000 protesters—some waving Viet Cong flags and peace flags, others shouting obscenities and "Kill the Pigs"—was Allen Ginsberg, who had risen to prominence in the fifties as a

"Beat Generation" poet. Also in the crowd that was demonstrating for the release of Tom Hayden was Tom Hayden himself, who had been let out of jail that afternoon, only to be arrested for the second time in twelve hours and then released again. During the remainder of the convention he moved about in disguise, wearing one outfit that included a woman's wig, a moustache and beard, and pink sunglasses.

During the demonstration on Monday, one youngster called to a policeman, "Why don't you go home to your wife and kids." "While you still have them," another added.

"Why don't we go up and clear them out," the policeman said under his breath.[3]

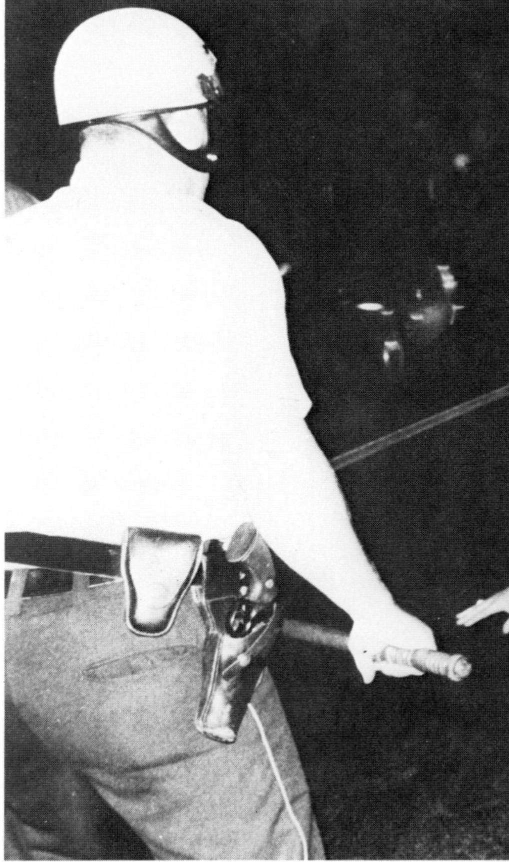

The next day, Tuesday the 27th, violence continued on the streets while the delegates at the convention wrangled over the party platform. Twenty-one reporters claimed that they had been assaulted and that the attackers had been policemen who had removed their badges and nameplates so they couldn't be later identified. The police had seemed to make a point of singling out reporters, who in each case had identified themselves as press. When asked about the attacks, Mayor Daley said that he was investigating and that any misconduct would bring a reprimand. Other clubbings occurred as police chanting "Kill, kill, kill" and using tear gas and night sticks marched into Lincoln Park and cleared out several thousand protesters, driving them into the streets. On Tuesday the 27th, an unbirthday party for Lyndon Johnson was held, attended by thousands of young people who chanted "I ain't marching anymore." Folk-singer

Phil Ochs sang, "It's always the old who lead us to war/It's always the young who fall." Writer Jean Genet spoke, calling the Chicago police "mad dogs."[4] At the convention, Dan Rather, a CBS television reporter, was punched in the stomach and pushed to the ground by a security guard. The incident was seen by millions of viewers.

On Wednesday night, the Vietnam plank was brought to the floor of the convention and passed by an unsurprising majority of 1,567¾ votes to 1,041¼. During the nominating speeches that followed, Mayor Daley, seated up front at the head of the Illinois delegation, was denounced from the speaker's platform by Senator Abraham Ribicoff, who was nominating George McGovern. The Connecticut senator said that there had been incidents of "gestapo tactics in the streets of Chicago."[5] Daley cupped his hand over his mouth and shouted back at Ribicoff, but the mayor's voice was lost in a sea of noise.

Out in the streets, police and National Guardsmen were battering protesters in downtown Chicago. Over one hundred people were injured, including twenty-five policemen; one hundred seventy-eight were arrested. Young demonstrators who broke out of the cordon surrounding the Grant Park area in an attempt to reach the convention site were driven back by clubs, rifle butts, and mace.

"How hard it is to accept the truth," said Ribicoff from the platform of the convention hall.[6]

A group of policemen charged the barricades surrounding the Hilton Hotel and shoved bystanders against the windows, splintering the glass and

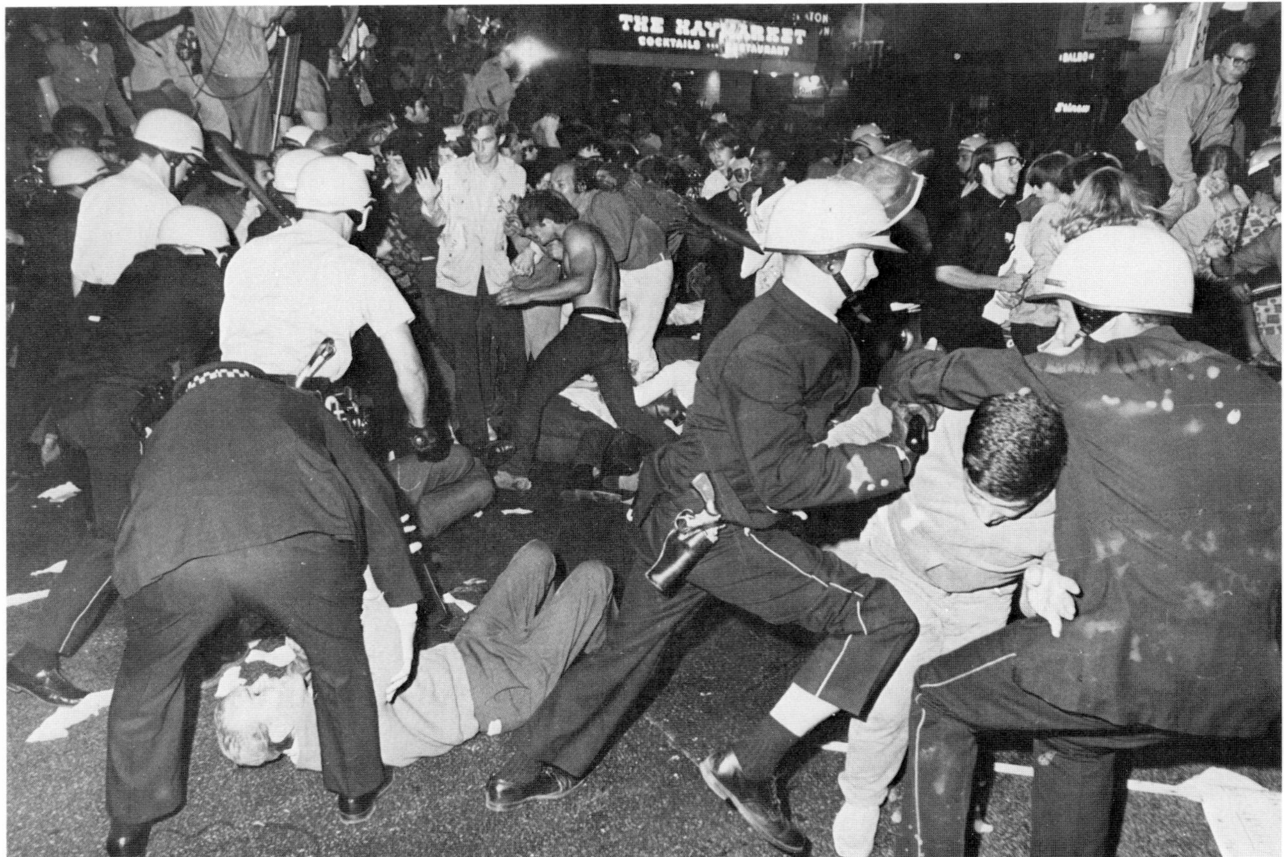

Police battle with demonstrators in front of the Haymarket Lounge.

sending people hurtling through the shards into the hotel restaurant, the Haymarket Lounge. Police then ran into the restaurant, beat up some of those who had fallen through the windows, and arrested them. Other policemen were clubbing demonstrators in the streets, in full view of television cameras and spectators looking out of the hotel windows.

At the convention, Hubert Humphrey's name was placed in nomination by Joseph Alioto, mayor of San Francisco.

In the streets outside the hotel where the spectators had been pushed through the window, reporters counted over two dozen shoes, women's purses, and other items of clothing, scattered for two blocks in each direction. Other observers saw a young news photographer who ran into the street, his hands covering his head, shouting "Press, Press, Press" as he was being clubbed to the

Much of the raging melee outside was visible from his suite, although it was about 20 stories below. I remember he insisted on leaning out the open window to get a better view of the battling cops and students, and the tear gas that floated in through the window engulfed us all. Humphrey stood shaking his head sadly, a look of incredulity on his face, saying over and over, "No, no, no."

ISABELLE SHELTON
WASHINGTON STAR
JANUARY 22, 1978

At the 1968 Democratic National Convention—as youthful anti-war activists chanted "Dump the Hump"—the late Senator Paul Douglas, then 76 years old, sat with the Illinois delegation. Suddenly he clutched his chest in agony. Turning to a friend, he gasped that he was having a heart attack. The friend told Douglas not to worry: he would be rushed immediately to a waiting ambulance. "No," Douglas answered. "I'm not leaving until I vote for Hubert Humphrey."

ROGER SIMON
CHICAGO SUN-TIMES

ground. As he was dragged off, he asked, "What did I do? What did I do?"

"If you don't know you shouldn't be a photographer," was the answer.[7]

Meanwhile, the delegates at the convention were casting their votes for the Democratic presidential candidate. When the roll of the states was called for the counting of ballots, the votes of the Pennsylvania delegation gave Humphrey the total he needed for the nomination. "Pennsylvania started it and Pennsylvania put us over,"[8] said Humphrey as he watched the convention from his hotel suite.

Exuberant, he jumped up and kissed Mrs. Fred Harris, who was watching with him; then, seeing Muriel's face flash on the screen, he went and gave the television image a quick kiss.

Outside the convention hall, the violence and the rhetoric continued. A minister, the Reverend John Bayles, was arrested and charged with breach of the peace when he protested the clubbing of a girl he knew from the McCarthy staff. "They were beating her on the head with clubs and I yelled 'Don't hit a woman!' At that point, I was slugged in the stomach and grabbed by a cop who arrested me."[9]

Allen Ginsberg, speaking to a crowd, said, "I lost my voice chanting in the park the last few nights. The best strategy for you in cases of hysteria, overexcitement, or fear is to chant 'Om.' It helps quell flutterings or butterflies in the belly. Join me now as I try to lead you."[10]

Norman Mailer made a speech in which he said, "I'm a little sick about all of this and also a little mad. I've got a deadline on a long piece and I'm not going to go out marching and get arrested. I just came here to salute all of you."[11]

Dick Gregory also had words of praise for the protesters. "You just have to look around you at all the police and soldiers to know you must be doing something right."[12]

A doctor reported, "I was hit and pushed by a cop while I was coming back from dinner, while wearing my white coat and red cross. When a friend said I was a doctor, the cop said, 'I don't give a damn.' "[13]

One black, seeing the police beating up the

My differences with Hubert over the Vietnam War began to develop slowly, and in discussions with him, he told me many times that he wished he could take a different course other than having to support the President's position. . . . Our differences finally caused me to lend my support in the 1968 convention to Eugene McCarthy and later to nominate Eugene McCarthy for president, all of which was very trying for me in my relationship with Mr. Humphrey and his staff. Hubert himself was always very courteous and friendly, an ever-forgiving man. Immediately after the convention was over, we were great friends and if he ever held any ill-will because of it, it certainly was never apparent to me or any of my friends.

HAROLD E. HUGHES

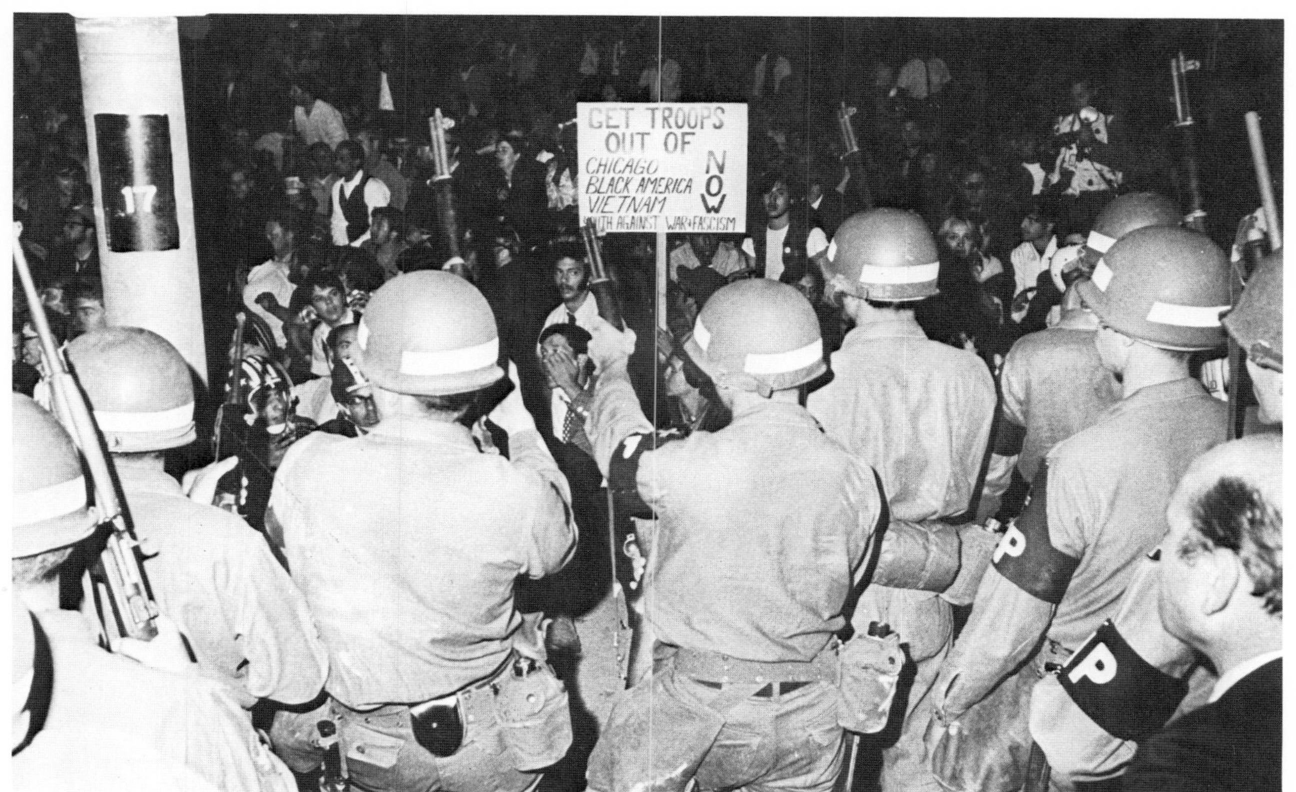

rioters, commented, "I'm so glad it's the white ones out there raising hell."[14]

When the roll call of states was completed at the convention, the final vote showed Humphrey with 1,760¼, McCarthy with 601, and McGovern with 146½. The next night, before an estimated eighty-nine million Americans watching on television, Hubert Humphrey would accept his party's nomination for president and begin the campaign he had worked toward for a lifetime. This night, twenty-five floors beneath him on the streets of Chicago, as those same eighty-nine million watched, Humphrey's chance of winning the election was slipping away.

Day after day during the convention, a juxtaposition of incongruous images had flashed across the television screen and into the nation's consciousness: a smiling, jubilant Humphrey enjoying the greatest moment of his political career, then scenes of riot and mayhem; Humphrey jumping up from his chair with a whoop, a young girl being beaten to the ground; Humphrey kissing an image on the

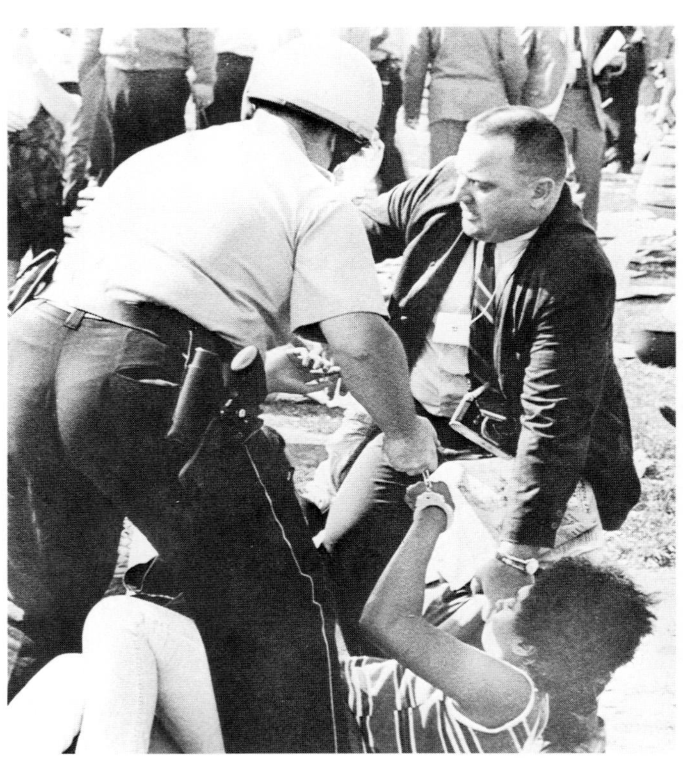

"A juxtaposition of incongruous images . . ."

television set, a minister, his head covered with blood, being dragged to the paddy wagon by two burly cops. Perhaps the most emotional and sensitive man ever to seek the presidency, Humphrey was incapable of suppressing a moment's pleasure at receiving his party's nomination or of hiding his optimism that at last he might have the opportunity to change the conditions that created the riots in the streets below. Yet his exuberance, seen against a background of tragedy, had a devastating impact. Humphrey was made to appear indifferent to the suffering going on about him, so self-involved

Not too long ago when I came back from Vietnam, somebody reported that I was "exuberant" over the prospects there. What nonsense! Who could come back from that tragic scene and be exuberant? . . . *Nobody wants to see this war in Vietnam come to an end any quicker than I do, so that we can bring our boys back home. What I'd really like to see in Vietnam is a cease-fire so that we can have peace while we talk peace.*

HUBERT H. HUMPHREY

with his personal triumph that nothing could penetrate his bubble of happiness, his politics of joy.

Humphrey was sharply aware that this was the picture that had gone out to the nation, and he was furious. "We're going to win," he said. "We have to. But that instrument there—if that instrument would stop playing up the kooks and rioters, they put them on only when the cops are fighting with them; that instrument just recruits trouble."[15] "I'm going to be president someday. I'm going to appoint the FCC—we're going to look into all this,"[16] said Humphrey, enraged as NBC switched from Carl Stokes' seconding of his nomination to scenes of carnage. A day after his nomination, Humphrey remarked bitterly that the real beneficiary of the conflict was far removed from the battlefield; Richard Nixon would eventually be the one to profit from the madness in the streets of Chicago.

But Humphrey had no time to brood over the events of the last few days or worry about the future. He had an immediate job, and that was to unite the two factions of the Democratic Party. First he tried one of the traditional methods, the selection of a vice-presidential candidate from the losing side at the convention. Humphrey had long wanted Edward Kennedy as his running mate, but Kennedy had repeatedly refused. Now George McGovern took himself out of the running. Eugene McCarthy was still completely estranged; he had not even indicated that he would support Humphrey, and in fact there was much talk of his running as an independent candidate. Finally Humphrey turned to a supporter and fellow senator, Edmund Muskie of Maine. Though a political unknown from a small state, with few geographic, ideological, or ethnic assets to bring to the ticket other than his Catholicism, the choice of tall, craggy-faced Ed Muskie was a wise one. Muskie proved to be a great benefit to the Democrats, presenting a sharp contrast to the Republican candidate, Spiro T. Agnew of Maryland, who brought geographic and ethnic balance to the ticket but ran an inept campaign.

I didn't say I wouldn't go into ghetto areas. I've been in many of them, and to some extent I would have to say this, if you've seen one city slum, you've seen them all.

SPIRO T. AGNEW

Mr. Nixon's first decision.

Spiro T. Agnew

In 1962, he began his elective career as County Executive of Baltimore County (not including the City of Baltimore), after several years of local prominence as member of a zoning board, president of a junior high school P.T.A. and active Kiwanis.

In 1966, he became the Governor of Maryland.

Mr. Humphrey's first decision.

Edmund S. Muskie

In 1946 he was elected to the Maine House of Representatives.

Re-elected in 1948 and 1950.

Served as Minority Leader of the Democrats in the Maine House of Representatives from 1949 through 1951.

Director of the state's Office of Price Stabilization from 1951 through 1952.

Democratic National Committeeman from Maine from 1952 through 1956.

In 1954, Mr. Muskie became Maine's first Democratic Governor in 20 years.

In 1956, he was re-elected Governor.

In 1958, he became the first popularly elected Democratic Senator in Maine's history.

Re-elected to the U.S. Senate in 1964.

Member of the Senate Committees on Public Works, Banking and Currency, Government Operations and the Special Committee on Aging.

Chairman of Inter-governmental Relations Subcommittee and generally recognized as one of the country's outstanding authorities on federal-state-municipal relations.

Hubert blows a kiss to Muriel before beginning his acceptance speech.

After selecting his running mate, Humphrey turned his attention to the acceptance speech he was to deliver Thursday evening, August 29. The evening began inauspiciously with a confrontation between the occupants of the galleries and the delegates on the floor of the convention. Mayor Daley, angered at being depicted as the villain in the drama unfolding about him, had filled the galleries with a claque of his party faithful—the precinct captains and city workers who were the cogs and wheels in the Daley Machine. Overflowing the balconies, rising and waving their "We Love Mayor Daley" placards on cue, they were silenced only when a memorial film tribute to Bobby Kennedy was shown. After the film the "We Love Mayor Daley" chant began again, evoking a counter-offensive from the floor, which, no one knows why, took the form of singing "The Battle Hymn of the Republic," that great Protestant hymn and Republican call to arms. Two hours later the convention was finally brought to order so that it could hear the address of its nominee for president.

Battered, exhausted, struggling to overcome the aura of violence that hung over the convention, searching for the words that would spark some hope for victory, Humphrey came to the platform to accept the nomination of his party. He began by acknowledging with sadness the brutal events that had disrupted the convention, and he recited the prayer of St. Francis of Assisi in a plea for healing and peace: "Where there is hatred, let me sow love. Where there is injury, pardon. Where there is doubt, faith. Where there is despair, hope. Where there is darkness, light." Then Humphrey called the roll of the Democratic Party's greats; not ducking Lyndon Johnson, he boomed out the name, the first time that the president of the United States had been mentioned from the speaker's podium since the opening night of the convention. The response was a mixed chorus of cheers and boos, but Humphrey courageously continued, "I truly believe that history will surely record the greatness of his contribution to the people of this land, and tonight to you, Mr. President, I say thank you. Thank you, Mr. President."

Continuing his speech, Humphrey touched on the subject of Vietnam: "If there is any one lesson that we should have learned, it is that the policies of tomorrow need not be limited by the policies of yesterday. My fellow Americans, if it becomes my high honor to serve as president, . . . I shall apply that lesson to search for peace in Vietnam. . . ." Finally, he concluded by addressing himself to the nation: "Put aside recrimination and dissension. Turn away from violence and hatred. Believe—believe in what America can do and believe in what America can be. . . . With the help of the vast, unfrightened, dedicated, faithful majority of Americans, I say to this great convention tonight and to this great nation of ours, I am ready to lead the country."[17]

At about the same time that Humphrey began his acceptance speech, the first cannisters of tear gas were thrown into the crowds in the street. More than 150 people were arrested from among the 3,000 who were stopped by the National Guard as they marched toward the amphitheatre. In an-

It was almost 4 a.m. on that tumultuous night in August 1968, and as I stood in the middle of a frenetic hotel ballroom in Chicago—tear gas wafting in the windows, police sirens wailing endlessly on Michigan Avenue below, chants of "Dump the Hump" cascading from Grant Park across the street—it seemed clear to all but his most devout acolytes that this was the end, not the beginning, of Hubert Humphrey's elusive quest for the Presidency.

But there on a small platform directly in front of me stood Hubert Humphrey, his ruddy face crisscrossed in smiles from the oversize forehead to the Bob Hope chin, preaching to the often disappointed faithful the politics of joy and the gospel of victory in November. Even for Humphrey, who could make Pollyanna look like a worrywart, the exuberance appeared ill-timed and out of place. Nudging one of Hubert's aides standing nearby, I asked: "Al, Hubert doesn't really mean all that stuff, does he?" The aide leaned over and whispered: "If you think that, then you don't know the man. Hubert always means it."

MEL ELFIN
NEWSWEEK
JANUARY 23, 1978

A truck spews out tear gas in Grant Park.

other skirmish, police stormed McCarthy's fifteenth floor headquarters in the Conrad Hilton and beat up the people they found there, claiming they had been throwing trash out the window. The marching, rioting, and beating continued through the night.

Humphrey's speech on Thursday evening

marked the end of the 1968 Democratic National Convention. For those who had been in Chicago and had witnessed the events that took place there, memories of the convention faded very slowly. In 1978, two men—lifelong friends, both lawyers, both delegates from Minnesota, the state that produced the party's two leading candidates for president—remembered what they had seen and heard. Ed Schwartzbauer was a McCarthy delegate:

> In the beginning, everything seemed to be going very well for McCarthy, we thought. The young people in Chicago had decorated all the light posts downtown with the famous McCarthy flower symbol. That kind of thing seemed to be everywhere you turned—everything was all McCarthy. There were movie stars in town, people like Dinah Shore, Paul Newman, and Joanne Woodward, doing free

t wasn't McCarthy who brought he students back into politics—it as the students who brought the ountry back into politics.

MARC LANDY
EDITOR OF STUDENT MAGAZINE
AT OBERLIN COLLEGE

shows for McCarthy. Everything was extremely well organized. McCarthy delegates were planted, so to speak, at a number of social gatherings held on Sunday and on the first days of the convention in people's homes in the suburbs, country clubs, and other places. Uncommitted delegates were invited to those gatherings, and there was a huge, carefully selected group of young people—college students from everywhere from New York State to California—who had volunteered to be drivers. They had a large number of automobiles in Soldier Field, and they communicated with McCarthy people in the hotels by walkie-talkies so that everybody got to the parties they were supposed to go to. Television stars and movie stars were in attendance at most of the meetings, so the first couple of days were really optimistic. Everybody in the McCarthy camp, I thought, was riding very high.

Sunday night some of the violence started in a kind of small way. I remember hearing stories after dinner about police attacking McCarthy supporters and chasing them out of the park, stories of clubbings, that kind of thing. As the days went on, the whole situation turned from kind of a high-flying mood to an uglier and uglier mood because every evening the relationship worsened between the police and the Yippies, as they were being called. Some of them were there, I guess, to make trouble as much as anything else; they were camping in Grant Park across the street from our hotel, the Conrad Hilton.

Arrests got more frequent every day. People were pushing and shoving one another, and the young people were shouting and the police were getting edgier and edgier. The young people wouldn't get out of the streets. They were standing in the streets and shouting, and there was pushing and shoving, and people started being knocked through windows. Everything began to get more gruesome. After a couple of days the situation

really deteriorated. The young people in the streets were throwing excrement at the hotel building, and people on the 15th floor, or thereabout, were throwing cans and bottles out of the windows. Fighting started. I remember young people being brought into the hotel on stretchers with blood streaming from their heads. The McCarthy headquarters on the 15th floor sort of turned into a hospital. There were young people on the floor, on blankets, and on stretchers, with wounds like you see in the war

We are called upon to pass a reasoned judgment and a moral judgment upon our Vietnam program. We are called upon in mid-course to make a decision. This is a difficult demand to make on a nation that has not known failure and always thought it was morally right. This is not a historic role for the United States. . . . The fact is that the napalm that is being dropped on primitive people in Asia is our napalm. We must raise a challenge to this program and this policy.

EUGENE McCARTHY

movies. It was a very, very emotional episode.

I agree with those people who said after the election that the demonstrations, both in the convention hall and on the streets, that people saw over TV probably cost Humphrey the election. I think the whole situation was one in which everybody behaved badly. I cannot think of anybody who behaved well. McCarthy behaved badly. I saw him many times. It seemed to me that he had made up his mind when the convention started that he had lost it, whereas most of us thought he was winning it when we arrived in town. We would have our McCarthy caucuses from time to time during the week, and he always spoke as though the convention was over, as if there was no chance, everything was stacked. He started talking like the bombthrowers that had joined the McCarthy movement in its waning moments, maintaining that the system simply wasn't able to function, that the system wasn't able to accommodate a challenge such as his. That was the kind of thinking he betrayed from the first, and that was the kind of thing he kept on saying until the very end, when he refused to go to the platform with McGovern, who was also an unsuccessful candidate, and stand beside Humphrey. He wouldn't acknowledge that it was he, McCarthy, who hadn't been able to make it because of the fact that he didn't have the votes. Rather it was the system that was corrupt, ineffective, and undemocratic, and no independent candidate could succeed in that kind of government. He began talking at the convention like a fuzzy-headed anarchist.

Also, there were a couple of things that happened during the convention that shattered all of us, I guess. I remember there was an announcement in the news with respect to the abortive uprising in Czechoslovakia. The McCarthy delegates were carrying on a continuing dialogue with the people who said that they were uncommitted,

trying to persuade them that McCarthy was really the one who could win the election, and then McCarthy made the statement on Czechoslovakia that it was "not the greatest crisis in the world." That ended the dialogue with the uncommitted people. There was no sense talking to them any more.

In any event, the convention started out as the best organized McCarthy effort that I had ever been involved in. . . . I was terribly impressed when I got to Chicago and observed the well-oiled, well-thought-out plans that were underway. But by the time the convention was half over, there was no longer any doubt as to the outcome. All of a sudden, it was just another protest, another confrontation—marching down Michigan Boulevard at 2 o'clock in the morning, burning candles, all those things. You know, I can never be grateful enough for the fact that McCarthy took a movement which was largely grass roots and he gave it leadership in the beginning. He gave it a dignity and an authenticity that it didn't possess when it was being led by Al Lowenstein. He did give it a focal point and he did step forward and he did become the figurehead for the movement. But he was the figurehead for the movement and he never led it.[18]

Dave Graven, a Humphrey alternate delegate, describes some of the things he saw at the convention:

There was one little girl, a little angelic thing with long blonde hair, wandering through the hotel, and as she wandered, smiling, I saw that with one hand she was throwing stink bombs. Later, I was witness to what I considered chicanery. We were some place one night, and we came back to the hotel. It was late at night when we got there, and around

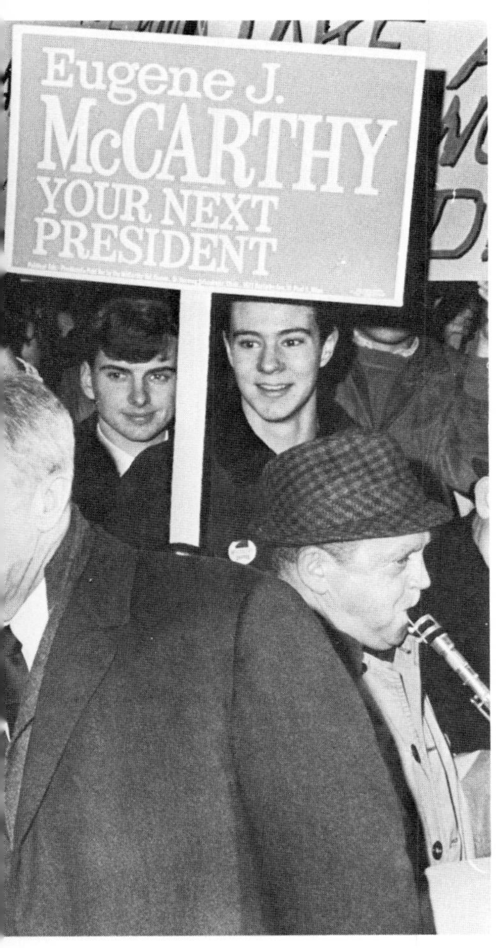

the elevator bank were these McCarthy kids, surrounded by police, sitting on the floor in pajamas and stuff. They were really scared but there was no one holding them. If anyone wanted to get up and walk, there was nothing to stop them, and I think one or two did. It seemed to me that one of the McCarthy people was saying, "Stay there, stay there," because they wanted to hold a press conference around those kids. It was clear to me that they were being exploited. I had two thoughts: First, the kids were scared because they were sitting in pajamas and there were people standing all around, and just being on the floor would be pretty scary anyway. Second, no one that I could see had put them there.

There were McCarthy aides around—Dick Goodwin was one. What really got me going was that a guy came out of one of the elevators and he had on phony bandages, that is to say, if you looked, you could see the bandages didn't fit anything that could be injuries. Moreover, there wasn't blood on his bandages—catsup or something, but it wasn't blood. I got a very good look at it. He was laughing and joking, and as he came out of the elevator, Goodwin said, "Not yet." So he went back into the elevator, which was stalled there. He was just sitting there laughing and joking, and Goodwin said, "Don't worry, Senator McCarthy is going to have you all under his personal protection." Pretty soon people with television cameras started coming around, and Goodwin motioned to the guy with the bandages and he came out, laid down on the floor, and started moaning. Goodwin rushed over there and said, "Give him air, give him air." I can still see Goodwin saying, "Give him air," while the cameras were focusing on them. It was the phoniest charade I have ever seen in my life. At that point, Goodwin said, "Don't worry, the Senator will be here." And then McCarthy showed up and said,

"You're safe with me. I'll get you out of here. Go two by two to my room." So two people would get up and leave and go in the elevator, then two more would get up, and then two more. Then the guy who was lying there got up and wandered off into the elevator, and a couple of us followed him, clapping, and he took the elevator up.

I thought, "Oh God, this is what high-minded people resort to to make a point or something." These kids were being exploited for high political purpose. I was sitting there when the TV cameras were grinding in on this guy moaning on the floor—it was clearly phony. If you just had a picture you could see that it was clearly someone's idea of what a bandaged person looked like. I'm not saying that the guy didn't have a cut somewhere, but you couldn't see it, and it wasn't blood on his bandages. In any event, I was sitting there, and I said to the guy next to me—he looked like a Czechoslovakian secret agent, but he was actually a liberal—I said to him, "Say, you know that's phony. That guy hasn't been injured." And he looked at me in his hate and said, "You lie!" Things were getting heated there. . . .

It was strange that last night of the convention. I have it in my home—one of those crazy signs—"We Love Mayor Daley." Daley was going to show, by God, that this was his Chicago, and then someone starts the gallery, and then at a signal all the signs went up, "We Love Mayor Daley." Isn't that funny—it's not "We *Like* Daley"—or "Hurray for Daley, Three Cheers for Daley." It's "We *Love*"—I've got one at home. It's a collector's item. "We Love Mayor Daley." One of the signs came floating down from above and I grabbed it.[19]

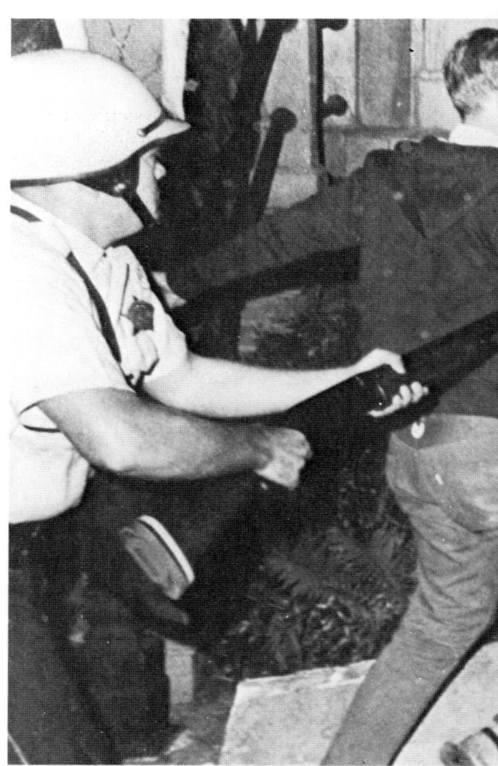

After it was all over, one of the young demonstrators, Bonnie Vendig, said, "If I had kids of my own, I wouldn't know how to explain it. We nominated a man for president with the Army in the middle of Michigan Avenue."[20]

But Hubert Humphrey said it best. "My wife and I went home heartbroken, battered and beaten. I told her I felt just like we had been in a shipwreck."[21]

The saddest thing about Humphrey was that he did not stand up for the right in 1968. At the end of his life, he emerged with great dignity just as he began his public life. The totality of his life and his contribution is very much the story of America in these times.

BETTY FRIEDAN

WE
LOVE
MAYOR
DALEY

chapter 17

ALMOST

Gene McCarthy was not around on the final day of the Democratic Convention. After Humphrey was nominated, McCarthy had gone over to Grant Park and had given some of his followers a brief talk: "I am happy to be here to address the government of the people in exile," he said, and indicated he would be campaigning for the antiwar candidates in the fall elections. He saw "great difficulty"[1] in backing Humphrey since he felt that Humphrey would be unable to change his position on the war. Soon McCarthy was off on a ten-day vacation in Nice, followed by a stint covering the World Series for *Life* Magazine.

At the convention's conclusion, Hubert Humphrey saw clearly that the prize he had fought so hard to win had more than a few cracks and dents in it. The party was badly divided. Though George McGovern had announced his support of the ticket, the split with the McCarthy supporters would continue to fester and to weaken Humphrey's position. From his experience at the convention, Humphrey knew that his greatest problems on the war issue would come in those areas of the country where the supporters of the minority Vietnam plank had shown the most strength—the states of California, Colorado, Iowa, Massachusetts, Michigan, Nebraska, New York, Oregon, South Dakota, Vermont, and Wisconsin.

When Humphrey won the presidential nomination, his campaign organization was virtually nonexistent. Larry O'Brien had agreed to manage the Humphrey effort only through the convention. Senators Mondale and Harris had both signed on as convention delegate hunters, not campaign

The Humphreys with Ed Muskie and his wife, Jane, at the Democratic Convention

aides. The day before Humphrey was nominated, there was still no plan for the election campaign until Joseph Napolitan, a long-time O'Brien associate, banged one out on the typewriter in his hotel room in Chicago. Humphrey could expect no assistance from the Democratic National Committee, which would normally provide at least the structural framework of a national campaign. The committee had been badly mauled during the Johnson years; the president had taken no interest in it, preferring to work through his own network, and there were neither funds nor personnel available to help Humphrey.

To make matters worse, Humphrey's finances were in grim shape. Though he had spent far less in winning the nomination than any other major candidate in either party, he was completely broke. A Gallup poll taken in late August that showed

Humphrey trailing Nixon by 16 percent had a brutal effect on Humphrey's hopes for improving his financial situation. There is little money to be found for a candidate who appears likely to lose; moreover, now that Humphrey had won the nomination, the money that had come in only because the donors wanted to lick Bobby Kennedy or Gene McCarthy or Teddy Kennedy had dried up. Robert Short, Humphrey's finance chairman, began the campaign having to borrow enough simply to get the day-to-day operations moving. For the moment, a media campaign was simply out of the question. Said Short,

Larry O'Brien

> Once we got out of Chicago, we measured so low in the polls that there was no chance of a campaign. I was elected Treasurer, and I went in with about $500,000 deficit—and there was no chance of raising any money. Money, like trucking, goes both ways. Railroads, tobacco industry, everything was going to Nixon and not to us at all. Humphrey was so far behind in the polls that for a while it didn't look like we could get the campaign off the ground. . . . It was probably the first time any national campaign was run where we included a coupon with our ads, to send money to a post office box.[2]

With only eight weeks to go before the election, leading a divided party, lacking money, a campaign plan, or even a campaign schedule, and almost out of contention in the polls, the Humphrey team limped back to Minnesota. They had solved only one of their problems in Chicago: Humphrey had managed to persuade Larry O'Brien to stay on to manage the campaign.

O'Brien long had wanted to get out of professional politics and to pursue a more ulcer-free and financially rewarding career, but his loyalty to his party and Humphrey's unquestioned need combined to persuade him to give it one last hurrah. Even that minor victory wasn't accomplished without cost. Orville Freeman, who had been informally helping his old friend Humphrey, was hurt at being passed over, and stayed on as a top adviser only at Humphrey's urging. Freeman had drafted a campaign plan before the convention, but either because the media costs involved made it too expensive to execute or because it simply got lost in the shuffle, the Freeman plan never became an operative part of Humphrey's effort.

As for Humphrey's initial strategy, there was none, and it showed. The Democratic presidential candidate was simply shoved out the door by his staff and told to free-fall until a plan could be worked out. After catching his breath for two days in Minnesota, Humphrey made his first post-convention statement—a spirited defense of Richard J. Daley that proved to be a disaster. In fairness to Daley (and to Humphrey), it must be said that some of the Mayor's critics hardly displayed a level of tolerance any loftier than that which they attributed to him. When the American Sociological Association voted to hold no convention in Chicago for ten years as a protest against Mayor Daley, one member, Peter Rossi, was moved to remark, "Mayor Daley is losing his cool and becoming the fundamental Irish bigot he is."[3]

Humphrey soon moderated his favorable remarks on Daley, but his campaign had gotten off

I served as an advertising consultant during the '68 campaign and I remember going up to the Doyle, Dane & Bernbach office in New York City. Well, we got in the elevator and a couple of people got in with us and they were wearing McCarthy buttons. I didn't think too much of it, but then they got off at the same floor we did and walked into the same agency we were walking into. Of course I know a little something about advertising from being in the food business, and I know I wouldn't be too pleased selling Chun King and walking into my advertising agency and seeing them all wearing LaChoy buttons.

My next shock came when I saw the commercials the agency had prepared. You know if your heart really isn't in a piece of advertising, it really shows. Well, the first ad they showed me was something with an elephant in it. It was an attempt to ridicule the GOP, but the advertisement itself was ridiculous. The one that was really the topper had a woman with a tiara on and a very elaborate hairdo and a beautiful high-style dress, and she started reciting why she was for Hubert Humphrey. It turned out that the reason she supported Humphrey was that he was so much for the common people, and my reaction to it was that . . . my gosh, she looks like Mrs. Harry Winston. So I got hold of Doyle, or Dane, or one of those people, and I fired them. I said, "You are a great agency, you've got terrific people, but your heart really isn't in it." And I don't think they really put up too much of an argument. Later on, they were threatening to sue us for non-payment, and I said that if they tried to sue us, we ought to counter-sue them for helping lose the election.

JENO PAULUCCI

to an undeniably bad start. His next move just four days after the Chicago convention took him to New York for the Labor Day Parade. He had ducked the traditional Labor Day kickoff in Detroit's Cadillac Square because of the prospects for violence. There was no violence in New York, but Paul O'Dwyer, an antiwar candidate who was running for a Senate seat, stayed clear of Humphrey during the parade and marched to a different drummer.

Humphrey marches in a Labor Day Parade in New York City.

Humphrey got in trouble again a week later in Philadelphia at the official kickoff of the campaign. He predicted that the United States would soon be removing some of its troops from Vietnam, but the president quickly contradicted him by saying no one could know when troops were going to be withdrawn. In Philadelphia Humphrey was subjected to the kind of intense heckling that would dog his campaign throughout September. His appearance in the city was also handicapped by bad work on the part of his campaign staff. The motorcade through the streets of Philadelphia had attracted only a small crowd, and the staff had placed the press bus so far back in the line of march that reporters could see none of the enthusiastic response from the few onlookers. Observers suggested that Humphrey's staff had "convinced itself that it can't generate crowds, so it won't even try."[4]

The following Saturday in Pittsburgh was perhaps the low point of Humphrey's campaign in terms of organizing gaffes. Having scheduled the candidate to spend twenty hours in a city normally deserted downtown on Saturdays, his aides could come up with only one public event, a picnic of government women employees to be held that afternoon, twelve miles from town. The best campaign opportunity of the day, a rare parade in downtown Pittsburgh, hadn't even been included in the schedule because it was sponsored by a local television station as a device to plug its fall programs. Humphrey's schedulers had been too pure of heart to permit the presidential candidate to lend himself to such a crassly commercial enter-

Sometimes Humphrey was a victim of his own people. I remember once he came to Sanford, Florida, which is where my winter home is, and I had a dinner for him at the Holiday Inn there. He came in a helicopter, but when he looked for his suitcase, he couldn't find it. No one had bothered to put it in the helicopter, so he was without a shave and a change of clothes. Finally when he got straightened out, he came over to my house and we went to the dinner. Later he had to leave and go to another meeting, so they are leading him out of the building, and where did they lead him but straight into the kitchen. He had to wander around there for five minutes before they could find their way out.

JENO PAULUCCI

I think the choice of Nixon is a proper choice. He is truly a Republican candidate.

EUGENE McCARTHY

prise. But as Humphrey left his hotel in the morning, he heard parade music. Heading for the sound, he was soon in the thick of the parade. As a toddler Humphrey had once gotten lost and had re-emerged leading the Norwegian Day Parade in Wallace, South Dakota; at the age of three he had learned never to let a parade pass him by. Using that knowledge, he salvaged what he could that Saturday in Pittsburgh. On Sunday a picture of Humphrey amid the crowds appeared on the front page of the *New York Times.*

The Republican candidate, Richard Nixon, didn't have to depend on a parade turning up at his front door in order to get press coverage. Even when one did turn up, like the Labor Day Parade that had passed under the window of his New York apartment at 812 Fifth Avenue, he wasn't about to participate in any event that wasn't carefully structured to show off his candidacy at its maximum

Richard Nixon campaigning in New Jersey

advantage. Nixon's campaign manager, his law partner John Mitchell, had never managed a national campaign. He *had* had thirty years of experience as a New York municipal bond lawyer, a profession that might seem light years removed from the rough and tumble of politics. In reality, however, the connection was not so obscure. The success of a New York municipal bond lawyer was dependent on his knowledge of the strengths and weaknesses of thousands of the nation's state and local officials. Officials in many communities looked to their New York bond counsel both to help them win favorable attention from the New York bond rating services, which could make or break a municipal credit, and also to show them a good time when they came to New York or when they met at the various conventions that municipal officials loved to attend. In return, a municipal bond lawyer like Mitchell depended on these officials for the success of his highly lucrative business. Over a lifetime of practice, Mitchell had become a walking encyclopedia of information on the people who held the power in the nation's states and municipalities. Unknown outside his own field, fanatically dedicated to Nixon's candidacy, possessing a nationwide network of contacts, John Mitchell was Nixon's Allard Lowenstein.

The Nixon campaign team included other able men from the law firm where Nixon and Mitchell were partners, among them Len Garment and Tom Evans. Also on the staff were several Southern Californians—Herb Klein, John Ehrlichman, and Bob Haldeman; a top-flight fund-raiser, Maurice Stans; bright young men like Ray Price, Patrick

The long dark night for America is about to end. . . . The time has come for us to leave the valley of despair and climb the mountain so that we may see the glory of the dawn of a new day for America, a new dawn for peace and freedom to the world.

RICHARD M. NIXON
ACCEPTANCE SPEECH FOR
REPUBLICAN NOMINATION

Buchanan, and Martin Anderson; former Goldwater loyalists such as Dick Kleindienst; and middle-of-the-roaders like Rodgers Morton and Clark MacGregor. The varied backgrounds of the campaign staffers were indicative of the kind of support that Nixon's candidacy had. Although the candidate himself commanded a deep personal affection only among a few, even within his own party, his victory at the Republican Convention in Miami had left no lingering bitterness. Richard Nixon led a unified party.

Organization was another strength of Nixon's

Republican vice-presidential candidate Spiro Agnew greets a young admirer dressed in a Greek national costume.

campaign. The planning that went into the campaign had been evolving throughout the spring and summer of 1968 and had been finalized during a relaxed and pleasant ten-day meeting in San Diego after the Miami convention. The gathering was staged to provide both showmanship and substance. While an inside group did the actual planning, an outside group, which included celebrities like Wilt Chamberlain, conducted public seminars and held press conferences that occupied all but the most intensely curious observers.

The campaign that emerged from the San Diego meeting would be professionally staffed, and it would be handsomely financed: the polls that showed Nixon with a seemingly insurmountable lead over Humphrey guaranteed that. Since financing and staffing were no problem, the efforts of important, well-meaning, well-heeled but amateur Nixon supporters were often unnecessary and in fact a nuisance. But how to deflect such supporters without offending them and possibly even driving them into the hands of the enemy? The answer was Citizens for Nixon-Agnew. If a Nixon-minded citizen walked in the door with a check and a desire to help and if his profession happened to be, say, running a bowling alley, he was asked to form "Bowling Alley Operators for Nixon." Each of these groups raised its own money, organized its own members, and placed its own ads, under the supervision of Charles Rhyne, Nixon's old law school classmate at Duke, Tom Evans of the Nixon law firm, and, later, John Warner, who became Secretary of the Navy in the Nixon administration.

Time is running out for the merchants of crime and corruption in America. The wave of crime is not going to be the wave of the future in the United States of America.

RICHARD M. NIXON
ACCEPTANCE SPEECH

And if we are to restore order and respect for law in this country, there's one place we're going to begin: We're going to have a new Attorney General of the United States.

RICHARD M. NIXON
ACCEPTANCE SPEECH

All the careful planning and hard work of Nixon's staff paid off. The candidate's campaign schedule was leisurely, permitting him to appear relaxed and well-rested at his public appearances. There was no dashing off to Alaska or Hawaii just to fulfill a foolish promise to visit all fifty states, as had happened in Nixon's 1960 campaign. In 1968, Nixon's public appearances were made before friendly, hand-picked audiences. The candidate's statements on the issues were guarded, but to give the semblance of openness and spontaneity, a "man-in-the-arena" format was used. Nixon appeared standing alone on a small open-pit stage, ringed by a panel of citizens free to question him

Nixon at the taping of a question-and-answer session in St. Louis. His audience is made up of local high-school students.

on whatever issues they chose. Asking questions is a skill that both lawyers and journalists spend years to hone, and Nixon handled the puffballs that these amateurs threw him with no difficulty. The device proved quite effective and showed the candidate at his most attractive.

In the final analysis, Richard Nixon's greatest advantage as a presidential candidate was neither his organization nor his campaign chest nor his personality. It was his correct assessment of the national mood in 1968. James Reston, writing in the *New York Times,* described that mood in a series of carefully chosen phrases: ". . . it is a combination of Watts and Berkeley. It's beatniks. It's hippies. It's draft card burners. It's demonstrators. It's blacks. It's high taxation. It's easy sex and dope and kids running away from home. It's uncertainty, fear, madness, murder—all these appearing day after day on the television and in the newspapers, adding up to a feeling that something is deeply wrong and must be changed."[5]

George Wallace was another presidential candidate who benefitted from the disgust and fear that many Americans felt toward current social trends. His message, far less subtle and more openly racist than Nixon's, was an appeal to many Americans who felt that their values were being mocked and their lives and their children's lives being used as cannon fodder in the social revolution by people who despised them. The candidacy of the former Alabama governor cut into the muscle of Democratic strength among white Southerners and blue-collar workers in the north.

Richard Nixon was well aware of the many

Now what are the real issues that exist today in the United States? It is the trend of pseudo-intellectual government, where a select, elite group have written guidelines in bureaus and court decisions, have spoken from some pulpits, some college campuses, some newspaper offices, looking down their noses at the average man in the street, the glassworker, the steelworker, the autoworker, and the textile worker, the farmer, the policeman, the beautician and the little businessman, saying to him that you do not know how to get up in the morning, or go to bed at night, unless we write you a guideline. . . .

GEORGE WALLACE

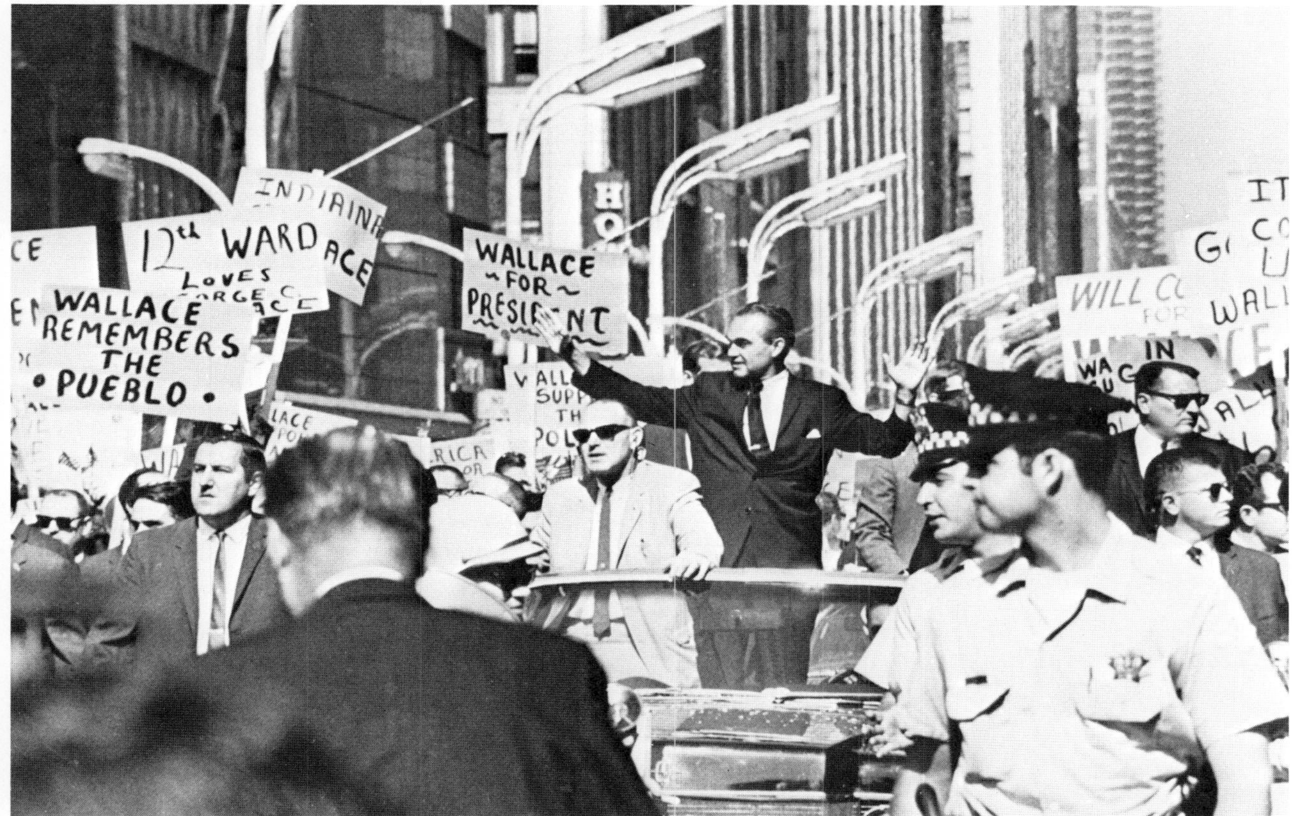

George Wallace campaigns in the streets of Chicago.

There is not a dime's worth of difference between Richard Nixon and Hubert Humphrey.

GEORGE WALLACE

advantages that he held over the Democratic candidate, Hubert Humphrey. To dramatize the contrast he could draw with Humphrey, Nixon made a move that was the only real political gamble of his campaign. On Wednesday, September 4, exactly six days after the Democratic National Convention ended, Nixon opened his campaign with a spectacular gesture—a parade through downtown Chicago, on the very streets where protesters and police had battled less than a week earlier. The whole event took only forty minutes. There was no violence, no demonstrations, no obscenities—just a few placards with mildly abusive messages. The principal damage to the city of Chicago lay in the tons of confetti and streamers that littered the parade route. Nixon's demonstration of the differences in style and mood between his campaign and Humphrey's succeeded brilliantly, and his successes continued. The only sour note in the whole first month of Nixon's campaign came when Spiro T. Agnew charged that Hubert Humphrey was "squishy soft on communism." Forced to retract after both Gerald Ford and Everett Dirksen defended Humphrey against the charge, Agnew said, "I have never been one to take the low road in politics."[6]

For Humphrey, the first week of the campaign was only the beginning of a nightmare month. The organizational chaos began to fade as Larry O'Brien took hold, but Humphrey's standing in the Gallup poll improved only marginally. At the time

You can look [Agnew] in the eye and know he's got it. This guy has got it. . . . Under pressure he is one of the best.

RICHARD M. NIXON

Humphrey and Nixon with Senator Everett Dirksen

of the convention, he trailed Nixon 45 percent to 29 percent, with 18 percent going to Wallace. By mid-September, Gallup showed 43 percent for Nixon, 31 percent for Humphrey, and 19 percent for Wallace. Humphrey's financial situation hadn't improved much either; there was still no money for a media campaign. Asked how the campaign was going, Wendell Anderson, head of the Humphrey effort in Minnesota, said, "Our number one priority is money. Number two is money. Also number three and four." Anderson added that he could not "honestly say that we have McCarthy people calling and offering their support."[7]

The same day that Anderson gave his pessimistic report, Nixon spoke through a closed circuit television network to a friendly audience that had raised $5 million for his campaign at twenty fund-raising dinners. "You've made a good bet,"[8] he said.

Even more discouraging than lack of funds was the public reception that Humphrey was receiving. His appearances were being savaged by protesters. Straining to make himself heard in city after city, Humphrey found his message swamped by chants and bullhorns, drowned out by obscenities and taunts, the protest escalating with each appearance. Perhaps the worst moment of the campaign came during a rally in Seattle on Saturday, September 28. Jim Klobuchar, a reporter for the *Minneapolis Star,* tells what happened as Humphrey faced the crowd:

> He is stunned, standing there in mid-platform, to hear himself called a warmonger, a murderer and

even . . . a racist, to see himself depicted on posters as an American Adolph Hitler.

He tries reason and humor, eloquence and tough talk, gentle, paternal chiding and hard-eyed ridicule, but none of it works. They stand in the second-deck galleries, singly and in clusters and now in full groups, and scream "Stop the war, stop the war!" and then, "Dump the Hump, dump the Hump!"

Demonstrators at the Seattle rally

You don't know me and I am certain you do not remember my rude and inconsiderate behavior during 1968 in the city of Boston. You came to speak and I, along with a large crowd of unfair individuals, would not allow you to voice your opinions. I certainly want to ask your forgiveness for my actions on that day. I know you are very ill now, but I also want you to know that the prayers of my family are with you on a daily basis.

LETTER FROM A "CONNECTICUT MAN" SENT TO HUMPHREY IN OCTOBER 1977

And Humphrey finally squares about to face them directly, wordlessly, his arms crossed. He is enraged but immensely sad, and he seems to be saying, "Why me? Why me?" . . .

Humphrey is now introduced and walks to the microphone, smiling, . . .

[He] turns from the lectern to regard them, seemingly with good humor. He offers them time to speak. A few voice standard antiwar slogans but now a mousey brunette with frozen smile holds up a battery-operated loudspeaker and a bearded youth speaks into a small hand microphone.

"In Vietnam there's a scream that will not end," he begins. . . .

"In Vietnam there's a wound that does not cease its bleeding. . . . We have not come to talk with you, Mr. Humphrey. We have come to arrest you. We charge you with crimes against humanity. . . .

[The gallery speaker finally stops and Humphrey begins his talk, but he is interrupted by more jeering.]

"I shall not be driven from this platform by a handful of people who believe in nothing," he declares.

And now he puts his hands on his hips and glares at them. He has been conditioned to their words and manner but he is seemingly appalled tonight by their rage and bitterness. Some of them verge on derangement in their shouting, blood vessels distended, eyes glazed. . . .

"Knock it off, will you please," he says coldly. They do not . . . .

Scuffling breaks out between a few of the hard core protesters and the police. There is no bloodshed. Some of them are pushed toward the exits. Some stay. Humphrey is now free to talk. He starts in on Nixon. The speech is crisp but mechanical. The candidate cannot forget the spectacle of the last half hour. He returns to it extemporaneously, with a voice quavering and eyes moist in emotion.

The protesters, he says, are driving thousands of voters into the arms of "another candidate who takes no stand." . . .

He finished his talk and they applaud earnestly, but the camaraderie of an hour ago has been deadened.

The heavily guarded candidate returns to his hotel from the back door of the arena.[9]

Seattle was the absolute low—the pits. Humphrey had had enough. The bitterness of his opponents had finally corroded his own spirits. He had been hectored from every side: president, press, party, staff, hawk, dove, friend, foe. Whatever subtle shades of difference he had tried to draw to distinguish his Vietnam position from Johnson's had been drowned out by the drum beat of the protesters.

The debacle in Seattle was to be followed by one of the most important events in Humphrey's campaign. Larry O'Brien had set aside enough funds to provide for a half-hour national television broadcast in which Humphrey would discuss the Vietnam issue. The speech was to be taped in Salt Lake City on Monday, September 30, and broadcast Monday evening. On Sunday, the campaign flew into Salt Lake City. No decision had been reached on the content of the speech, and a marathon planning session was held in Humphrey's suite at the Hotel Utah. At four in the morning, Humphrey, conducting the meeting in his bathrobe, finally became so weary of all the tugging and hauling over his Vietnam position that he kicked

Humphrey and Larry O'Brien confer during the flight from Seattle to Salt Lake City.

all of his advisers out of the room so that he could decide for himself. He described his reasoning later: "On the Vietnam issue, there was no way you could say anything about Vietnam that wasn't going to get you in trouble, some way or another, so I did what I thought was right. I didn't worry about whether the President liked it, whether McCarthy liked it, or whether the academic community liked it, or who liked it. I made up my mind in this campaign, so help me, I said, I may not win this election, but I'm going to be true to myself and I refuse to compromise on the fundamental issues."[10]

Within a short time, Humphrey had dictated the key elements of the speech he had decided upon. After a few hours of sleep, he went to a breakfast with the leaders of the Utah Democratic Party, at which he told them that "if the election were held today, we wouldn't have a prayer."[11] That afternoon, Humphrey did some more polishing on the speech, and fifteen minutes before the taping was to take place, he called Johnson at the White House. Humphrey told the president what he was about to say and added hopefully, "I don't think this is going to impair your hand."[12] "I gather you're not asking my advice,"[13] replied Johnson.

For the first time in the campaign, Humphrey spoke from a lectern shorn of the vice-presidential seal, a symbolic break with Johnson. The substantive break came a few moments later in the speech itself:

> As President, I would stop the bombing of the North as an acceptable risk for peace because I believe it could lead to success in the negotiations and a shorter war. This would be the best protection for our troops.
>
> In weighing that risk, and before taking action, I would place key importance on evidence, direct or indirect, by deed or word, of Communist willingness to restore the demilitarized zone between North and South Vietnam.
>
> If the government of North Vietnam were to show bad faith, I would reserve the right to resume the bombing.[14]

The difference between the policy described in Humphrey's speech and the official administration line was so thin that a number of reporters assigned to the Humphrey campaign thought he was simply giving still another facelift to the Johnson bombing position. What Johnson had been saying was that he required a show of good faith as a condition for halting the bombing. What Hum-

After delivering his speech in Salt Lake City, Humphrey visited the city's famed Mormon Temple.

phrey said at Salt Lake City was that he would stop the bombing first and then look for a gesture of good faith from the North, while reserving the right to resume bombing. It was a distinction that would have gladdened the heart of a Philadelphia lawyer. For the benefit of those reporters who hadn't understood the significance of the statement, Humphrey issued a release the next day, underlining his pledge to stop the bombing and indicating that the mention of some gesture from North Vietnam was simply included out of respect for the efforts being made at the Paris peace talks.

Even though some of the press did not find anything new in Humphrey's speech, it was enough to turn the campaign around. Its effect was immediate. Republicans Everett Dirksen and Gerald Ford claimed that Humphrey's statement was politically motivated. Nixon said that he would not alter his stand of requiring reciprocity from the Communists before he would undertake a bombing halt. The *New York Times* endorsed Humphrey's candidacy, saying, "The Times is not finding the statements of either candidate satisfactory on the war issue but Mr. Humphrey has shown unmistakable signals that he intends, if elected, to move away from the errors of the past."[15]

. . . I*t appears that the great debate this year is going to be Humphrey versus Humphrey, and I'm going to have to ask for equal time.*
RICHARD M. NIXON

President Johnson, as expected, was not impressed with Humphrey's speech. In an interview a year after the election, Johnson claimed that the speech had actually cost Humphrey the presidency: "I think as a result the South Vietnamese . . . decided they wouldn't go to the peace talks table until after the election, that they would hold back and so for several days we had a very difficult position and the people didn't have much hopes of an immediate prospect for peace. So I think it hurt us in the election."[16] The president also noted that Nixon "did not make any changes in policy"[17] on his Vietnam position during the campaign. Johnson was certainly right in believing that had Saigon gone to the Paris peace table, giving rise to the prospect of a prompt settlement, then Humphrey might have stood a better chance of being elected. What makes his theory implausible, however, is Johnson's suggestion that peace in Vietnam could have been brought about by the presence of the South Vietnamese at the Paris talks or that the American people could be made to believe that this was the case. The Saigon government may have hoped to damage Humphrey's candidacy by shunning the talks, but if so, American voters paid little mind to the gambit. Instead, they began to take another look at Humphrey. He had finally broken away from Johnson. He had begun to unite his party.

In Nashville, the next campaign stop after his Vietnam speech, Humphrey could see young people with signs saying, "Humphrey, if you mean it, we're with you."[18] At the rallies, the heckling began to die down. With such encouragement, Humphrey's spirits and natural optimism quickly revived, and the old Hubert Humphrey was in evidence again; in a Nashville hotel, he broke into impromptu dance with two of his women campaign workers when he heard a band playing "Balling the Jack." As the mood of the public continued to improve, that unmistakable omen of glad tidings, the local politician—so long absent from the Hum-

In the 1968 campaign, when he came through Illinois, I got a chance to hop on the plane and go around with him a little bit. We were always behind schedule. Somehow the candidate for President always spoke longer than the schedule called for. . . . Once he got through speaking, officials tried to rush him along so we could catch up with our schedule. But all of a sudden, behind a barrier, Hubert Humphrey spotted a little 11- or 12-year-old retarded girl. He stopped and went over and shook hands and chatted with her. That really symbolized Hubert Humphrey for me. He was always reaching out for the disadvantaged, whoever they are, wherever they are—the retarded, the hungry, the unemployed, those who are oppressed for whatever reason.

PAUL SIMON
REPRESENTATIVE FROM ILLINOIS

phrey's campaign stops—suddenly began to reappear, first in ones and twos, then in droves, nesting on speaker's platforms to be seen with Humphrey, sticking their beaks into camera lenses to be photographed with Humphrey. In the course of one frantic month, Humphrey had succeeded in getting off the defensive on Vietnam, putting the issue behind him, and going on the attack against Nixon and Wallace.

Humphrey campaigns in a canning factory.

George Wallace's candidacy began to fade as Humphrey's strengthened. Wallace's running mate, Air Force General Curtis LeMay, had been a disaster from the moment he had opened his mouth at his first press conference and expressed his fondness for the use of nuclear weapons. (Wallace had tugged at LeMay's coattails in a vain effort to tone him down.) LeMay grew increasingly less visible as the campaign wore on. With a week to go before the election, his campaign schedule for a typical day involved a flight from Oklahoma to Evansville, Indiana, and then a leisurely motor trip to Paducah, Kentucky. "Thus, the bulk of the day's time was spent in going to and from Paducah and with short stops at Brown's Grocery at the midway point and at Halloman's Grocery at Mott City, along the way."[19]

But LeMay was only part of Wallace's problem. More significant was the dwindling of his constituency as Humphrey's message started to get through to blue-collar families in the North with the help of organized labor. Throughout Humphrey's campaign, even in its darkest hours, the AFL/CIO had stuck loyally with Humphrey. When the local politicians had deserted him and the liberal idealogues were heaping calumny on him, the labor chiefs still marched beside him in the parades, clapped dutifully at his speeches, and provided much of what little he had in the way of organization and money. Labor's message to its members was clear: Under Governor George Wallace, Alabama had had poor public education, high sales taxes, low pay, and miserable working conditions, and had been a hotbed of hostility to organized labor. It would be bad enough for working people to vote for Wallace as an expression of anger and resentment against hippies and blacks. Even worse, a vote for Wallace would be a vote

The voice of Hubert Humphrey has been heard loud and clear—and often—on the great social issues of our time. When others would mute their voices and duck their heads to avoid the impending fight, that was when you were most likely to see Hubert Humphrey standing tall, out in front.

PETER BOMMARITO
VICE-PRESIDENT OF THE AFL-CIO

against their own interests. As governor, George Wallace had been no friend of labor—he would be no better a friend as president. Throughout October, Wallace's northern support began to shear off rapidly under the weight of this argument.

Humphrey's case against Nixon also started to be heard. With the uproar of protest diminishing, Humphrey could key his message to the bread-and-butter issues that had sustained Democratic candidates since the New Deal. Democrats would do more for working people, more for the elderly, more for the blacks, more for the farmers. A Democrat in the White House meant good times.

A Republican would bring tight money, trickle-down economics, and hard times. Nixon's strategy of playing the campaign close to the vest made him an inviting target for Humphrey's attacks. Why won't Nixon debate? Where does Nixon stand on Social Security benefits? Aid to education? Why won't Nixon speak out on the issues? Can you trust a man who won't tell you where he stands? Can you trust Nixon?

It was not long before the new spirit in Humphrey's campaign began to show in the polls and in the campaign chest. Trailing Nixon in the Gallup poll 45 percent to 29 percent at the time of the convention, by October 12 Humphrey had moved up to 31 percent while Nixon had dropped to 43 percent. Then, as Wallace faded, the figures reached 44 percent to 36 percent by October 21. Money started to flow into the campaign, though Humphrey refused either to sell himself to the oil industry or to grovel for the funds that were available from several of the more arrogant and overbearing doves. Politicians who had jumped ship began to climb back on board. Jesse Unruh of California belatedly resurfaced; Stephen Mitchell, who was Gene McCarthy's floor manager in Chicago, joined the Humphrey campaign; Paul O'Dwyer, the New York senatorial candidate who had refused to march beside Humphrey on Labor Day, ended his holdout and backed Humphrey for president. On Tuesday, October 29, even Eugene McCarthy gave Humphrey a tepid endorsement, at the same time announcing that he would not be running for re-election to the Senate in 1970—at least not as a Democrat.

Humphrey waves to a crowd in the Los Angeles garment district.

Hubert Humphrey should have been President of the United States. He narrowly missed it in 1968. During the campaign I was stuck in Paris trying to get the Vietnam peace negotiations started. We finally did reach an agreement after unnecessary delay caused by the South Vietnamese government, but it was only a couple of days before the election and too late to affect the results.

AVERELL HARRIMAN

There was more good news for Humphrey on Thursday, October 31. President Johnson announced that he had ordered a halt in the bombing of North Vietnam to commence Friday, November 1. "I have reached this decision on the basis of developments in the Paris talks," said Johnson, "and I have reached it in the belief that this action will lead to progress for a peaceful settlement of the Vietnam war."[20] Humphrey was elated. "I have been hoping for months that it would happen. For months,"[21] he said. Nixon, who had been girding himself for several weeks against the possibility that a bombing halt might occur, maintained his policy of "saying nothing that might jeopardize chances for peace."[22] The next day, Humphrey, campaigning in Chicago for the first time since the convention, received the news that the South Vietnamese refused to join the Paris peace talks. Though President Thieu had supported the bombing halt at first, he became balky when several rockets landed in Saigon a few hours before the halt was to go into effect.

The situation was complicated further when Anna Chan Chennault, a Nixon supporter, was discovered to have been working behind the scenes to undermine the peace talks so that Humphrey would be unable to benefit by them. Knowledge of her activities was brought to Johnson, who turned the information over to Humphrey. Humphrey did not believe that Nixon knew of Mrs. Chennault's plans. He was also afraid that disclosure of her interference could have destroyed whatever chance remained to get South Vietnam to the peace table and could have caused irreparable damage to Nixon's presidency if he were elected. For these reasons, Humphrey rejected the advice of some of his aides to attack Nixon with the story. Of Humphrey's forbearance, Theodore White said, "I know of no more essentially decent story in American politics."[23]

During the final week before the election, Humphrey's campaign continued to build momentum. On Sunday, November 3, at the Astrodome in Houston, Lyndon Johnson made his only appearance on a platform with Humphrey during the campaign. Humphrey and Johnson walked side by side into the arena, where Johnson told 50,000 cheering Texans that Humphrey's election meant the preservation of the American Union. While he spoke, 50,000 light bulbs flashed out "HHH" on the world's largest scoreboard, four stories high and 474 feet long. Johnson's gesture undoubtedly helped Humphrey carry Texas, but Bob Short felt that the president never did signal his Texas backers to provide Humphrey any financial support.

I think the grandest night of all was that one in the Astrodome in Houston on Saturday before the November 1968 election. One more week and Humphrey would have overtaken the opposition. One more week and we would have been spared the tragedies of the years 1969 through 1974.

RALPH W. YARBOROUGH
FORMER SENATOR FROM TEXAS

The final Gallup poll before the election showed Nixon leading Humphrey 42 percent to 40 percent, while the final Harris poll showed Humphrey in the lead for the first time, 43 percent to 40 percent. John Mitchell called the Harris poll a "concoction" and referred to Harris as "the former Democratic pollster."

Humphrey wound up his campaign in Los Angeles, where he and Ed Muskie did a two-hour telethon together. Later he attended a party at the home of Lloyd Hand, a former chief of protocol, and the exuberant mood made the gathering seem like a victory celebration. When Humphrey returned to Minnesota at 7:45 A.M. on election day, a number of loyal DFLers were at the airport to meet him, including Art Naftalin, his old college pal and now the mayor of Minneapolis. Two hours later, Humphrey waded through the mud in front of the Marysville Town Hall, where he greeted the election judge by name ("He does that to everybody. Once he's seen you, he don't hardly forget you," said the judge, Earl Bodin[24]) and cast his ballot. After asking several people "Did you see the telethon last night? Was it good? Was it good?"[25] Humphrey went back to his home at Lake Waverly and took a long nap while Muriel spent the day getting her hair done and working a needlepoint pillow for her granddaughter Amy. Later in the afternoon, Humphrey drove into the

nearby town of Buffalo for a "while-U-wait" press job on his blue suit. He had a cup of hot chocolate at the Buffalo Drug Store and went over to Bridgeman's Ice Cream Store, where he bought two quarts of ice cream—vanilla and butter pecan—and a can of peanuts. Then Humphrey went home to prepare for the evening.

The Humphreys ate a pheasant dinner off TV trays in the home of one of Hubert's oldest supporters, Dwayne Andreas, while other supporters, aides, and members of the press began to gather at the Leamington Hotel in downtown Minneapolis, Humphrey's election eve headquarters. They were eating Jeno's Pizza Rolls, courtesy of Jeno Paulucci, and some were less than enthusiastic. They liked Jeno's Pizza Rolls, but they had been eating little else for two days.

The early returns were encouraging as some of the big northeastern industrial states began to fall into Humphrey's column—Massachusetts (never in doubt), Connecticut, New York, Pennsylvania, Michigan. But the euphoria faded quickly. New Jersey had been lost; Illinois was going to Nixon this time, as was Ohio, usually a bellwether state. Texas, another big state, was still uncertain, but California, with the second largest bag of electoral votes in the nation, looked as if it would be won by Nixon. George Wallace was managing only to hold on to his regional base of support in the South. Ironically, if Humphrey had not been so successful in discrediting Wallace's candidacy, the former governor might have won enough states to have thrown the election into the House of Representatives.

The Humphreys had joined the vigil at the Leamington, but as the evening wore on, Muriel retired to a suite on the twelfth floor. At 3 A.M., Hubert came up to bid her goodnight, knowing that there was little chance left. By 4 A.M., he too went to bed, and when he woke four hours later, all hope had gone.

The electoral vote showed Nixon with 31,785,-480 (43.40 percent) to Humphrey's 31,275,166 (42.72 percent) and Wallace's 9,906,473 (13.53 percent). The difference between Nixon and Humphrey was 510,314 votes. Nixon carried thirty-two states with an electoral total of 301; Humphrey carried thirteen states and the District of Columbia for an electoral vote of 191; Wallace won five states and had an electoral vote total of 46.

Facing his supporters in the Leamington ballroom that Wednesday morning, Humphrey read his telegram of congratulations to Nixon:

> According to unofficial returns, you are the winner in this election. My congratulations. Please know you will have my support in unifying and leading the nation. This has been a difficult year for the American people and I am confident that if constructive leaders in both our parties join together, we shall be able to go on with the business of building the better America we all seek in the spirit of peace and harmony. Signed Hubert H. Humphrey.

To his supporters, Humphrey said, "I have done my best. I have lost. Mr. Nixon has won. The democratic processes worked its will, so now let's get on with the urgent task of uniting our country.

Surrounded by family members and supporters, Humphrey acknowledges his defeat in the 1968 election.

Thank you." But his supporters didn't want to let him go. He returned to the stage, his eyes filled with tears: "Now go and have some fun. It has been a lot of hard work. I don't want anybody to have any extra sympathy—as a matter of fact—but what I would like to have you do is just redouble your effort to do what you thought you were doing and what I thought I was doing and maybe we can make an even greater contribution to the things that are important to this country."[26]

Characteristically, Humphrey did not lock himself into a room and go into a sulk after his defeat. That afternoon he and Freddie Gates went out to lunch at a popular Jewish delicatessen. Humphrey was as comfortable with Jews as any leading political figure in the nation, and they were among his strongest supporters. The patrons of the deli kept popping up at his table, commiserating with him at his loss, and the mutual affection helped ease the pain of the day.

When an election is as close as the Humphrey-

Maybe what he left behind was a record of a great man who lived by his convictions and didn't compromise them in order to become president. That's a hell of a lot more than can be said for Richard Nixon. When you think about it, Richard Nixon, even though he was president, will leave an awful lot less behind than Hubert Humphrey did. The country lost, all right, when Nixon was elected. Maybe Humphrey actually won. He stood by what he believed in.

JENO PAULUCCI

Nixon contest in 1968, any number of things might have changed the outcome: if McCarthy had supported Humphrey sooner and with more enthusiasm . . . if the Chicago convention had not been so disruptive and the media coverage of the violence so painfully thorough . . . if the convention had not been held so late . . . if there had been more early money . . . if the Humphrey forces had been better organized . . . if Humphrey had broken with Johnson earlier . . . if the bombing halt had come sooner. The possibilities are endless.

James Reston, writing in the *New York Times* two days after the election, saw it this way: "[Humphrey] was the right man at the wrong time."[27]

Humphrey himself, reflecting several years later in a newspaper interview, said: "I was like a man riding a tiger. It wasn't a question so much whether I was going to get across the finish line as whether I was going to be eaten up. . . . I was almost president once. Almost president."[28]

chapter 18

ANOTHER TRY

"In writing my concession speech, I told myself, 'This has to be done right, because it is the opening *speech of your next campaign.' "*

Hubert H. Humphrey

Reader's Digest, *August 1977*

On January 20, 1969, Richard Nixon was sworn in as president of the United States. For the first time in nearly a quarter of a century, Hubert Humphrey, Nixon's opponent in the 1968 election, was out of public office. He was not without prospects, however. Nixon had offered him the position of ambassador to the United Nations.

Richard Nixon takes the oath of office while Hubert Humphrey and Lyndon Johnson look on.

> It was a hot day, but Nixon was perspiring more than one would expect. And his hands shook perceptibly when he greeted me. I was struck by how ill at ease he seemed. He asked me to be the Ambassador to the United Nations and, to sweeten the offer, proposed to grant me control over any Democratic appointments he was required to make. I had a special feeling about the United Nations, but I was not eager to go from Lyndon Johnson's vice president to Richard Nixon's Ambassador.[1]

One of the more exotic proposals to come Humphrey's way had been made by Democratic Con-

In January 1969, the Humphreys visited the Sannes farm in Norway, where Hubert's mother was born.

gressman Benjamin S. Rosenthal of New York. Rosenthal had pointed out that the Speaker of the House of Representatives did not have to be a member of Congress and urged Humphrey to seek the post. Humphrey declined. What he needed was a chance to decompress, to shed some of the habits he had acquired over the years in Washington, to try on new ideas and new people, but in familiar surroundings. Humphrey wanted to go home to Minnesota.

On December 13, barely a month after the election, Humphrey accepted a joint offer to teach at the University of Minnesota and Macalester College, where he had last held a post before he was elected mayor in 1945. He was to be the first to fill Macalester's Hubert Humphrey Endowed Fellowship of International Affairs, which had been created the year before in his honor. The arrangement provided that he would spend two-thirds of his teaching time at Macalester and one-third at the university.

In addition to the salary he would receive from his teaching job, Humphrey had several sources of income: his pension as vice-president, a syndicated newspaper column, a contract with Doubleday to write his memoirs, numerous speaking engagements, and, most lucrative of all, positions as director and consultant to Encyclopaedia Britannica, acquired with the aid of his old friend, ex-Senator William Benton of Connecticut. All together, his income for 1969 would be close to $200,000, nearly four times what he had earned as vice-president.

Humphrey's teaching duties began on February

23, 1968, with a keynote address at Macalester's annual Political Emphasis Week. His address, a formal speech open to the public, dealt mostly with domestic issues. He reviewed his call for a Marshall Plan for American cities and a Model States plan patterned after the Model Cities program. Humphrey also addressed the need for national urban development and urban homestead banks and turned his attention to a favorite theme, arms control, asking for permanent suspension of the ABM system.

Humphrey's spring teaching schedule at Mac-

Humphrey addresses a class at the University of Minnesota.

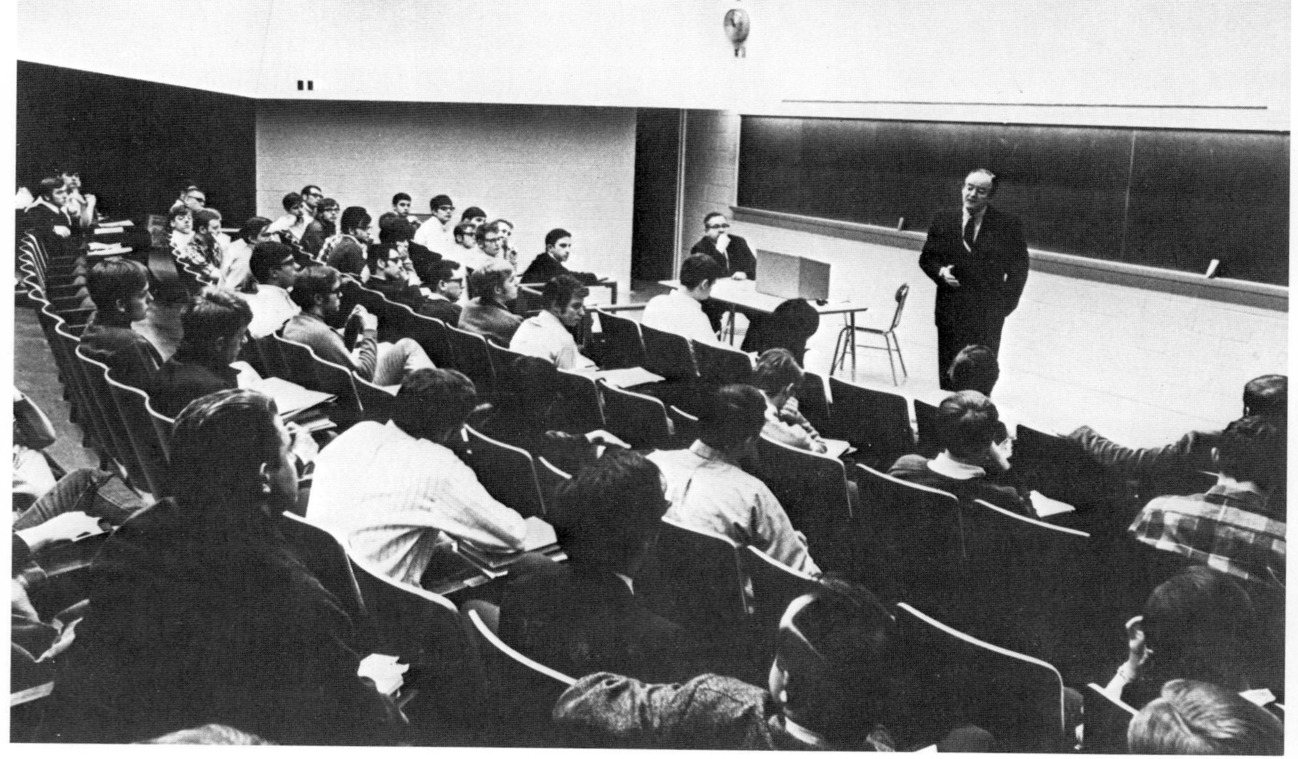

alester called for him to speak in five public affairs seminars, which were open to the public, and to conduct at least one class in each of the thirteen political science courses offered that term. Facing a class for the first time in March, he was nervous and rambled in his delivery. He had been away from teaching for many years, and he was also handicapped by the knowledge that, of late, he had not exactly been the darling of the nation's campuses. After an uncertain start and mixed reviews from his young critics, Humphrey settled down when one of his students suggested bluntly that he seemed to be wallowing in self-pity and that he should stop dwelling on the past. The comment, which might have devastated a more fragile personality, got Humphrey's juices flowing again, and his bouyancy and optimism returned. He had come prepared for demonstrations—"surprisingly, there haven't been any."[2] Instead, Professor Humphrey found himself the object of the students' admiration. He received a standing ovation in a black history class when he described the passage of the 1964 Civil Rights Act and the role he had played in working behind closed doors with Everett Dirksen. "Now you may call that hanky-panky, but I call it being a liberal. I don't think the only way to be a liberal is to suffer."[3] While at Macalester, Humphrey had an opportunity to demonstrate his continuing dedication to civil rights. When a St. Paul landlord refused to rent an apartment to a black student couple, he cancelled his class to take part in an open-housing march. The landlord relented. Humphrey was proud of his students for achieving their goals nonviolently; in the young

people's eyes, Humphrey had gained new stature by his participation in their demonstration.

Humphrey seemed happy in his role as a teacher and leader of the young, but events were taking place that made him think about his political future. In July, Gene McCarthy announced unequivocally that he would not seek re-election in 1970, either as a Democrat or, as many DFLers feared, as a third-party candidate. In August, Chappaquiddick weakened Teddy Kennedy's chances for achieving the presidency. And by November, Nixon's honeymoon was over.

During the summer of 1969, Humphrey turned his attention from domestic politics for a while and took a month-long trip abroad that included thirteen days spent in the Soviet Union. He met with

When he was at Macalester, I asked him to come to my class to speak on the Middle East. One time, he called me fifteen minutes before the class and asked me to come to his office. I went to his office, and who did I see there but Ambassador to the United Nations and former Supreme Court Justice Arthur Goldberg. He introduced me and said, "Well, Mr. Goldberg was just passing through and I've called you to find out whether you would permit me to bring him into the class." Well, naturally I was overjoyed. And he brought Mr. Goldberg and we really had the time of our lives with the two people who were on the top of making foreign policy and executing it. He was willing to share practically every important person who passed through with the students in my class.

YAHYA ARMAJANI
PROFESSOR, MACALESTER COLLEGE

Humphrey chats with Premier Aleksei Kosygin (second from right) **during his trip to the Soviet Union in 1969.**

Soviet Premier Aleksei Kosygin—the first meeting that year between the Russian premier and a leading American politician. The two men discussed U.S. and Soviet arms negotiations, as well as the situations in the Middle East and Southeast Asia. When Humphrey returned, he sent President Nixon a report on his meeting with Kosygin, in which he focused primarily on Soviet concerns over the development of offensive weapons systems.

In October, Humphrey met with President Nixon in the White House, a session that generated a lot of criticism from Democrats who disapproved of Humphrey's trafficking with the enemy. When he emerged from the meeting, Humphrey told reporters that he supported "to the best of [his] ability"[4] Nixon's efforts to end the war in Vietnam. Humphrey also revealed that he had promised the president that he would never say Nixon lost the war "if the President undertakes accelerated systematic withdrawal from Vietnam."[5] But there was a cautionary note. Humphrey said that Nixon continued to cling to the belief that the United States could end the war "on minimum acceptable terms, but the question is, If Hanoi doesn't agree, then do we stay five years more? Ten years more?"[6] As for the South Vietnamese, he felt that the United States had met its treaty obligations to them and bought them time to achieve self-determination: "We have done as much for our friends as a friend can be expected to do."[7]

On domestic policy, Humphrey was far more critical, faulting the Nixon administration for establishing priorities that put military hardware and supersonic transports ahead of controlling inflation, dealing with the problems of the nation's poor, and achieving meaningful tax reform.

With increasing frequency, Humphrey directed his public remarks toward the bread-and-butter issues that concerned Minnesota voters, while stating that he was "giving serious consideration"[8] to running for the Senate seat McCarthy was vacating. Humphrey's fellow DFLers were not strongly opposed to his plans. Some of the bitterness that had infected the DFL in 1968 had begun to fade. Forrest Harris, a leading McCarthy delegate to the 1968 convention, said he saw "little carry-over from '68 to'70. Most people think that Humphrey

Nixon is riding the bandwagon of Vietnam disengagement but he's not driving recklessly, he's not drag-racing. He's going around torturous curves and corners, and he's saying, "Please don't grab the wheel and please stop fighting in the back seat." On that, I support him. . . . He not only intends to withdraw our forces faster than anyone thinks, he is compelling the South Vietnamese to accept responsibility for their own defense—and I want to help him.

HUBERT H. HUMPHREY

Humphrey with fellow DFLers Eugene McCarthy and Congressman Donald Fraser at the DFL State Convention in 1970

was a good Senator, particularly in domestic issues. By and large, they will support him for the Senate, regardless."[9]

Before he began his campaign to regain a Senate seat, Humphrey had an opportunity to learn firsthand how empty his role as titular head of the Democratic Party was. The position, a residue of having been the party's presidential candidate in 1968, entitled Humphrey to name the chairman of the Democratic National Committee, a choice that would normally be confirmed in perfunctory fashion by the party's Executive Committee. When Fred Harris, Humphrey's original selection for the post, resigned, Humphrey badly fumbled the selection of a successor. Larry O'Brien, Humphrey's candidate to succeed Harris, accepted, then withdrew under circumstances that made it appear that Humphrey had misled him about the depth of the party's support for him. Humphrey then persuaded former Governor Matthew Welsh of Indiana to take the job. The Executive Committee promptly rejected Welsh and went back to O'Brien, and the whole embarrassing episode got in the papers.

While the story set Washington tongues atwitter, Minnesotans took no notice of this tale of high intrigue.

On June 13, 1970, Humphrey formally announced his candidacy for the Senate. He had assembled a new campaign team and a new image. Among the fresh faces around him were Jack Chestnut, a young Minneapolis lawyer, and John Morrison, a businessman who had parlayed a $5,000-stake into a million-dollar investment in a franchising business. Chestnut and Morrison planned a new kind of campaign for Humphrey.

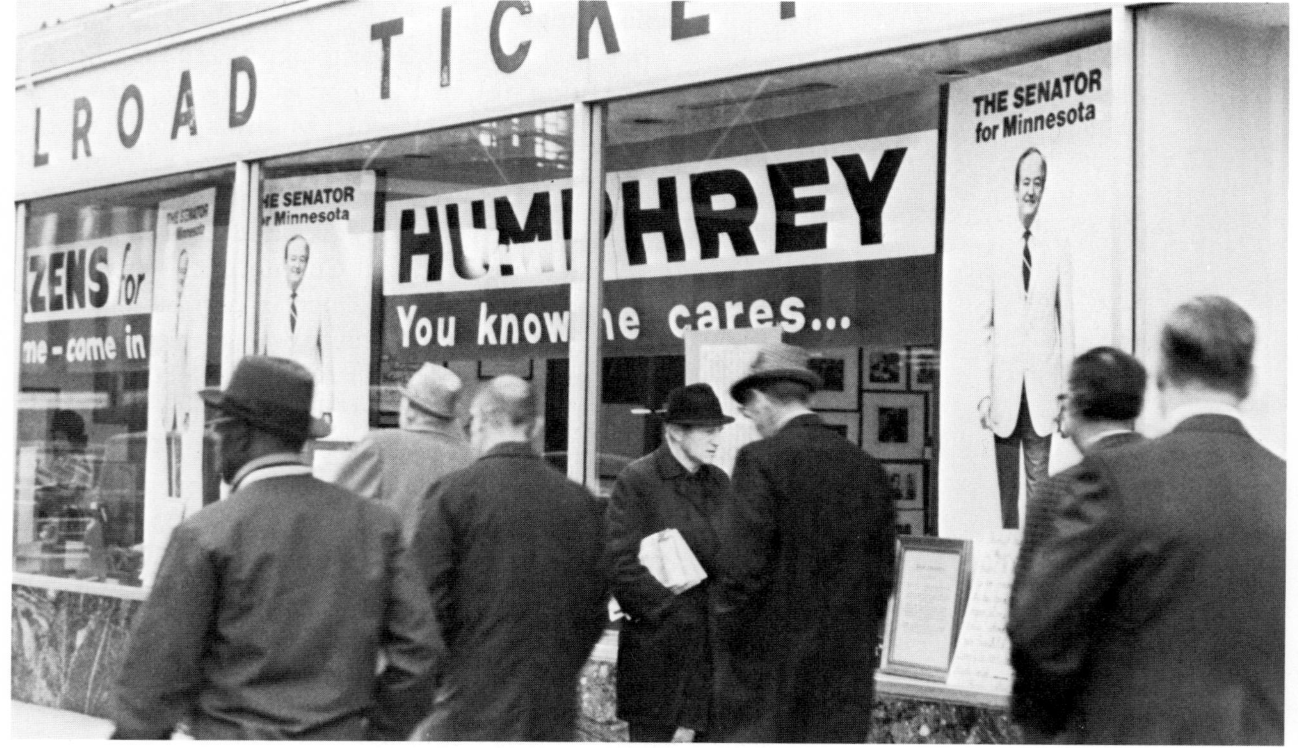

The 1970 Humphrey campaign office in Minneapolis

By the time the 1970 campaign rolled around, Humphrey really knew how to get his advance work done. Before he showed up at one of these county fairs, he had his people out there, usually young college students passing out flyers and telling the folks, "Humphrey is coming . . . Humphrey is coming." He would land in a helicopter and it was all very exciting and was drawing big crowds. Well, I ran again, and there weren't very many big crowds for me. . . . What I learned to do was to time my arrival as close to Humphrey's as I could. Then I would find out where he was speaking or holding his rally, and I would join him. I would just coattail him all over Minnesota.

After that happened twice, he finally turned around to me and said, "Forsythe, are you going to be with me at all these fairs?" And I said, "I am if I can just find out your schedule." "Well," he said, "there's no use your standing way back there in the crowd, you might as well come right up here." And so I would get up there on the platform with him and he would introduce me and say, "Well, now this is Bob Forsythe, and he's from the other party. You can't vote for him, but he's not such a bad guy after all."

ROBERT FORSYTHE

The gypsy days of bouncing along country roads in Freddie Gates' car from one county fair to another were over. His arrivals and departures were by helicopter or airplane and were staged to be events in themselves. They were preceded by careful advance work, and there were cheering crowds to meet the candidate at every stop. As part of his new image, both Humphrey's suits and his haircut acquired a more modish cut; his hair was mysteriously darker and his figure noticeably slimmer.

Humphrey's Republican opponent, Clark MacGregor, had served five terms in Congress representing the well-to-do suburban areas southwest of Minneapolis. He had been an early and ardent Nixon supporter, though the state's Republican delegation to the Miami Beach convention in 1968 had given the majority of its votes to Nelson Rockefeller. MacGregor, who had been planning his Senate race since 1966, had been hoping that his campaign would be against Gene McCarthy, or better yet, against both McCarthy and Humphrey, who would split the liberal vote. No such luck. On election day 1970, Humphrey buried MacGregor by 220,000 votes and helped elect a DFL governor, Wendell Anderson, as well as a host of other office seekers.

One of the small ironies of the campaign was that Humphrey's coattails carried a DFL attorney-general, Warren Spannaus, into office. Humphrey originally had opposed the selection of Spannaus for the ticket at the state convention, though once the matter was settled, no hard feelings lingered. During the campaign, Spannaus waged a lonely struggle for gun control, while Humphrey, not unaware of the strong hunting lobby in the state, ran newspaper ads that showed him walking through the woods with a gun slung over his shoulder. In his television commercials, cops hitched up their pants and talked about what a tough law-and-order mayor Humphrey had been. No two campaigns or campaigners could have been more unalike, yet without Humphrey leading the ticket and working hard to build up a cushion of DFL votes, Spannaus might not have pulled through.

Senator Humphrey was welcomed back to Washington in grand style at a party in his honor held at the Shoreham Hotel in late January, 1971. Several dozen of the Democratic Party's wealthiest contributors and a cross-section of office-holders, past and present, attended. There were no political speeches, but it was the sort of gathering that couldn't help but be noticed and remarked upon further up the street on Pennsylvania Avenue.

The Senate had changed in the six years since Humphrey had left, and his role there would be a much different one. Many of the old Senate types like Richard Russell were gone. Liberalization of Senate traditions, which had shown the greatest progress during Johnson's years as Majority Leader, now insured that freshmen senators would receive significant committee assignments during the first term and not be automatically put on the Post Office and the District of Columbia committees. Freshman Senator Humphrey asked for a seat on Appropriations, but was denied and wound up on Agriculture instead; his other committees were Government Operations and Joint Economics. A

I was invited one time to the opening of the new golf course out in Chanhassen. I was running for something at the time—it must have been the Senate—and they invited me, and they also invited Humphrey for this ground-breaking. They wanted both of us to hit a drive for the opening of this thing. Well, he got up there—he wasn't much of a golfer—and he swung and he sliced. I said, "Hubert, that's the best drive you've made in

Senators Humphrey, Muskie, Bayh, McGovern, and Hughes at the opening of the 92nd Congress in January 1971

a golf game in a long time." And he said, "Why?" And I said, "You finally went to the right." The crowd got a big kick out of that. So I got up and hit the ball. It didn't go very far, but at least it went down the middle. Humphrey said, "Well, that's the trouble with Forsythe, you never know where he is going to land." We had a good time with that one. Of course there was no problem having a good time—he was always a lot of fun to be with.

ROBERT FORSYTHE

greater disappointment than his committee assignments was Humphrey's realization that the legislative areas he had hoped to develop had been staked out by others during the years of his absence. No longer the Majority Whip, no longer holding chairmanship of Senate subcommittees or carrying sixteen years of seniority, he was Minnesota's junior senator, number ninety-one on the Senate seniority list, sandwiched between Adlai Stevenson III of Illinois and Lloyd Bentsen of Texas. If there was any particular distinction attached to his status, it was that he was the sixth former vice-president in the nation's history to return to the Senate: John Calhoun, John Breckenridge, Hannibal Hamlin, Andrew Johnson, and Alben Barkley had preceded him.

The first speech that Humphrey made on his return to Washington was to the Women's National Democratic Club, where he told a warmly approving audience of 300 that he refused to rule out the possibility of another race for the presidency in 1972.

In the Senate itself, Humphrey's freshman efforts met with mixed success. On the floor, he felt constrained by the Majority Whip, Robert Byrd, a martinet who permitted little latitude in the matters of Senate business. Even after Humphrey had succeeded in re-establishing himself, he could still be subject to the kind of legislative setback that would have been unthinkable in his own days as whip. Late in 1971, Humphrey was embarrassed when he realized that his amendment to postpone production of the Multiple Independent Re-entry Vehicle (MIRV) was in trouble. Sensing that he was about to lose the vote, he tried, and failed, to have the matter postponed. Then, seeing Quentin Burdick, a fellow Democrat from North Dakota, about to enter the Chamber, he attempted to persuade him to stay out long enough to create the absence of a quorum. Burdick refused. The resulting vote was a lopsided 39 to 12 against Humphrey's amendment. The defeat provided another item for the Washington gossip circuit but had little impact in the hinterlands.

Humphrey's legislative successes attracted more public attention than his failures. His first speech on the Senate floor called for the United States to temporarily limit development of the defensive nuclear missile, the ABM, while awaiting Russian

In July 1971, Humphrey gave testimony concerning the ABM before a Senate subcommittee headed by his old running mate Ed Muskie.

responses to a call for limitations of offensive weapons. The speech renewed Humphrey's credentials as the Senate's leading expert on armament. Together with an earlier vote against funding for the supersonic transport (SST)—a litmus test for re-establishing his relations with the liberals—it gave rise to speculation in the media that he might be making another run for the presidency. Humphrey did not discourage the talk. "If you decide to be an elder statesman, they give you a second-hand desk somewhere. I have no intention of becoming an elder, I would like to be a statesman—but I'd like to have a little power."[10]

As he performed fund-raising duties around the country, Humphrey began to take some soundings.

Talking to reporters outside the Foreign Relations committee room

A considerable number of people offered support and encouraged him to try again, and it was not long before he was musing aloud about his prospects in 1972. The bitterness and division within Democratic ranks over the war seemed to have abated, and there were early indications that neither of his two likeliest rivals, Edward Kennedy and Edmund Muskie, was likely to run away with the prize.

On the morning of May 27, he dropped a broad hint about his intentions as reporters joined him at breakfast to help celebrate his sixtieth birthday. "I've got the sails up and I'm testing the winds. I'm not really salivating but I'm occasionally licking my lips,"[11] he said, mixing his metaphors but making his intentions clear enough.

By October 1971, Muriel had joined the ranks of those who wanted Humphrey to run. She explained, "I have made up my mind, Daddy, as long as I have to campaign for a Democrat for president, I'm sure I want you as my candidate."[12]

Encouraged both by his family and by his closest political advisers to try again, Humphrey added more meetings, more travel, and more contacts with local Democratic leaders to an already overburdened schedule. Through the rest of the year he laid the political, financial, and organizational foundations for another run. During October he visited twenty states. In November, while visiting Atlanta, he stopped just short of a formal announcement, saying, "I look forward to the opportunity of a rematch with President Nixon next year."[13] On December 26, a nationwide Gallup poll taken of 560 Democrats showed him with a lead

The third party is beginning to look like a good risk, especially as it now appears that the Democrats and the Republicans are again going to come to the people, as they did in 1968, without offering any real choice and without raising the important issues for public examination.

EUGENE McCARTHY

over the candidates who had already announced that they were in the running. Assuming Kennedy out of the race, Hubert Humphrey was the preferred choice of 36 percent; Edmund Muskie got 31 percent; John Lindsay, 8 percent; George McGovern, 8 percent; Henry Jackson, 5 percent; Eugene McCarthy, 5 percent; Sam Yorty, 1 percent; and 8 percent polled had no opinion. A private poll commissioned by Humphrey and completed on December 1 showed virtually the same results

Leading contenders for the Democratic presidential nomination with party chairman Larry O'Brien: (left to right) **Henry Jackson, Hubert Humphrey, O'Brien, Ed Muskie, Fred Harris, and George McGovern.**

nationwide; another private poll of 449 Florida Democrats showed Wallace leading in Florida with 27 percent, Humphrey next with 23 percent, Muskie a close third with 22 percent, Jackson with 7 percent, and the rest of the pack trailing off.

The polls might have made Humphrey a front-runner, and the "atta boy"s he had heard on the banquet circuit may have been encouraging, but he knew that the surge of popularity could be subject to rapid erosion once he became an active candidate. As a candidate, he would no longer be above the battle but would be just another member of the pack, all of them lusting for the nomination. His narrow loss to Nixon would no longer be regarded solely as a tragic historical aberration; his rivals could easily portray it as the result of a fumbling campaign. His legislative achievements would be dissected, his experience would be derided as old age, and his role in the development of Vietnam policy would be ceaselessly criticized.

On January 10, 1972, Humphrey boarded a chartered 737 jet in Washington and flew to Philadelphia, where he had first made his presence felt nationally at the 1948 Democratic convention. With Muriel at his side, Humphrey took the plunge again and became the eighth announced candidate for the Democratic presidential nomination in 1972: "I was defeated for mayor the first time I ran for office, but I was elected the second time. I was defeated for the vice presidential nomination the first time, but I was nominated and later elected. I was defeated for the presidential nomination in 1960, but I was nominated in 1968. I was defeated in the presidential election of 1968. But I returned to the battle determined to do my best to achieve victory in 1972."[14]

To shake the loser's image and avoid being charged with lying in wait until he could arrange a brokered nomination in some smoke-filled room at the convention, Humphrey decided to enter a representative number of primaries. It was not a strategy he chose willingly.

I remember our granddaughter Amy, who was just seven, asking Hubert during the 1972 campaign, "Grandpa, are you mad at Mr. Nixon?" When he indicated that he was not, she said, "Then why do you want to take his job away?" So he sat down to explain very patiently and carefully why he was running for the presidential nomination. No reporter's question had been any more difficult or required a more thoughtful answer.

MURIEL HUMPHREY

Humphrey, like most politicians, was well aware that primaries offer the entrants few advantages. They are ruinously expensive, depleting funds that candidates need in the general election. Primaries often divide a party against itself at the very moment it faces the opposition party, when the greatest strength and unity are needed. They magnify errors, provide future ammunition to the opposing party, lock candidates into awkward positions, deplete their fund of issues, and exhaust them physically and mentally. For a presidential candidate less than certain of winning his party's nomination, about the only choice worse than entering the primaries is not entering them.

Humphrey decided to duck the March 7 New Hampshire primary in Ed Muskie's back yard and to begin his effort in Florida a week later. Muskie faced only one serious opponent in New Hampshire, George McGovern, and he managed to win the campaign with 46.4 percent of the vote to McGovern's 37.1 percent. But, like Lyndon Johnson's 1968 victory over Eugene McCarthy, the win was disastrous. Muskie's margin of victory was well below earlier predictions; even worse, the candidate destroyed his image as a strong statesmanlike leader by allowing himself to be televised

Too long this party has been controlled by the so-called intellectual snobs who feel that big government should control the lives of American citizens from the cradle to the grave.

GEORGE WALLACE

as he wept while denouncing the editor of the *Manchester Union Edition* for articles attacking his wife.

The next week in the Florida primary, George Wallace won, as expected, and Humphrey came in second. Muskie staggered in fourth and, the day after the election, made another emotional statement, this time attacking Wallace. The sudden collapse of the Muskie campaign enabled Humphrey to emerge in the role of the centrist Democratic candidate, but Humphrey's showing in Florida was not encouraging. He had made a major effort in the state, operating a computer-based campaign that involved 250,000 mailing pieces and 250,000 phone calls, as well as television, newspaper, radio, and billboard ads. Humphrey had spent twenty-two of the thirty days before the primary campaigning in Florida. In Washington on the day that a crucial Senate vote had been scheduled but then cancelled, he had rushed to the airport while his Florida advance team scurried about to develop an appearance that would be useful. In the time it took Humphrey to get to Florida, they had set up a booth at the State Fair in Tampa where he was seen by some 30,000 Floridians. Spending four hours in St. Petersburg, he had led Head Start classes singing "Old MacDonald Had a Farm," played basketball with ghetto youth, danced with an elderly woman to the tune of "Let Me Call You Sweetheart," and played shuffleboard with some retirees in the park.

But all the energy that Humphrey expended in Florida had been to no avail. Wallace had finished with 526,651 votes (41.6 percent), while Hum-

George Wallace with an enthusiastic crowd in Indiana

Humphrey rides in a 1920s model truck during a campaign parade.

phrey's second place showing of 234,658 (18.5 percent) was not even close. More disturbing to some was the report coming out of Florida a few days after the primary that some of Humphrey's radio ads had featured an attack on "lazy welfare chiselers." Northern editorial writers criticized the ads as an attempt to capitalize politically on black-white tensions, which were particularly severe in Florida, where anti-busing had been the theme of the Wallace campaign.

Humphrey, four years ago, when I said get the loafers and chiselers off the welfare rolls, he said I was a demagogue. And you know what he said this time? "Get the loafers and chiselers off the welfare rolls."

GEORGE WALLACE

The Florida primary also affected the fortunes of several other candidates. John Lindsay had campaigned hard and spent lavishly in Florida. His campaign featured clever ads in which Carroll O'Connor, television's Archie Bunker, delivered a liberal message that belied his image as a television bigot. Lindsay finished fifth with 82,386 (6.5 percent). George McGovern, who finished sixth behind Lindsay with 78,232 (6.1 percent), had not campaigned at all in Florida. By the peculiar mathematics of primaries, McGovern was therefore counted a winner and Lindsay a loser in Florida.

The next lap would be run in Wisconsin on April

George McGovern campaigns in a market in Buffalo, New York.

4, and it was here that McGovern would begin to emerge from the pack. McGovern workers had been organizing in Wisconsin since November 1970; since that time McGovern himself had been making a three-day tour of the state every ninety days. "By the last week in March 1972, every one of Wisconsin's seventy-two counties had a McGovern volunteer nucleus; thirty-five to forty paid organizers (most of them paid $50 a week) had opened storefronts in some counties, housewives had opened their homes in others, to cover the state. Two thousand unpaid volunteer workers were walking blocks and country roads, marking voters on precinct sheets in the familiar one-two-three-four patterns of preferences indicating the degree of pressure to be exerted to bring them out on primary day. $232,000 had been spent in Wisconsin, the largest expenditure ($65,000) on an eight-page reprint in eighteen Wisconsin newspapers that reached 1,256,000 people in February."[15]

Humphrey had been unable to match the McGovern effort in Wisconsin. Moreover, Ed Muskie was still going through the motions, and when the primary was held on April 4, he and Humphrey split the centrist vote. Humphrey still managed to finish third, with more than twice as many votes as Muskie, but McGovern had buried John Lindsay, his opponent for supremacy on the party's left, with over four times as many votes. McGovern's total was 333,528 (29.5 percent); George Wallace came in second with 248,676 votes (22 percent); Humphrey got 233,748 (20.7 percent); Muskie, 115,811 (10.2 percent); Jackson, 88,068 (7.8 percent) and Lindsay, 75,579 (6.6 percent). George Wallace's ability to draw more votes in Wisconsin than Hubert Humphrey was a pointed commentary on the racial fears that had swept the North.

We want to tell the world to vote
For Hubert Humph-erey.
We want you all to know why he
Is the best for the presidency.
He's the man who started Medicare
For the elderly.
He's always fought for the little guy
And folks like you and me.
The people really need him now,
He's a fighter tried and true.
To get our country back on track
Elect Humphrey '72.

CAMPAIGN SONG BY JIMMY WOLFORD

On April 25 was the Pennsylvania primary, with 182 delegate votes at stake. Humphrey won with strong union backing, getting 481,900 (35.0 percent) to Wallace's 292,437 (21.2 percent), McGovern's 280,861 (20.4 percent), and Muskie's 279,983. On the same day, McGovern swamped his opponents in Massachusetts with 325,673 (52.6 percent) to Muskie's 131,709 (21.2 percent) and Humphrey's 48,929 (7.9 percent). Surprisingly, in all his years of campaigning for the nomination, Pennsylvania was the first presidential primary that Hubert Humphrey had won. In the next two weeks, he was to win three more—Indiana, West Virginia, and Ohio, another delegate-rich state that Humphrey took with 499,680 (41.2 percent) to McGovern's surprisingly strong 480,320 (39.6 percent) and Muskie's 107,806 (8.8 percent). During the early weeks of May, Humphrey lost to George Wallace in Tennessee and to McGovern in Nebraska.

On May 16, two more important primaries would be held, Maryland and Michigan. The day before the election, in a parking lot in Laurel, Maryland, George Wallace was shot by a crazy, Arthur Bremer, who earlier had wanted to kill Nixon but, finding him too heavily guarded, had settled for Wallace. Wallace, who was paralyzed by his injuries, won both primaries held the next day: Maryland with 219,687 (38.9 percent) to Humphrey's 151,981 (26.9 percent) and McGovern's 126,978 (22.5 percent); and Michigan, where

On May 18, George Wallace spoke at a shopping center in Wheaton, Maryland. Later that same day, he was shot during a campaign appearance in Laurel, Maryland.

busing was the overriding issue, with 809,239 (50.9 percent) to McGovern's 425,694 (26.8 percent) and Humphrey's weak 249,798 (15.7 percent). Wallace had made good on his campaign promise to "send them a message," but the gunman had eliminated him as a factor in the presidential race. The contest was now between McGovern and Humphrey, and the issue would be settled on June 6 in California, in a winner-take-all primary for 271 delegate votes.

Once again, McGovern's superb campaign organization had been at work long before the primary. The McGovern forces made use of computer cards carrying the names and voting preferences of millions of Californians, all of whom received personalized letters emphasizing their political concerns.

McGovern talks with a resident of a home for the elderly in San Francisco.

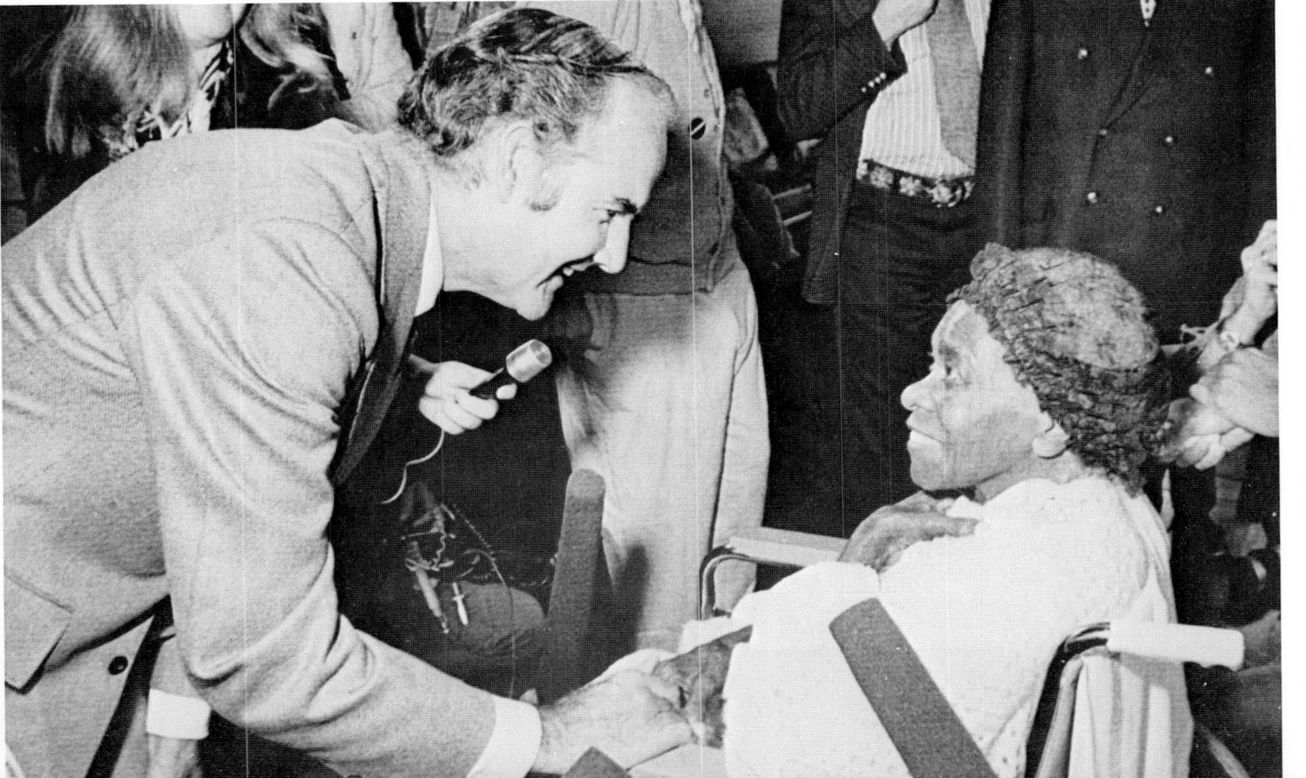

Humphrey addresses the congregation of t Macedonia Mission Church in San Francis

By election day, 283 McGovern store-fronts had sprung up; block workers had been busy block-working, telephoners telephoning.

Humphrey counted on the traditional sources of his strength, labor unions, blacks, and Jews, to deliver the votes in California. Finances, always the bane of a Humphrey campaign, were in even worse shape than usual. By mid-April a large gift program had gotten Humphrey $800,000 in contributions, but he was still $700,000 in debt. "What are you going to say about a campaign when you go into headquarters and the biggest question is how are we going to get $280 in cash *now* or else the staff gets tossed out of their motel rooms this afternoon?"[16] said Robert J. Keefe, part of the AFL/CIO team that had been sent into California to help pull Humphrey through. Ten days before the primary, Humphrey's California media funds, which had been carefully husbanded by his campaign treasurer, Eugene Wyman, suddenly were needed in Washington if those who had been writing checks for the campaign against nonexistent balances were to avoid going to jail. The money went to Washington and with it any possibility of a Humphrey television campaign.

There remained one chance for Humphrey to win in California—if he could score heavily in the three television debates with McGovern that would take place late in May, first on CBS's "Face the Nation," then on NBC's "Meet the Press," and finally on ABC's "Issues and Answers."

In the first debate on May 28, Humphrey wasted no time going on the attack, immediately zeroing in on what would seem to be McGovern's

Harry S Truman couldn't even get on the radio in 1948 until somebody raised $70,000 for him. . . . You've got to have the money—cash on the line—or they won't let you on the radio, they won't let you on the television, they won't put your ad in the newspaper. They want cash on the line. Every campaign I've ever been in I've been short of money.

HUBERT H. HUMPHREY

greatest strength, his Vietnam record. Humphrey hit McGovern's slogan "Right from the start" and pointed out that McGovern, like Humphrey, had been wrong from the start in voting both for the Tonkin Gulf resolution and for Vietnam appropriations. (McGovern later said that he was "somewhat amazed"[17] by both the vigor of the attack and the very fact that Humphrey would criticize his record on Vietnam.) On defense spending, Hum-

Humphrey and McGovern during their debate on "Meet the Press," May 30

phrey charged that McGovern's plan to lop $20 billion from the defense budget cut "into the muscle, the very fiber of our national security,"[18] a point not lightly taken in a state whose largest employer is the defense industry and whose population includes countless retired servicemen. Humphrey's most telling criticism was directed against McGovern's plan to provide a $1,000 federal grant to everyone in the country, a scheme that Humphrey estimated would cost $409 for every family earning over $12,000. In his response, McGovern wobbled on his figures and acknowledged he could not produce a true cost estimate because of the effect of other tax changes pending in Congress.

The effect of the first debate on viewers was not clear-cut. Mostly there was no effect, since the program had been aired on a weekend and Californians had preferred the beach to the tube. Humphrey's camp felt their candidate had been too strident, and in the next two meetings, Hum-

My greatest single asset is truth-telling. I don't duck the issues, and I'm not capable of deception. I'm open, honest, Midwestern and rural in background. People think I come across like a Sunday school teacher, that I'm not an effective communicator. I think a lot of the American people are tired of flash and charisma and show business spectacles or candidates getting special instruction in television techniques and image-changing. I think truthfulness and trustworthiness are more important than flash appeal and charisma.

GEORGE McGOVERN

Campaigning on San Francisco's Fisherman's Wharf

Humphrey and S. Harrison Dogole

In mid-June of 1972, after Senator Humphrey's narrow loss in the California presidential primary, I had arranged to hold a fund raising event in Florida for the benefit of expenditures that had to be met at the upcoming convention in Miami Beach. The event, which produced about $20,000, found Humphrey in his usual jovial mood, pressing the flesh and exhilarating the audience. When the evening's activities came to a close, the Senator and I returned to a hotel suite in Miami Beach, where we were staying. As was his custom, he turned on the television set in his bedroom to watch a late-night western movie. I asked him for his present assessment of the situation. He turned around and, in an un-Humphrey succinct manner, answered "Gloomy."

S. HARRISON DOGOLE
PHILADELPHIA BUSINESSMAN
AND HUMPHREY FUND RAISER

phrey's delivery was much gentler. McGovern may have won some points on style during the debates, but he lost convincingly on substance. For the first time in the campaign, the issues on which McGovern had based his candidacy were openly challenged. From that time on, his message began to unravel. Before the campaign was over in November, his opponents had made his call for a $1,000 payment synonymous in the public mind with fuzzy-headed liberalism.

On June 6, California voted, and the totals gave McGovern 1,550,652 (44.3 percent) to Humphrey's 1,375,064 (39.2 percent). Earlier, the polls had indicated that McGovern might win by 15 to 20 percent over Humphrey, rather than the 5 percent margin he did achieve. Humphrey had done far better than expected, but with California's 271 delegates presumably now in McGovern's bag, it appeared that the contest was all over.

The next morning, Humphrey flew to Houston for a meeting with Democratic governors. He spoke about withdrawing from the race, but all of them, except Pat Lucey of Wisconsin, a long-time McGovern supporter, urged him not to quit. Still undecided, Humphrey reached George Meany, at sea aboard the *Queen Elizabeth,* by ship-to-shore phone. Meany also urged him to stay in the race.

The 1972 Democratic Convention, to be held at Miami Beach in mid-July, presented Humphrey with one final opportunity for the nomination. His effort got underway before the convention began. While McGovern's people were preoccupied with counting delegates and with obtaining a strong representation on the Platform and Rules committees, the ABM (anybody-but-McGovern) forces quietly packed the Credentials Committee. Suddenly, the seating of the 271 McGovern delegates won in the winner-take-all California primary was in doubt. The new reform rules of the Democratic Party, which had thus far worked so well for McGovern, were turned against him by the Credentials Committee. Meeting in Washington on June 27, several weeks in advance of the convention, the committee issued a majority report stating that the California winner-take-all primary contradicted the reform rules and that McGovern was therefore entitled only to the proportion of the delegates corresponding to his primary vote—44.3

Humphrey visits the Texas delegation to the Democratic National Convention in Miami Beach.

percent, or 120 delegates. The rest of the delegates would go to the other California candidates in proportion to their vote. The decision of the Credentials Committee was promptly taken to the Supreme Court, where it was affirmed.

McGovern's reaction was both predictable and understandable. He described the committee's actions as "an incredible, cynical, rotten political steal. A corrupt, spiteful deal. . . . I can't believe what happened. Senator Humphrey was delighted with the California rules before the election. He said even if he lost, he wasn't going to be a spoil sport. Now this effort is being led by Senator Humphrey and it shocks and grieves me to see an old friend participate in a shabby, underhanded deal. I can't believe that it happened. It's the old corrupt politics,"[19] said McGovern. He was so upset that he said he might bolt the party if denied the nomination. Humphrey countered by leading the opposing forces, the Wallace, Muskie, Jackson, and Wilbur Mills supporters, in issuing a statement saying that they would support whomever the convention selected. When asked why he had changed his mind about abiding by the voters' decision in California, there wasn't much he could say except "Sometimes I just talk too much."[20]

When the Democratic Convention convened on Monday July 10, the decision on the California question was to be put to the delegates in the form of a minority report that dissented from the action of the Credentials Committee. The key to the outcome lay in the answer to two questions: who would be permitted to vote on the report, and what would constitute a majority vote. If the entire

Presidential candidates Humphrey, McGovern, and Shirley Chisholm, Congresswoman from New York, on the platform at the Democratic Convention

California delegation, including the 120 delegates conceded to McGovern under the majority report, were barred from voting on the theory that no menber of a contested delegation should be permitted to vote on the delegation's credentials, then the ABM forces felt they had an excellent chance of defeating the minority report. If the 120 McGovern delegates were permitted to vote, then it seemed likely that the McGovern forces would win and all 271 McGovern delegates would be seated.

Larry O'Brien, the convention chairman, ruled that the 120 McGovern delegates would be allowed to vote on the minority report.

On the question of what constituted a majority, the convention parliamentarian, James O'Hara, ruled that the 151 contested delegates would be subtracted from the total delegate vote of 3,016, with the result that the McGovern forces needed only 1,433 rather than 1,509 votes to win their challenge.

With both rulings from the chair against Humphrey, the result was a foregone conclusion. On Tuesday, July 11, at 2:30 A.M., the minority report won, 1,689.52 to 1,162.23. Humphrey told his people to drop any further procedural tactics. His last hope for the nomination was gone, and there remained only the final painful ceremony.

Later Tuesday morning, Humphrey stood with

Muriel by his side and, in an emotional scene, announced that he was leaving the race. "My withdrawal from the Presidency is a withdrawal of candidacy only. It is not a withdrawal of spirit or . . . of determination to continue the battle I have waged all my public life on behalf of those who had no voice."[21]

After Humphrey spoke to his workers, many of them the idealistic and the young whom the press had insisted were so little in evidence in his campaign, one young man remarked: "I wish that everyone who called Hubert Humphrey a fuddy-duddy and a spokesman for the old politics could have heard what he told us today. He's a great man. I don't know of another politician who has done so much for his people in the years that Mr. Humphrey has been in office."[22]

What appeared to be his last grab for the brass ring was now over—hard fought, expensive, and a failure. Humphrey admitted, "It's a mission unaccomplished and a dream unrealized. There is no use pretending. It was a tremendous goal in my life and one that I am not going to achieve. I really felt if I was President, I could do great things for this country, and that's why I ran again. . . . Once again, I've got to be one of the architects instead of the architect."[23]

Later, he tried to isolate the cause of his defeat:

> People have known me for so long there's nothing left to know. . . . The media wanted something new. . . . It was incredible, but we just couldn't break in. They were interested only if I was waffling on busing or dyeing my hair. You'd never have known that I won a few major primaries, or

In 1972, as defeat in the battle for the Democratic Presidential nomination loomed, I put it to Humphrey, as politely as I could, that perhaps he was a bit past it. "Aren't you simply too nice a man to be President of the United States?" I asked. The Humphrey chin stuck out, as it had done in the cartoons for a quarter-century, and he said a very touching thing. "Goddam it, what this country needs is a nice man as President."

PETER JENKINS
NEW YORK TIMES MAGAZINE

Hubert hugs Muriel after announcing his withdrawal from the race for the Democratic nomination.

> that George McGovern had lost a few. My total popular vote was bigger than George's, but no one examined what that meant, and we had plenty of young people working in our campaign, but nobody paid any attention. They said we were old hat. I suppose it was true.[24]

I was ready in '68 and I was ready in '72 but the times weren't ready for us. Politics is timing and events.
HUBERT H. HUMPHREY

Among those who had stood by with tears in their eyes when Humphrey announced his withdrawal had been Jack Chestnut, his campaign manager, and the other members of the Humphrey team. They knew that the uncharacteristic toughness of the campaign had bothered Humphrey. "You almost got the feeling that he hated some of the things he was driven into the last three or four weeks," one of them said. "I think he would rather go back to the old, rollicking, cornball Humphrey. . . ."[25]

For Humphrey, the time for tears had been that morning at 8:50 when he announced his withdrawal. At 9:30, some long-faced supporters came up to the man who had lost his last bid for the presidency, and Humphrey told them, "The trouble with you guys is that you all get depressed."[26]

chapter 19

LAST TRY

"Frankly we had to scramble for money all the time . . . . I had desperate financial needs."
Hubert H. Humphrey

Following the McGovern debacle in November of 1972, I picked up Senator Humphrey in a fishing boat at Caneel Bay in the Virgin Islands. His son Douglas was also with us at the time. We were not having much success in our fishing endeavors, so . . . I asked Humphrey to implore the fish to start taking our bait. He did so without any success, at which point I said, "Perhaps they don't know who you are." I followed up with the statement that "it's too bad the press is not here now. They would say that old Humphrey had gone bananas. He does not have any people to talk to, so he is now talking to fish." All three of us had a good laugh.

S. HARRISON DOGOLE

When election day came in 1972, Humphrey cast his vote in the same place as he had in 1968, the little township hall in Marysville, near his home at Lake Waverly. But this time, the scene was different than it had been when he was a presidential candidate. There were no television cameramen following him in and out of the polling place, no newsmen tripping over each other, no townspeople crowding around their famous neighbor. There was only a lone reporter tramping after Humphrey as he panhandled Muriel for $20 so he could pay the township supervisors for having the snow plowed from his driveway that winter. After handing over the money, Humphrey asked Muriel, "Are you ready, Mom?"[1] and they went over to the wooden polling booths and voted. Recalling the scene that had taken place four years earlier at Marysville, township supervisor Emery Jenkins said, "It will never happen again. It was really something."[2] Humphrey agreed.

After voting, the Humphreys returned to the house at Lake Waverly, which had been their home in Minnesota since 1967. The Waverly property had originally been purchased from Republican dairyman Ray Ewald, and its acquisition had been the cause of a mild flutter in the closing days of the 1968 election. As the *New York Times* began to run stories of Spiro Agnew's wheelings and dealings in Maryland, the *Chicago Tribune* revealed that Humphrey's purchase from Ewald had come at about the same time that the dairyman was involved in a price fixing case. There was never any indication that Humphrey had intervened in Ewald's behalf, and the only satisfaction

The Humphreys' home at Waverly

the Republicans ever got from the incident was a grudging slap on Humphrey's wrist delivered in a *Times* editorial a few days before the election.

The minor controversy over the acquisition of the Waverly property had no effect on the pleasure that the Humphreys derived from the lakefront home they had built there. Forty miles from the Twin Cities and several miles from the nearest small town, it was called the "HHH Ranch," but unlike the LBJ Ranch, Humphrey's home was a refuge, not an empire. Here he could observe the normal rituals of family life, mundane to most, but precious to a public man, particularly one as warm and affectionate as Humphrey. Here he could watch his four children grow to adulthood, establish careers, start families of their own: Nancy, the oldest, the first to marry and to make the Humphreys grandparents; Hubert III—Skip—who became a politician like his father, winning election to the Minnesota Senate in 1972; Bob, pursuing a career in public service as a city planner in Minneapolis; and Doug, the youngest, who joined the business world and became president of a local distributing company.

We encouraged our children to be independent and to think for themselves. With a father prominent in politics, we wanted them to make their own choices and to have their own experiences. I am proud of how well they have succeeded.

MURIEL HUMPHREY

Muriel enjoys a sunset over Lake Waverly.

Hubert, Muriel, and assorted grandchildren in one of the Humphreys' antique cars

After they were married, all the Humphrey children made their homes in the Twin Cities, and the house at Lake Waverly was a gathering place for the whole family, including ten lively grandchildren. Old friends also came to visit and to join in the family sing-alongs, which were accompanied and led by Muriel. An accomplished pianist, she had studied music as a young woman and had maintained her skills over the years. Besides sing-alongs, Waverly offered a wide variety of diversions for guests and residents alike. Depending on the season, there was ice skating, snowmobiling, waterskiing, swimming in lake or pool, boating—sail or motor—and plenty of fishing. Hubert found many hours of enjoyment in tinkering with and tuning an old Model A. He also enjoyed hunting

The Humphreys celebrate their fortieth wedding anniversary with their four children: (from left to right) **Doug, Muriel, Hubert, Nancy, Skip, and Bob**

At a time when my boys and Humphrey's boys were about 12 to 14 years old, we took a fishing trip up north. We had a truck on a one-way road through the wilderness at a portage, and the truck broke down. It blocked the passage of a big bus loaded with tourists and canoes and gear. Humphrey said he'd try to figure out what was wrong with the truck, and I ran to the bus.

I said, "How do you do, folks. Welcome to Minnesota, land of clean air and good water. I want to point out a little local color to you: There's a fellow here who pretends he's a U.S. senator. In fact, he even looks like a senator. But he's harmless. He might try to spear a few drinks off you, but he won't hurt you. Here, I'll show you. Hubert, come here. These people want to see you."

So Humphrey came running to the bus, and I said to the tourists, "Folks, now humor him along but don't lend him any money." Humphrey got on the bus and said, "Hi, folks, I'm Senator Humphrey." Someone from the back of the bus yelled, "And I'm Soapy Williams." Someone else said, "And I'm Pat Brown." Humphrey realized something was up and he said to me, "Miles, what have you done to me this time?"

MILES LORD
U.S. DISTRICT JUDGE

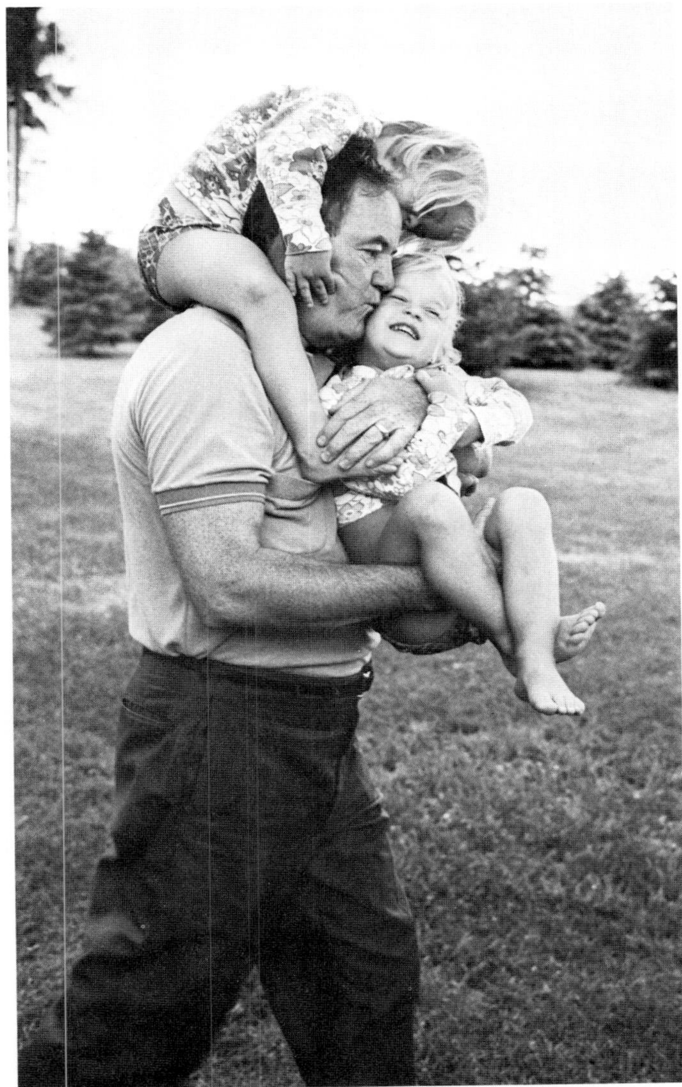

Humphrey with two of his grandchildren

and was an excellent shot, having the rare ability to switch guns—from a slide action to an automatic, from a side-by-side to an over-and-under—with no noticeable fall-off in marksmanship.

Some of the time that Humphrey spent at Waverly was occupied by his ongoing battle against spiders and dandelions, the only unwelcome guests at the HHH Ranch. Harold Chapman, the caretaker at Waverly, swore that Humphrey could spot a dandelion a mile away. No matter how tired he was or how pressing any other business might be, once Humphrey had sighted one of the offending plants, its dispatching took precedence over everything else. Spiders and spider webs suffered the same fate. Broom in hand, Humphrey would probe the corners and eaves of the buildings until he was satisfied that the trespassers had been rooted out. Humphrey's almost compulsive tidiness was manifested in other situations. On one occasion, he and Miles Lord took their sons on a fishing trip in northern Minnesota, and Humphrey spent most of his time cleaning Lord's somewhat rundown vacation cabin, too busy dealing with the mess ever to get much fishing done. Humphrey's picture-straightening, table-wiping frame of mind may have been fixed in him as part of his early training as a small town merchant or during his days earning the roof over his and Muriel's heads as a janitor of their apartment building. Whatever the source, Humphrey believed that hard and dirty work was not just something to talk about—it was something to pitch in and do. "I hear people say, 'I don't like that kind of work.' Well, who the hell does? I used to swab out the toilets when I went to

In Texas, as Lyndon Johnson's guest, you did things his way. Early one morning . . . , we climbed into his Lincoln, and Johnson, guns at the ready, drove slam bang and lickety split across the countryside until we spotted one of the many deer that grazed on his ranch. He slammed on the brakes, and in his commanding voice said, "Hubert, there's one for you. Get it!"

I am a good shot and have hunted duck and pheasant and quail fairly frequently throughout my life. . . . But I never liked to shoot four-legged creatures, deer particularly. Nevertheless, I got slowly from the car, lifted my rifle, set myself for its kick, and brought down the deer. I turned to Johnson with a mixture of satisfaction at having done so well what he wanted and revulsion at having killed the deer.

"Well," he said, "Bobby Kennedy got two of them. You're not going to let Bobby get the best of you, are you?" Before there was time for an answer, the car sped on its way again, until we sighted another deer. As he slammed on the brakes once again, Johnson said, "Now's your chance. Hit that one." I hit it, and the deer fell.

HUBERT H. HUMPHREY

college and we were caretakers for a fourplex. I repaired the roof, fixed the plumbing, cleaned the sewers, shoveled the snow and besides that, worked six hours a day in a drugstore for 20¢ an hour. So, when I hear people say, 'I don't like that kind of work,' I say, 'Well, isn't that too bad!' "[3]

The chores that Humphrey performed at Waverly were not really burdensome but rather a pleasant part of the private family life that he cherished and enjoyed so much. Humphrey continued to enjoy a full and active public life as well. Soon after the 1972 election, he made a trip abroad that included his fourth visit to Moscow as well as stops in Warsaw, Bonn, London, and Dublin. Humphrey's duties in the Senate also kept him active and visible. Late in 1972, he led a successful fight to deny President Nixon the authority to withhold the spending of funds that had been

Humphrey met with members of the Ministry of Agriculture during his visit to the Soviet Union in December 1972.

One day when we were visiting the Vatican, Humphrey had a private meeting with the Pope. Then he asked the Pope whether he could introduce him to some of his staff and Secret Service Agents who were Catholic. One staff member was very devout, churchgoing, very serious about his religion and very close to Humphrey. That was David Gartner. When he introduced him to the Pope, Humphrey said, "Your Holiness, David is a member of my staff and a member of your church, but I simply cannot get him to go to Mass." David just turned purple with embarrassment. The Pope went along with the joke, and he took David's hand in both of his and said, "My son, you must go to Mass!" Humphrey in the most serious of times had a way of relieving the pressure and the tension and did it beautifully.

NORMAN SHERMAN

authorized by Congress. Humphrey was able to attract some conservative support to his cause by arguing that the president's action would violate the Constitutional separation of powers: if Nixon were to refuse to spend funds authorized by Congress, then he would be usurping the authority that the Constitution had conferred on Congress. The thirty-nine-to-twenty-seven vote confirming Humphrey's position helped enhance his status as a legislative leader and fueled speculation that when Mike Mansfield stepped down as Majority Leader in 1977, the fight to succeed him would be between Humphrey and the new Whip, Robert Byrd of West Virginia.

Pope Paul VI welcomes Humphrey to the Vatican in November 1973.

There was no talk of another presidential try. Not only would Humphrey be sixty-five by the time of the next election, but he also carried the battle scars of his previous efforts. In addition, a Humphrey protege, Walter Mondale, now Minnesota's senior senator, was exploring his own presidential prospects. If one lesson had been learned in 1968, it was that while some quirk in American politics seemed to require that there always be one presidential hopeful from Minnesota, one per election was quite enough.

Another factor entered into Humphrey's decision not to pursue his presidential prospects. In the backwash of the Watergate scandal, which had

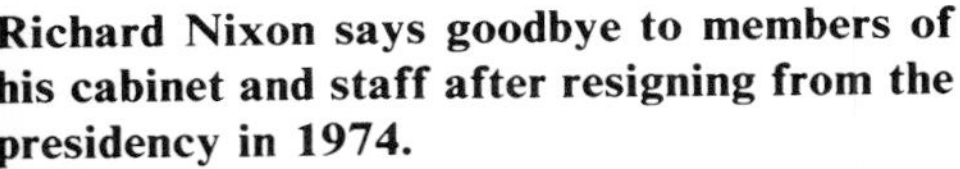

Richard Nixon says goodbye to members of his cabinet and staff after resigning from the presidency in 1974.

swept the country in 1973, illegal activities had been uncovered in several past Humphrey campaigns. For years Humphrey had encouraged dairy co-operatives to establish legal political funds supported by voluntary contributions from their members, just as labor unions and businessmen had done. Humphrey had supported the legislative program of dairy interests since he entered the Senate in 1949, and when he first started getting contributions from the American Milk Producers, Inc., in 1968, he thought: "The dairy farmers in politics: it's almost like getting it from church."[4] It wasn't. It turned out that the funds had not come from voluntary contributors. Illegal corporate funds were used, in 1968 and again in 1970 and 1972, both because the voluntary funds had not been in existence long enough to have much money in them and also because the reports required for contributions from voluntary funds would have revealed to the Republicans the existence of the Milk Producers' donations. Humphrey's campaign manager, Jack Chestnut, was subsequently convicted of arranging an illegal $12,000 contribution from American Milk Producers, Inc., and sentenced to jail for four months.

Once the first charges began to surface, a whole new set of incidents came to light. Humphrey's former press secretary Norman Sherman pleaded guilty to a criminal information filed by the Watergate special prosecutor, involving the purchase of computer lists for Humphrey's '72 campaign with $82,000 in corporate money. A $3,000 fine was assessed against John Loeb, a Wall Street financier, who made an illegal $48,000 contribu-

How he glowed when he involved his audience at a fund-raiser and matched Golda Meir, pledge for pledge. I nearly collapsed one night when he waggled his finger and said to Mrs. Meir, "Get busy, Golda, I'm raising more money than you are."
BURTON JOSEPH

tion to Humphrey's '72 campaign, and an illegal corporate contribution of $1,000 from Minnesota Mining and Manufacturing was also uncovered.

Also subjected to criticism were the large sums of money that Humphrey had received as a public speaker. During his years in the Senate he had come a long way from the $5 speech that marked his early days in politics. Between 1971 and 1974 he had earned honorariums that ranged between $29,135 and $83,451 annually, paid to him for speaking before groups eager to be addressed by a United States senator. Many of these appearances were made at fund-raisers for Jewish causes, where Humphrey was a master at soliciting large dona-

Humphrey and Connecticut senator William Benton with Golda Meir

tions. Burton Joseph, national chairman of the Anti-Defamation League of B'nai B'rith, remembers that sometimes Humphrey would get so swept away with his own oratory that in the enthusiasm of the moment he would donate back most of his speaker's fee.[5]

Humphrey also faced more controversy over the issue of campaign contributions. Early in 1972, he had asked businessman Dwayne Andreas, who had been managing a blind trust of Humphrey's assets since 1965, to transfer funds and stock worth $110,000 to his badly strapped campaign. At the same time that these transfers were made, Andreas, his daughter, and a friend of his daughter made personal contributions in the total amount of $276,000 in cash and stocks. When Humphrey publicly revealed his major financial supporters in March 1972, however, he listed only the contribution of Andreas himself. While the legal requirements both for mandatory disclosure and for limiting the amount of funds from any one source did not go into effect until the next month, Humphrey's omission of these significant contributions drew criticism in the press. Another flap developed when the tax deductions that Humphrey took for the contribution of his vice-presidential papers to the Minnesota Historical Society was disallowed by the IRS, costing him approximately $240,000 in additional taxes. Humphrey tried to point out the differences between his circumstances and those of Nixon, who also had a similar deduction disallowed; for one thing, he had not back-dated the donation, as had been attempted in the Nixon case. Nonetheless, Humphrey again drew heavy

Campaign financing is a curse. . . . It's stinky, it's lousy. I just can't tell you how much I hate it. I've had to break off in the middle of trying to make a decent, honorable campaign and go up to somebody's parlor or to a room and say, "Gentlemen and ladies, I'm desperate. You've got to help me."

HUBERT H. HUMPHREY

editorial criticism for his actions in an atmosphere highly sensitized by Watergate.

One of the more bizarre tales to emerge during this period was a charge made by Robert Maheu, a former Howard Hughes aide, who swore he personally handed over an illegal contribution of $50,000 (in some versions it was $100,000) to Humphrey in the back seat of a limousine in Las Vegas. The charge was never proven and was vigorously denied by Humphrey, but the melodramatic image of black bags and bundles of cash made a vivid impression on the public. "There's no way you can live this kind of thing down,"[6] said Humphrey.

The final reckoning of Humphrey's 1972 campaign showed that his efforts had cost $4.7 million, had directly resulted in three convictions for illegal campaign activities, had raised numerous other related and unrelated charges, had harmed a number of reputations, including Humphrey's, and had left some $900,000 in unpaid campaign debts. The debts were settled much later for three and four cents on the dollar; the debtors were presumably satisfied by these token amounts because they were "close personal friends" who hadn't really expected repayment.

Surveying the ruins of his 1972 campaign, Humphrey called political fund-raising "the most disgusting, demeaning, depressing, disenchanting, debilitating experience of a politician's life."[7] "For a while there, I was damn close to quitting public life."[8] Eventually he was able to joke about it. "When I started out in this hard-drinking field of politics, I never thought I'd get in trouble over

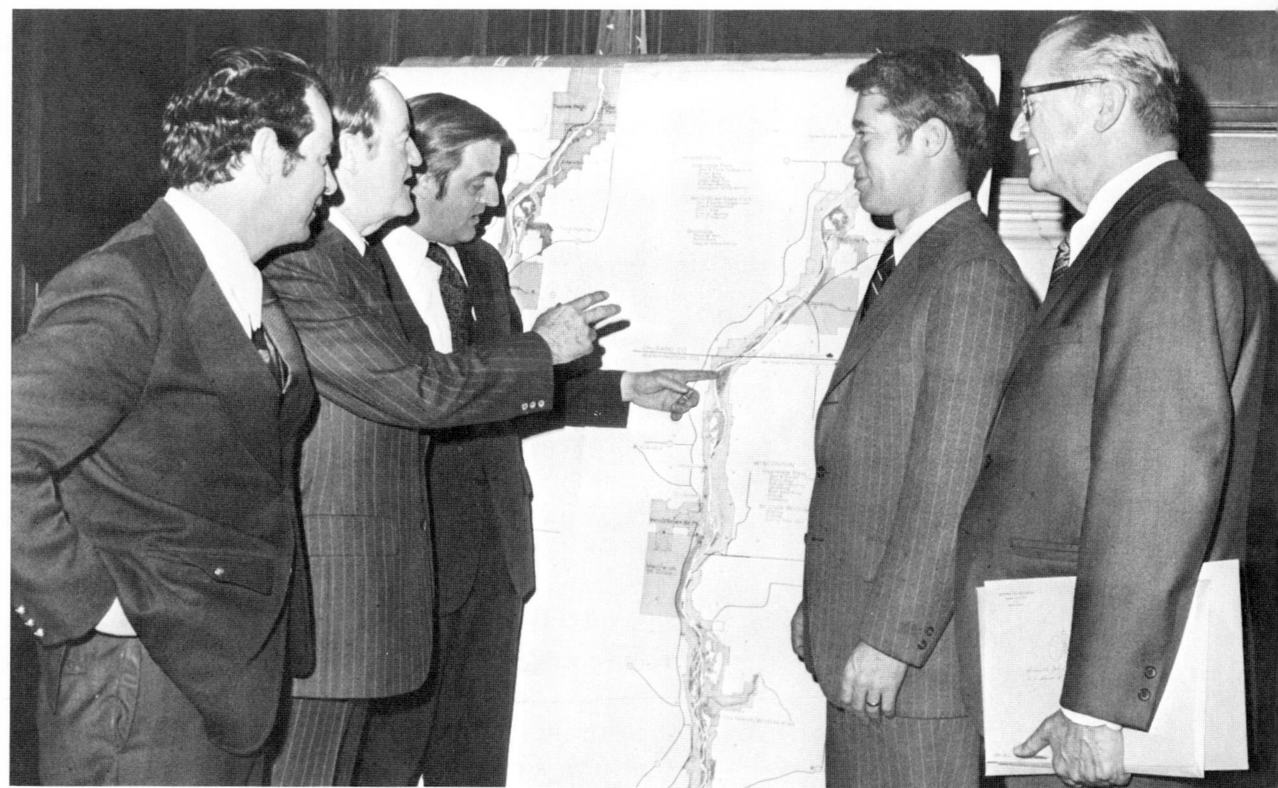

Humphrey with fellow DFL office holders (from left to right) **Congressman Donald Fraser, Senator Humphrey, Senator Walter Mondale, Governor Wendell Anderson, and Congressman John Blatnik**

milk,"[9] he said. The best line came from Wendell Anderson, a Humphrey campaign manager who became governor of Minnesota and eventually occupied a Senate seat. Anderson attended a $15 fund-raiser for Humphrey and claimed that he got in for 60¢: "I told the man at the door I was a close personal friend of Senator Humphrey, so we settled for 4¢ on the dollar,"[10] Anderson explained.

Although the fallout from the 1972 campaign was severe, it seemed to have no lasting effect on Humphrey's popularity. A Harris poll taken in early 1976 showed that 63 percent of the American people viewed him as a man of high integrity and only 13 percent disagreed. As long as Humphrey remained a noncandidate for president, he could expect that situation to remain fairly stable. He was enough of a realist to know, however, that the moment he began to look like a candidate again, he could expect no mercy from his opponents.

Humphrey's political difficulties could not be overlooked, but he faced problems of even greater

You can't be looked upon as a statistic. You're an individual. Some people conquer this disease. Some people are conquered by it. More are conquered by it than those who conquer it. One thing I know, positive thinking, the right attitude, not being afraid, doing your job, and living each day—that's what it's all about.

HUBERT H. HUMPHREY

significance. With no prior public awareness there had been anything wrong with his health, Humphrey entered Bethesda Naval Hospital on January 4, 1974, for what was described as a "check-up that will last three or four days."[11] At the same time it was announced that he had been receiving x-ray treatments during the past two months for a possibly malignant tumor in his bladder. The initial reports were as reassuring as possible under the circumstances. Dr. Edgar Berman, Humphrey's longtime personal physician, stated that he was "about 70 percent certain"[12] that the tumor was destroyed. "It was pinhead size,"[13] Dr. Berman said. Berman revealed that Humphrey's bladder problems dated back to 1966, when he had first noticed blood in his urine. Humphrey had been examined with a cystoscope, a small lighted instrument inserted through the urethra, and a wart-like growth called a papilloma had been discovered. The scope was used to locate the tumor, snip it off, and bring back the tissue for examination. Five or six papillomas had developed over the years and had been removed, but not until September 1973, did a growth arise that "didn't look right," Dr. Berman said.

Medical opinion was divided on the proper course of treatment. At least nine different doctors were consulted, and several recommended surgery immediately, regarding the tissue as malignant. But the decision was finally made to pursue a course of x-ray therapy, based on the theory that the situation was still marginal. From November 1 to December 19, 1973, Humphrey took deep x-ray treatments at 7 A.M. each morning while continuing his Senate duties in the afternoon. During this period, he was able to manage the Foreign Aid bill in the Senate, but about halfway through the x-ray series, the treatments began wearing him down and he started to stay home nightly instead of making his usual political rounds. After the treatments were completed, he had "a very serious and significant reaction."[14] He spent the Christmas holidays at home in Minnesota and when he en-

Christmas at Waverly

tered Bethesda on January 4, 1974, he "didn't feel particularly good."[15]

The check-up that was to last three or four days stretched into two weeks and included more x-ray treatments before Humphrey was released. The doctors pronounced themselves pleased with his recovery, making it clear that they would monitor Humphrey's condition closely. Though the tumor continued to be described as a "possible" malignancy, newspapers began publishing reports of the survival odds for bladder cancer—no more than five years in 60 to 90 percent of the cases. The odds would drop considerably if cancer had spread to the nearby lymph glands.

One of the toughest parts of Humphrey's ordeal had been telling his family:

> Mrs. Humphrey and I went home to Minnesota in October. It was a beautiful evening at our lake home. . . . I suggested we take a walk. We started walking out across the fields and I told her. "I know you must be wondering what the results of the checkup have been. Now look dear, we've got to face up to it now. We're at a point where the possibilities are that I could be suffering from a malignancy. There's argument among the doctors but no argument that something needs to be done."
>
> I said, "I'm not panicked by this and I don't want you to be. I'm going to tell you all I know about it and then we're going to stop talking about it." And I said, "My judgment is that my chances on this are pretty good."
>
> She listened to me and then she said, "Well, Daddy, I think that's all I need to know. We'll work together." It was just kind of a quiet talk between husband and wife over a very serious personal problem.[16]

Out of the hospital in mid-January, Humphrey was kept busy by his political duties. He had his hands full fending off the charges that had emerged during the post-Watergate period and assuming a new Senate responsibility. After twenty years in the Senate, a committee chairmanship had finally come his way. He had been appointed chairman of the Joint Economic Committee, which had thirty staff members and twenty Congressional members, ten from the House and ten from the Senate. The committee had no real legislative responsibilities; its function was to conduct studies and hold hearings, and it had been practically stillborn at its inception thirty years earlier. But with Arthur Burns, chairman of the Federal Reserve Board, Treasury Secretary William Simon, and other economic biggies in the witness chair and Humphrey conducting the hearings, the doings of the committee were soon featured with some frequency on the nightly television news. Economic

M*y recollection is of a luncheon we had in 1975 at which the senior figures of the ADA met with Hubert—it was part of the continuing effort to heal the wounds that developed over Vietnam. Hubert had just emerged from the radiological and other treatments for his first attack of cancer. It was the first time I ever heard anybody describe medical symptoms with exuberance, charm, and obvious enjoyment. The whole table listened with complete interest for what could have been the better part of an hour. I can't think that anybody but Humphrey was capable of this particular feat.*

JOHN KENNETH GALBRAITH

studies were ground out, like the 756-page report titled "China Economic Reassessment." The China study and others like it might have seemed to some to be rather far afield from the committee's original charter under the Full Employment Act of 1946, but Humphrey's talents were not easily confined.

The Joint Economic Committee provided Humphrey with a national forum and strengthened his position as a political figure of national significance. When President Ford announced his economic and energy programs, it was Humphrey who was designated to respond as the Democratic

Presiding over a meeting of the Joint Economic Committee

spokesman in a nationally televised address. In the Senate, Humphrey continued to promote his program for the Marshall Plan for the cities, and in January 1975, he introduced a new proposal called the Humphrey-Hawkins bill. In its original form, the measure represented an attempt to fulfill the promise of the Full Employment Act of 1946 by providing a definition of full employment to mean no more than 3 percent unemployment, a goal to be reached within four years of the bill's passage. The administration would be required to submit a comprehensive plan to Congress each year for achieving the objectives of full employment and balanced growth. If the objectives weren't met, then a program of grants, tax incentives, and training programs would be instituted. If these measures failed, then the bill provided that the government would become an employer of last resort, providing jobs at the prevailing wage in the public sector. This last provision generated the most controversy. Opponents of the measure estimated that costs could run as high as $80 billion and would require the adoption of complete federal wage and price controls. Supporters, while conceding that costs could be as much as $40 billion, countered with the argument that the lack of national planning and the continued high levels of unemployment had created a drag on the economy and dangerous social conditions among the unemployed that justified the measure.

While the Humphrey-Hawkins bill attracted the most attention, Humphrey's Senate work on arms control continued. He introduced a bill to transfer control of sales and gifts of American-made arms

I measure a politician by what he cares about, what he cares enough about to run risks for. What does Hubert Humphrey really care about? He cared about the old widow in the nursing home, and the family who had a son off at war, and a farmer who had to close up because he was going broke on the family mortgage . . . and he cared about the black kid in the ghetto and the family with a handicapped child—all of these people.

MORRIS UDALL
REPRESENTATIVE FROM ARIZONA

The Humphreys meet a group of school girls during a trip to China in September 1974.

from the president to Congress. The bill would require purchasing nations to take care of all administrative costs and other hidden subsidies now paid by the American taxpayers, representing a saving that Humphrey estimated at over $450 million.

Amid the flurry of his Senate activities, Humphrey's presidential prospects for 1976 had been all but forgotten until September 1974, when Walter Mondale unexpectedly dropped out of the race, saying he was tired of the endless tramping back and forth across the country and "sleeping in Holiday Inns."[17] It was not long before Humphrey began to resurface once more as a presidential prospect. For Humphrey even to be considered a possibility was nothing short of amazing. His age, the concern about his health, and the election follies of 1972 were all working against him, but nothing seemed to overcome his optimism or to erode his durability as a political figure. McCarthy and McGovern, the most recent of the Democratic Party's new faces, had been Roman candles, burning brightly for a few moments and then vanishing

Over the years the stature of Hubert Humphrey has risen steadily in the eyes of the American people. . . . Rarely has the character of a man been more tested by the vicissitudes of American politics than Hubert Humphrey's. But throughout it all, he never looked back. His political philosophy springs from a well of faith in people and an optimism about the future which inspires all of us who come under the spell of his extraordinary rhetoric.

DONALD FRASER
REPRESENTATIVE FROM MINNESOTA

from the nation's consciousness. Humphrey had remained in the forefront almost since the day he had given his civil rights speech at the Democratic Convention in 1948, and he had managed it without any of the juicy special assets like money, glamour, or famous relatives.

There were solid reasons for Humphrey's appeal. Except for the Vietnam period, his fortunes were never tied to a single issue. His range of interests was boundless; nothing of public importance occurred without his being a participant or a commentator. Humphrey could embroil himself in political controversy time and again and emerge not only without sacrificing his beliefs but also without making enemies of his opponents. He also

Young people visiting Washington always received a warm welcome from Senator Humphrey. In this picture he is surrounded by the members of a high school class from Eden Prairie, Minnesota.

Humphrey with Anwar Sadat during the Egyptian president's visit to the United States in November 1975

had the ability to make his views interesting to others, so much so that he was commonly referred to as the best political speaker in the nation.

No one should have been surprised, therefore, to see the unsinkable Hubert Humphrey pop up again as the Democratic candidates began to emerge for 1976. At the end of March 1975, the Gallup Poll showed George Wallace as the first choice for the Democratic presidential nomination with 27 percent; Humphrey was second with 16 percent and Henry Jackson third with 13 percent. By late October, however, Humphrey was first in the polls and Wallace second. Tom Wicker of the *New York Times* said, "In September of 1975, there is no talk about Humphrey. By October of '75, it's all Humphrey talk. . . ."[18] James Reston, also of the *New York Times,* wrote from Washington: "The idea is gradually getting around this town that Hubert Humphrey is going to be the Democratic Party's nominee for 1976."[19]

Humphrey himself had few illusions. He had heard the siren song before. "I have a vast area of support . . . and I know it. In fact, the longer I am not a candidate, the more I have."[20]

In November, Humphrey responded to questions about his candidacy on "Meet the Press," his twenty-fifth appearance on the program, a record for any guest. He said he would enter no primaries, would disavow any draft committees, and in states where his name was proposed for the ballot, he would file affidavits of noncandidacy. Humphrey pointed out that if he were to enter the race, the cries of "there he goes again"[21] would echo around the country. There was one possibility of his be-

coming a candidate, however. If the primaries did not produce a clear winner and if the Democratic convention were to turn to him, "I would readily accept the nomination."[22] He regarded the possibility of this happening, however, as "highly improbable."[23]

Humphrey's refusal to enter the primaries was not simply part of some exotic new strategy to win the nomination. For the first time in his career, the fires of his ambition had been banked. Yes, he wanted to be president, but no, he did not lust for the office, not enough to join the wolf pack on the campaign trail. The irony of his situation was not lost on him. The less he tried for the nomination, the more popular he seemed to become. For years he had been like the girl next door, available but unwanted. Now, when he had finally been noticed at last, the moment when it all could have worked seemed to have passed. "It isn't as if I'm above the battle," he said. "Not at all. I've fought the battle."[24] In Muriel's words, "We don't need the presidency at this stage of our lives. There are only a certain number of years left. It doesn't last forever and yet I know he would be the best president for our country at this time."[25]

Humphrey was well aware that to foreswear ambition in Washington was to abandon the hope of exercising any power. Despite his determination not to enter the contest, he couldn't help but be flattered by the predictions of the columnists and the results of the polls. By December, Gallup showed him leading Ford 52 percent to 41 percent, and old pros like George Meany were saying that Humphrey "is the most electable candidate."[26]

It's my judgment that right now the person that has no ambition, no declared ambitions, is more credible. He's freer; you don't have to go around weighing every word as you inevitably do when you become a candidate. I feel I have a role to play in the Party of keeping everybody on the beam. Not just a referee or a healer. Someone that's just a little cut above the pack. The minute you get in it, you're just another one of them.

HUBERT H. HUMPHREY

Whatever the outcome of the struggle for the 1976 Democratic nomination, the favorable publicity he was receiving would help dispel the post-Watergate election disclosures, ease the path for re-election to the Senate in 1976, and perhaps even help Humphrey's chances for winning the Majority Leader's post in January 1977, after Mansfield retired. With nothing to lose—unless he began to take it all too seriously—Humphrey kept the faintest of hopes alive.

The 1976 contest for the nomination differed from that of previous years in several respects. The

The candidates for the 1976 Democratic presidential nomination would be challenging President Gerald R. Ford in the November election. Here Ford is seen with Humphrey and fellow senators Hugh Scott (center) **and James Eastland** (right).

new federal campaign financing laws had made some public funding available for both the primary and the general election campaigns. The Democratic reform rules of 1972 had been unreformed a bit to permit up to one-fourth of a state's delegation to be selected through the state's party machinery rather than elected according to the complicated formulas that had served the New Politics so well in 1972 and had left so many of the old pols watching the convention on television. The structural changes, together with the ebb and flow of political fortunes that make change itself the only constant in the democratic process, generated new candidates for the Democratic nomination. Shriver, Bentsen, Bayh, Harris, Shapp, Udall, and Carter, all new faces, announced early, as did the old warhorses Sanford, Jackson, and Wallace. Muskie, McGovern, Church, Brown, and Humphrey stood on the sidelines waiting for the signal to enter.

Jimmy Carter

During the early stages of the race, Jimmy Carter, the former governor of Georgia, scored several surprising victories. The first direct confrontation between the candidates came in the Iowa precinct caucuses on January 19. The media would interpret this event as the first hard news story of success or failure in the campaign in 1976, but only Carter seemed to realize this. Because the Iowa caucuses were the only game in town, their importance was out of all proportion to the handful of delegates who would be elected. While the other candidates focused their energies elsewhere, Carter's hard work and organizational skills earned him 27.6 percent of the Iowa delegates, a two-to-

Everytime that something happens, there's a whole new group that comes down to you and says, "Now, you've got to do something, Hubert." After New Hampshire, you know, it was "Stop Jimmy Carter." After Massachusetts, "Hurry up, we've got to stop Scoop Jackson." And I keep telling them the Democrats better quit stopping and start starting. You know, we've been stopping each other around here for the last eight years. We stopped in '68; we stopped in '72. And Democrats better learn that what this country wants is somebody who can get up and go, not somebody that can stop.

HUBERT H. HUMPHREY

one margin over Birch Bayh, his nearest rival. The Iowa victory also provided an important psychological boost: Carter had broken into an early lead and had already challenged the myth that his appeal was primarily regional. Mississippi, another caucus state, was next, and while Carter's second-place finish was disappointing to him, the state had been so long conceded to Wallace that the outcome had no real national significance. In the Oklahoma caucuses, Carter managed to virtually tie Fred Harris, a native Oklahoman, and to preserve the momentum he had first established in Iowa. Then came the New Hampshire primary on February 24. Udall, Bayh, and the rapidly fading Harris all split the liberal vote, and Shriver made his first showing, a weak fifth-place finish. Carter finished first again.

Carter's early successes were well deserved. He had worked harder than the other candidates. He had done a better job of sensing the mood of an electorate grown weary of solutions from Washington that seemed to solve nothing. He had brought the voters a message of love and trust uncomplicated by ideology of either the right or the left, and they responded.

After his triumph in New Hampshire, Carter miscalculated by entering the March 2 Massachusetts primary too late to make any impact. Jackson won in Massachusetts, but his victory provided him only a short-lived moment of glory. Carter even managed to salvage something that same day by winning the Vermont primary over the hapless Shriver. The next week in Florida, on March 9, Carter accomplished what no other Democrat had

Al Hofstede (right) **managed Humphrey's senatorial campaign in 1976. Hofstede served as mayor of Minneapolis from 1974 to 1975 and was re-elected to the office in 1977.**

been able to achieve—beating George Wallace in a southern state. While the attention given to Wallace's physical problems and the wholly unsouthern character of much of the Florida electorate made Carter's task easier than it appeared, the image was more significant than the reality. Here was a man who could blow away George Wallace in the South without resorting to a racist message. Democratic liberals began to get interested, and Carter began to pull away from the pack. On March 16, Carter won in Illinois. The victory was downplayed in the media because Jackson and Udall, now thought to be the only announced candidates left with any hope of stopping Carter, had not entered the primary. While the media significance of Illinois was muted, this factor was now less important in Carter's overall strategy for capturing the nomination than the huge bag of delegates that the Illinois victory represented for him.

Carter's victory in Illinois was followed by another win in North Carolina, destroying whatever hopes had remained for Wallace. In the next important test, Wisconsin, Carter squeaked by Udall, who had made this primary the lynchpin of his campaign. Here, luck played a role in the significance of the Carter victory. On election day, Carter's two-to-one lead in the polls seemed to vanish, and Udall's strong showing in the early-reporting urban precincts led the press to believe that Udall had won. The next morning, the late-reporting rural results came in and brought with them news of another Carter victory. The Wisconsin primary story that the media brought to the nation the next day was not the story of Mo Udall's strong showing and near miss, but a picture of a grinning Jimmy Carter holding up the front page of the *Milwaukee Sentinel,* which carried the headline "Carter Upset by Udall."[27] The situation was instantly recognized as a replay of underdog Harry Truman's defeat of Tom Dewey in 1948. Wisconsin all but ended Udall's chances and left only Henry Jackson and the important Pennsylvania primary on April 27.

On April 8, 1976, Humphrey attended a dinner in St. Paul, Minnesota, honoring King Carl Gustaf of Sweden.

Hubert Humphrey played an unwitting part in the outcome of the Pennsylvania primary. He was restless in his unfamiliar role on the sidelines and not altogether comfortable with Carter's candidacy. Before the Wisconsin primary, Humphrey and Carter had engaged in some long-distance probing. Without naming Carter, Humphrey had said, "Candidates who make an attack on Washington are making an attack on government programs, on the poor, on blacks, on minorities, on the cities. It's a disguised new form of racism, a disguised new form of conservatism."[28] Carter responded in kind, saying that perhaps Humphrey's criticism arose "because some of the things that he was influential in passing fifteen or twenty or twenty-five years ago are challenged as perhaps not being perfect."[29]

With the two men warily circling each other and a mid-April Gallup Poll showing Carter barely edging Humphrey 32 percent to 31 percent among Democrats, Carter went into Pennsylvania to face Jackson, the last credible survivor of the announced candidates. Pennsylvania was a Humphrey stronghold. The state had been the scene of several of the high points of his career: the 1948 Democratic Convention, the announcements of his candidacy in 1968 and 1972, and his first primary victory in 1972. Its labor unions were large and well organized, and Jews and blacks were numerous in the urban areas. Humphrey's popularity in Pennsylvania and the growing signs of his availability worked to Jackson's disadvantage by undercutting his candidacy. Had Humphrey announced his own candidacy, he would instantly have blown Jackson away in Pennsylvania. Had he unequivocally withdrawn, he would have given Jackson a clear field to exploit the considerable anti-Carter feeling among union members and Jews. But Humphrey's ambivalence made Jackson appear to be no more than a Humphrey stand-in, a pale imitation of the candidate that many Pennsylvanians preferred. The result was predictable. Jackson's wishy-washy support translated into a wishy-

This man had a zest for life, an unceasing optimism, an unwavering faith in this country and its people, and a complete commitment to making this a better world. And he held to all of these convictions with a broad and happy smile in the face of outrageous attacks, smears, and lies from those who opposed Hubert's agenda for America. There were those of us who respond with anger to such attacks, but Hubert never stopped talking to the attackers, hoping that someday they will see the light—or surrender for a little peace and quiet.

GEORGE MEANY

Humphrey and Senator Henry Jackson

washy vote, while Carter support remained solid. Carter won, with 511,905 votes (36.9 percent) to Jackson's 340,340 (24.6 percent) and with the rest of the pack trailing far to the rear. Exit Henry Jackson.

Now only one primary remained where Humphrey might still have a significant chance of affecting the outcome of the race—New Jersey. The primary would be held on June 8, but the filing deadline was Thursday, April 29, just two days after the Pennsylvania primary. The possibility of a deadlocked convention, the basis of Humphrey's hopes for the nomination while staying out of the primaries, had all but vanished. Carter's steady progress was bringing him within reach of a first ballot nomination. If Humphrey were to stop Carter, he had to enter the New Jersey primary. Polls in New Jersey showed Humphrey with better than a two-to-one lead over Carter. Influential New Jersey politicians like House Judiciary Chairman Peter Rodino urged him to run. Newark's Mayor Kenneth Gibson, officially uncommitted, made it clear that if Humphrey was to have any chance, he must get into the race in New Jersey. The pressure built on Humphrey. With only hours to go before the filings closed, he shut himself in his Senate office on Thursday morning to make up his mind. The press conference he had scheduled to

With Muriel and Walter Mondale at his side, Hubert Humphrey announces that he will not enter the 1976 New Jersey primary.

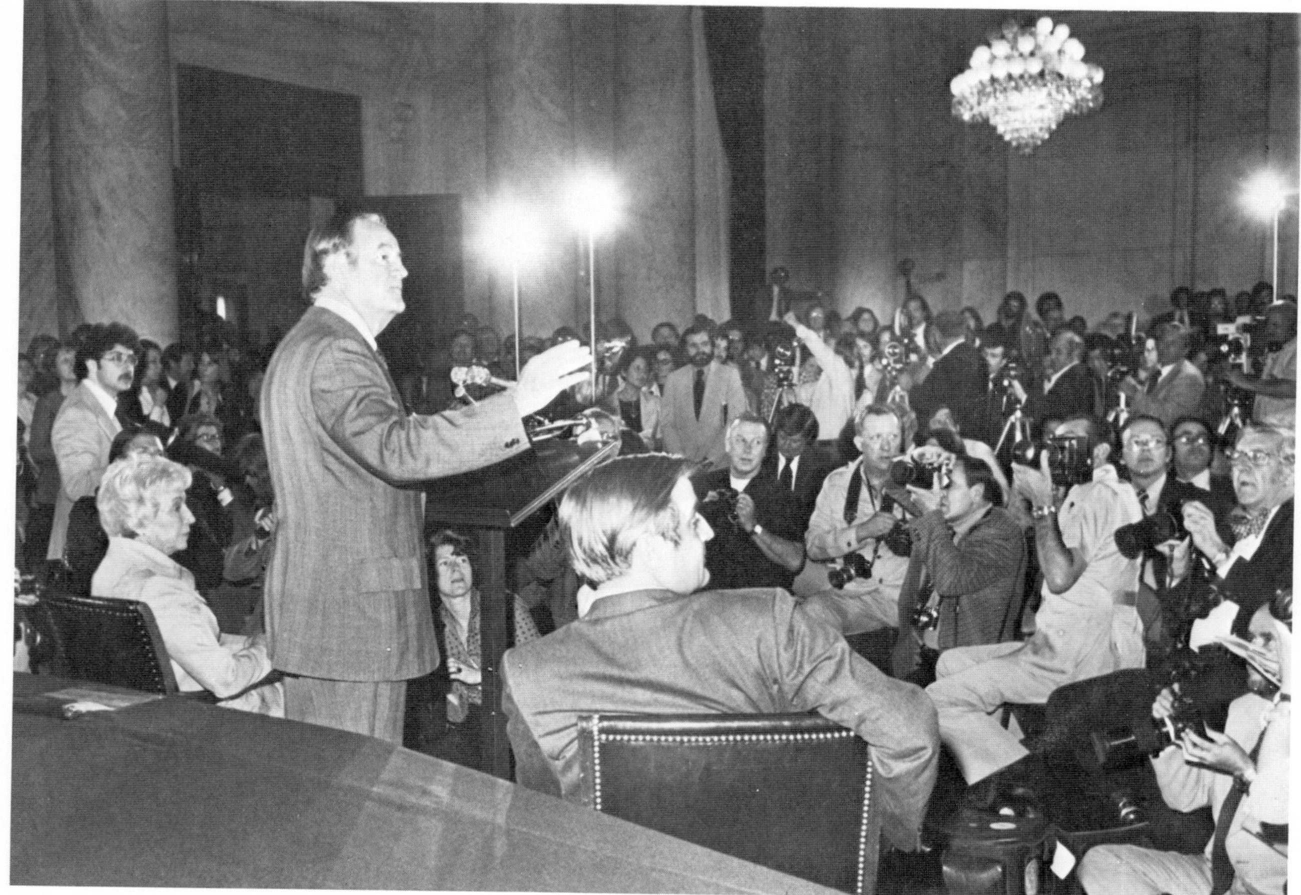

announce his decision was to be held that afternoon in the Senate Caucus Room, the launching pad for the Kennedy candidacies, supporting the consensus opinion that Humphrey would say he had decided to make the race. Entering a packed room ablaze with television lights, flanked by family and friends, Humphrey handshook his way to the podium. Then he announced that he would not be running in New Jersey, but that he would be available at the time of the convention if the party wanted him.

Humphrey's statement was no different than the ones he had been making throughout the year. Yet the expectation that had surrounded it and Carter's commanding lead in the contest had changed the meaning of those words. There now remained no real possibility that Hubert Humphrey would ever again be the Democratic Party's nominee for president of the United States. Later Humphrey said, "I still had the desire, but I knew I shouldn't be in it, politically, emotionally, and physically. If you've tried to climb the mountain before, and you are now considerably older than the first or second time that you didn't make it, and you know there are a number of people who can, maybe it's better that you just sit back and look at the mountain. Yearn a little, but not try to climb it."[30]

The "Happy Warrior" . . . never made it to the Presidency himself; he did not become the leader of the government; he became something rarer than that; he became the conscience of the government.

ERIC SEVAREID

chapter 20

UNDEFEATED

"I have enjoyed my life, its disappointments outweighed by its pleasures. I have loved my country in a way that some people consider sentimental and out of style. I still do, and I remain an optimist, with joy, without apology, about this country and the American experiment in democracy."

Hubert H. Humphrey

Humphrey's decision to stay out of the New Jersey primary and thus close forever his presidential dream had not put an end to his ambitions. He knew that had he challenged Carter and lost, he would have divided the party and harmed his chances to become Majority Leader, a prize that he felt was still within his reach. Realistically, his chances for defeating Carter had been remote. His age, the 1972 campaign irregularities, and his

Jimmy Carter was chosen as the Democratic candidate who would run against Gerald Ford in the 1976 presidential election.

health would all have been handicaps. He had failed in 1972 with fewer liabilities, and his opposition this time, Jimmy Carter, would have been far tougher to defeat than the bumbling George McGovern. Even had he won the nomination, he could have lost the election and with it his Senate seat.

Bob Short, who had been with Humphrey when he made his final decision not to run, said, "The road is just a rough one at this point and the price is so extreme, I don't think he wanted to pay for it."[1] Later Humphrey said, "There comes a time in your life when your whole psyche, your whole system reacts a different way. Of course, I would have loved to be President of the United States. That was a great ambition, but I also want to be a human being. I want to be well. I want to be happy. I want to live."[2]

Campaigning for re-election to the Senate in 1976

During the summer of 1976, Humphrey devoted his energies to his re-election to the Senate, to the race for Senate Majority Leader, to Fritz Mondale's selection as Carter's running mate, and to the election of Jimmy Carter as president of the United States. Then, on September 29, a little over a month before the fall elections, there came another surprise announcement concerning Humphrey's health. "In his regular checkup earlier this month, the bladder tumors which he had been subject to have shown a change in character which may require surgery,"[3] said David Gartner, his administrative assistant. It was later disclosed that Humphrey had experienced some bladder irritation and that the time for his regular six-month checkup had been advanced. The tumor had been found during the examination. Dr. W. Dabney

Jarman, Humphrey's urologist, said that further tests were required, but that recent cellular changes observed in Humphrey's bladder tissue gave rise to the possibility that all or part of Humphrey's bladder would have to be removed. A week later, on October 5, the doctors revealed that Humphrey's condition was no longer borderline or precancerous; the tests indicated that full-fledged cancer had developed. Humphrey's bladder, nearby lymph nodes, and prostate would be removed in an operation on October 7, to be performed by Dr. Willet Whitmore in New York City's Sloan-Kettering Memorial Hospital. During the operation, a short piece of the small intestine would also be removed and hooked up to the two ureters that serve to drain the kidneys. The intestine would serve to extend the drainage system, which would be redirected through an incision made in the outside of Humphrey's body.

"The worst moment in my life was when I discovered that I had cancer,"[4] Humphrey said later. But the disease was no stranger to him. In 1964, with the debate over the Civil Rights Act raging in the Senate and with Humphrey serving as floor manager, his son Bob, age twenty, was stricken with cancer of the lymph glands. Desperate to return home while his son was being operated on, he could not leave the Senate floor while the fate of the bill was still uncertain. Bob Humphrey fully recovered and there was no recurrence of the condition, but Humphrey's brother, Ralph, died of stomach cancer in 1967 with Hubert at his side.

In the hospital the day before his own operation, Humphrey "was walking down the hallway with a

brisk stride, greeting all the nurses and asking them where they were from."[5] The operation took eight hours; "The last stitch was in and 30 seconds later he spoke to me,"[6] the doctor said. Within a day Humphrey was on his feet and making the rounds of the hospital. But the good news of his steady recovery was followed eight days later by reports that the post-operative tests had revealed that the cancer had penetrated the bladder and that Humphrey's lymph nodes had also been cancerous. The chances for long-term survival of those whose cancer has reached the lymph nodes are calculated by the National Cancer Institute to be 23 percent. Nonetheless, Humphrey's doctors were still hopeful that the cancer cells had been surgically removed. To reinforce the surgery, a series of chemotherapy treatments was begun, involving powerful drugs introduced intravenously in a procedure similar to a blood transfusion. The procedure was so painful that Humphrey once referred to it as "bottled death."[7] Its effect on Humphrey's appearance was startling. His hair fell out by the handful and what was left turned white. His frame withered. In a few weeks, his appearance changed from that of a sixty-five-year-old man who looked as if he were fifty to that of a sixty-five-year-old man who looked eighty.

While Humphrey recuperated in the hospital, thousands of letters poured in, and the famous and not so famous streamed through his hospital room. Henry Kissinger, President Ford, and President-elect Carter came to visit, as did Mark Siegel, a Democratic Party official, who said, "He picked up my spirits more than I picked up his,"[8] noting a

My name is Lauren Markoe. I am 9 years old. When Senator Humphrey was in the Intensive Care Unit in Sloan-Kettering Memorial Hospital, he was in the same bed my cousin had been in before. My cousin's name is Robert Davidman, but we usually call him Bobby. I was waiting in the waiting room with my sister Nancy who is seven. I was writing a letter to Senator Humphrey. In the letter I wrote that he was in the same bed that Bobby was in before he was. My Aunt Joan came down and said she would bring the letter up to the guard. The guard said just give it to Mrs. Humphrey. So Aunt Joan and Mrs. Humphrey started talking too. Aunt Joan called my mother. So then all three of them started talking.

Mrs. Humphrey visited Bobby. This made Bobby feel very good.

The guard delivered Bobby a huge basket of flowers with four helium balloons attached. Mrs. Humphrey almost came down to see me.

Senator Humphrey read my letter. I am not quite sure of his reaction.

My cousin Bobby died March 23, 1977, at 15 years old; two more weeks, and he would have been 16.

I learned that the Humphreys are a very nice family.

LAUREN MARKOE

unique Humphrey ability to gain comfort by giving comfort at the time of his own greatest need. Nurse Helen Craig said, "I think it's going to be a very boring place when he leaves. He's the most cheerful person I've ever taken care of."[9] While he was in the hospital, Humphrey phoned Deschler Welsh, a schoolmate through his childhood years in Doland and the man Humphrey regarded as the "smartest kid in our class." Welsh too had intestinal cancer and Humphrey called to cheer him up. "He did, too. I wanted to talk about anything but cancer. I wanted to talk about wheat prices. Anything but cancer. But not Hubert. He talked about it. He wanted me to buck up and fight it with everything I've got."[10]

Discharged on October 30, pale but smiling, Humphrey walked firmly out of the hospital to a waiting car. Three days later, for the first time unable to attend his own victory celebration, he won re-election by the largest margin in his career, 812,000 votes. His Independent-Republican opponent had been Gerald N. Brekke, an elderly and amiable professor of education at Gustavus Adolphus College who had never before run for public office except for a position on a local school board. Brekke ran an elderly and amiable kind of campaign that proved no match for Humphrey's popularity.

Despite his illness, Humphrey never broke stride in his race for Majority Leader. Eleven days after he left the hospital, he restated his determination to stay in the contest. Humphrey's principal opponent, Robert Byrd, had maintained for a year that he had the votes of the majority of the sixty-five

Democrats in the Senate that he needed to win. Then, in the fall elections, three of Byrd's supporters, Hartke of Indiana, McGee of Wyoming, and Montoya of New Mexico, lost their seats and Humphrey thought that he had a chance. His prospects appeared to brighten when the other two contenders for the job, Ed Muskie and Ernest Hollings of South Carolina, withdrew and endorsed Humphrey. But Byrd had built up an insurmountable lead. His position as Whip had given him the opportunity to do countless favors for his fellow Democrats in all manner of Senate business: scheduling legislation to avoid embarrassing absences, arranging the pairing of opposing votes so that senators did not have to be present when the actual voting took place. Byrd also served as chairman of the Interior Appropriations Subcommittee, which controlled millions of dollars of federal funds important to nearly every state. And finally, there were no concerns about Byrd's health.

Some of the votes that Humphrey had been counting on began slipping away as Byrd announced the names of his supporters: Huddleston and Ford of Kentucky, Durkin of New Hampshire, Melcher of Montana, and Abourezk of South Dakota, an especially tough one for Humphrey to lose because he had campaigned up and down his native state on Abourezk's behalf when Abourezk first ran for the Senate in 1972. When the executives of the AFL-CIO, Humphrey's oldest and most loyal national political allies, quietly indicated that they would not support him and even signaled a tilt towards Byrd, it was all over.

I called some of Hubert's old buddies from the early days to help celebrate the seventy-fifth birthday of my father-in-law, Brad Mintener. It was December 22, 1976, and we had a luncheon at the Minneapolis Club. Hubert came, and of course everyone was thrilled. There was Brad and Ed Ryan and Van Konynenburg and Harry Fiterman and Stu Leck. Brad started the meeting and wanted them all to join hands for a prayer. Well, there was Harry Fiterman on one side, Jewish and a little deaf, and there was Ed Ryan on the other, Catholic and a little deaf. Half way through the prayer, Brad looks up and says, "Harry and Ed, you're not joining hands. Now let's be ecumenical." So they finally got the circle closed and there was a prayer with much concern about Hubert's health, and you could sense the emotion and feeling among these elderly gentlemen who had known Hubert and loved him for so long. When the prayer was over, Hubert said, "By golly, I'm sure that's one that got through."

PETER HEEGAARD

The Senate is a special body whose character and actions are shaped not only by its official nature but also by the personalities and commitments of those who serve in it at any given time. The presence of Hubert Humphrey in the Senate enhances the greatness that already inherently belongs to this distinguished Chamber.

ROBERT C. BYRD

On January 4, 1977, Humphrey, who had been ill with the flu for three days, telephoned Byrd to say he was withdrawing from the race and then got up from his bed to deliver the message in person. Humphrey asked the Democratic caucus for a unanimous ballot for Byrd when the Senate convened to open the 95th Congress. The next day,

Democratic leaders of the Senate in 1976: (from left to right) **Hubert H. Humphrey, Deputy President Pro Tempore; Alan Cranston, Majority Whip; James Eastland, President Pro Tempore; Daniel Inouye, Secretary of the Democratic Congress;** (seated) **Robert Byrd, Majority Leader**

perhaps acting out of a sense of guilt at having rejected the nation's most articulate spokesman for liberal causes in favor of a bloodless technocrat, the Senate invented a job for Humphrey, the position of Deputy President Pro Tempore of the Senate. Humphrey might have resented being tossed a sop, but he was delighted. The perks, an increased salary, and a car and driver were welcome, but the chance to have the president's ear as an official member of the Senate Democratic leadership meant much more at this stage. Humphrey had no great need for any additional money. In October 1976, his and Muriel's net worth had been reported at $636,584, including the value of the home at Waverly and a condominium in Washington where they had moved when Humphrey was vice-president. As for the new Senate position being concocted and without any formal powers, said the man who thirty years before had made something out of a no-power job as mayor of Minneapolis and who had just resurrected the Joint Economic Committee, "If you have a position, you can make power."[11] Humphrey also had some thoughts on his loss of the race for Majority Leader: "I find you can win when you lose. A good deal of what Bob Byrd, the winner, is doing now—he's doing because there was a threatened contest. Commitments were made and we're modernizing the Senate, and he is holding the caucus meetings we need and the openness we require."[12]

Before the Ford administration left office, Humphrey visited with the outgoing president, who, like Humphrey, had suffered a narrow and painful defeat. It would not be the loss to Jimmy Carter

I work for the Committee on International Relations, which is the House of Representatives counterpart to the Senate Foreign Relations Committee, of which Mr. Humphrey was a member. On March 10, 1977, both my Committee and the Senate Committee hosted a luncheon for Prime Minister James Callaghan of Great Britain during his visit to the United States to meet with President Carter. As Prime Minister Callaghan was in the midst of his remarks, Senator Humphrey entered. My initial reaction was one of shock and despair because the Senator's appearance had so altered since the discovery of his illness. The white hair and the loss of weight changed his appearance so completely from the picture that Americans remember of the dark-haired, cherubic Senator, Vice-President, and Presidential candidate that one could not help but feel an instantaneous rush of pity. However, this initial reaction was short-lived. It seemed as if every *Congressman spoke to him as he walked across the room to his seat at the head table. I was amazed to see the Prime Minister interrupt his speech and greet the Senator with a "Hello Hubert," a warm handshake, and a moment of personal conversation. I do not know how long these two men have known each other, but they appeared to have been life-long friends.*

I have often heard of people who have such an aura about them that when they enter a room the entire atmosphere is changed, but I have never encountered such an experience until that day.

EMILY C. HOWIE

that Ford would be remembered for, Humphrey told him, but for having restored a sense of integrity to the office of the presidency. "Mr. President, you've had two and a half years in this house. I'd have given ten years of my life to have two days or two weeks here. It was the heartache of my life."[13]

Within three weeks, Humphrey was pushing the new Carter administration on a whole range of issues from his seat in the Senate. Black concerns were among the first; "these little tidbit measures are about as effective as spearmint chewing gum is

Humphrey watches as Jimmy Carter is sworn in as president of the United States.

for a serious case of the flu,"[14] he said. Humphrey introduced a Youth Employment Package far more ambitious than the timid administration program, a new version of the Humphrey-Hawkins bill, a comprehensive health care program for children, a federal housing bank program to help lower- and middle-income people own their own homes, a package of reform measures directed at Congress, a bill to re-establish a national ocean council that would oversee orderly development of the nation's ocean resources, and even a bill calling for federal help for the beleaguered honey industry (not to forget that Minnesota is the nation's number-one honey producer). Humphrey also made some contributions to Carter's fledgling administration. He helped rescue the president's floundering nomination of Griffin Bell for Attorney General by putting his own reputation on the line with blacks and liberals, and he did the same on behalf of Paul Warnke's nomination as head of the Arms Control and Disarmament Agency when conservative opposition developed. But his efforts went largely unappreciated by the administration, which was uncertain of itself and suspicious of Humphrey's motives.

By May, Humphrey had regained some weight, the gaunt look had vanished under a tan, and his hair, though permanently whitened, had begun to grow back a bit and even take on the distinguished appearance popularly associated with a senator. As his energy was restored, his importance to the Carter administration grew. Humphrey became the new administration's most important ally on Capitol Hill, just as he had been during John

On June 14, 1977, Bill Connell, Max Kampelman, Humphrey, and I had a little reunion dinner at a restaurant in D.C. After a long day on the Senate floor, Humphrey was tired, but he was happy to be with his old friends. We talked about many things, including the Mid-East situation, his plans for the future, and his role in the leadership of the Senate. Senator Humphrey spoke about how much he enjoyed the White House meetings with the President, and how well his input was being received. He further stated that at the conclusion of almost all of the meetings that the leadership had with the President, he, Humphrey, gave the benediction (or the final say).

S. HARRISON DOGOLE

Muriel gives Hubert a kiss during a celebration of his sixty-sixth birthday on NBC's "Today" show, while Vice-President Walter Mondale looks on.

Kennedy's administration. He played a major role in drafting the Senate version of the Agriculture bill and managed a complex series of foreign aid authorizations through Congress. Because he met on a regular basis with the president in his role as deputy president of the Senate, Humphrey could give Carter the kind of disinterested advice he needed to hear and learned to rely upon. "Mr. President, I'm not running for re-election. There's

A Humphrey family picture taken at the baptism of granddaughter Heather Harriet in May 1977

not a thing you can do for me. The only way I can prove to you that I am your friend is to tell you what I really think."[15] And he did. Humphrey urged Carter to introduce multi-year budgeting as a means of getting away from the unpredictability of year-to-year planning. He called for the adaptation of a medical program based on preventive care, instead of programs that begin only after illness strikes. It was not long before the president came to regard the man whom he had once referred to as "too old" as the "number one Democrat in our country."[16]

Just as Humphrey seemed restored to the full range of his powers, another of those ominous releases was issued by his office: Senator Humphrey had entered University Hospital in Minneapolis on Tuesday, August 16, for a checkup. He had been having stomach cramps. On Wednesday, it was announced that he would be operated on the next day to relieve a blockage in his colon. The blockage could have been caused by scar tissue built up as a result of the extensive radiation treatments he had taken. On Thursday, the operation took place and the worst became known. The blockage had come from the development of a large and deep inoperable cancerous tumor that stretched across Humphrey's pelvis. Dr. John Najarian, his surgeon, said, "It is a terminal situation if you accept the fact that he has cancer we can't treat surgically."[17] The blockage itself was relieved by a colostomy, which involved creating another new intestinal pathway for the removal of waste. There would be more radiation, more chemotherapy, new drugs would be tried; the doctors were hopeful of being able to prolong Humphrey's life. For how long? "It could be months," said Dr. Najarian. "It could be years."[18] The doctor reported that when Humphrey was given this news, "he was sad and disappointed, but only momentarily."[19]

I met Senator Humphrey just a year ago when both he and my mother (who has since passed away) were patients on the 8th floor of the Memorial Sloan Kettering hospital for cancer in New York. It was a casual meeting though my family and I were shaken by the idea that a famous and/or important person could also be inflicted with such a degrading and humiliating condition.

Upon hearing the diagnosis of terminal cancer, I had only the most extreme compassion for a man who, because of who he was, had to come before the press to express his feelings about being told he had only perhaps a few months yet to live.

DEBBIE ELIAN

Within a week, the president and the vice-president, who had called to wish Humphrey well, were asking his advice and help in getting the Panama Treaty ratified. It was the best therapy he could have gotten. Back on his feet, he began making rounds of his ward. "He has been walking so fast we almost had to give him a speeding ticket,"[20] said one surgeon. On the 12th of September, Humphrey was released, now more gaunt and weaker than ever before. His flesh seemed to have died while his eyes burned with the desire to live. One commentator described him with cruel accuracy as looking like a "skull on a stick."[21] One week later, he walked onto the stage at the Minnesota AFL-CIO Convention. Everyone in the audience was shamelessly overcome with emotion as

Humphrey is welcomed to the platform of the AFL-CIO Convention by Dave Roe, president of the Minnesota AFL-CIO.

I've probably looked through the viewfinder at Humphrey more than any other American photographer, and I've often wondered what was wrong with his eyes. They seemed to be watering, and I thought it was the wind or a speck in his eye. Later on, I came to the conclusion—I never discussed this with him—that he would be talking about America and he would get emotional about it. He never broke down but he was just on the verge, he was holding back a tear, his eyes were misty. After a while I knew it was his love for this country that put him in that state.

MARTY NORDSTROM

Humphrey said, "You'll find out as we go through this speech, I may start out a little wobbly, but I am going to end up damn good and strong."[22] He did. He spoke to them for forty-six minutes, and at one point, his eyes filled with tears. "Mom said, 'Yeah, they'll take your picture if you wipe your eyes with a Kleenex.' Well, take it. People who don't have any tears, don't have any heart."[23] He spoke about the future, the needs of the cities, the need for jobs, pounding the lectern until it jumped. If surgery and x-rays and drugs wouldn't cure him,

Humphrey and Carter at the airport in Minneapolis

then perhaps faith in God and hard work would, or at least they might make the awful burden somehow easier to bear.

On October 23, President Carter stopped in Minnesota to pick up Humphrey on Air Force One and return with him to Washington. On October 25, a special tribute was presented on his return to the floor of the Senate. "I've been here 27 years and I've never known anything like it,"[24] said one Senate staffer, overcome by the outpouring of love and emotion that greeted Humphrey's appearance. "To those who feel there are no longer any heroes left in the world," said his colleague Wendell Anderson, "to them I say they have never known Hubert Humphrey."[25] The next week, in an action

Hubert Humphrey is the greatest American that I know, the number one Democrat in our country, and the man who has been admired and is admired throughout the world.

. . . If there is a retarded child in our country who hasn't been helped by Senator Humphrey, I don't know about it. Every elderly person in our nation, every poor person in our nation, every black person in our nation, everyone who has come here from overseas who doesn't speak English well, everyone who lives in something of despair, knows that they have one staunch and undying friend in Senator Hubert Humphrey.

JIMMY CARTER
MINNEAPOLIS STAR
OCTOBER 24, 1977

Some people have suggested that it would be difficult to come to the U.S. Senate and serve as a junior Senator to Hubert Humphrey. Nothing could be further from the truth. The greatest honor that can come to anyone interested in public service is to serve an apprenticeship under that perfect gentleman.

WENDELL ANDERSON
SENATOR FROM MINNESOTA

unprecedented in American history, the House of Representatives asked Humphrey to speak and paid him honor.

Several weeks before his second cancer operation had taken place, an announcement was made that a Hubert Humphrey Institute was being planned on the campus of the University of Minnesota. Twenty-two million dollars in private funds

Muriel accompanied Hubert when he returned to the Senate on October 25.

would be raised in a drive sponsored by Vice-President Walter Mondale and Irving Shapiro, president of DuPont. Humphrey was pleased by the plans for the Institute. He said, "My prayer is to see it come into being, to finish out this term in the Senate, and go home to that Institute and I'll have an office and I'll sit and talk and visit about politics and problems with the young people who come there. God, won't that be great! I just pray that I can do it."[26]

But it was not to be. When Humphrey returned to Waverly for the Senate's Christmas recess in

On Saturday evening, November 26, 1977, at 7:00 P.M., while dining at home with my wife, who was recuperating from recent major surgery, the phone rang. It was Senator Humphrey. He said that he was calling merely to find out how his old friends in Philadelphia were feeling, particularly because he had not heard from me recently. In a lighter vein, my wife, Marilyne, offered to compare incisions. He said that he would win hands down for he had more to compete with. I asked how he was feeling and he said that during the previous week, due to the arterial chemotherapy, "I damn near died." Then he said that progress had been made. "Son-

The Humphreys with Golda Meir, November 1977

ny, I will be around for a while. I have got too many important things to do yet." He further assured me that he would be at the dinner which was being held in his honor the following Friday, December 2, 1977; he already had his tuxedo laid out. When the call was over, my wife and I were stunned by the thought that here was a man with so much on his mind, with a body racked with pain and withered by disease, wanting to know how we were feeling.

S. HARRISON DOGOLE

On December 8, 1977, Humphrey attended the dedication of the new Health, Education and Welfare building, which was named in his honor.

December, he had made his final trip home. He had fought his disease with all the strength that remained in him, struggling each day to make a little progress, to stay on his feet a little longer, to walk a little farther than he had the day before. During the second week in January, cancer finally overwhelmed a body grown too weak to sustain life. Wanting to stay alert, Humphrey refused any kind of medication for pain until January 11. About that time, he even stopped telephoning—there were no more calls to President Carter, Secretary of State Vance, Henry Kissinger, "everybody."[27] On the afternoon of Friday, January 13, he sank into a coma. At 9:25 P.M. Friday evening, Hubert Humphrey died quietly and without any further suffering.

Characteristically, Humphrey's final public acts reflected his life-long dedication to civil rights and to the search for world peace. Shortly before his death, he had written a few words to be read at a ceremony commemorating the forty-ninth anniversary of the birth of Martin Luther King, Jr., a ceremony at which Humphrey himself would be honored for his contributions to the civil rights movement. His message was read at the Ebenezer Baptist Church on January 14, the day after his death: "I am deeply moved by this tribute bestowed on me tonight. To be linked to Dr. King in the battle for equal rights is a distinct honor. My only regret is that I cannot be with all of you tonight to share in your warm friendship."[28] A few days before he died, Humphrey had also drafted a letter to Prime Minister Menachem Begin of Israel in which "he made a personal plea . . . for

It was the afternoon of New Year's Eve when we got the call. "I was thinking of calling you tomorrow but tomorrow might be too late," Humphrey said. His voice was almost too weak to hear on the phone.

DAVE ROE

He was absolutely the greatest user of the telephone of anybody I know, even recently when he's been so ill. The phone would ring and there would be Hubert Humphrey at the other end of the phone. I can remember times calling out to Waverly to talk to Muriel. They always had lots of Secret Service during the time he was vice-president. You never expected to get him on the phone but you usually got him on the phone. He couldn't stand to have anyone answer the telephone. I've talked to a number of his friends in recent days, and so many of them said, "Oh, he called me just last week." "He called me just the other day."

GERI JOSEPH

It has been said of Hubert that he was asked to speak at a tree-planting ceremony in Israel and by the time he finished talking he was standing in the shade. But who can fail to remember the purpose of his eloquent oratory—his pleas for compassion, for brotherhood, for equal rights and simple decency? Who can fail to have been inspired by this courageous fighter who practiced what he preached over a career so long and distinguished that few of us dare imagine what our national life would have been without him. This buoyant, bubbling, lovable warrior demonstrated through a lifetime of service that in America man achieves nobility not by his beginnings but by his ends.

HENRY KISSINGER

The lives of millions of Americans—the old, the young, the disadvantaged—are better today because Hubert Humphrey has not hesitated to champion unpopular causes. He is a man of uncommon decency and compassion. The people of the United States, whatever their party affiliation, whatever their philosophy, are fortunate to have Hubert Humphrey in their service.

ROBERT DOLE
SENATOR FROM KANSAS

flexibility and restraint in the search for peace"[29] in the Middle East.

During that final week, Humphrey had taken part in the arrangements for his own funeral. Fully aware of his condition, he had discussed plans for the service with Reverend Calvin Didier of the House of Hope Presbyterian Church, the oldest Protestant congregation in Minnesota. Humphrey requested that his funeral be a "celebration" rather than a somber memorial; "I've had enough eulogies for two lifetimes,"[30] he said.

The public outpouring of grief at Humphrey's death and the public ceremonies of mourning were the most extensive that the nation had seen since John Kennedy's assassination fifteen years earlier. On Saturday Humphrey's body was flown to Washington on Air Force One to lie in state in the Capitol Rotunda. On Sunday a memorial service was held there. Then the casket was taken back to St. Paul, where it was displayed to the public at the State Capitol from Sunday night until the funeral service on Monday.

As the ceremony unfolded, many of the nation's great and powerful gathered—public figures who spanned the decades when Humphrey stood at the center of the country's political life. Among those who came to honor Humphrey were Teddy Kennedy, Tip O'Neill, Jacob Javits, Mike Mansfield, Theodore Hesburgh, Billy Graham, Coretta King, Frank Church, Robert Byrd. There was also Richard Nixon, returned to Washington for the first time since his exile three and a half years earlier. He and Humphrey had been rivals but not enemies. Humphrey had spoken with Nixon on

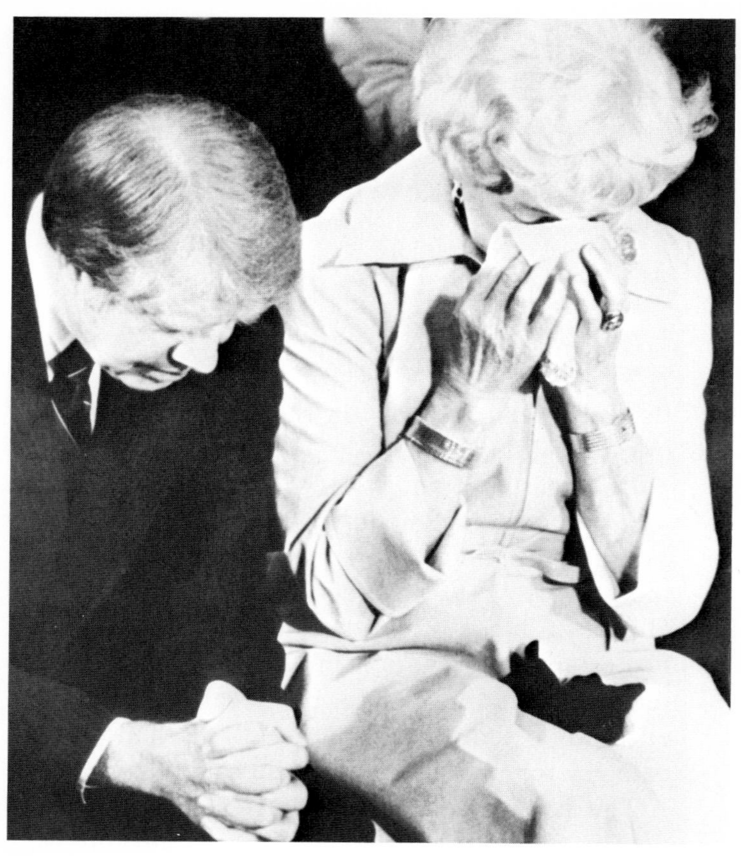

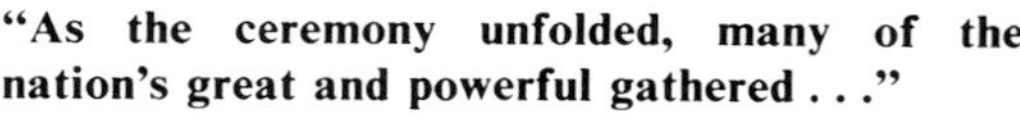

"As the ceremony unfolded, many of the nation's great and powerful gathered . . ."

Christmas Day and had telephoned him the week before he died to wish him a happy birthday. Nixon called Humphrey "a great and good man. To the extent that few others in the political arena ever had, he commanded the genuine respect and affection of his political opponents and allies alike."[31] Nixon's successor, Gerald Ford, was also there to give his tribute: "Hubert was an idealist in the purest sense. He was a man of character, compassion, enthusiasm, dedication, and tremendous ability."[32] Lady Bird Johnson recalled, "The country met him as a buoyant young man and we watched him grow in grace. He gave so much love and earned so much in return."[33] Ed Muskie, Humphrey's running mate in 1968, spoke of his old friend's final days: "Being Hubert, he made it seem so easy that he succeeded in covering up what

Like a modern Ben Franklin, Humphrey embodied old-fashioned virtues. Be loyal to your friends. Bear the slings and arrows of public life with fortitude. Never bear a grudge. Make friends of your enemies. Never feel sorry for yourself. Always be optimistic.

HENRY REUSS
REPRESENTATIVE FROM WISCONSIN

When history weighs the great social advances of our time, the impact of the man who never became President may outweigh them all.

LORNE GREENE

Shortly before his death, one of his doctors told him that a poll just published indicated that he was ranked as the best legislator of the century, and Humphrey nodded. And then the doctor indicated that Lyndon Johnson finished second. And Hubert just thought for a moment, smiled, and then said, "When Lyndon finds out, he'll be mad."

WENDELL ANDERSON

must have been excruciating pain. Earlier in the week I asked him how he was doing. He said, 'Oh, I'm feeling much better.' He gave you the feeling he would survive somehow . . . It was more than courage; it was faith as well—an unquestionable faith in the future, even the future that lies beyond the curtain."[34] George Wallace said, "We had our philosophical differences on political issues, but I knew him as a compassionate man, a concerned man, who truly loved his country and his family."[35] Another old opponent, George McGovern, expressed the feelings of many when he said, "We are comforted now in the knowledge that he crowded half a dozen careers into all too brief a life."[36]

During the ceremony in Washington, President Carter spoke of the growing reliance and trust that he had come to place in Humphrey during the last year of his life. "He has been an inspiration and a conscience to us all. His personal attribute was that he really knew how to love."[37] Humphrey's friend, his political ally, and the most successful of all the many Minnesotans who had advanced with Humphrey's help through the ranks of the DFL and into national prominence was the vice-president, Walter Mondale, who gave the final valediction: "He taught us all how to hope and how to live, how to win and how to lose. He taught us how to live and, finally, he taught us how to die."[38] The ceremony in Washington, both a funeral for a fallen leader and a celebration to honor the love and joy he brought to those he touched, ended with the whole audience singing "America the Beautiful," moving many to tears.

It was not only the great and powerful who had come to say goodbye. There were many whose names were unknown and whose lives were lived in obscurity. As he filed past the bier in Washington, Charles Hambel said, "Everyone knows him for the big things. But Lord knows how many people like me in this town he helped in a very personal way when we needed it. I didn't know him from Adam. But he was touched by my situation. He got me running an elevator that used to be right over there," he said, pointing off the Rotunda. "It wasn't much. But it got me started in school. I'll never forget it. He was a great man." "I have a great admiration for the man," said Perry Maiden, a young history teacher. "I grew up in Mississippi during the Civil Rights movement. It seemed we were surrounded by enemies. Our governor was a segregationist; our senators were segregationists. It seemed everyone around us was against civil rights. But every now and then we'd hear the voice of Hubert Humphrey saying that racial justice and equality are what the country is all about. You can't imagine how refreshing and encouraging that voice was." Reverend and Mrs. Robert J. Westerberg brought their two teenage daughters from Altoona, Pennsylvania, to pay their respects. "The snow was deep there when we left," Lorraine Westerberg said. "People thought we were crazy. But we didn't think we were. We had to come here. We all just loved Hubert Humphrey for all the work he's done for the underdogs of this country. We couldn't let the snow keep us away. We just loved him."[39]

I heard a student from Macalester say, "I lost a dear and good friend, but I never met him."
WENDELL ANDERSON

A day later, as the body lay in the State Capitol

Some of the thousands who waited through the night at the Minnesota State Capitol

in St. Paul from Sunday evening until the funeral on Monday, the people of Minnesota had their turn to pay a final tribute to Humphrey. Some waited as long as three hours in the subzero cold to file slowly past the flag-draped casket. As they waited, and slowly froze, they too burst into singing "America" and "The Star Spangled Banner" and "The Battle Hymn of the Republic." Why had they come, in the middle of the night, to stand in the cold for hours just for a few seconds' glimpse of that casket? Some wanted to be a part of history, even bringing tiny children in the hope that they would someday remember having been there. For others, it was a kind of pilgrimage to show that they too could sacrifice for him as he had for them: a woman whose ninety-one-year-old husband had finally been "pardoned" by his government, due largely to Humphrey's efforts, for a crime he did not commit; a union worker, whose retirement

Humphrey performed a great service to the people of the United States, greater than that which many presidents have rendered and certainly greater than the disservice that some of them have rendered.

RALPH W. YARBOROUGH

party Humphrey had attended twenty years before; a Vietnam protester, who, having forgiven Humphrey his views on the war, came to ask forgiveness for his own behavior. They filed past, the serious and the light-hearted, a thrill-seeker or two, but most of them were there to reach out and give, through the sacrifice of sleep and warmth and comfort, some small measure of the devotion they felt that Humphrey had given them.

"I dreamed I saw Joe Hill last night
Alive as you and me.
Says I, 'But Joe, you're ten years dead.'
'I never died,' says he. . . .

'Joe Hill ain't dead,' he says to me.
'Joe Hill ain't never died.
Where the working men are out on strike,
Joe Hill is at their side.' . . .

I dreamed I saw Joe Hill last night
Alive as you and me.
Says I, 'But Joe, you're ten years dead.'
'I never died,' says he."

LYRICS FROM THE SONG *JOE HILL*
READ AT HUMPHREY'S FUNERAL

Then, on Monday afternoon, the final prayer had been said, the service at the House of Hope had ended. The body had been laid to rest in Lakewood Cemetery in Minneapolis; the last of the great and near-great and not so great had gone home. Muriel had endured it all bravely, though tension and weariness were etched deeply into her face. There was a gathering after the funeral at the Leamington Hotel in Minneapolis, the same hotel

THE NOYES MEMORIAL CARILLON PRELUDE	**Theophil Rusterholz**
ORGAN PRELUDE	
Partita "O Gott, du frommer Gott"	Bach
Wir glauben all' an einen Gott, Vater	Bach
Sonata III in A Major	Mendelssohn
Prelude and Fugue in Eb Major (St. Anne)	Bach
Liebster Jesu, wir sind hier	Bach
Wir glauben all' an einen Gott, Schopfer	Bach
Sharon Kleckner, organ	
INSTRUMENTAL PRELUDE	
Sonata Number 1 in G Major, Movement 1	Brahms
Isaac Stern, violin Eugene Istomin, piano	
SOLO Ave Maria	Schubert
Robert Merrill, baritone	
INVOCATION	Calvin Whitefield Didier Pastor, House of Hope Church
HYMN A Mighty Fortress Is Our God	Ein feste' Burg
OLD TESTAMENT LESSON Psalm 8	Rabbi Max A. Shapiro Senior Rabbi, Temple Israel, Minneapolis, Minnesota
SOLO He'll Understand, Well Done	Tom Tipton, Baritone
SPIRITUAL	Sabathani Baptist Church of Minneapolis William J. Perry, Minister of Music
I'm Going Up Yonder	
REMARKS	Dr. Robert Schuller
SOLO The Lord's Prayer	Malotte
Mr. Merrill	
NEW TESTAMENT LESSON John 14	The Most Reverend John R. Roach Archbishop of the Archdiocese of St. Paul and Minneapolis
ANTHEM Hallelujah (Mount of Olives)	Beethoven House of Hope Choir
REMARKS	Walter F. Mondale, Vice President of the United States
REMARKS	Jimmy Carter, President of the United States
MUSIC Sonata Number 1 in G Major, Movement 2	Brahms
Mr. Stern Mr. Istomin	
MEDITATION	Mr. Didier
PRAYERS	
RESPONSE Alleluia	Randall Thompson
HYMN America The Beautiful	Materna
BENEDICTION	
RESPONSE Hallelujah Chorus (Messiah)	Handel
POSTLUDE Prelude and Fugue in C Minor	Bach

Joan and Walter Mondale with Muriel Humphrey at Lakewood Cemetery

where Humphrey had conceded the presidency to Richard Nixon in 1968. Muriel thanked them all for having come to show their respect, and then it was over, finally over.

On June 14, 1976, a year and a half before he died, Hubert Humphrey had returned to Doland to speak at the dedication of an auditorium named in his honor. Back among the friends, the teachers, the relatives whom he cherished and who cherished him, once more renewing his vows to that stark land, he spoke from his heart:

> I've had the opportunity to see most of America first-hand, and unlike some people today, I'm not a pessimist. I know that there is a sort of mood that people talk about in the country—they call it cynicism and despair—I think it is in the eye of the beholder. I see hundreds of thousands of people and I spend time with people. . . . I like to hold their hand and shake hands and see their children, and I am here to tell you that this country is filled with boundless faith—boundless energy and great faith—it's just waiting to be released. . . .
>
> I want people to know that America's greatness is not because it produces massive weapons, even though we do, that America's greatness is not because we put a man on the moon, even though we have, and America's greatness is not only because we have championed the cause of many

Hubert could no more deride people than he could avoid returning a smile or accepting an outstretched hand. He would have been the perfect leading character for any play by Oscar Hammerstein; he was in love with the whole human race, and especially that portion of it that lived in the United States.

NORMAN COUSINS
SATURDAY REVIEW
MARCH 4, 1978

nations and have been generous as a victor, even to the vanquished, even though all of that we have done. America's greatness is because it cares about people. Maybe not as much as we could, but we are growing and we are getting better all the time.

I have been listening to the politicians this year and I'm one of them, and what do we mean? Do we have more missiles than they have? Are ours better than theirs? . . . Well, ladies and gentlemen, there's no doubt we have the muscle, let me tell you that. I know of this country's strength. We have incredible power, we have massive military power, we are without a doubt unequalled in military power. . . . But what is it that makes for security? Not just weapons, but love of country. When people love their country, when they feel they are a part of it, when they feel that their country gives them a chance, then they are true patriots. . . . A great English philosopher—John Stuart Mill was his name—said, "Let a person have nothing to do for his country, and he shall have no love for it." America needs to be loved, and if it is going to be loved then it has to have people that feel they are a part of it, that they belong, that they are wanted, whether they are black or white, whether they are urban or rural, whether they are rich or poor. They have got to feel that this country cares about them and that their government cares about them and they have to feel that they care about their country.

Dear friends, I find that there is a lot of that caring and feeling around America. I am here to give you a report on the state of the nation, and the state of the nation is this—that our people are not satisfied with the yesterdays. That does not mean that they are bitter or embittered. It means that they know that they can do better. They know that America can set its own goals, that we can have our own standards, that we have to have achievements that are meaningful to us, and there are people in America today by the hundreds of thousands that are restless to get on with the job. Not only of America being number one in military power but, dear friends, to be number one in caring for each other. To be number one in cleaning up our cities, to be number one in trying to have a community that is free of violence and crime, to be number one in health and health care, to be number one in education for everyone—the handicapped, the normal, the child, the adult—to be number one in housing of our people, to be number one in jobs for our people.

These are the things that we ought to aspire to and, dear friends, if we can be number one in caring for one another, . . . I'll tell you we'll be the strongest nation that the world ever knew. We'll be strong not only in the cutting edge of our military, but we'll be strong in body, strong of heart, strong of mind. The real security of a nation is not in its machines, but in its people. And that's what I mean when I talk about Doland High School. Doland High School didn't make me rich, it didn't add a lot of big honors. Doland High School just gave me an understanding about people. It gave me a sense of caring, it gave me some kind of a desire to do better, and the people of this community helped me. So I come back here tonight as your neighbor, your friend, just to say "Thank you, and let's try from here on out to do even better than we've already done." God bless you. Thank you very, very much.[40]

The day he was buried, the prairie around Doland lay under a thin cover of snow, but next year, next year, there was always the chance that if the rains came at the right time and the winds were not too strong and everyone worked like hell, why, next year could turn out to be the best year of all.

He expected other people to be happy with his achievements, not because they were Hubert Humphrey's achievements, but because he was—and you often heard him say this—"a boy from the prairies," and if it could happen to him, it could happen to just anybody. He really believed that. Of course, it couldn't happen to just anybody, but he really believed this. I couldn't tell you the times in which he evidenced great satisfaction in some distinction that had been bestowed upon him. But not to say, "Look what a wonderful guy I am," never that, but to say, "Gee, you know this is the sort of thing that could happen to an American kid from the prairie." And his love of his region and of the country was, in my judgment, as spontaneous and unrehearsed and lacking in self-serving as his affection for just human beings.

JULIAN HARTT

Hubert H. Humphrey

ELECTION RESULTS
1943-1976

Mayor of Minneapolis, Minnesota*
1943

May 10	Primary Election
Marvin L. Kline	29,752
Hubert H. Humphrey	16,148
T. A. Eide	13,566
Henry J. Soltau	5,875
John G. Alexander	2,345
Owen Cunningham	2,169
Earl Kallestad	1,152
V. R. Dunne	793
Arthur D. Russell	350
Frank J. Hess	311

*First two nominated

Source: *Minneapolis Times*, May 14, 1943

Mayor of Minneapolis, Minnesota
1943

June 14	General Election
Marvin L. Kline	60,075
Hubert H. Humphrey	54,350

Source: *Proceedings of the City Council of the City of Minneapolis, Minnesota from July 1942 to July 1943*. Published by Authority of the City Council, 1942–1943

Mayor of Minneapolis, Minnesota
1945

May 14	Primary Election
Hubert H. Humphrey	49,550
Marvin L. Kline	26,091
T. A. Eide	12,090
Lewis E. Lohmann	5,459
Roland L. Hill	2,019
S. C. Bolstad	1,107
Harry J. Todd	666
Hjalmer O. Johnson	549
Gil Carmichael	447
John J. O'Brien	447
Edward J. Toohey	248
Olaf Pederson	222
Rev. O. S. Winther	215

Source: *Proceedings of the City Council of the City of Minneapolis, Minnesota from July 1945–July 1946*. Published by Authority of the City Council, 1945–1946

Mayor of Minneapolis, Minnesota
1945

June 11	General Election
Hubert H. Humphrey	86,377
Marvin L. Kline	55,263

Source: *Minneapolis City Council Proceedings, 1945–1946*

Mayor of Minneapolis, Minnesota
1947

May 12	Primary Election
Hubert H. Humphrey	68,056
Frank J. Collins	30,459
Robert J. Kelly	1,783
John McIlvaine	1,185
Roland L. Hill	1,086
Perley McBride	987
Vincent R. Dunne	908
Bernard E. Ericsson	838
Earl Kallestad	800
H. G. Knight	754
Barton C. Brown	647
Edward G. Toohey	415
Bert D. Page	203

Source: *Proceedings of the City Council of the City of Minneapolis, Minnesota from July 1946–July 1947*. Published by Authority of the City Council, 1946–1947.

Mayor of Minneapolis, Minnesota
1947

June 9	General Election
Hubert H. Humphrey	102,696
Frank J. Collins	52,358

Source: *Minneapolis City Council Proceedings, 1946–1947*

United States Senator, State of Minnesota
1948

September 14		Primary Election
Republican:	Joseph H. Ball	269,594
	Lenore Irene Bussman	18,060
	Earl L. Miller	51,801
DFL:	*Hubert H. Humphrey*	204,175
	James M. Shields	25,051

Source: *Minnesota Legislative Manual*. Compiled for the Legislature of 1949 by Mike Holm, Secretary of State

United States Senator, State of Minnesota
1948

November 2	General Election
Hubert H. Humphrey	729,494
Joseph H. Ball	485,801
Vincent R. Dunne (Socialist Workers)	4,951

Source: *Minnesota Votes: Election Returns by County for Presidents, Senators, Congressmen, and Governors, 1857–1977.* St. Paul: Minnesota Historical Society, Public Affairs Center Publications, 1977

Nomination for President
Democratic National Convention
Chicago, 1952

July 26	First Ballot
Estes Kefauver, Tenn.	300½
Richard Russell, Ga.	267½
Adlai Stevenson, Ill.	248½
W. Averell Harriman, N. Y.	126
Robert Kerr, Okla.	69
Alben Barkley, Ky.	49½
G. Mennen (Soapy) Williams, Mich.	40½
Paul Dever, Mass.	37½
Hubert H. Humphrey, Minn.	26
William Fulbright, Ark.	22
James McMahon, Conn.	16
James Murray, Mont.	12
Harry Truman, Mo.	6
Oscar Ewing, N.Y.	4
Paul Douglas, Ill.	3
William O. Douglas, Wash.	½

Source: *Congress and the Nation, A Review of Government and Politics in the Postwar Years.* Washington, D.C.: Congressional Quarterly Service, 1965

United States Senator, State of Minnesota
1954

September 14		Primary Election
Republican:	Val Bjornson	237,690
	Arthur D. Russell	17,253
	Richard S. (Dick) Wilcox	16,347
DFL:	*Hubert H. Humphrey*	319,194
	Harold Strom	11,707
	A. B. Gilbert	8,863

Source: *Minnesota Legislative Manual,* 1955. Compiled by Joseph L. Donovan, Secretary of State

United States Senator, State of Minnesota
1954

November 2	General Election
Hubert H. Humphrey	642,193
Val Bjornson	479,619
Frank P. Ryan	12,457
Vincent R. Dunne	4,683

Source: *Minnesota Votes*

Nomination for Vice-President
Democratic National Convention
Chicago, 1956

August 18	First Ballot	Second Ballot
Estes Kefauver, Tenn.	483½	551½
John F. Kennedy, Mass.	304	618
Albert Gore, Tenn.	178	110½
Robert Wagner, N.Y.	162½	9½
Hubert H. Humphrey, Minn.	134½	74
Luther Hodges, N. C.	40	½
Pitt Tyson Maner, Ala.	33	—
Clinton Anderson, N.M.	16	—
Frank Clement, Tenn.	13½	½
Leroy Collins, Fla.	1½	—
Edmund (Pat) Brown, Calif.	1	½
Stuart Symington, Mo.	1	—
Lyndon B. Johnson, Texas	½	—

"After switches the totals were: Kefauver 750, Kennedy 593, Gore 11½, Wagner 6, Humphrey 5½, Clement ½. Following the roll call, the nomination was made unanimous."

Source: *Congress and the Nation*

Democratic Presidential Primary
Wisconsin, 1960

April 5	
John F. Kennedy Slate	476,024
Hubert H. Humphrey Slate	366,753

Source: *America Votes 4.* Compiled and edited by Richard M. Scammon. Pittsburgh: University of Pittsburgh Press, 1962

Democratic Presidential Primary
Illinois, 1960

April 12

There were no candidate names on the ballot, and all preference votes were written in.

John F. Kennedy	34,332
Adlai E. Stevenson	8,029
Stuart Symington	5,744
Hubert H. Humphrey	4,283
Lyndon B. Johnson	442
Scattered	337

Source: *America Votes 4*

Democratic Presidential Primary
Pennsylvania, 1960

April 26	(all write-ins)
John F. Kennedy	183,073
Adlai E. Stevenson	29,660
Richard M. Nixon	15,136
Hubert H. Humphrey	13,860
Stuart Symington	6,791
Lyndon B. Johnson	2,918
Nelson Rockefeller	1,079
Scattered	4,297

Source: *America Votes 4*

Democratic Presidential Primary
West Virginia, 1960

May 10	
John F. Kennedy	236,510
Hubert H. Humphrey	152,187

Source: *America Votes 4*

Democratic Presidential Primary
Nebraska, 1960

May 10	
John F. Kennedy	80,408
Stuart Symington (write-in)	4,083
Hubert H. Humphrey (write-in)	3,202
Adlai E. Stevenson (write-in)	1,368
Lyndon B. Johnson (write-in)	962
Scattered	669

Source: *America Votes 4*

Democratic Presidential Primary
Oregon, 1960

May 20	
John F. Kennedy	146,332
Wayne Morse	91,715
Hubert H. Humphrey	16,319
Stuart Symington	12,496
Lyndon B. Johnson	11,101
Write-ins	9,134

Source: *America Votes 4*

Democratic Presidential Primary
South Dakota, 1960

June 7	
Hubert H. Humphrey Slate	Unopposed

Source: *America Votes 4*

Nomination for President
Democratic National Convention
Los Angeles, 1960

July 13	First Ballot
John F. Kennedy, Mass.	806
Lyndon B. Johnson, Tex.	409
Stuart Symington, Mo.	86
Adlai E. Stevenson, Ill.	79½
Robert Meyner, N.J.	43
Hubert H. Humphrey, Minn.	41½
George Smathers, Fla.	30
Ross Barnett, Miss.	23
Hershel Loveless, Iowa	1½
Orville Faubus, Ark.	½
Edmund (Pat) Brown, Calif.	½
Albert Rosillini, Wash.	½

Source: *Congress and the Nation*

United States Senator, State of Minnesota
1960

September 13	Primary Election
Republican: P. Kenneth (P. K.) Peterson	256,641
James Malcolm Williams	30,242
DFL: *Hubert H. Humphrey*	289,525

Source: *Minnesota Legislative Manual, 1961–1962.* Compiled by Joseph L. Donovan, Secretary of State. Published by the State of Minnesota at the State Capitol, St. Paul, Minnesota

United States Senator, State of Minnesota
1960

November 8	General Election
Hubert H. Humphrey	884,168
P. Kenneth (P. K.) Peterson	648,586
Carl Feingold (Socialist Workers)	4,085

Source: *Minnesota Votes*

Nomination for Vice-President
Democratic National Convention
Atlantic City, 1964

August 26	Nomination for Vice-President
Hubert H. Humphrey	Nominated by acclamation

Source: *Congress and the Nation*

Presidential Election 1964

November 3

	Popular Vote	Electoral Vote
Lyndon B. Johnson-*Hubert H. Humphrey*	43,129,484	486
Barry Goldwater-William Miller	27,178,188	52
Other	336,838	0

Source: *America Votes 6*. Compiled and edited by Richard M. Scammon. Washington, D.C.: Congressional Quarterly, 1966

Democratic Presidential Primary New Hampshire, 1968

March 12

Lyndon B. Johnson (write-in)	27,520
Eugene McCarthy	23,263
Richard M. Nixon (write-in)	2,532
John Crommelin	186
Richard E. Lee	170
Jacob J. Gordon	77
Scattered	1,716

Source: *America Votes 8*. Compiled and edited by Richard M. Scammon. Washington, D.C.: Congressional Quarterly, 1970

Democratic Presidential Primary Wisconsin, 1968

April 2

Eugene McCarthy	412,160
Lyndon B. Johnson	253,696
Robert F. Kennedy (write-in)	46,507
No preference	11,861
George C. Wallace (write-in)	4,031
Hubert H. Humphrey (write-in)	3,605
Scattered	1,142

Source: *America Votes 8*

Democratic Presidential Primary Pennsylvania, 1968

April 23

Eugene McCarthy	428,259
Robert F. Kennedy (write-in)	65,430
Hubert H. Humphrey (write-in)	51,998
George C. Wallace (write-in)	24,147
Lyndon B. Johnson (write-in)	21,265
Richard M. Nixon (write-in)	3,434
Scattered	2,556

Source: *America Votes 8*

Democratic Presidential Primary Massachusetts, 1968

April 30

Eugene McCarthy	122,697
Robert F. Kennedy (write-in)	68,604
Hubert H. Humphrey (write-in)	44,156
Lyndon B. Johnson (write-in)	6,890
Nelson Rockefeller (write-in)	2,275
George C. Wallace (write-in)	1,688
Scattered	2,593

Source: *America Votes 8*

Democratic Presidential Primary District of Columbia, 1968

May 7

"No primaries as such, but party officers and delegates to the national conventions were elected. A slate of Robert F. Kennedy delegates (top vote 57,555) defeated a slate of Hubert H. Humphrey delegates (top vote 32,309) and an independent Hubert H. Humphrey slate (top vote 2,250)."

Source: *America Votes 8*

Democratic Presidential Primary Indiana, 1968

May 7

Robert F. Kennedy	328,118
Roger D. Branigan	238,700
Eugene McCarthy	209,695

Source: *America Votes 8*

Democratic Presidential Primary Florida, 1968

May 28

George Smathers	236,242
Eugene McCarthy	147,216

Source: *America Votes 8*

Democratic Presidential Primary Nebraska, 1968

May 28

Robert F. Kennedy	84,102
Eugene McCarthy	50,655
Hubert H. Humphrey (write-in)	12,087
Lyndon B. Johnson (write-in)	9,187
Richard M. Nixon (write-in)	2,731
George C. Wallace (write-in)	1,298
Scattered	646

Source: *America Votes 8*

Democratic Presidential Primary
Oregon, 1968

May 28

Eugene McCarthy	163,990
Robert F. Kennedy	141,631
Lyndon B. Johnson	45,174
Hubert H. Humphrey (write-in)	12,421
Ronald Reagan (write-in)	3,082
Richard M. Nixon (write-in)	2,974
Nelson Rockefeller (write-in)	2,841
George C. Wallace (write-in)	457

Source: *America Votes 8*

Democratic Presidential Primary
California, 1968

June 4

Robert F. Kennedy	1,472,166
Eugene McCarthy	1,329,301
No-preference slate	380,286

Source: *America Votes 8*

Democratic Presidential Primary
New Jersey, 1968

June 4	(all write-ins)
Eugene McCarthy	9,906
Robert F. Kennedy	8,603
Hubert H. Humphrey	5,578
George C. Wallace	1,399
Richard M. Nixon	1,364
Scattered	596

Source: *America Votes 8*

Democratic Presidential Primary
South Dakota, 1968

June 4

Robert F. Kennedy	31,826
Lyndon B. Johnson	19,316
Eugene McCarthy	13,145

Source: *America Votes 8*

Democratic Presidential Primary
Illinois, 1968

June 11	(all write-ins)
Eugene McCarthy	4,646
Edward Kennedy	4,052
Hubert H. Humphrey	2,059
Scattered	1,281

Source: *America Votes 8*

Nomination for President
Democratic National Convention
Chicago, 1968

August 28	First ballot voting before switches
Hubert H. Humphrey, Minn.	1,760¼
Eugene McCarthy, Minn.	601
George McGovern, S. Dak.	146½
Channing Phillips, D. of C.	67½
Dan Moore, N.C.	17½
Edward Kennedy, Mass.	12¾
Ferris Bryant, Fla.	1½
George C. Wallace, Ala.	½
Other	½
Abstain	14

Source: *The 24th Annual Congressional Quarterly Almanac.* 90th Congress, 2nd Session–1968. Vol. XXIV. Washington, D.C.: Congressional Quarterly, Inc., 1968

Presidential Election
1968

November 5	*Popular Vote*	*Electoral Vote*
Richard M. Nixon-Spiro T. Agnew	31,785,480	301
Hubert H. Humphrey- Edmund Muskie	31,275,166	191
George C. Wallace-Curtis Lemay	9,906,473	46
Other	244,756	0

Source: *America Votes 8*

United States Senator, State of Minnesota
1970

September 15	Primary Election
No Republican Primary	
DFL: *Hubert H. Humphrey*	338,705
Earl Craig, Jr.	88,709

Source: *Minnesota Legislative Manual, 1971–1972.* Compiled by Arlen I. Erdahl, Secretary of State. Edited by Larry K. Anderson. Published by the State of Minnesota at St. Paul

United States Senator, State of Minnesota
1970

November 3	General Election
Hubert H. Humphrey	788,256
Clark MacGregor	568,025
Nancy Strebe (Socialist Workers)	6,122
William C. Braatz (Industrial Government)	2,484

Source: *Minnesota Votes*

Democratic Presidential Primary New Hampshire, 1972

March 7

Edmund Muskie	41,235
George McGovern	33,007
Sam Yorty	5,401
Wilbur Mills (write-in)	3,563
Vance Hartke	2,417
Edward Kennedy (write-in)	954
Hubert H. Humphrey (write-in)	348
Edward T. Coll	280
Henry Jackson (write-in)	197
George C. Wallace (write-in)	175
Scattered	1,277

Source: *America Votes 10*. Compiled and edited by Richard M. Scammon. Washington, D.C.: Congressional Quarterly, 1973

Democratic Presidential Primary Florida, 1972

March 14

George C. Wallace	526,651
Hubert H. Humphrey	234,658
Henry Jackson	170,156
Edmund Muskie	112,523
John Lindsay	82,386
George McGovern	78,232
Shirley Chisholm	43,989
Eugene J. McCarthy	5,847
Wilbur Mills	4,539
Vance Hartke	3,009
Sam Yorty	2,564

Source: *America Votes 10*

Democratic Presidential Primary Illinois, 1972

March 21

Edmund Muskie	766,914
Eugene J. McCarthy	444,260
George C. Wallace (write-in)	7,017
George McGovern (write-in)	3,687
Hubert H. Humphrey (write-in)	1,476
Shirley Chisholm (write-in)	777
Henry Jackson (write-in)	442
Edward Kennedy (write-in)	242
John Lindsay (write-in)	118
Scattered	211

Source: *America Votes 10*

Democratic Presidential Primary Wisconsin, 1972

April 4

George McGovern	333,528
George C. Wallace	248,676
Hubert H. Humphrey	233,748
Edmund Muskie	115,811
Henry Jackson	88,068
John Lindsay	75,579
Eugene J. McCarthy	15,543
Shirley Chisholm	9,198
None of the Names Shown	2,450
Sam Yorty	2,349
Patsy Mink	1,213
Wilbur Mills	913
Vance Hartke	766
Edward Kennedy (write-in)	183
Scattered	559

Source: *America Votes 10*

Democratic Presidential Primary Massachusetts, 1972

April 25

George McGovern	325,673
Edmund Muskie	131,709
Hubert H. Humphrey	48,929
George C. Wallace	45,807
Shirley Chisholm	22,398
Wilbur Mills	19,441
Eugene J. McCarthy	8,736
Henry Jackson	8,499
Edward Kennedy (write-in)	2,348
John Lindsay	2,107
Vance Hartke	874
Sam Yorty	646
Edward T. Coll	589
Scattered	760

Source: *America Votes 10*

Democratic Presidential Primary Pennsylvania, 1972

April 25

Hubert H. Humphrey	481,900
George C. Wallace	292,437
George McGovern	280,861
Edmund Muskie	279,983
Henry Jackson	38,767
Shirley Chisholm (write-in)	306
Scattered	585

Source: *America Votes 10*

Democratic Presidential Primary
Indiana, 1972

May 2

Hubert H. Humphrey	354,244
George C. Wallace	309,495
Edmund Muskie	87,719

Source: *America Votes 10*

Democratic Presidential Primary
Ohio, 1972

May 2

Hubert H. Humphrey	499,680
George McGovern	480,320
Edmund Muskie	107,806
Henry Jackson	98,498
Eugene McCarthy	26,026

Source: *America Votes 10*

Democratic Presidential Primary
Tennessee, 1972

May 4

George C. Wallace	335,858
Hubert H. Humphrey	78,350
George McGovern	35,551
Shirley Chisholm	18,809
Edmund Muskie	9,634
Henry Jackson	5,896
Wilbur Mills	2,543
Eugene McCarthy	2,267
Vance Hartke	1,621
John Lindsay	1,476
Sam Yorty	692
Scattered	24

Source: *America Votes 10*

Democratic Presidential Primary
Nebraska, 1972

May 9

George McGovern	79,309
Hubert H. Humphrey	65,968
George C. Wallace	23,912
Edmund Muskie	6,886
Henry Jackson	5,276
Sam Yorty	3,459
Eugene McCarthy	3,194
Shirley Chisholm	1,763
John Lindsay	1,244
Wilbur Mills	377
Edward Kennedy (write-in)	293
Vance Hartke	249
Scattered	207

Source: *America Votes 10*

Democratic Presidential Primary
West Virginia, 1972

May 9

Hubert H. Humphrey	246,596
George C. Wallace	121,888

Source: *America Votes 10*

Democratic Presidential Primary
Maryland, 1972

May 16

George C. Wallace	219,687
Hubert H. Humphrey	151,981
George McGovern	126,978
Henry Jackson	17,728
Sam Yorty	13,584
Edmund Muskie	13,363
Shirley Chisholm	12,602
Wilbur Mills	4,776
Eugene McCarthy	4,691
John Lindsay	2,168
Patsy Mink	573

Source: *America Votes 10*

Democratic Presidential Primary
Michigan, 1972

May 16

George C. Wallace	809,239
George McGovern	425,694
Hubert H. Humphrey	249,798
Shirley Chisholm	44,090
Edmund Muskie	38,701
Uncommitted	10,700
Henry Jackson	6,938
Vance Hartke	2,862
Scattered	51

Source: *America Votes 10*

Democratic Presidential Primary
Rhode Island, 1972

May 23

George McGovern	15,603
Edmund Muskie	7,838
Hubert H. Humphrey	7,701
George C. Wallace	5,802
Uncommitted	490
Eugene McCarthy	245
Henry Jackson	138
Wilbur Mills	41
Sam Yorty	6

Source: *America Votes 10*

Democratic Presidential Primary
Oregon, 1972

May 23

George McGovern	205,328
George Wallace	81,868
Hubert H. Humphrey	51,163
Henry Jackson	22,042
Edward Kennedy	12,673
Edmund Muskie	10,244
Eugene McCarthy	8,943
Patsy Mink	6,500
John Lindsay	5,082
Shirley Chisholm	2,975
Wilbur Mills	1,208
Scattered	618

Source: *America Votes 10*

Nomination for President
Democratic National Convention
Miami Beach, 1972

July 13	First Ballot (after adjustments for switches)
George McGovern, S. Dak.	1,864.95
Henry Jackson, Wash.	485.65
George C. Wallace, Ala.	377.5
Shirley Chisholm, N.Y.	101.45
Terry Sanford, N.C.	69.5
Hubert H. Humphrey, Minn.	35.0
Wilbur Mills, Ark.	32.8
Edmund Muskie, Me.	20.8
Edward Kennedy, Mass.	10.65
Wayne Hays, Oh.	5.0
Eugene J. McCarthy, Minn.	2.0
Walter F. Mondale, Minn.	1.0
Abstentions	9.7

Source: *The 28th Annual Congressional Quarterly Almanac.* 92nd Congress, 2nd Session-1972. Vol. XXVIII. Washington, D.C.: Congressional Quarterly, Inc., 1972

Democratic Presidential Primary
California, 1972

June 6

George McGovern	1,550,652
Hubert H. Humphrey	1,375,064
George C. Wallace (write-in)	268,551
Shirley Chisholm	157,435
Edmund Muskie	72,701
Sam Yorty	50,745
Eugene McCarthy	34,203
Henry Jackson	28,901
John Lindsay	26,246
Scattered	20

Source: *America Votes 10*

Democratic Presidential Primary
New Mexico, 1972

June 6

George McGovern	51,011
George C. Wallace	44,843
Hubert H. Humphrey	39,768
Edmund Muskie	6,411
Henry Jackson	4,236
None of the Names Shown	3,819
Shirley Chisholm	3,205

Source: *America Votes 10*

The primaries listed here for 1976 are only those for which ballots were cast for Humphrey. The exception is New Jersey, where Humphrey's name did not appear on the ballot but the "uncommitted" slate was regarded as pro-Humphrey.

Democratic Presidential Primary
New Hampshire, 1976

February 24

Jimmy Carter	23,373
Morris Udall	18,610
Birch Bayh	12,510
Fred Harris	8,863
Sargent Shriver	6,743
Hubert H. Humphrey (write-in)	4,296
Henry Jackson (write-in)	1,857
George C. Wallace (write-in)	1,016
Ellen McCormack	1,008
Edward Kennedy (write-in)	140
Other/scattered	3,522

Source: *Campaign '76: A CBS News Reference Book.* Compiled and edited by Warren J. Mitofsky and Catherine C. Krein. New York: Arno Press, 1977

Democratic Presidential Primary
Massachusetts, 1976

March 2

Henry Jackson	164,393
Morris Udall	130,440
George C. Wallace	123,112
Jimmy Carter	101,948
Fred Harris	55,701
Sargent Shriver	53,252
Birch Bayh	34,963
Ellen McCormack	25,772
Milton Shapp	21,693
Hubert H. Humphrey (write-in)	7,851
Edward Kennedy (write-in)	1,623
Lloyd Bentsen	364
Other/scattered	4,905
Uncommitted	9,804

Source: *Campaign '76*

Democratic Presidential Primary
Pennsylvania, 1976

April 27

Jimmy Carter	511,905
Henry Jackson	340,340
Morris Udall	259,166
George C. Wallace	155,902
Ellen McCormack	38,800
Milton Shapp	32,947
Birch Bayh	15,320
Fred Harris	13,065
Hubert H. Humphrey (write-in)	12,729
Other/scattered	5,067

Source: *Campaign '76*

Democratic Presidential Primary
Nebraska, 1976

May 11

Frank Church	67,297
Jimmy Carter	65,833
Hubert H. Humphrey	12,685
Edward Kennedy	7,199
Ellen McCormack	6,033
George C. Wallace	5,567
Morris Udall	4,688
Henry Jackson	2,642
Fred Harris	811
Birch Bayh	407
Sargent Shriver	384
Other/scattered	1,467

Source: *Campaign '76*

Democratic Presidential Primary
Idaho, 1976

May 25

Frank Church	58,570
Jimmy Carter	8,818
Hubert H. Humphrey	1,700
Jerry Brown (write-in)	1,453
George C. Wallace	1,115
Morris Udall	981
Henry Jackson	485
Fred Harris	319
Uncommitted	964

Source: *Campaign '76*

Democratic Presidential Primary
Oregon, 1976

May 25

Frank Church	145,394
Jimmy Carter	115,310
Jerry Brown (write-in)	106,812
Hubert H. Humphrey	22,488
Morris Udall	11,747
Edward Kennedy	10,983
George C. Wallace	5,797
Henry Jackson	5,298
Ellen McCormack	3,753
Fred Harris	1,344
Birch Bayh	743
Other/scattered	2,957

Source: *Campaign '76*

Democratic Presidential Primary
Tennessee, 1976

May 25

Jimmy Carter	259,243
George C. Wallace	37,256
Morris Udall	12,420
Frank Church	8,026
Henry Jackson	5,672
Jerry Brown (write-in)	1,939
Ellen McCormack	1,782
Fred Harris	1,628
Milton Shapp	507
Hubert H. Humphrey (write-in)	132
Other/scattered	77
Uncommitted	6,244

Source: *Campaign '76*

Democratic Presidential Primary
New Jersey, 1976

June 8	
Jimmy Carter	132,585
Morris Udall	59,933
Frank Church	31,052
George Wallace	28,614
Ellen McCormack	19,907
Uncommitted	199,796

Source: *Campaign '76*

Nomination for President
Democratic National Convention
New York, 1976

July 14	First Ballot
Jimmy Carter, Ga.	2,238.5
Morris Udall, Ariz.	329.5
Jerry Brown, Calif.	300.5
George C. Wallace, Ala.	57
Ellen McCormack, Mass.	22
Frank Church, Idaho	19
Henry Jackson, Wash.	10
Hubert H. Humphrey, Minn.	10
Fred Harris, Okla.	9
Others	12.5

Source: *Campaign '76*

United States Senator, State of Minnesota
1976

September 14	Primary Election
Independent-Republican:	
Gerald Brekke	76,183
Richard "Dick" Franson	32,115
John H. Glover	13,014
Roland "Butch" Riemers	9,307
Bea Mooney	9,150
DFL:	
Hubert H. Humphrey	317,632
Dick Bullock	30,262

Source: *Minneapolis Star,* September 30, 1976

United States Senator, State of Minnesota
1976

November 2	General Election
Hubert H. Humphrey	1,290,736
Gerald Brekke	478,602
Paul Helm (American)	125,612
William Peterson (Socialist Workers)	9,380
Robin E. Miller (Libertarian)	5,476
Matt Savola (Communist)	2,214

Source: *Minnesota Votes*

NOTES

Chapter 1. Doland

Opening quotation: Hubert H. Humphrey, Jr., "My Father," *Atlantic Monthly*, November 1966, p. 83

1. Personal interview, August 1977
2. *St. Paul Pioneer Press,* April 4, 1965
3. *Time,* February 1, 1960, p. 14
4. Hubert H. Humphrey, "My Father," p. 83
5. Personal interview, August 1977
6. Personal interview with Olive Doty, August 1977
7. Richard P. Jennett, "That Man from Minnesota" (Minneapolis: Joyce Press, 1965), p. 21
8. Personal interview, August 1977
9. Ibid
10. Hubert H. Humphrey, "My Father," p. 82
11. Ibid
12. *Doland Times Record,* January 30, 1930

Marginal quotations: p. 19, Doland speech taken from tape supplied by Deschler Welch; p. 23, Hubert H. Humphrey, Jr., "My Father," *Atlantic Monthly,* p. 84; p. 27, telephone conversation with the author, November 1977; p. 28, personal interview, August 1977; p. 31, telephone conversation, November 1977; p. 37, personal interview, August 1977

Chapter 2. To Minnesota

Opening quotation: Doland speech, June 14, 1976

1. Charles Bailey II, "Hubert H. Humphrey," in *Candidates 1960,* ed. Eric Sevareid (New York: Basic Books, 1959), p. 158
2. Ibid
3. *St. Paul Pioneer Press,* May 12, 1968
4. *Time,* February 1, 1960, p. 14
5. Interview with Hubert H. Humphrey rebroadcast over KTCA-TV, St. Paul, Minnesota, on January 14, 1978
6. Hubert H. Humphrey, *The Education of a Public Man: My Life and Politics* (Garden City, N.Y.: Doubleday & Co., Inc., 1976), p. 53

Marginal quotations: p. 45, quoted by Herbert E. Harris II, U.S., Congress, House, *Congressional Record,* 95th Cong., 1st sess., 1977, 123: H12136; p. 54, C. Donald Peterson—letter to the author, November 17, 1977.

Chapter 3. Becoming Someone

Opening quotation: Doland speech, June 14, 1976

1. Personal interview, September 1977
2. Eric Sevareid, *Not So Wild a Dream* (New York: Alfred A. Knopf, Inc., 1946), p. 58
3. Conversation with Max Shulman, 1958
4. Quoted in "Tom Heggen and Mr. Roberts" by Dan Cohen, *Ivory Tower* (University of Minnesota Daily), April 30, 1956
5. Interview on "Minnesota Issues," KTCA-TV, St. Paul, Minnesota, January 18, 1978
6. *Minneapolis Tribune,* May 10, 1966
7. Ibid
8. Personal interview, February 1978
9. *Minneapolis Tribune,* June 18, 1967

Marginal quotations: p. 62, telephone conversation with the author, August 1977; p. 64, telephone conversation, December 1977; p. 67, telephone conversation, September 1977; p. 69, letter to the author, November 17, 1977; p. 71, telephone conversation, November 1977; pp. 72–3, ibid.

Chapter 4. Party Politics

1. Arthur Naftalin, "A History of the Farmer-Labor Party" (Ph.D diss., University of Minnesota, 1948), p. 92
2. Ibid, pp. 205–6
3. Ibid, p. 210, n. 74
4. Ibid, p. 226
5. Ibid, p. 236
6. Ibid, p. 357

Marginal quotations: p. 79, telephone conversation with the author, August 1977; p. 81, telephone conversation, April 1978; p. 87, letter to the author, November 17, 1977

Chapter 5. Elected

1. *Education of a Public Man,* pp. 73–4
2. *Minneapolis Times,* May 26, 1943
3. Ibid
4. "Meet Muriel Humphrey" (Campaign pamphlet circa 1972), p. 6
5. *Minneapolis Star,* August 26, 1964
6. *Minneapolis Tribune,* January 26, 1969
7. *Education of a Public Man,* p. 81
8. Ibid, p. 85
9. Collection of Charles Hyneman

10. *Minneapolis Tribune,* July 24, 1968
11. Personal interview with Harry J. Lerner, January 1978

Marginal quotations: p. 91, introduction to the Pillsbury Centennial Lectures, University of Minnesota, October 1969; p. 92, telephone conversation with the author, December 1977; p. 94, letter to the author, November 17, 1977; p. 95, interview on WCCO-TV, Minneapolis, Minnesota, January 15, 1978; p. 96, personal interview, January 1978; p. 99, personal interview, January 1978; pp. 100–1, personal interview, January 1978; p. 102, telephone conversation, September 1977; pp. 106, 108, Arthur Naftalin—interview on WCCO-TV, Minneapolis, Minnesota, January 15, 1978; pp. 108–9, Harry J. Lerner—personal interview, October 1977; pp. 109–10, William F. Buckley, Jr., "A Tribute to Hubert Horatio Humphrey—from the Opposition," *National Review,* December 23, 1977, p. 1490

Chapter 6. Mayor

Opening quotation: "Minnesota Issues," KTCA-TV, St. Paul, Minnesota, January 18, 1978

1. *Minneapolis Times,* June 12, 1945
2. Ibid, July 9, 1945
3. *Minneapolis Star Journal,* June 16, 1945
4. Letter to the author, October 29, 1977
5. *Minneapolis Morning Tribune,* July 6, 1946
6. Max Kampelman, "Hubert H. Humphrey: Reflections," included in a letter to the author, October 17, 1977
7. Interview with Carey McWilliams, *Minneapolis Tribune,* November 7, 1946
8. *Minneapolis Times,* January 3, 1946
9. Kampelman, "Reflections"
10. *Minneapolis Times,* June 4, 1946
11. "Minnesota Issues," KTCA-TV, St. Paul, Minnesota, January 18, 1978
12. Ibid
13. *Minneapolis Star,* August 27, 1964
14. Kampelman, "Reflections"

Marginal quotations: p. 114, speech given at Temple Israel, Minneapolis, Minnesota, January 20, 1978; p. 116, telephone conversation with the author, March 1978; p. 118, telephone conversation, August 1977; p. 128, Marilyn Harstad Moynahan—letter to the author, September 20, 1977; pp. 128–9, Robert Forsythe—personal interview, September 1977

Chapter 7. To Washington

Opening quotation: *Education of a Public Man,* p. 459

1. Kampelman, "Reflections"
2. *Minneapolis Star,* August 26, 1964
3. "Reflections"
4. *Current Biography 1948* (New York: H. W. Wilson Co., 1949), p. 599
5. Winthrop Griffith, *Humphrey: A Candid Biography* (New York: William Morrow & Co., 1965), p. 153
6. *Education of a Public Man,* p. 459
7. *Minneapolis Tribune,* September 27, 1948
8. *Minneapolis Star,* September 21, 1948

Marginal quotations: p. 135, personal interview, November 1977; p. 139, telephone conversation with the author, September 1977; pp. 142–3, letter to the author, October 28, 1977; p. 144, personal interview, November 1977; p. 146, personal interview, September 1977

Chapter 8. Freshman

Opening quotation: *Time,* January 17, 1949, p. 16

1. "Reflections"
2. *Time,* January 17, 1949, p. 16
3. Ibid
4. "Reflections"
5. *Minneapolis Tribune,* February 5, 1949
6. *Time,* January 17, 1949, p. 16
7. October 1, 1949, p. 30
8. *Education of a Public Man,* p. 124
9. Albert Eisele, *Almost to the Presidency: A Biography of Two American Politicians* (Blue Earth, Minn.: The Piper Co., 1972), p. 94
10. *Education of a Public Man,* p. 148
11. Griffith, p. 190
12. Ibid
13. *Education of a Public Man,* p. 138
14. *Minneapolis Tribune,* May 27, 1967

Marginal quotations: p. 155, personal interview, September 1977; p. 156, quoted in the *Daily Texan,* January 16, 1978; p. 158, letter to the author, November 29, 1977; pp. 160–1, letter to the author, September 13, 1977

Chapter 9. Recovery

1. Letter to the author, October 3, 1977
2. Ibid
3. Ibid
4. Ibid
5. *St. Paul Pioneer Press,* January 5, 1964
6. *Minneapolis Tribune,* May 28, 1951
7. Bailey, pp. 172–3
8. Griffith, p. 214
9. *Education of a Public Man,* p. 164
10. *Minneapolis Tribune,* November 8, 1954
11. Ibid, November 7, 1954

Marginal quotations: p. 168, personal interview, September 1977; pp. 171–2, telephone conversation with the author, December 1977; p. 173, Norman Sherman—interview on WCCO-TV, Minneapolis, Minnesota, January 15, 1978; p. 173, Lee Loevinger—telephone conversation with the author, September 1977; p. 176, personal interview, January 1978; pp. 178–9, personal interview, September 1977; pp. 180–1, ibid

Chapter 10. Recognition

Opening quotation: Doland speech, June 14, 1976

1. *Congress and the Nation: A Review of Government and Politics in the Postwar Years* (Washington, D.C.: Congressional Quarterly Service, 1965), p. 1726
2. Bailey, p. 152
3. Ibid, p. 153
4. "Reflections"
5. Ibid
6. *Minneapolis Tribune,* May 12, 1965
7. Bailey, p. 147
8. *St. Paul Pioneer Press,* June 29, 1975
9. Ibid, January 5, 1964
10. *Minneapolis Star,* June 6, 1957
11. Ibid
12. *Minneapolis Tribune,* December 9, 1958
13. Ibid

Marginal quotations: pp. 188–9, personal interview, September 1977; p. 195, ibid; p. 198, letter to the author, December 1, 1977

Chapter 11. Setback

Opening quotation: Courtesy of Jimmy Wolford

1. Bailey, p. 145
2. *Minneapolis Tribune,* December 7, 1958
3. Ibid, December 4, 1958
4. Ibid
5. Jennett, p. 86
6. Ibid
7. Bailey, p. 149
8. *Minneapolis Star,* December 2, 1958
9. Eisele, p. 136
10. Theodore H. White, *The Making of the President, 1960* (New York: Atheneum Publishers, 1961), p. 40
11. *Minneapolis Star,* August 27, 1964
12. *Minneapolis Tribune,* July 15, 1959
13. Ibid, January 24, 1960
14. Eisele, p. 143
15. *Education of a Public Man,* p. 209
16. Eisele, p. 149
17. White, p. 113
18. Ibid, p. 114
19. Griffith, p. 246
20. White, p. 128
21. *Education of Public Man,* p. 215

Marginal quotations: p. 206, personal interview, December 1977; p. 207, *New Haven Register,* January 15, 1978; pp. 208–9, letter to the author, October 11, 1977; p. 212, speech given at the First International Symposium on Famine Prevention, December 19, 1977, quoted in a letter from Zahedi Ardeshir, Ambassador from Iran, January 1978

Chapter 12. Whip

Opening quotation: Quoted in the *Washington Post,* January 14, 1978

1. *Education of Public Man,* p. 221
2. Eisele, p. 152
3. Griffith, p. 247
4. Eisele, p. 156
5. *Minneapolis Tribune,* October 31, 1960
6. Vivian Cadden, "A Special Child Indeed," *McCalls,* January 1972, p. 110
7. Ibid, p. 112
8. Ibid
9. "Meet Muriel Humphrey," p. 4
10. *St. Paul Pioneer Press,* September 9, 1962
11. Ibid
12. Ibid
13. *Minneapolis Herald,* June 7, 1962
14. Griffith, p. 266
15. *Minneapolis Star,* November 23, 1963
16. Letter to the author, October 28, 1977

Marginal quotations: p. 228, personal interview, September 1977; p. 230, personal interview, September 1977; p. 233, *Washington Post,* January 16, 1978; p. 234, *The Papers of Adlai Stevenson,* ed. Walter Johnson (Boston: Little, Brown & Co., 1977), 7: 561; pp. 234–5, letter to the author, January 19, 1978; p. 236, letter to the author, September 13, 1977; p. 237, letter to the author, September 16, 1977; p. 240, personal interview, September 1977

Chapter 13. Winning

1. *St. Paul Pioneer Press,* January 5, 1964
2. *Minneapolis Star,* August 15, 1964
3. Eisele, p. 205
4. Letter to the author, October 28, 1977
5. *Minneapolis Star,* August 26, 1964
6. Eisele, p. 219
7. Ibid
8. *New York Times,* August 28, 1964
9. Personal interview, December 1977
10. *Minneapolis Star,* November 11, 1964
11. *Minneapolis Tribune,* October 11, 1964
12. *Minneapolis Star,* September 27, 1964

Marginal quotations: p. 246, U.S., Congress, House, *Congressional Record,* 95th Cong., 1st sess., 1977, 123: H12130; p. 248, Eugene McCarthy—*Minneapolis Tribune,* November 12, 1967; p. 248, Harold E. Hughes—letter to the author, September 16, 1977; p. 252, speech given at a Chamber of Commerce luncheon, Leamington Hotel, Minneapolis, Minnesota, October 1977; p. 255, *Private Faces, Public Places* (Garden City: Doubleday & Co., Inc., 1972), p. 266; p. 257, letter to John R. Lowrie of the *Watertown Public Opinion,* Watertown, South Dakota, September 14, 1977; p. 260, *Education of a Public Man,* p. 306

Chapter 14. Hawk

1. *Minneapolis Tribune,* January 20, 1965
2. Ibid, March 7, 1965
3. Ibid
4. *Minneapolis Star,* May 27, 1965
5. *Minneapolis Tribune,* April 10, 1966
6. Ibid
7. Ibid
8. *Education of Public Man,* pp. 323, 324
9. *Minneapolis Tribune,* December 27, 1965
10. Ibid, February 20, 1966
11. Ibid
12. Ibid
13. Ibid, February 24, 1966
14. Eisele, p. 244
15. *Minneapolis Tribune,* April 10, 1966
16. *St. Paul Pioneer Press,* January 29, 1967
17. Ibid
18. Ibid
19. *Education of Public Man,* p. 321
20. *Minneapolis Tribune,* March 20, 1968
21. Ibid
22. Ibid, July 21, 1966

Marginal quotations: p. 265, telephone conversation with the author, November 1977; p. 272, *What They Said in 1969,* ed. Alan F. Pater and Jason N. Pater (Beverly Hills, Calif.: Monitor Book Co., Inc., 1970), p. 236; p. 274, letter to the author, September 14, 1977; p. 276, *Los Angeles Herald-Examiner,* January 12, 1970; p. 278, *What They Said in 1969,* p. 239; p. 281, *New York Times Magazine,* October 11, 1970; p. 284, *New York Times,* January 11, 1971

Chapter 15. To Chicago

1. *Minneapolis Tribune,* November 2, 1967
2. *New York Times Magazine,* November 13, 1977
3. Theodore H. White, *The Making of the President, 1968* (New York: Atheneum Publishers, 1969), p. 9
4. Eisele, p. 284
5. *New York Times Magazine,* November 13, 1977
6. Letter to the author, November 2, 1977
7. *New York Times Magazine,* November 13, 1977
8. Eisele, p. 320
9. *New York Times Magazine,* November 13, 1977
10. Personal interview, August 1977
11. Eisele, p. 339
12. White, *Making of President, 1968,* p. 345
13. Ibid
14. Eisele, p. 332
15. *New York Times,* February 3, 1972
16. *Minneapolis Tribune,* June 21, 1968
17. Ibid, June 19, 1968

Marginal quotations: p. 293, *What They Said in 1969,* p. 238; p. 296, *New York Times,* March 10, 1968; p. 297, *New York Times,* May 13, 1968; p. 302, Ralph G. Martin, *Hubert H. Humphrey: A Man for All People* (New York, Grosset & Dunlap, 1968), unpaged; p. 309, *New York Times,* January 14, 1968; p. 311, *What They Said in 1969,* p. 160; p. 313, letter to the author, November 29, 1977; p. 315, *New York Times,* January 7, 1968

Chapter 16. Chicago

Opening quotation: *New York Times,* August 30, 1968

1. *New York Times,* August 21, 1968
2. Ibid, August 26, 1968
3. Ibid, August 27, 1968
4. Ibid, August 28, 1968
5. Ibid, August 29, 1968
6. Ibid
7. Ibid
8. Ibid
9. Ibid
10. Ibid
11. Ibid
12. Ibid
13. Ibid
14. Ibid
15. White, *Making of President, 1968,* p. 292
16. Ibid, p. 302
17. *New York Times,* August 30, 1968
18. Telephone conversation with the author, November 1977
19. Ibid
20. *New York Times,* August 30, 1968
21. White, *Making of President, 1968,* p. 303

Marginal quotations: pp. 324–5, letter to the author, November 23, 1977; p. 326, *What They Said in 1969,* p. 246; p. 327, ibid, p. 233; p. 328, personal interview, September 1977; p. 333, quoted in "Remembering Hubert Humphrey," *Reader's Digest,* May 1978, p. 110; p. 334, letter to the author, September 16, 1977; p. 337, Martin, *A Man for All People;* p. 338, *New York Times,* October 19, 1968; p. 343, *New York Times,* May 13, 1968; p. 345, *New York Times,* January 14, 1968; p. 349, personal interview, November 1977

Chapter 17. Almost

1. *New York Times,* August 29, 1968
2. Personal interview, December 1977
3. *New York Times,* August 30, 1968
4. Ibid, September 15, 1968
5. Ibid, August 26, 1968
6. Ibid, September 13, 1968
7. *Minneapolis Star,* September 20, 1968
8. Ibid
9. Ibid, September 30, 1968
10. *St. Paul Pioneer Press,* January 26, 1969
11. Eisele, p. 377
12. White, *Making of President, 1968,* p. 355
13. *Education of Public Man,* p. 403
14. Eisele, p. 378
15. *New York Times,* October 6, 1968
16. *Minneapolis Tribune,* December 27, 1969
17. Ibid
18. White, *Making of President, 1968,* p. 356
19. *New York Times,* November 1, 1968
20. Ibid
21. Ibid
22. Ibid
23. *Minneapolis Tribune,* July 9, 1969
24. *Minneapolis Star,* November 5, 1968
25. Ibid
26. Ibid
27. *New York Times,* November 7, 1968
28. *St. Paul Pioneer Press,* March 21, 1971

Marginal quotations: pp. 356–7, personal interview, September 1977; p. 358, ibid; p. 359, *New York Times,* August 9, 1968; p. 360, ibid; p. 362, ibid; p. 363, ibid; p. 364, *New York Times Magazine,* April 7, 1968; p. 365, *New York Times,* September 7, 1968; p. 366, *New York Times,* August 10, 1968; p. 369, quoted in the *Minneapolis Tribune,* December 19, 1977; p. 373, *New York Times,* September 7, 1968; p. 374, U.S., Congress, House, *Congressional Record,* 95th Cong., 1st sess., 1977, 123: H12132; p. 376, "News from the AFL-CIO," May 9, 1974; p. 379, letter to the author, November 29, 1977; p. 380, letter to Hubert Humphrey, November 30, 1977—copy sent to the author, December 2, 1977; p. 385, personal interview, September 1977

Chapter 18. Another Try

Opening quotation: "You Can't Quit," *Reader's Digest,* August 1977, p. 59

1. *St. Paul Pioneer Press,* May 2, 1976
2. *New York Times,* July 6, 1969
3. Ibid, March 26, 1969
4. *Minneapolis Star,* October 10, 1969
5. Ibid, October 16, 1969
6. Ibid
7. *Minneapolis Tribune,* October 23, 1969
8. *Minneapolis Star,* July 29, 1969
9. Ibid
10. *Minneapolis Tribune,* May 28, 1971
11. Ibid
12. *Minneapolis Star,* May 28, 1972
13. *Minneapolis Tribune,* November 16, 1971
14. Ibid, January 11, 1972
15. Theodore H. White, *The Making of the President, 1972* (New York: Atheneum Publishers, 1973), p. 105
16. Ibid, p. 130
17. *Minneapolis Tribune,* May 29, 1972
18. White, *Making of President, 1972,* p. 134
19. *Minneapolis Tribune,* June 30, 1972
20. Ibid
21. Ibid, July 12, 1972
22. Ibid
23. *St. Paul Pioneer Press,* July 23, 1972
24. *Minneapolis Tribune,* August 13, 1972
25. *Minneapolis Star,* July 12, 1972
26. *Minneapolis Tribune,* July 12, 1972

Marginal quotations: p. 394, telephone conversation with the author, December 1977; p. 396, *What They Said in 1969,* p. 233; pp. 398–9, personal interview, September 1977; pp. 400–1, ibid; p. 404, *New York Times,* March 14, 1971; p. 407, notes contributed by Muriel Humphrey, April 1978; p. 408, *San Francisco Examiner,* January 13, 1972; p. 409, *Dallas Times Herald,* April 16, 1972; p. 411, contributed by Jimmy Wolford, May 1977; p. 414, *New York Times,* October 13, 1972; p. 416, *Parade,* August 1, 1972; p. 417, letter to the author, January 23, 1978; p. 422, quoted in "Remembering Hubert Humphrey," *Reader's Digest,* May 1978, p. 110; p. 432, 1976 interview rebroadcast on WCCO-TV, Minneapolis, Minnesota, January 15, 1978

Chapter 19. Last Try

Opening quotation: *St. Paul Pioneer Press,* July 23, 1972

1. *Minneapolis Tribune,* November 8, 1972
2. Ibid
3. *Minneapolis Star,* January 16, 1978
4. *Minneapolis Tribune,* April 18, 1975
5. Speech given at Temple Israel, Minneapolis, Minnesota, January 20, 1978
6. *St. Paul Pioneer Press,* April 7, 1974
7. Ibid
8. *Minneapolis Tribune,* May 18, 1975
9. *New York Times,* March 11, 1976
10. *Minneapolis Star,* January 31, 1976
11. *Minneapolis Tribune,* January 5, 1974
12. Ibid
13. Ibid
14. Ibid, January 27, 1974
15. Ibid
16. Ibid

17. Jules Witcover, *Marathon: The Pursuit of the Presidency, 1972–1976* (New York: Viking Press, 1977), p. 127
18. *New York Times,* October 28, 1975
19. Ibid, October 17, 1975
20. *Minneapolis Tribune,* October 12, 1975
21. *New York Times,* November 3, 1975
22. *Minneapolis Star,* December 25, 1975
23. *New York Times,* November 3, 1975
24. *Minneapolis Star,* December 25, 1975
25. *Minneapolis Tribune,* January 26, 1976
26. *Minneapolis Star,* February 17, 1976
27. Witcover, p. 286
28. Ibid, p. 294
29. Ibid
30. *St. Paul Pioneer Press,* January 23, 1977

Marginal quotations: p. 427, letter to the author, January 23, 1978; p. 428, notes contributed by Muriel Humphrey, April 1978; p. 431, *Minneapolis Tribune,* January 22, 1978; p. 432, *Education of Public Man,* pp. 306–7; p. 434, interview on WCCO-TV, Minneapolis, Minnesota, January 15, 1978; p. 437, speech given at Temple Israel, Minneapolis, Minnesota, January 20, 1978; p. 438, *New York Times,* October 13, 1972; p. 441, 1976 interview rebroadcast on WCCO-TV, Minneapolis, Minnesota, January 15, 1978; p. 444, letter to the author, September 14, 1977; p. 446, U.S., Congress, House, *Congressional Record,* 95th Cong., 1st sess., 1977, 123: H12132; p. 448, ibid, H12130; p. 450, *Washington Post,* November 3, 1975; p. 453, *What They Said in 1976,* ed. Alan F. Pater and Jason N. Pater (Beverly Hills, Calif.: Monitor Book Co., 1977), p. 241; p. 456, "News from the AFL-CIO," March 16, 1977; p. 459, quoted by Herbert E. Harris II, U.S., Congress, House, *Congressional Record,* 95th Cong., 1st sess., 123: H12136

Chapter 20. Undefeated

Opening quotation: *Minneapolis Tribune,* January 14, 1978

1. *Minneapolis Tribune,* April 20, 1976
2. Ibid, July 17, 1976
3. *Minneapolis Star,* September 29, 1976
4. "You Can't Quit," *Reader's Digest,* August 1977, p. 57
5. *Minneapolis Tribune,* October 7, 1976
6. Ibid, October 8, 1976
7. *Washington Post,* January 14, 1978
8. *Minneapolis Star,* October 23, 1976
9. *Minneapolis Tribune,* October 23, 1976
10. Personal interview, August 1977
11. *Minneapolis Star,* January 6, 1977
12. *St. Paul Pioneer Press,* January 23, 1977
13. Ibid
14. *Minneapolis Star,* January 28, 1977
15. *Minneapolis Tribune,* May 29, 1977
16. *Minneapolis Star,* July 15, 1977
17. *Minneapolis Tribune,* August 19, 1977
18. Ibid
19. Ibid, August 20, 1977
20. Ibid, August 29, 1977
21. *Twin Cities Reader,* January 20, 1978
22. *Minneapolis Tribune,* September 20, 1977
23. Ibid
24. *Newsweek,* January 23, 1978, p. 23
25. Ibid
26. *Minneapolis Tribune,* September 29, 1977
27. *Washington Post,* January 15, 1978
28. Ibid
29. *Minneapolis Star,* March 28, 1978
30. *Minneapolis Tribune,* January 15, 1978
31. *St. Paul Pioneer Press,* January 15, 1978
32. Ibid
33. Ibid
34. *Minneapolis Tribune,* January 15, 1978
35. Ibid
36. Ibid
37. Ibid, January 23, 1978
38. *Minneapolis Star,* January 16, 1978
39. *Washington Post,* January 15, 1978
40. Doland speech, June 14, 1976

Marginal quotations: pp. 466–7, letter to the author, September 21, 1977; p. 468, personal interview, January 1978; p. 469, U.S., Congress, Senate, *Congressional Record,* 95th Cong., 1st sess., 1977, 123: S17676; pp. 470–1, letter to the author, September 19, 1977; p. 472, letter to the author, January 23, 1978; p. 475, letter to the author, September 18, 1977; p. 477, personal interview, April 1978; p. 479, U.S., Congress, Senate, *Congressional Record,* 95th Cong., 1st sess., 1977, 123: S17677; pp. 480–1, letter to the author, January 23, 1977; p. 482, Dave Roe—personal interview, May 1978; p. 482, Geri Joseph—speech given at Temple Israel, Minneapolis, Minnesota, January 20, 1978; p. 483, speech given at a dinner of the National Council of Christians and Jews in September 1977—contributed by Max Kampelman; p. 485, Henry Reuss—U.S., Congress, House, *Congressional Record,* 95th Cong., 1st sess., 1977, 123: H12137; p. 485, Lorne Greene—quoted by Senator Wendell Anderson in *Congressional Record,* S17677; p. 485, Wendell Anderson—telephone conversation with the author, January 23, 1978; p. 486, interview on WCCO-TV, Minneapolis, Minnesota, January 15, 1978; p. 487, from a letter to Hubert Humphrey, November 30, 1977—copy sent to the author, December 2, 1977; p. 489, lyrics of "Joe Hill" by Alfred Hays—from the *West Virginia Hillbilly,* April 15, 1978, contributed by George Birklein; p. 492, telephone conversation with the author, November 1977

Author's note: On January 26, 1978, Rudy Perpich, the governor of Minnesota, appointed Muriel Humphrey to fill her late husband's Senate seat until the election in November. On April 8, Senator Humphrey announced that she had decided not to run in the fall election.

INDEX

Page numbers in *italic* type refer to material in marginal quotations; page numbers in **bold** type refer to photographs.

PHOTO ACKNOWLEDGMENTS: In addition to the sources and individuals listed below, the photographs appearing on the following pages were provided through the courtesy of the Office of Senator Hubert H. Humphrey and the Hubert H. Humphrey Collection, Minnesota Historical Society: 2, 96-97, 167, 172, 178, 191 (bottom), 199, 200-201, 201, 208, 223, 228, 235, 336, 390, 397, 398, 403, 429, 430, 433, 437, 440, 442, 444, 447, 448, 449, 451, 455, 458, 469, 474, 481 (top and bottom), 493. Humphrey family photos: pages 19, 20 (top and bottom), 21 (top left, top right, and bottom), 24 (top), 34-35 (top), 44 (top and bottom), 45, 50, 51, 64, 68 (top and bottom), 67, 113, 148 (bottom); Frances Humphrey, Smithsonian Institution: 22, 156; Mark Lerner: 23 (top), 34 (bottom); Olive Doty: 23 (bottom), 28 (left), 29 (bottom), 30 (left and right); Ellis Flint: 24-25 (bottom); Deschler Welch: 25 (top); Julian Hartt: 26 (top), 27 (left); Irven Herther: 26 (bottom); Homer Krentz: 27 (right), 28-29 (top), 37; South Dakota Historical Society: 32-33 (bottom), 33 (top), 47; Norbert "Tip" Miles: 35; Minnesota Historical Society: 42-43, 48, 59, 60-61 (top and bottom), 77 (Charles A. Zimmerman photo), 78, 81 (*St. Paul Daily News* photo), 82-83 (George Luxton Collection), 86, 87, 100-101 (George Luxton Collection), 116-117, 133, 140, 145 (top), 194 (top); *Minneapolis Times* newspaper file, Minneapolis Public Library Collection: 49 (*Minneapolis Tribune* photo), 79, 80, 84 (*Minneapolis Tribune* photo), 91 (*Minneapolis Tribune* photo), 94, 126 (George Luxton photo); Wide World Photos: 52, 141, 143, 159, 162, 175, 205, 210, 220-221, 222, 250, 256, 265, 267, 275 (top), 279, 284, 285, 301, 302, 319, 327 (bottom), 353, 366, 400-401, 402, 405, 409, 414, 416, 418, 423, 471, 473, 484 (top left, top right, and bottom); *The Minneapolis Star*: 55, 68, 115 (top), 123, 127 (left and right), 148 (top), 152, 157, 193, 307, 480; School of Journalism and Mass Communication, University of Minnesota: 63; C. Donald Peterson: 65; Louisiana State Library (John H. Williams Studio): 70 (top); New York Public Library: 70 (bottom); *The Saturday Evening Post* (Ollie Atkins): 72; Charles Hyneman: 73; Independent Picture Service: 93, 110, 124-125; Minneapolis Public Library and Information Center: 98, 115 (bottom) (George Miles Ryan Studio), 489 (Minneapolis History Collection); United Press International, Inc.: 104 (top), 104-105 (bottom), 238 (top and bottom), 239 (top and bottom), 245 (top), 249, 258, 260, 261 (top), 277, 291, 292, 294-295 (Kyoichi Sawada), 296, 299, 303 (top), (Sam Parrish), 303 (bottom), 306, 312 (top and bottom), 320, 321, 323, 326-327 (Kyoichi Sawada), 330-331, 332, 335, 336 (right), 339, 341, 342, 343, 344, 346-347, 348-349, 354, 355, 359, 361, 363, 365, 368, 371, 373, 376, 383, 389, 408, 410, 412, 413, 415, 421, 435, 452, 463; Harry J. Lerner: 107, 109; Ed Ryan: 108, 119, 120, 121; Max Kampelman: 122; Bob Forsythe: 129; Eugenie Anderson: 137; Robert Y. Fluno: 138, 145 (bottom); *Minneapolis Tribune*: 147, 192, 194-195, 216, 259, 289, 375, 381, 384, 385, 392, 394, 429 (top), 477, 478, 479, 487; Eddie Schwartz: 151; Marty Nordstrom: 153, 155 (Tommy Lee photo), 179, 180, 181, 228, 231, 232, 233, 234 (*Minneapolis Tribune* photo), 237, 242, 245 (bottom), 261 (bottom), 262, 270-271, 324-325, 333, 336 (left), 370, 377, 378-379, 428, 434; Julius Passerman, Lincoln Drugs: 154; United States Historical Society (George F. Mobley, *National Geographic* photographer): 160-161; Indiana State University Library: 163; Judge Luther W. Youngdahl: 168-169, 170 (top); Sid Glanzer: 170 (bottom); State Historical Society of Wisconsin: 174, 215; *Life* Magazine, © Time, Inc.: 177, © 1959 (Hank Walker), 190-191, © 1956 (Francis Miller), 206, © 1959 (Alfred Eisenstadt), 214, © 1960 (Stan Wayman), 218, © 1960 (Paul Schutzer); National Archives: 186; Del Ankers Photography: 189; Bert Brandt and Associates: 196; Hans H. Pinn: 197; Chancellor Willy Brandt: 198; Genack Studio: 212; Joseph Rauh: 253; United States Marine Corps: 268, 269; USIS Photo Lab, Manila: 273; Air Force Photo: 275 (bottom); U.S. Army Photo (S/Sgt. Gilbert L. Meyers): 280, 281; U.N.C. Photo Lab: 282; USIS Photo Lab, Mexico City: 298; *Time* Magazine, © Time, Inc.: 304, © 1968 (Louis Glanzman); Religious News Service: 310; Lyndon Baines Johnson Library: 316; Gordon Twiss: 338; David Graven: 349; Archer Associates: 357; Embassy of the USSR, Washington, D.C.: 395; S. Harrison Dogole: 417; Dev O'Neill: 420; Stan Wayman: 431; *The Washington Post* (James K. W. Atherton): 445; Gene O'Brien, *Sun* Newspapers: 454; Senator Henry M. Jackson: 457; Corey Gordon: 464; Lauren Markoe: 466, 467; Dave Roe: 476; Mattox Photography: 480; *Dayton Daily News*, © 1978: 488; Robert Schoenbaum: 490. Efforts have been made to credit all of the photographs included in this book; any unintentional omissions or errors will be remedied in future printings.

Portions of G. Theodore Mitau's introduction first appeared in the *St. Paul Sunday Pioneer Press*, January 15, 1978. Used by permission.

Designer: Richard J. Hannah
Typesetters: TriStar Graphics, P & H Photocomposition, Headliners, Inc.
Typefaces: Text—Times Roman modified for this book
Display—Helvetica in regular and specialty styles
Printer: Meyers Printing Company
Paper: Body—Plainwell's Publishers Matte 60 lb.
End Sheets—Coral Red Curtis Tweedweave
Binder: North Central Publishing Company, Smyth sewn
Cover Material: Joanna Western Centennial
Cover Process: Stamped, one color ink
Jacket: Offset, 4 colors by Johnson Printing Company
Laminated with polyester film by United Coating & Laminating, Inc.